THE GUINNESS
DICTIONARY
OF
SPORTS
QUOTATIONS

COMPILED BY COLIN JARMAN

Happy birthday Peter —
Love — Mother & Father.

Think you will especially appreciate
pages 183-4.

8.4.93.

GUINNESS PUBLISHING

Editor: Charles Richards

Design and Layout: Cathy Shilling

© Colin M. Jarman and Guinness Publishing Ltd, 1990

Published in Great Britain by Guinness Publishing Ltd,
33 London Road, Enfield, Middlesex

Typeset in Plantin Light
by Ace Filmsetting Ltd, Frome, Somerset
Printed and bound in Great Britain by The Bath Press, Bath

'Guinness' is a registered trademark of Guinness Superlatives Ltd

British Library Cataloguing in Publication Data

The Guinness dictionary of sports quotations
1. Sport
I. Jarman, Colin M.
796

ISBN 0-85112-924-2

Born in Welling, Kent in 1958, COLIN M. JARMAN was educated locally at Bexley Grammar School, where he earned colours in cricket. Since leaving school he has won honours in many sports ranging from American football to road-running.

A former Chief Executive of the Budweiser American Football League, he is now sports editor for the *Satellite Times* magazine, an assistant editor of *Roy of the Rovers*, and runs his own sports promotion company.

CONTENTS

PREFACE

Sport has been written and talked about ever since Apple Bowl I, when the Snake pipped Adam in Eden Square Gardens, with the main point of record coming when the Chief Umpire showed Adam the world's first 'red card'.

This personal collection of sporting quotes is the end product of many hours spent thumbing through scores of sports books, newspapers, magazines and standard literary works. The final result is the literary equivalent of a sporting highlights film; the essence of sport through the ages, represented by quotations – written, spoken and attributed.

If you want a definition of a sporting quotation, don't bother to ask Joe DiMaggio, the legendary baseball player. He recalled the first time a New York reporter asked him for a quote, 'I didn't know what a quote was. I though it was some kind of drink.'

When placed alongside the classics of literature, a book of sporting quotations is probably held in about the same regard as a football match between the Lake Poets and the Algonquin Round Table, although the idea of William Wordsworth nutmegging Alexander Woollcott is rather appealing.

But my view is that the wide world of sport is part of the global entertainment culture; Dame Flora Robson and Bryan Robson, Vaughan Williams and J. P. R. Williams, Dr Samuel Johnson and Magic Johnson, and Max Miller and Mick the Miller have all, in some way, been involved in entertaining the public. The underlying principle of sport is to have fun, an ideology that this book aims to reflect.

COLIN M. JARMAN

HOW TO USE THIS BOOK

This book, like a game of soccer, is divided into two halves – sports and themes. Both run alphabetically – Aerial Sports to Wrestling, and Advice to Women, respectively.

The individual sports quotes are listed alphabetically under either the originator of the quote or the subject of the quote, with preference given to the subject. For example, where John Arlott, the TV commentator and writer, comments on Ian Chappell, the Australian cricketer, this is found under Chappell (as a subject), although Arlott has his own individual section of non-specific cricket quotes.

Where a specific sport has a great many quotes, it has been divided into sub-sections. The above 'Arlott/Chappell' quote concerns Chappell as a player and is found in the 'Australian players' sub-section under Cricket; while a quote by Mike Brearley on Chappell's leadership qualities will be found in the 'Captaincy & Tactics' sub-section. The opening contents page lists all the sports, themes and sub-sections.

The quotes within the thematic sections are listed alphabetically by component sports, except where indicated.

An extensive subject index is provided for referencing all quotes either by, or on, a particular individual.

EDITORIAL NOTES

Biographical details include dates of birth and death where known. This information is given to place the quotes in a 'time' context rather than in the interests of providing a definitive biographical reference for the subject of each quote.

Where possible, nationalities other than British are given. The Home Countries have been identified where relevant (e.g. in the sections on Football, Rugby Union and Snooker). The sections on the major American sports (American Football, Baseball, Basketball and Ice Hockey) see nationalities assumed as US unless otherwise stated.

As many players from various team sports have played for a number of different teams, the teams listed as part of a player's biographical details are either specific to the quote in question, or they are the teams most readily associated with the subject's career. This applies equally to managers, trainers and coaches in individual and team sports.

AERIAL SPORTS

GENERAL

Colin M. Jarman – *(b 1958) sportswriter*
Daedalus and Icarus were two of the earliest
sporting pioneers. In one afternoon they
invented hang-gliding and free-fall parachuting:
1988

BALLOONING

Christine Turnbull – *writer*
Ballooning is an art, not a science, and is surely
the only form of flying, or even locomotion
where one has no controls to turn left or right,
accelerate or brake: *1970*

GLIDING

Peter Scott – *glider*
Gliding is largely a matter of ups and downs – a
battle against gravity.

Bill Scull – *National coach of the British Gliding
Association*
Gliding is a team sport, up to the point at
which you become airborne.

HANG-GLIDING

Anon
Hang gliding, blast baseball, and sod cycling.

There is nothing quite like hang-gliding.
Nothing. Sex is the nearest, but hang-gliding
lasts forever. Once you've done it, you can
hardly wait till you do it again.

Martin Hunt – *Chairman of the British Hang
Gliding Association*
Hang-gliding will be commonplace by the year
2000. They will be the bicycles of the air: *1977*

PARACHUTING

Anon
If at first you don't succeed – so much for sky
diving.

Peter Moran – *writer & parachutist*
Chapter titles – 'The Sky is Neutral' and 'No
Going Back': *A Speck in the Sky (1987)*

Bud Sellick – *US sky diver & writer*
If ever there was a sport that requires self-
confidence and independence, parachuting is
that sport: *1971*

Sally Smith – *writer*
In freefall, the body can do everything an
aeroplane can do, except go back up!: *1978*

AMERICAN FOOTBALL

GENERAL

Anon
Football is the perfect expression of American
life. Its demarcation lines are very clear; they
even draw lines across the field.

A drawback is a player who is more hindrance
than help.

The worst thing about football is that none of

the cheerleaders ever gets injured.

Jacques Barzun – *(b 1907) Provost of
Columbia University*
To watch a football game is to be in prolonged
neurotic doubt as to what you're seeing. It's
more like an emergency happening at a distance
than a game.

Harry Blaha – *writer*
Rugby is a beastly game played by gentlemen.

Soccer is a gentleman's game played by beasts. Football is a beastly game played by beasts:

1972

Pete Dexter– *writer*
It's a world in itself, designed in a way that condenses most of the things you hate to see coming in this life into a very short period of time: decision, pain, fear, embarrassment, confrontation, spit hanging from the bars of your face-mask:

1983

Wilfrid Diamond – *sportswriter*
If a football player isn't tough as nails to begin with and in good, hard condition, he's flirting with a wheelchair.

Paul Dietzel – *writer*
You can learn more character on the two-yard line than you can anywhere in life.

F. Scott Fitzgerald – *(1896-1940) novelist*
Life was a damned muddle – a football game with everyone offside and the referee gotten rid of – everyone claiming the referee would have been on his side.

David Harris – *writer*
The game proceeds in short bursts of synchronized combat broken by pauses to regroup. At each break, the stakes escalate. The strategy is enormously complex and the execution brutally simple. The object is to dominate:

1984

Doug Ibbotson – *British sportswriter*
American Football is not so much a sport, but a way of strife. It might be best described as Rugby League with knobs on, or feinting by numbers.

Thomas Jable
In hiring the gifted player or professional, the athletic club shattered the amateur ideal upon which it was founded, that is, participation for the sheer love of the game:

1892

Glenn Jackson – *Canadian Football linebacker*
It's pitiful to see some of the kids trying to deal with a playbook. It's as though they've been given some obscure formula in a foreign language.

Colin M. Jarman – *(b 1958) British sportswriter*
Muscle-bound chess.

Sue Lawley – *British TV presenter*
American Football makes rugby look like a Tupperware party.

James Lawton – *British sportswriter*
If all of sport is a magnificent triviality, American Football seems least tolerant of the limitation.

Dan Leno – *(d 1904) comedian*
I see the world as a football, kicked about by the higher powers, with me clinging on by my teeth and toe-nails to the laces.

Tex Maule – *sportswriter*
When a game is well on the way to being lost, the bench is quiet and the strong faces grow still and watchful. The only happiness for the proud ones is victory.

PROFESSIONAL

New York Giants playbook
A.R.A.P.A.H.O.E. – A Run, A Pass, A Hit On the Enemy:
[*The Giants successfully called this play on 4th down in Super Bowl XXI. More routinely it is called 'Check roll tide'*]

Pete Rozelle – *(b 1926) NFL commissioner*
Pro football is the greatest success story in American sport.

When two 250lb players run into each other, it's like ammunition.

Irwin Shaw – *novelist & college quarterback*
On the NFL – It is the Alamo every Sunday, with the cavalry coming in on a long pass. Pro football is show business, and where are you going to find a better show than the Alamo?:

1965

'Red' Smith – *(1905-82) sportswriter*
On conditions at a Chicago Bears v New York Giants game – It was an ideal day for football – too cold for the spectators and too cold for the players:

1963

2

Jim Tunney - *referee*
On the average NFL fan - He'll scream from the sixtieth row of the bleachers that you have missed a marginal call in centre field, but then he won't be able to find his car in the parking lot.

COACHES

Anon
A football coach is a person who is willing to lay down your life for the good of the team.

George Allen - *Washington Redskins*
The future in football is now: *1971*

A football team is a lot like a machine. It's made up of parts. I like to think of it as a Cadillac. A Cadillac's a pretty good car. All the refined parts working together make the team. If one part doesn't work, one player pulling against you and not doing his job, the whole machine fails. Nobody is indispensable. We try to improve and replace some of the parts each year.

Heywood Broun - *(1888–1939) writer*
God is always on the side which has the best football coach.

Hank Bullough - *(b 1934) Buffalo Bills*
We keep beating ourselves, but we're getting better at it.

Jerry Burns - *(b 1927) Minnesota Vikings*
I am like the captain of the Queen Mary. I have got navigational officers and people in the boiler room. So, I am not running down there to tell them how to stoke the boiler. Still, I do have the final decision. If the ship runs aground, the captain is responsible. But I don't like that idea about going down with the ship. So I've instructed my first mate to pull me off in that event.

Hugh Campbell - *LA Express [USFL]*
Too often football forgets that it is involved in human beings, people as vulnerable as anyone walking down the street.

Marion Campbell - *(b 1929) Atlanta Falcons*
On resigning from the inept Falcons - I've coached for 36 years and it's time to go fishing: *1989*

I hope he has more success catching fish than his receivers have had catching passes:
Rick Donnelly - Falcons (1989)

Johnny Giles - *(b 1940) Irish soccer player*
In American Football, the play becomes just an extension of the will and imagination of the two coaches. This can be fascinating, but I'm not certain it has much to do with sport, certainly as Europeans know sport.

Bud Grant - *(b 1927) Minnesota Vikings*
A good coach needs a patient wife, a loyal dog and a great quarterback, but not necessarily in that order.

Tom Landry - *(b 1924) Dallas Cowboys*
Most people don't realise that to perform well in whatever you do, especially in an athletic contest which is extremely emotional, concentration is the key. If you can keep concentration, then you have a tremendous opportunity to perform at maximum efficiency. When you break your concentration, then you start to let other thoughts enter. So I'm constantly thinking about what's coming.

Nothing funny ever happens in football.

The biggest misconception about me is that I am unemotional. I am not a cheerleader.

When Tom Landry says something is so, it's true today, it's true tomorrow, and it's true until he says it isn't:
Billy Joe DuPree - Cowboys tight end

Tom Landry smile? I don't know, I was only there nine years:
Walt Garrison - Cowboys running back

He's a perfectionist. If he was married to Raquel Welch he'd expect her to cook:
Don Meredith - Cowboys quarterback

Vince Lombardi - *(1913-70) Green Bay Packers*
If we create something, we must be something.

If you're not fired with enthusiasm, you'll be fired with enthusiasm.

Perfection is not attainable, but if we chase

perfection, we can catch excellence.

Tackling is more natural than blocking. If a man is running down the street with everything you own, you won't let him get away. That's tackling.

Coaches who can outline plays on a blackboard are a dime a dozen. The ones who win get inside their players and motivate.

Football is first and foremost a running game.

When we don't use our ability to the fullest, we're not only cheating ourselves and the Green Bay Packers, we're cheating the Lord. He gave us our ability to use to the fullest.

Running a football team is no different from running any other kind of organization – an army, a political party, a business. The problems are the same. The objective is to win!

Nobody is hurt. Hurt is in the mind. If you can walk, you can run.

Vince Lombardi was fair, he treated us all the same – like dogs: *Henry Jordan – Packers*

The first real superstar in modern professional football was not Jim Brown or Joe Namath, but a coach – Vince Lombardi. He was much more of a celebrity across the country than any of his players: *Bill Russell*

John Madden - *(b 1936) Oakland Raiders*
To me discipline in football occurs on the field, not off of it.

I don't know that I ever had a great player that was normal. To get outstanding performance you get some people that are a bit left of plumb: *1983*

John McKay - *Tampa Bay Buccaneers*
Providing I don't ask them to pass or block, we're OK.

Bill Parcells - *New York Giants*
To me there is no such thing as history in pro football, people are only really worried about whether you're going to win the next game.

Hell, I've lost six pounds on the way to the Super Bowl. Mind you, that's like throwing a deck chair off the Queen Mary: *1987*

John Ralston - *Denver Broncos*
I resigned as Head Coach because of illness and fatigue. The fans are sick and tired of me: *1978*

Don Shula - *(b 1930) Colts & Miami Dolphins*
If a nuclear bomb is ever dropped on the United States, the only things that will survive are Astro-turf and Don Shula:
Charles 'Bubba' Smith

He can take his'n and beat your'n, or he can take your'n and beat his'n:
O. A. 'Bum' Phillips – Houston Oilers

Joe Walton - *(b 1935) New York Jets*
There's not a lot of good football being played in the NFL, and we're at the forefront.

DEFENSE

Lyle Alzado - *LA Raiders*
I never met a guy that I didn't want to fight. 'Cos if it takes a street fight to get something done, that's what I'm going to do.

If me and King Kong went into an alley, only one of us would come out. And it wouldn't be the monkey.

On Alzado's retirement – I definitely miss him. There are times I wish we could have come into the league together. If he had come into the league the same time as I did, forget about it. We might have been wanted in four or five states: *Howie Long – Raiders*

Dan Birdwell - *Oakland Raiders*
You have to play this game like somebody just hit your mother with a two-by-four.

Hardy 'The Hatchet' Brown - *San Francisco 49ers*
Pound for pound, inch for inch, he was the toughest football player I ever met. He was so tough, he was damn near illegal:
Y. A. Tittle - New York Giants quarterback

Dick Butkus - *(b 1942) - Chicago Bears*
Some people think I have to get down on all

fours to eat my couple of pounds of raw meat every day. Others think that George Halas taught me to walk upright and that I have an agent to do my reading and writing for me. But, people who really know me, know that I can read a little. I move my lips sometimes, but I can read things on a second grade level – like newspapers. I don't need a rubber stamp to give an autograph.

With the highest respect, I've got to say Dick Butkus is an animal. He works himself up to such a competitive pitch that on the day of a game he won't answer a direct question. He'll grunt: *Mike Ditka – Bears coach*

Major Frank Cavanagh
There is something in the swoop and shock of a hard tackle which stirs a racial memory and satisfies an ancient desire.

Bruce Clark – *(b 1958) New Orleans Saints*
On making a tackle – You have all kinds of mixed feelings. Like do I want to just hit him or bury him? Is he a nice guy, or a jerk? It's a funny feeling, time stops, all the noise stops. I enjoy the feeling.

Lester 'The Molester' Hayes – *LA Raiders*
This is a game played by mere mortals, and mere mortals make mistakes.

Playing cornerback is like being on an island. You see boats passing by, but you can't be helped – there is no rescue.

Mark Haynes – *(b 1953) Denver Broncos*
On his demotion to the bench – Now, I'm not even a nickel back, I'm a penny back.

Ted 'Mad Stork' Hendricks – *LA Raiders*
The Raiders are responsible for many rule changes. There is the no-clothes line rule. The no spearing rule. The no hitting out-of-bounds rule. No fumbling forward in the last two minutes of the game. No throwing helmets rule. The no stickum rule . . . So, we are not all bad.

Sam Huff – *New York Giants*
You can run on a football field but you can't hide out there. Sooner or later you are going to get hit.

Cecil Johnson – *(b 1955) Tampa Bay Buccaneers*
Playing middle linebacker is like walking through a lion's cage dressed in a three-piece pork-chop suit.

Alex Karras – *Detroit Lions*
To me, football is a contest in embarrassments. The quarterback is out there to embarrass me in front of my friends, my team-mates, my coaches, my wife, and my three boys. The quarterback doesn't leave me any choice. I've got to embarrass him instead.

Tim Krumrie – *(b 1960) Cincinnati Bengals*
Tim Krumrie is like a shark out there – he smells blood: *Cris Collinsworth – Bengals*

Jack Lambert – *Pittsburgh Steelers*
Godzilla the middle linebacker – an animal at the point, an obsessed pursuer and a human radar station tracking down receivers: *Anon*

James Lawton – *British sportswriter*
Offense is the shop window of football. Defense is the heart and conscience and, often, the entrails.

Robert Lyles – *Houston Oilers*
We don't go out to hurt anybody. We go out to tackle them hard on every play. If the sucker's moving, our goal is to get eleven guys on him. Put the flag up. Surrender. He's dead. It's over. He's a landmark. It's hit, crunch and burn: *1989*

Merlin Olsen – *(b 1940) LA Rams*
So many moves you can make, so many stunts. But the best philosophy is to simply keep hitting them with your best lick.

They don't call the middle of the line 'The Pit' for nothing. We really do get like animals in there. It is very hard in 'The Pit'. No matter what the score is, it's always hard.

William 'The Refrigerator' Perry –
(b 1962) Chicago Bears
On his time for running 40 yards – It all depends on what speed you run the projector! :
                    Buddy Ryan – Bears
                    defensive coach (1986)

Andy Robustelli – *(b 1925) New York Giants*
The key blocks which pry a crack in the defense
are almost always hidden in the hurly-burly at
the line of scrimmage.

Jack Tatum – *Oakland Raiders*
Al Davis [*owner*] left me with the impression
that my only marketable talents in pro football
were those of an intimidator. My job with the
Raiders was that of a paid assassin.

My idea of a good hit is when the victim wakes
up on the sidelines with train whistles blowing
in his head. I like to believe that my best hits
border on felonious assault.

Lawrence Taylor – *(b 1959) New York Giants*
A hitter, that's me. In college, we'd hit people
in practice. We'd even hit people in the
lunchroom.

Once you see Lawrence Taylor, you never
forget him: *George Young – Giants owner*

Jack Reynolds – *Rams & 49ers*
We got more than a player when 'Hacksaw'
Reynolds came here. We got a lot of emotion.
We got an idea: *Bill Walsh – 49ers coach*

Otis Wilson – *(b 1957) Chicago Bears*
If I'm not selected to the Pro Bowl this year,
Stevie Wonder must be counting the ballots:
1985

Jack Youngblood – *LA Rams*
There are no opportune times for a penalty,
and this is not one of them.

KICKERS

Alex Karras – *Detroit Lions defensive lineman*
Placekickers aren't football players – they're
hired feet.

Mike Lansford – *(b 1958) LA Rams*
I pick out a drunk behind the goal posts, aim at
him and kick it through.

Mark Malone – *(b 1948) Washington Redskins*
On being named the NFL's most valuable player – I
didn't even think kickers were eligible: *1982*

Buddy Ryan – *Philadelphia Eagles coach*

Kickers are like taxi-cabs. You can always go
out and hire another one: *1989*

Billy Van Heusen – *Denver Broncos*
After a bad day kicking inside the Superdome – I
figured I was kicking against the air
conditioning!

OFFENSIVE LINE

Anon
I guess you need a certain mentality to play the
offensive line, knowing that you've done well is
enough. You don't need the band to play
everytime you accomplish something.

Julius Adams – *(b 1948) New England Patriots*
On the Raiders' line illegally holding – Put it this
way. Every time I rushed the passer, I had to
turn around and tuck my shirt back in.

Mike Baab – *(b 1959) Cleveland Browns*
Mike Baab is about as strong as nine acres of
Texas onions:
Doug English – Detroit Lions defensive lineman

Jimmy Breslin – *(b 1930) journalist & novelist*
They're killing the game with this phoney
mystique – telling people that a guy needs the
abilities of a brain surgeon to play left-guard for
the Colts. Football is simply a game to keep the
coalminers off the street.

Larry Csonka – *Miami Dolphins running back*
Guards make the running. If you don't have
good guards, you can't run inside.

Bill Curry – *Baltimore Colts*
An offensive lineman is programmed. I move
my right foot and the offensive guard next to
me puts his left foot where my right foot was.
Everything is done in concert.

Conrad Dobler – *St Louis Cardinals*
I have never knowingly bitten another player.
For one thing I believe in good hygiene.

Henry Lawrence – *LA Raiders*
In this game you can't be like a cabbage – all
head and no butt.

Gene Upshaw – *(b 1945) Oakland Raiders*
You have to laugh, when you get knocked on

your butt, and get up. Everyone gets knocked down, but the winners are the ones who get up. That's the key – how fast you get up.

Gene Upshaw & Art Shell – *Oakland Raiders*
They could block out the sun:
Doug Sutherland – Vikings

OWNERS

Al Davis – *(b 1929) LA Raiders*
Team motto – We have a total commitment to excellence.

The Raider organisation is the most respected, imitated, and feared in pro football. If I had my choice, I'd rather be feared.

My football philosophy advocates attack and pressure.

Being a Raider means that you perform on the field and win for Al. You give everything from the deepest part of your soul:
Lyle Alzado – Raiders

Al Davis is a good guy not to play gin rummy with:
Mike Holovak – Patriots coach

We're about as well matched as Amos and Costello; 1974 was the last time we spoke without lawyers being paid:
Gene Klein – Chargers owner

Every tale must have its villain. Every Peter Pan must have its Captain Hook. Every tenant must have a landlord. Every divorced husband must have his ex-wife's attorney. The National Football League has Al Davis: *Gene Klein*

Most head coaches have to make their reports to people who aren't football men, guys who don't understand. Would you rather talk to Al Davis or to a guy who owns an oil company?:
John Madden – Raiders coach

He is a field marshal, not a PR man. He is shrewd, cunning, aggressive, and, if need be, ruthless. Davis is Rocky Marciano swarming at you from all angles and not especially grief-stricken if a stray blow hits below the belt:
Larry Merchant – writer

Al always had information nobody else had. He was always looking for an edge. He's a very smart man. He's probably the only one who knows the serial number of the Unknown Soldier:
Sam Rutigliano – Cleveland Browns coach & former high school classmate

George Halas – *(1895-1983) Chicago Bears*
A big city is filled with various attractions for a young athlete. If a player has to report for early morning practice, he won't do much playing of a different sort at night.

George Halas didn't invent football, it just seemed that way: *Arthur Daley – sportswriter*

Barron Hilton – *Chargers & hotel magnate*
I really don't know the difference between a three-point field goal and a 3pm checkout time.

Lamar Hunt – *(b 1932) Kansas City Chiefs*
On the increasing problems of litigation in the NFL – My definition of utter waste is a coach-load of lawyers going over a cliff, with three empty seats.

Bob Irsay – *(b 1923) Colts*
Welcoming speech in Indianapolis, after his team had moved from Baltimore – It's not your ball team or our ball team, it's my family's ball team. I paid for it and worked for it.

Gene Klein – *San Diego Chargers*
Football is a very funny business. It's the only business I've ever been in where the more successful you are, the less money you make.

My two happiest days were when I bought a controlling interest in the San Diego Chargers and when I sold my controlling interest in the San Diego Chargers.

The men and women who control NFL franchises are called owners because they are used to getting things their *own* way.

Rankin Smith – *Atlanta Falcons*
The reason why we always have the toughest schedule is because we don't play us!

7

QUARTERBACKS

Dave Archer – *Atlanta Falcons*
The White House ought to send for Dave
Archer, he'll be able to overthrow any
Government: *Anon*

George Blanda – *(b 1927) Oakland Raiders*
George Blanda had a God-given killer instinct:
                                    Al Davis – owner

Terry Bradshaw – *Pittsburgh Steelers*
Bradshaw couldn't spell 'CAT', if you spotted
him the 'C' and the 'A':
                        Thomas 'Hollywood' Henderson

John Elway – *(b 1960) Denver Broncos*
*After Elway had refused to play for Baltimore and
joined Denver* – As former Bishop of Baltimore, I
have come to admire the choice of John Elway:
                Francis Stafford – Archbishop of Denver

John Elway is a time-bomb waiting to go off:
                        Sam Wyche – Bengals coach

Dan Fouts – *(b 1951) San Diego Chargers*
When you have a pure passer like Dan Fouts,
from a receiver's standpoint, it's like dying and
going to Heaven: *Wes Chandler – Chargers*

Sonny Jurgensen – *Washington Redskins*
The defense tells you when to throw, where to
throw and how to throw. The most important
thing a quarterback has to learn is how to react
to the defense.

I have to be the only quarterback ever booed in
Berlin. I have that distinction. What other
quarterback's been booed there? Hitler? Did he
play?

Joe Montana – *(b 1956) San Francisco 49ers*
You have to be somewhat crazy to play the
game; crazy about the game.

Joe Montana is not human. I don't want to call
him a god, but he's definitely somewhere in
between: *Cris Collinsworth (1989)*

*On Montana's surprise return to the starting line-up,
after major back surgery* – I feel like the guy who
was dancing with Juliet when Romeo cut in:
                Jeff Kemp – 49ers quarterback (1987)

Chuck Morton – *Denver Broncos*
I kind of like Chuck Morton. I think he's an
over-achiever. The main reason I like him,
though, is because he can't run outside the
pocket: *Jack Lambert – Steelers linebacker*

Joe Namath – *(b 1943) New York Jets*
The name of the game is kill the quarterback.

If you aren't going all the way, why go at all?

Joe Namath is the hottest thing since fire:
                Jerome Barkum - Jets wide receiver

Sam Rutigliano – *Cleveland Browns coach*
A quarterback doesn't have to play an
extraordinary game. He simply has to do the
ordinary, extra-ordinarily well.

Ken Stabler – *Oakland Raiders & Houston
Oilers*
On personal game statistics – It doesn't matter
when you lose. It's like ear-rings on a pig. It
doesn't make a whole lot of difference: *1981*

Bart Starr – *(b 1934) Green Bay Packers*
I'm for the upperdog. I was for the underdog
because I was one. Now I see the pressures that
are on the upperdog. The average fan cannot
appreciate the pressure and the emotional peak
you must reach each week to keep from getting
knocked off your perch at the top.

Bart Starr was one of the purest gentlemen
you'll ever want to meet, but on the football
field he'd cut your heart out and show it to you:
                Zeke Bratkowski – Packers quarterback

Fran Tarkenton – *(b 1940) Minnesota Vikings*
Remember an 80-yard drive is better than an
80-yard 'bomb'. The bomb can be dismissed by
the other team as a lucky, one-time fluke,
which it probably is. The sustained drive that
systematically pushes the other team back over
its own goal line shows them that you play
sound, unbeatable football, and is far more
demoralising to your opposition.

We think Fran Tarkenton uses audibles when
we're chasing him. Audibles like 'Help!':
                Roger Brown – Lions defensive tackle

Joe Theismann – *(b 1949) Washington Redskins*

Q. Why doesn't Joe Theismann answer his
phone?
A. 'Cos he can't find a receiver!   *Joke*

Johnny Unitas – *(b 1933) Colts & Chargers*
Being in the huddle with Johnny Unitas is like
being in the huddle with God:
John Mackey – Colts & Chargers tight end

RECEIVERS

Anthony Carter – *(b 1960) Minnesota Vikings*
I've never seen such skinny legs on a football
player before. Wonder if he ever caught the
rustler who stole his calves?:
Steve Jordan – Vikings tight end

Mark Bavaro – *(b 1963) New York Giants*
If I were in a foxhole, I'd want Mark Bavaro to
be sitting next to me:
Gerry Faust – Notre Dame coach

Raymond Berry – *(b 1933) Baltimore Colts*
My whole life and ambition could be summed
up in one sentence: I just had to play football.

Cris Collinsworth – *(b 1959) Cincinnati
Bengals*
On reaching the Super Bowl in his rookie year – I
feel like some guy who picked up the Rubik
Cube and got it right first time: *1982*

Don Hutson – *(b 1913) Green Bay Packers*
For every pass I caught in a game, I caught a
thousand passes in practice.

John Jefferson – *San Diego Chargers*
That man could fly, and if a ball was thrown
anywhere within his zip code, he would catch
it: *Gene Klein – Chargers owner*

Lee Roy Jordan – *Dallas Cowboys*
Football is like a day off. I grew up picking
cotton on my daddy's farm and nobody asked
for your autograph or put your name in the
paper for that.

Steve Largent – *(b 1954) Seattle Seahawks*
Having great hands is a cliché that doesn't go
very far when you try to describe what catching
a football is all about.

Ozzie Newsome – *(b 1956) Cleveland Browns*

He makes a one-handed catch, in full stride,
look as easy as an ant-eater snapping out its
tongue and collecting an ant for a snack:
Handbook of Pro Football

RUNNING BACKS

Anon
Two halves make a hole, and the fullback goes
through.

Sayings
Five yards and a cloud of dust.

Jim Brown – *(b 1936) Cleveland Browns*
Every time I tackled him, I heard a dice game
going on in my mouth:
Don Burroughs – Eagles

I hit him, I hit him good, and we both went
down. It was one of the few times in my life when
my body was aching all over. Only my pride
made me get up: *Willie Davis – Packers*

Earl Campbell – *Houston Oilers*
It's like standing blindfolded in the middle of
Interstate 75, dodging cars and trying to tackle
the biggest truck out there:
Gary Burley – Bengals

Larry Csonka – *Miami Dolphins*
When Larry Csonka goes on safari, the lions
roll up their windows: *Anon*

Eric Dickerson – *(b 1960) LA Rams &
Indianapolis Colts*
People think of me as being selfish, egotistical,
cocky or all the above. I'm just confident and
will let you know I'm confident.

Tony Dorsett – *(b 1954) Dallas Cowboys*
In football, you just can't stand still. If you do,
they come along and eat you up.

Tom Franckhauser – *Dallas Cowboys*
On the early Dallas Cowboys – We had some pretty
talented players. But just not enough of them. We
were a lot like an oil slick. We came from
everywhere, but we weren't very deep.

Walt Garrison – *Dallas Cowboys*
If you needed four yards, you'd give the ball to
Walt Garrison and he'd get you four yards. If you

needed twenty yards, you'd give the ball to Walt Garrison and he'd get you four yards:

Don Meredith – Cowboys quarterback

Harold 'Red' Grange *(b 1903) Chicago Bears*
He was a streak of fire, a breath of flame; eluding all who reach and clutch.
A grey (galloping) ghost thrown into the game, that rival hands rarely touch:

Grantland Rice – sportswriter

Freeman McNeil – *(b 1959) New York Jets*
Getting hurt is no bed of roses, but it's part of the business. Football is like the game of life. You could be on top of the world one minute, and flat on your back the next.

Bronko Nagurski – *(b 1908) Chicago Bears*
He was the only man I ever saw who ran his own interference: *Steve Owen*

Walter Payton – *(b 1954) Chicago Bears*
I guess my running comes by instinct. I don't try to define it or explain – only to improve it.

Trying to tackle Payton is like trying to rope a calf: *Bobby Bryant – Vikings cornerback*

On the reason for his success – Simple! He's got a big butt: *Frank Caito – Bears trainer*

Walter Payton is the all-time greatest. Remember the word all-time! All-time means that he's the greatest since they started keeping records. Maybe there was some other guy, who is unknown to man, who carried a stone for more yards. Or maybe those guys who carried messages from city to city covered more yardage. You know, the guys in Greece. But as far as we know, Payton's the greatest:

Darryl Grant – Redskins defensive lineman

To the Saints' defence after Payton had broken Jim Brown's career rushing record – All right you guys, don't tackle him for a loss on the next play and make us go through all that again:

Jay Hilgenburg – Bears (1984)

The first time I saw Walter Payton in the locker room, I thought, God must have taken a hammer and chisel and said to himself, 'I'm going to make me a half-back':

Fred O'Connor – Bears team doctor

George Rogers – *(b 1958) New Orleans Saints*
I want to gain 1500 or 2000 yards, whichever comes first: *1984*

Gale Sayers – *Chicago Bears*
Gale Sayers was as sleek as a greyhound, fluid as a panther, deceptive as a wildcat:

Handbook of Pro Football

O. J. Simpson – *(b 1947) Buffalo Bills*
The harder you work, the luckier you get.

To O. J. Simpson, running backs might be categorised as bulldogs, but he was a cat, a beautiful black cat:

James Lawton – British sportswriter

Duane Thomas – *Dallas Cowboys*
If the Super Bowl is the 'Ultimate Game', why are they playing it again next year?

Duane was the best football player in the world, except that that world was not the same one in which the rest of us live:

Gene Klein – Chargers owner

Jim Thorpe – *(1888–1953) Chicago Bears*
On his method for avoiding tackles – I give 'em the hip, then I take it away.

COLLEGE

GENERAL

Anon
A college football team is an organisation that an American boy joins in order to see the USA.

An American university is an institution that has two thousand seats in the classrooms and eighty thousand in the stadium.

Charles Horton Cooley
There is a function of a quasi-religious nature performed by a few experts but followed in spirit by the whole university world, serving indeed as a symbol to arouse in the students and in the alumni certain congregate and hieratic emotions. I refer, of course, to football.

Paul Gallico – *(1897–1976) writer & journalist*
College football today is one of the last great strongholds of genuine old-fashioned American

10

hypocrisy: *Farewell to Sport (1938)*

Elbert Hubbard - *(1856-1915) writer*
College football is a sport that bears the same relation to education that bullfighting does to agriculture.

Robert M. Hutchins - *(1899-1977) educator*
I don't see the relationship of the highly industrialised affairs on Saturday afternoon to higher learning in America.

Henry L. Mencken - *(1880-1956) editor*
College football would be more interesting if the faculty played instead of the students – there would be a great increase in broken arms, legs and necks.

Grantland Rice - *(1880-1954) sportswriter*
On Notre Dame v Army – Outlined against a blue-grey October sky, the four horsemen rode again. In dramatic lore they were known as Famine, Pestilence, Destruction and Death. These are only aliases. Their real names are Stuhldreher, Miller, Crowley and Layden: *1924*
[*Fellow sportswriter 'Red' Smith wondered how Rice saw the players 'outlined against the sky' from high up in the press box!*]

Y. A. Tittle - *(b 1926) New York Giants*
Kids in my part of Texas would rather play football than eat.

Robert Zupke - *sportswriter*
Many an All-American has been made by a long run, a weak defense, and a poet in the press-box.

A pro game is motion. A college game is emotion.

COACHES

Anon
There are two kinds of colleges in the USA: those that fired the football coach before the season started, and those that wish they had.

'Slinging' Sammy Baugh - *(b 1914)*
Washington Redskins quarterback
The algebra teacher used to be the football coach. Now the football coach is the algebra teacher: *1962*

Dick Bestwick - *Georgia Tech*
When you play guard, it's because you're not smart enough to play quarterback, not fast enough to be a halfback, not rugged enough to be a running back, not big enough to be a tackle and don't have the hands to be an end.

Dana X. Bible - *Texas A & M 'Aggies'*
Five word pep-talk, at half-time, after his team had been trounced in the first half – Well girls, shall we go?
[*The Aggies went on to win*]

Jimmy Cannon - *(1910-73) sportswriter*
A college alumni is a group of graduates who attend football games on a Saturday to find reasons to fire the coach on Monday.

Duffy Daugherty - *Michigan State University*
Football is not a collision sport – it's a contact sport. Dancing is a contact sport.

When you're playing for the national championship, it's not a matter of life and death. It's more important than that.

Carl De Pasqua - *University of Pittsburgh*
Football is not a democracy. There's nothing to debate. The players can debate in political science class.

Dixon Ryan Fox
I listened to a football coach who spoke straight from the shoulder – at least I could detect no higher origin in anything he said.

Woody Hayes - *(1913-87) Ohio State University*
When you put the ball in the air, three things can happen, and two of them are bad – incompletions and interceptions.

Joe Kapp - *University of California, Berkeley*
They say football is America's greatest game, but it's not. The greatest game in America is called opportunity. Football is merely a great expression of it.

Jerry Moore - *Texas Tech*
If the meek ever inherit the earth, our defensive line is going to end up owning Texas.

Ara Parseghian - *University of Notre Dame*

Every successful coach must have a successful quarterback: *1964*

Knute Rockne – *(1888-1931) University of Notre Dame*
Never tell 'em how many lettermen you've got coming back. Tell 'em how many you lost.

When the going gets tough, the tough get going.

It isn't necessary to see a good tackle, you can hear it.

Knute Rockne wanted nothing but 'bad losers'. Good losers get into the habit of losing:
George Allen – Redskins coach

Darryl Rogers – *Arizona State University*
You don't get fired for cheating, you get fired for losing.

Darrell Royal – *University of Texas*
A coach likes to have a lot of those old trained pigs who'll grin and jump right in the slop for him.

Ben Schwartzwalder – *coach*
A successful coach is one who is still coaching:
1963

Jock Sutherland – *University of Pittsburgh*
Fewer than three touchdowns is not enough and more than five is rubbing it in.

A forward pass is not only cowardly – it is immoral.

Pappy Waldorf – *University of California*
Pappy Waldorf could make one game look like the Punic Wars: *Anon*

ANGLING

Anon
Nothing grows faster than a fish from the time it bites until he gets away.

There are two periods when fishing is good – before you get there and after you leave.

Most people who do great things are alone, especially on a river bank.

Maybe the fish goes home and brags about the size of bait he stole.

Always bait with minnows, so that anything you catch will be a size larger.

Truth is when one fisherman calls another fisherman a liar.

How far an angler will stretch the truth depends upon how far he can stretch his arms.

The reason some fish get so big is because they're the ones that got away.

Springtime is when fishermen get that faraway lake in the eyes.

Many fishermen catch their fish by the tale.

No honest man is a successful angler.

Never a fisherman need there be;
If fish could hear as well as see.

Bragging may not bring happiness, but no man having caught a large fish goes home through an alley.

Caution is the most valuable asset in angling, especially if you are the fish.

There are two types of fisherman – those who fish for sport and those who fish for fish.

A thoughtful wife is one who has a juicy steak ready when her husband returns from a day's fishing.

Old fishermen never die – they just smell that way.

Proverbs
To angle all day and catch a gudgeon at night.

An angler eats more than he gets.

The fisherman with a rod eats more than he earns.

Sea has fish for every man.

All is fish that cometh to net.

The best fish swim near the bottom.

If you wish to be happy forever, learn to fish:
Chinese

The Gods do not deduct from man's allotted span the hours spent in fishing: *Babylonian*

The net of the sleeper catches the fish: *Greek*

It is not a fish until it is on the bank: *Irish*

He fishes well who uses a golden hook: *Latin*

Fish are not to be caught with a bird-call:
Old English

It is ill fishing if the hook is bare: *Scottish*

Riddles
Fisherman – one who lives on the waves and makes his living from the wind.

Fishing net – a thousand knots and a thousand holes.

Thomas Adams - *(d 1620) printer & warden*
When the fish is caught, the net is laid aside:
1615

Vivian Bailey - *writer*
Fishing differs from all other sports in one essential detail; it is the only sport, in which the quarry has to co-operate and play its own active and willing part: *1961*

Thomas Bastard - *(1566-1618) satirist*
Fishing, if I, a fisher, may protest,
Of pleasures is the sweetest, of sports the best,
Of exercises the most excellent;
Of recreations the most innocent;
But now the sport is marred, and wot ye why?
Fishes decrease, and fishers multiply: *1598*

Dame Juliana Berners - *(1343-1443) prioress*
The Salmon is the most stately fish that any man may angle to in fresh water.

Ambrose Bierce - *(1842-1914) US journalist*
Overwork is a dangerous disorder affecting high-public functionaries who want to go fishing: *1906*

William Blake - *(1757-1827) poet*
The weather for catching fish is that weather, and no other, in which fish are caught.

William Browne - *(1591-1643) poet*
Lays down his rod, and takes his line in hand.
And by degrees, getting the fish to land: *1613*

John Buchan - *(1875-1940) Scottish writer*
The charm of fishing is that it is the pursuit of what is elusive but attainable, a perpetual series of occasions for hope.

Samuel Butler - *(1612-80) poet*
Trouts are tickled best in muddy water.

Miguel de Cervantes - *(1547-1616) Spanish novelist & poet*
There's no taking trout with dry breeches.

Jack Charlton - *(b 1935) Republic of Ireland football manager*
I won't die at a match. I might die being dragged down the River Tweed by a giant salmon, but at a football match, no: *1988*

Peter Chippenham - *writer*
Catching salmon in Britain is not a sport, it is an art: *1978*

Thomas Churchyard - *(1520-1604) poet*
Some say there is no fishing to the seas: *1575*

Samuel Daniel - *(1562-1619) poet & dramatist*
They thought best fishing still in troubled streams: *1595*

Sir William Davenant - *(1606-1668) poet & dramatist*
For angling rod he took a sturdy oak,
For line a cable that in storm ne'er broke.
The hook was baited with a dragon's tail,
And then on rock he stood to bob for whale.

Delamothes
Still fisheth he that catcheth one: 1592

John Dennys - *(1657-1734) writer*
Then may you safely strike and hold him short,
And at your will, prolong or end your sport:
The Secrets of Angling (1613)

And with this bait hath often taken been, the
Salmon fair, of river fish the best.

Norman Douglas - *(1868-1952) novelist*
Don Francesco was a fisher of men, and
women. He fished ad maioerem Dei gloriam,
and for the fun of the thing. It was his way of
taking exercise.

Fergusson
He that fishes before the net,
   Lang or he fish get: 1641

Eugene Field - *(1850-95) US poet & critic*
   I never lost a little fish. Yes, I am free to say.
It always was the biggest fish I caught that got
   away.

Phineas Fletcher - *(1582-1650) poet*
The fish long playing with the baited hook.
At last is caught; thus many nymph it took: 1633

Richard Franck - *(1624-1708) Army Captain*
Experience is my master, and angling my
exercise.

Thomas Fuller - *(1608-61) clergyman*
That fish will soon be caught that nibbles at
every bait.

The end of fishing is not angling, but catching.

It is rare to find a fish that will not some time
or other bite.

John Gay - *(1685-1732) poet & playwright*
   If or chance or hunger's powerful sway
Directs the roving trout this fatal way.
   He greedily sucks in the twining bait
And toys and nibbles the fallacious meat.

Francois Guyet - *(1575-1655) French editor &
critic*
The line with its rod is a long instrument whose

lesser end holds a small reptile while the other
is held by a great fool.

Hardy Brothers Catalogue
A good rod is, without doubt, the Angler's chief
requisite: 1886

Gabriel Harvey - *(1545-1630) poet & satirist*
There never was a fish taken out of the sea, but
left another as good behind: 1573

Ernest Hemingway - *(1898-1961) novelist*
Someone just back of you while you are fishing
is as bad as someone looking over your shoulder
while you write a letter to your girl.

George Herbert - *(1593-1633) poet*
It is no sure rule to fish with a crossbow.

The fish adores the bait.

You must lose a fly to catch a trout.

Oliver Herford - *(1863-1935) writer &
illustrator*
There are more fish taken out of a stream, than
ever were in it.

Sir Alec Douglas Home - *(b 1903) Prime
Minister*
Fishing is undoubtedly a form of madness but,
happily for the once-bitten, there is no cure: 1976

Edgar Howe - *(1853-1937) US editor &
novelist*
A woman who has never seen her husband
fishing doesn't know what a patient man she
has married.

Colin M. Jarman - *(b 1958) sportswriter*
Does the chairman of an angling club ever use
his casting vote?

Samuel Johnson - *(1709-84) lexicographer*
Fly fishing may be a very pleasant amusement;
but angling or float fishing I can only compare
to a stick and a string, with a worm at one end
and a fool at the other.

Baites, Sir, for the people! And they will bite
like fishes.

Franklin P. Jones - *US humorist*
Fishing is a laborious way of taking it easy.

Juvenal - *(60-140) Roman satirist*
The fisherman could, perhaps, be bought for less than the fish.

Bishop Hugh Latimer - *(1485-1555)*
Well, I have fished and caught a frog; brought little to pass with as much ado: *1555*

William Lauson
The trout makes the angler the most gentlemanly and readiest sport of all other fishes.

Stephen Leacock - *(1869-1944) Canadian humorist and scientist*
It has to be observed that angling is the name given to fishing by people who can't fish.

Every man, deep down, is a fisherman.

No true fisherman ever wants to eat the darned things.

Thomas McGuane - *(b 1939) US essayist & philosopher*
What is emphatic in angling is made so by the long silences – the unproductive periods:
Essays on Sport (1980)

Don Marquis - *(1878-1937) US humorist*
Fishing is a delusion entirely surrounded by liars in old clothes.

Leonard Marshall
It is a great pleasure for a man sometime to take with his angle a dish of fish in those waters whereas fish is plenty and well-preserved and not use any other engines but with the hook:
1599

'Beachcomber' [John B. Morton] - *(1893-1979)*
Doctor Strabismus of Utrecht is carrying out research with a view to crossing salmon with mosquitoes. He says it will mean a bite every time for fishermen.

H. I. Phillips - *US writer*
A trout is a fish known mainly by hearsay. It lives on anything not included in a fisherman's equipment:
On White or Rye

Charles Ritz - *fly fisherman & writer*
All rods can catch fish; their success depends on the hand that uses them.

Fly rods are like women; they won't play if they are maltreated.

William Shakespeare - *(1564-1616) playwright*
Tawny-finn'd fishes; My bended hook shall pierce their slimy jaws: *Antony & Cleopatra*

A man may fish with the worm that hath eat of a king; and eat the fish that hath fed of that worm: *Hamlet*

The pleasantest angling is to see the fish cut with her golden oars the silver stream, and greedily devour the treacherous bait:
Much Ado About Nothing

A fish hangs in the net, like a poor man's right in the law, 'twill hardly come out: *Pericles*

Bait the hook well! This fish will bite.

Sidney Spencer - *writer*
No one ever did consistently well with unsuitable tackle.

Moonlight may be magic to some people but it holds no magic for fishers.

Rex Stout - *(1886-1975) US writer*
Born with the attitude toward all attractive women that a fisherman has toward all the trout in the stream.

Jonathan Swift - *(1667-1745) satirist & poet*
Fish should swim thrice; first in the sea, then it should swim in butter, and, at last, sirrah, it should swim in good claret.

Gladys Taber - *(1899-1980) US author*
The curious thing about fishing is you never want to go home. If you catch anything, you can't stop. If you don't catch anything, you hate to leave in case something might bite:
Ladies Home Journal (1941)

Henry D. Thoreau - *(1817-1862) US poet*

Time is but the stream I go a-fishing in.

Mark Twain – *(1835-1910) US humorist & writer*
There is no use in your walking five miles to fish when you can depend on being just as unsuccessful near home.

Henry Van Dyke – *(1852-1933) US clergyman*
The attraction of angling for all ages of man, from the cradle to the grave, is in its uncertainty. 'Tis an affair of luck.

Robert Venables – *(1612-87) Army Lieutenant-Colonel*
Many have supposed a void of delight, never having tried it, yet have afterwards experimented it so full of content, that they have quitted all other recreations.

Richard Waddington – *writer*
The fish is the hunter, the angler the hunted:
1978

Izaak Walton – *(1593-1683) writer*
Angling may be said to be so like mathematics, that it can never be fully learnt:
The Compleat Angler

As for winter fly-fishing it is as useful as an almanac out of date.

As no man is a born artist, so no man is a born angler.

Angling is somewhat like poetry, men are born to do so.

God never did make a more calm, quiet, innocent recreation than angling.

We'll banish all sorrow
And sing till tomorrow
And angle, and angle, again.

Angling will prove to be so pleasant, that it will prove to be like Virtue, a reward to itself.

No life so happy and so pleasant as the life of the well-govern'd angler.

What Walton saw in angling was not the delight in the consciousness of accomplishment and intelligence which sends the true fisherman to the rivers, and keeps him there, rejoicing in his own strength, whether he kill or go away empty. It was rather the pretext – with a worm and perhaps a good supper at one end, and a contemplative man at the other – of a day in the fields: *W. E. Henley*

No matter what evidence may be cited as a proof of American crowd-mindedness, it is significant to note that the most popular form of recreation in the United States is Walton's lonely sport of fishing: *J. E. Morpurgo*

Carolyn Wells – *(1869-1942) US anthologist & humorist*
One man's fish is another man's 'poisson'.

Arthur Young – *(1741-1820) agricultural theorist*
Angling is incessant expectation and perpetual disappointment.

ARCHERY

Proverbs
As straight as an arrow.

In order to hit the bull's-eye, a person has to miss something.

Rev J. W. Dodd
In sportive round, without a sigh,

A Bowman varies thus the scene.
Smooth as his shafts the seasons fly;
His Mark – Contentment's golden mean.

Sir Thomas Elyot – *(1499-1546) diplomat & writer*
But this sufficeth for the declaration of shooting, whereby it is sufficiently proved that

it incomparably excelleth all other exercise, pastime and solace.

John Heywood – *(1497–1580) playwright*
A fooles bolte is soone shot, and fleeth oftymes fer,
But the fooles bolte, and the marke, aim few times ner.

A. E. Hodgkin – *writer*
When you have perfected the 'loose', you will have done what no other archer has ever done before: *1951*
[*The 'loose' is the action of releasing the arrow*]

Alice Blanche Legh – *23 times UK ladies' champion archer [1881–1922]*
It is the very difficulty of hitting that round target with its bright and open countenance that makes archery so engrossing.
[*Alice won her last title aged 67!*]

C. J. Longman – *writer*

Neither dancing, nor hunting, nor any other sport has played a part in the history of the world which can compare with that of Archery: *1894*

W. M. Moseley – *essayist*
The Bow! That weapon of remote antiquity, once so destructive – so bloody, so cruel; that weapon, by which Nations have subverted Nations – among us now known only as an instrument of polite amusement:
Essays on Archery (1792)

William Shakespeare – *(1564–1616) playwright*
A well-experienc'd archer hits the mark, his eye doth level at: *Pericles*

Joseph Strutt – *(1749–1802) writer & engraver*
Among the arts that have been carried to a high degree of perfection in this kingdom, there is no one more conspicuous than that of Archery: *1801*

ATHLETICS

ANCIENT

The Bible
Know ye not that they which run in a race run all, but one receiveth the prize? So run, that ye may obtain: *I Corinthians 9:24*

Cicero – *(106–43 BC) Roman orator & statesman*
If a man is running a race in the stadium, he ought to use every effort to win, but on no account must he cut in on a rival or push him with his hand. So too in life, it is not wrong for a man to try to satisfy his needs, but it is not right for him to take anything from another.

Horace – *(65–8 BC) Roman poet & satirist*
What local athlete would spurn the chance of an Olympic victory, if he could get it without the struggle involved?

The man who wishes to achieve the longed for victory in a race must as a boy have trained

long and hard, have sweated and groaned, and abstained from wine and women.

If you prefer discus throwing, then aim high in the yielding air with your discus.

Ovid – *(43 BC–AD 17) Roman poet*
If you hurl a discus into the empty air, may it hit you and fell you to the ground like hyacinthus.

Philostratus – *(c 210) Greek author*
Rarely does God allow a man to run the race of life to the end without stumbling or tripping, and permit him to avoid both kinds of foul, intentional and accidental, by sweeping past the other runners with a sudden surge of speed which they cannot match.

Statius – *(45–96) Latin poet*
When the bar fell and left the threshold level, the speedy runners leaped onto the track.

MODERN

GENERAL

Anon
God made a home in the sky for the sun, it comes out every morning, like an athlete eager to run a race.

Never worry about a competitor who imitates you, because he can't pass you while following in your tracks.

Proverbs
What is the use of running if you are on the wrong road?

It is not enough to run, one must start in time:
French

Chris Brasher - *sportswriter*
The athletes here in Edmonton are beginning to open wide their legs and show their form:
1976

Noel Carroll - *Irish writer & double Olympian*
Running is the classical road to self-consciousness, self-awareness and self-reliance. Independence is the outstanding characteristic of the runner. Runners only get promoted through self-conquest:
1981

J. Kenneth Doherty - *writer*
A man runs with his mind and emotions, just as much as with his legs and circulatory system:
Modern Track & Field (1953)

Finlay Peter Dunne - *(1867–1936) US humorist*
In my younger days, it was not considered respectable to be an athlete. An athlete was always a man that was not strong enough to work.

Colin M. Jarman - *(b 1958) sportswriter*
Early rounds of an athletics meeting are called heats, because that is when the competition begins to hot up:
1988

Paul Joseph and James Robbins - *US sociologists*
Running represents a quiet but legitimate rebellion against the unwarranted hegemony of work as the primary focus of self- identity:
1981

E. R. Loader - *writer*
The athlete does not embark upon a sport, but upon a way of life:
Testament of a Runner (1960)

Alice Meynell - *(1847–1922) writer & poet*
With the first dream that comes with sleep, I run, I run.

Ron Pickering - *TV commentator*
Watch the time - it gives you a good indication of how fast they are running.

Alf Shrubb - *(b 1878) multi-world record holder*
We have not heard the last word of running:
1908

Charles H. Sorley - *(1895–1915) Scottish poet*
We swing with girded hips,
And lightened are our eyes,
The rain is on our lips,
We do not run for prize.

We run because we like it, through the broad bright land.

Dr Thomas Tutko & Dr Umberto Tosi - *US psychologists*
The psychological factors are the most important, yet most neglected in our approach to sports. Most great athletes acknowledge state of mind as the key to success.

Rex Van Rossum - *writer*
The need to compete with other athletes and with oneself and with nature is the driving force of all athletes:
1964

Athletics is not a sport for the half-hearted. It is an all-or-nothing sport. There is nothing to be won, no honour, glory, pleasure or satisfaction from dabbling in it:
1964

Paul Weiss - *(b 1901) US philosopher & essayist*
Athletics, because it enables one to move from a poor to a better state of being, can be viewed as a branch of medicine, but one which fortunately finds room for the expression of

spontaneity, ingenuity and judgement:
Sport - a philosophic inquiry (1969)

P. G. Wodehouse - *(1881-1975) novelist*
One of the foulest cross-country runs that ever occurred outside Dante's inferno.

ALL ROUNDERS

Fanny Blankers-Koen - *Dutch multi-Olympic champion [1948]*
Newspaper headline after the Olympics - The world's fastest woman is an expert cook:
Daily Graphic (1948)

Mildred Didrikson [Babe Zaharias] - *(1914-56) US multi-Olympic champion [1932]*
Before she won 2 golds and a silver in Los Angeles -
I came out here to beat everybody in sight and that is exactly what I am going to do. Sure, I can do anything!: *1932*
[*She was awarded the silver in the high jump despite finishing equal with Jean Shiley. The judges decided that Didrikson's style was illegal and relegated her to second place*]

My goal was to be the greatest athlete that ever lived.

Jackie Joyner-Kersee - *US Olympic heptathlon champion [1988]*
Jackie's got to think of the world record as another competitor. I've named it Wilhemina World Record: *Bob Kersee - husband & coach*

Carl Lewis - *(b 1961) US multi-Olympic champion [1984 & 1988]*
I never developed the macho side as a lot of boys do. Even my sister, Carol, shows more masculinity, but that doesn't make me a homosexual. They say I am, but I am not. They say it because nobody knows what I'm doing. I don't even sleep in the same hotel as the other athletes. I could be sleeping with a horse, for all they know: *1987*

There's going to be some serious celebrating when Carl gets beaten:
Larry Myricks - US long jumper (1984)

Slogan on his warm-up T-shirt - Is the world's second-best athlete gay?:
Daley Thompson (1984)

Steve Ovett - *(b 1955) middle-distance runner*
The decathlon is nine Mickey Mouse events and the 1500 metres.

Jesse Owens - *(1913-80) US multi-Olympic champion [1936]*
I let my feet spend as little time on the ground as possible. From the air, fast down, and from the ground, fast up.

Jesse Owens glides over the track with the grace of a streamlined express flying over the open prairie: *Arthur Daley - US sportswriter*

When Jesse Owens ran it was like water flowing downhill: *Marty Glickman*

Daley Thompson - *(b 1958) Olympic decathlon champion [1980 & 1984]*
As a runner he is excellent, as a jumper he is excellent, and as a thrower he is an excellent runner and jumper:
Cliff Temple - sportswriter (1978)

Jim Thorpe - *(1888-1953) US Olympic decathlon champion [1912]*
On presenting him with the gold medal - You sir, are without doubt the greatest athlete in the world: *King Gustav of Sweden*
To which Thorpe replied - Thanks, King! *1912*

Bill Toomey - *US Olympic decathlon champion [1968]*
Behind every good decathlete, there's a good doctor.

JUMPING

Anon
If you want a track team to win the high jump, you find one person who can jump seven feet, not seven people who can jump one foot.

Proverbs
He who leaps high must take a long run: *Danish*

Ethel Calderwood - *US Olympic high jump champion [1928]*
I'd rather gulp poison than try my hand at motion pictures.

Stuart Faulkner - *long jumper*
I'll let my legs do the talking this summer: *1988*

Dr R. V. Ganslen - *US athletic researcher at the University of Arkansas*
The pole vaulter, early in his career, must learn that the mind is something to think with, not just for worrying.

Pole vaulting is a religious experience: *1973*

Dwight Stones - *US world high jump record holder*
I know the high jump inside out. This is my job, in fact, I know more about it than anyone living. Who else knows what it's like to go over a bar at 7' 7"? Only I know.

I want to keep jumping until my legs fall off.

LONG DISTANCE RUNNING

David Bedford - *world 10,000 metres record holder*
Athletics is not a gentle school. It's a hard road to becoming a champion. I know, because I'm the one superstar who's been crucified by the press. The difference now is that I don't intend bleeding anymore.

Joan Benoit - *(b 1957) US Olympic marathon champion [1984]*
When I first started running I was so embarrassed, I'd walk when cars passed me. I'd pretend I was looking at the flowers.

Noel Carroll - *Irish writer & double Olympian*
If people were possessed by reason, running marathons would not work. But we are not creatures of reason. We are creatures of passion. We do need reason, of course, to steer the ship. But if the winds of passion are not in our sails, all the steering in the world will get us nowhere: *1981*

Derek Clayton - *Australian world marathon record holder*
The difference between my world record and many world class runners is mental fortitude. I ran believing in mind over matter: *1981*

Arnold Cooper - *US professor of psychiatry at Cornell University*
Scratch marathoners once - they tell you how wonderful they feel. Scratch them twice and they tell you about their latest injuries: *1981*

Monte Davis - *US runner*
Running long and hard is an ideal anti-depressant, since it's hard to run and feel sorry for yourself at the same time.

Leonard 'Buddy' Edelen - *US marathoner*
The miler knows that in just over 4 minutes the pain of severe effort will subside. But the marathoner must be able to tolerate pain and fatigue for over two hours: *1964*

Jim Fixx - *US runner & writer*
Runners are much like ordinary mortals. They can, sad to say, get sick. They can even die.
[*He died of a heart attack while out running, aged 43*]

Brendan Foster - *Commonwealth 10,000 metres champion [1978]*
By having a definite plan to follow, you feel that each ten mile run through the rain is a specific piece of the jig-saw, not just another run.

Every athlete has a certain number of races in him. There just isn't an infinite supply. When you get fit and good, you just can't keep churning them out week after week.

When the pace is slow, sometimes the athletes will make a move they hadn't planned to make earlier in the race than they planned to do it.

Jeff Galloway - *US runner & writer*
I'm convinced you run much better the skinnier you are.

Bob Glover & Pete Schuder - *US writers*
Rumour has it that there is life after running. There is even life after - or without - marathoning: *Runner's Handbook (1983)*

Brutus Hamilton
When you see 20 or 30 men line up for a distance race in some meet, don't pity them, don't feel sorry for them. Better envy them instead: *1957*

Mark Hanson - *US runner*
To run is to live - everything else is just waiting.

Joe Henderson - *US runner*

Running is a childish and a primitive thing to do. You strip away all the chains of civilisation. While you're running, you go way back in history.

Ron Hill - *Commonwealth marathon champion [1970]*
You don't know your best marathon time until you retire.

John Hopkins - *sportswriter*
In the marathon the contest is not so much between runner and runner but, in the tradition of this classic drama, between man and the Gods. The Gods in this instance being represented by distance, heat and time: *1966*

Derek Ibbotson - *world mile record holder*
There is no one formula that fits everyone. That is the fascination about distance running: *1960*

Nina Kuscsik - *Boston Marathon winner [1972]*
There isn't much freedom in our lives any more. Running gives you freedom. When you run, you can go at your own speed. You can go where you want to go and think your own thoughts. Nobody has a claim on you.

Vladimir Kuts - *Russian Olympic 5,000 & 10,000 metres champion [1956]*
Nature's attempt at an engine in boots:
Sir A. P. Herbert - MP & humorist

Marti Liquori - *US runner & writer*
What is pain or discomfort to a relatively inexperienced runner is merely information to the elite runner: *1980*

The athletes who truly make it are mentally some of the toughest people in the world. No one is born with that kind of toughness, and it doesn't come overnight. You must develop it, cultivate it, cherish it: *1981*

Tim Noakes - *South African physician, runner & writer*
The marathon race is less a physical event than a spiritual encounter: *1986*

Paavo Nurmi - *(1897-1973) Finnish multi-Olympic champion*
Standing water and a man that does not move

are the same. You must move otherwise you are bound for the grave.

Dorando Pietri - *Italian marathon runner*
After finishing 'first' in the 1908 Olympic Marathon -
It is horrible, yet fascinating, this struggle between a set purpose and an utterly exhausted frame: *Sir Arthur Conan Doyle (1908)*
[*Pietri was disqualified for receiving help to cross the line*]

Bill Rodgers - *(b 1947) US Boston & New York Marathon winner*
If I ever stopped running I'd feel terrible, as if I were slowly decomposing.

I'd rather run. The truth is I hate walking.

There are many doctors who would come out and say the same thing - that jogging is bad. Take a look at them. See how fat and overweight they are. Ask them their own physical history. Don't take anything for granted. Just because they have M.D. after names, they are not Gods: *1982*

Henry Rono - *Kenyan multi-world record holder*
The man with asbestos lungs:
Ron Pickering - TV commentator

Alberto Salazar - *(b 1958) New York Marathon winner [1980-82]*
I like the marathon because it's one race where you can find out who's really toughest. On the track, sometimes a guy can just pull away, and you want to stay with him but you don't have the leg speed. The marathon is slow enough that anyone can stay with you if he wants, if he has the will. The marathon is ultimately a test of will: *1981*

William Shakespeare - *(1546-1616) playwright*
He has no pace, but runs where he will:
All's Well That Ends Well

Dr George Sheehan - *US cardiologist*
The music of the marathon is a powerful martial strain, one of those tunes of glory. It asks us to forsake pleasures, to discipline the body, to find courage, to renew faith and to become one's own person, utterly and completely: *1978*

Frank Shorter – *US Olympic marathon champion [1972]*
You don't run 26 miles at five minutes a mile on good looks and a secret recipe.

Kitei Son – *Japanese Olympic marathon champion [1936]*
The human body can do so much. Then, the heart and soul must take over.
[*Son previously ran under the name of Kee Chung Sohn for Korea*]

Mao Tse-Tung – *(1893-1976) Chinese political leader*
Long-distance running is particularly good:
1918

Lasse Viren – *Finnish Olympic 5,000 & 10,000 metres champion [1972 & 1976]*
Some do well in other races, some run fast times, but they cannot do well in the ultimate – the Olympics. The question is not why I run this way; but why so many cannot.

After the Olympic 5,000 metres – This guy, Viren, just mesmerised the rest of the field like a rattlesnake: *Brian Kidd (1976)*

Emil Zatopek – *(b 1922) Czechoslovakian multi-Olympic champion [1948 & 1952]*
Zatopek isn't human in his achievement. While he goes for a 20 mile run on his only free day, we lie here panting and moaning that the Gods are unkind to us: *Roger Bannister – miler*

In every area and in every field of man's achievement there is one man who stands out, as the greatest. Politically, the man would be a Churchill or de Gaulle; musically, a Beethoven or even a Beatle; and athletically, a Zatopek:
Derrick Young

MIDDLE DISTANCE RUNNING

Roger Bannister – *(b 1929) world mile record holder*
On his sub-four-minute mile – I leapt at the tape like a man taking his last spring to save himself from the chasm that threatens to engulf him. My effort was over and I collapsed almost unconscious with an arm on either side of me. It was only then that the real pain overtook me.

I felt like an exploded light-bulb with no will to live: *1954*

Running is creative. The runner does not know how or why he runs. He only knows that he must run, and in so doing he expresses himself as he can in no other way: *1955*

No one can say, 'You must not run faster than this, or jump higher than that.' The human spirit is indomitable: *1956*

Filbert Bayi – *Tanzanian world 1500 metres record holder*
It is fun to run as fast as one can until you are dead-tired.

From running I derive not just physical but aesthetic pleasure.

World records are like shirts. Anyone can have one if he works for it.

Amos Biwott – *Kenyan Olympic steeplechase champion [1968]*
Amos Biwott leaped the water jump as if he thought crocodiles were swimming in it:
Joe Henderson – sportswriter

Zola Budd – *British/South African world 3000 metres record holder*
After tripping up Mary Decker in the 1984 Olympics and being booed by the Los Angeles crowd – My legs may be sore, my spirit may be bruised, but in my heart I'm still a runner. And there are a lot more races waiting to be run:
1984

Zola Budd – the transplanted South African, the put-upon matchstick mite:
Frank Keating – sportswriter

Zola Budd, so small, so waif-like, you literally cannot see her; but there she is:
Alan Parry – TV commentator

We gave Zola Budd a passport of convenience and she has abused that by not living here. It is a flag of convenience:
Ron Pickering – TV commentator

Sebastian Coe – *Olympic 1500 metres champion [1980 & 1984]*

I'm inclined to feel far from taking me into imbalance, sport adds a sort of balance to the equation.

I never went into a race believing I was invincible.

I'm too mentally alert to be a selector.

On 'the' rivalry – Coe and Ovett are chicken-hearted, they are pussy cats masquerading as tigers: *Bob Hersh*

The public has always known that I was never the beast that I was painted and Seb was never the saint some people made him out to be:
Steve Ovett

Steve Cram – *(b 1960) world mile record holder*
I even time myself driving to training.

Mary Decker – *US world 1500 & 3000 metres champion [1983]*
What is the use of doing something if you don't try to be the best?

On her tripping over Zola Budd in the 1984 Olympics – The most famous collision since the Titanic and the ice-berg: *Pat Butcher*

In the Eastern Bloc, it's just not necessary to look like Mary Decker, who looks like she goes two hours before the meet and puts on make-up and curls her hair: *Ria Stalmach – Dutch Olympic discus champion (1984)*

Derek Ibbotson – *world mile record holder*
In the moment of victory I did not realize that the inner force which had been driving me to my ultimate goal, died when I became the world's fastest miler: *1960*

Alberto Juantorena – *Cuban Olympic 400 & 800 metres champion [1976]*
Every time he opens his legs he shows his class:
Ron Pickering – TV commentator (1976)

Steve Ovett – *(b 1955) Olympic 800 metres champion [1980]*
I enjoy being myself 90 per cent of the time and Steve Ovett, the runner, just 10 per cent of the time.

You find out a lot about yourself through athletics. If you're cut out to be a winner or a failure or a quitter, athletics will bring it out of you. You're always stripping yourself down to the bones of your personality.

Sure, I immerse myself in athletics, but I won't let myself drown. If you're a sportsman in Britain, people won't leave it at that. They want to own a bit of you.

On his physical running style – It's got to the stage where I'm beginning to come out like a cross between Attila the Hun and Genghis Khan, and I wouldn't like the kids coming into the sport to think you have to be mean to get on.

Had Dr Frankenstein turned his hand to creating athletes, there is little doubt that the summit of his aspirations would have been cast in the mould of Steve Ovett: *James Coote*

I am sure he enjoys being the anti-hero:
Alan Pascoe

There is not one British athlete who has ever given more to the handicapped than Steve Ovett. He is the sort of person who doesn't support charities at arms length:
Ron Pickering – TV commentator

One can state with some authority that Steve Ovett is the greatest big-time competitor ever to wear a British vest:
Mel Watman – coach & writer

Fate was kind to him, dealing him a hand of five aces: *Harry Wilson – coach*

Kirsty Wade – *Commonwealth 800 & 1500 metres champion [1986]*
To run well involves a lot of pain, time and commitment.

Fred Wilt – *US miler*
In every race there comes a critical point when victory hangs in the balance. Only then does the athlete's powers of physical and mental courage, will-power, tenacity and competitive desire stand naked and exposed in a moment of truth, which cannot be denied.

ATHLETICS

SPRINTING

Proverbs
He that runs fastest gets most ground.

Valeriy Borzov - *Russian Olympic 100 & 200 metres champion [1972]*
For success, first, athletes must have talent; second, they must work, and third, they must have control of mind.

John Carlos - *US Olympic 200 metres silver medallist [1968]*
After his Black Power salute at the medal ceremony –
White America will only give us credit for an Olympic victory – they'll say I'm an American, but if I did something bad, they'd say I was a negro: 1968

Harvey Glance - *USA*
Harvey Glance, the black American sprinter, with the white top and black bottom:
Ron Pickering – TV commentator

Bob Hayes - *(b 1942) US Olympic 100 metres champion [1964]*
Bob Hayes doesn't so much run a race, as beat it to death: *Anon*

On the final leg of the Olympic 4 ×100 metres relay – Bob Hayes just exploded, he was absolutely fantastic, just like a clenched fist travelling down the track: *Neil Allen – sportswriter*

Colin M. Jarman - *(b 1958) sportswriter*
The Olympic 100 metres final is the modern equivalent of a Gold Rush: 1988

Ben Johnson - *Canadian 'world's fastest man'*
The human cheetah: *Colin M. Jarman (1988)*
[Johnson finished first in the 1988 Olympic 100m final but was subsequently disqualified]

Brian Mitchell - *coach & journalist*
The true sprinter is, by nature, necessity and training, a physical spendthrift.

Bobby-Joe Morrow - *US Olympic 100 metres champion [1956]*
Whatever success I've had is due to being so perfectly relaxed that I can feel my jaw muscles wiggle.

Charlie Paddock - *US Olympic 100 metres champion [1920]*
I'm going to win. I've known it all along. I can trim any sprinter whoever lived: 1920

William Shakespeare - *(1564-1616) playwright*
Where run'st thou so fast?: *Comedy of Errors*

Franz Stampfl - *coach*
Muscle speed is inborne. To this extent, one might say an athlete and particularly a sprinter, is born not made: 1955

Allan Wells - *Olympic 100 metres champion [1980]*
The feeling of running fast is unforgettable, the exhilaration you feel running around a bend, it's like you're in charge, you're a Ferrari.

THROWING

Geoff Capes - *double Commonwealth shot put champion*
Somewhere inside that flabby body was an athlete trying to get out: *Stuart Storey – coach*

J. Kenneth Doherty - *writer*
Sound field event coaching should have three bones – a wish-bone on which to fix goals and ideals; a back-bone with which to maintain persistence; and a funny bone with which all the work can be made to seem worth while.

Al Oerter - *(b 1936) US Olympic discus champion [1956-68]*
Technique is something I never had: 1978

I make sure that I work out everyday. Anything else good that happens, that's gravy.

When you throw against Al Oerter, you don't expect to win, you just hope: *Jay Silvester*

Howard Payne - *triple Commonwealth hammer champion*
Mention that you are a hammer thrower to someone who is not an athletics enthusiast and you will be met with any reaction from a puzzled frown to raucous laughter. If you have the misfortune to say it to a groundsman, you may face physical violence.

Fatima Whitbread – *world javelin champion [1987]*
People think of me as the Incredible Hulk.

TRAINING

Anon
Before the Paris Olympics – We have reduced our athletics to a science. You shall see:
Finland coach (1924)
[*The Finns won 9 gold medals*]

Noel Carroll – *Irish double Olympian & writer*
There is a time to run and there is a time to rest. It is the true test of the runner to get them both right: *1981*

Percy Cerrutty – *Herb Elliott's coach*
If you do not have that almost constant feeling of dissatisfaction with everything, recognizing that no sooner is one pinnacle achieved, one goal realized, there will be another, success may well elude you: *1964*

Peter Coe – *Seb's father & coach*
If speed is the name of the game, don't get too far away from it.

Jumbo Elliott & Theodore Berry – *US writers*
Athletics are an extension of the classroom:
1982

Marti Liquori – *US runner & writer*
Much of running is mental, and the guru coaches probably have been successful more because they knew how to harness a runner's heart and mind, than because of any mysterious secret training formula: *1980*

Over-training is, to my way of thinking, the biggest medical problem incurred by talented runners who lack the experience or discipline to cope with their own enthusiasm: *1981*

E. R. Loader – *writer*
Training schedules were not handed down with the Tablets of the Law on top of Mount Sinai, to be lost sight of and only recently disinterred with the Dead Sea Scrolls. No magic inheres in

a training schedule. Sometimes the slavish following of schedules can be an indication that the runner isn't able to think for himself: *1964*

If you define poetry as the right words in the right order, then good running is the right movements in the right tempo.

Sam Mussabini – *Harold Abrahams' coach*
You can't put in what God left out:

Arthur Newton – *5 times Comrades Marathon winner [1922-7]*
Training is, in some ways at any rate, just cleaning the channels through which energy flows: *1947*

We must wake up to the fact that athletics is not, nor ever can be perfected; there will always be more to learn: *1949*

Nine rules for training –
1. Train frequently all year round.
2. Start gradually and train gently.
3. Train first for distance, only later for speed.
4. Don't set yourself a daily schedule.
5. Don't race in training.
6. Specialize.
7. Don't overtrain.
8. Train the mind.
9. Rest-up before the race.

Perhaps the greatest debt of all is owed to Arthur Newton, who, more than any other man, showed the way to success by daily and hard training, in season and out:
Percy Cerruty (1964)

Ron Pickering – *Lynn Davies' long-jump coach*
The great joy days were the training days. The competition days were always the stress days.

Alf Shrubb – *(b 1878) multi-world record holder*
The less serious running of any description which an athlete indulges in before the age of 18, the better for his future prospects: *1910*

Franz Stampfl – *Roger Bannister's coach*
Training is principally an act of faith: *1955*

AUSTRALIAN RULES FOOTBALL

Anon
Aussie Rules OK   *Graffiti*

Thorold Merrett
Ninety-nine per cent of all Aussie Rules players are typical citizens.

BADMINTON

Anon
To play Shuttle-cock methinks is the game now: *1609*

John Arlott – *(b 1914) writer and commentator*
Badminton vies with hockey among British games in being, simultaneously, highly skilled, fast, competitive, satisfying, under-estimated, under-publicized and truly amateur.

The Badminton Gazette
The progress of badminton in the popular esteem has been so rapid that we can look forward to a time, not far distant, when it will be as well known as Lawn tennis: *1907*

Pat Davis – *Welsh national coach & editor of Badminton Gazette*
The shuttle is a prima donna: *1983*

John Oliff
A poetic pastime for the Parish Hall.

George Thomas *(1881–1972) IBF Founder-President*
The art of Badminton is to deceive.

BASEBALL

GENERAL

Anon
Calling it the World Series must impress the world as an example of America's modesty.

April showers bring May double-headers.

Franklin P. Adams – *(1881–1960) editor & humorist*
In spring, when it's cold out
Appears the baseball hold-out;
In spring, when it's warm out,
   He gets his uniform out.

Roger Angell – *(b 1920) sportswriter*
Whatever the pace of the particular baseball game we are watching, whatever its outcome, it holds us in its own continuum and mercifully releases us from our own.

Jacques Barzun – *(b 1907) Provost of Columbia University*
Baseball is a kind of collective chess with arms and legs in full play under sunlight.

Ambrose Bierce – *(1842–1914) journalist & poet*
Monday, in Christian countries, the day after the baseball game.

Changing Times
Los Angeles is a town where you can watch night baseball almost any afternoon.

Arthur Daley - *(1904-74) sportswriter*
Baseball must be a great game to survive the
people who run it: *1964*

Angus Evans - *British writer*
The Americans have a genius for taking a thing
apart, examining its every part and developing
each part to the utmost. This they have done
with the English game of rounders, and, from a
clumsy primitive pastime, have so tightened its
joints and put such a fine finish on its points
that it stands forth a complicated machine of
infinite exactitude: *1910*

James T. Farrell - *(1904-79) novelist*
Baseball is a self-enclosed world of competition
and action in which the emotions can have free
play without the consequences being
dangerous.

William Feather - *(b 1889) publisher*
A baseball game is twice as much fun if you're
seeing it on the company's time.

Stanley Frank - *sportswriter*
Once an asylum for amiable eccentrics, baseball
has become a lifeless charade by actors who
look as impersonal as motor-cycle cops: *1962*

Frankie Frisch - *St Louis Cardinals*
It's a beautiful day for a night game.

William B. Furlong
For all the psychologist could find out baseball
players are the stuff that telephone poles are
made out of: *1976*

Paul Gallico - *(1897-1976) writer & journalist*
No game in the world is as tidy and
dramatically neat as baseball, with cause and
effect, crime and punishment, motive and
result, so cleanly defined.

Joe Garragiola - *(b 1926) Pittsburgh Pirates &
TV commentator*
Baseball gives you every chance to be great.
Then it puts every pressure on you to prove
that you haven't got what it takes. It never
takes away the chance and it never releases the
pressure.

Garagiola is considered a humorist like Mark
Twain, who also came from Missouri. The

resemblance is purely residential:
Jim Brosnan - St Louis Cardinals

Ernest Hemingway - *(1899-1961) novelist*
They can't yank novelist like they can pitcher.
Novelist has to go the full nine, even if it kills
him.

Jay Johnstone - *Cleveland Indians*
The good thing about playing for Cleveland is
you don't have to make road trips there.

Roger Kahn - *sportswriter*
On retirement - Unlike most, a ball-player must
confront two deaths.

Ralph Kiner - *Pittsburgh Pirates*
That's the greatest thing about baseball; you
never know what is going on.

Oscar Levant - *(1906-72) humorist*
Ballet is the fairies' baseball.

William O. McGeehan - *(1879-1933) editor*
Baseball is a circus, and as is the case in many a
circus, the clowns and the sideshows are
frequently more interesting than the big stuff in
the main tent.

Henry L. Mencken - *(1880-1956) editor*
An opera in English is, in the main, about as
sensible as baseball in Italian.

Jim Murray - *sportswriter*
Is baseball a business? If it isn't, General
Motors is a sport.

Ogden Nash - *(1902-71) poet & humorist*
  All winter long,
I am one for whom the bell is tolling;
I can arouse no interest in basketball,
  Indoor fly casting or bowling;
  The sports pages are strictly no soap!
And until the cry Play Ball! I simply mope:
1957

Michael Novak - *(b 1933) critic, writer &
philosopher*
Baseball is a Lockean game, a kind of contract
theory in ritual form, a set of atomic
individuals who assent to patterns of limited
co-operation in their mutual interest: *1976*

Scott Ostler - *sportswriter*
In the competition for spring training optimism award, all twenty-six teams are tied for first.

Louis Phillips - *writer*
If the connection between the 'new' theatre and baseball once seemed tenuous, recent trends in the theatre have now rendered the distinction between sport and theatre, between theatre and baseball, obsolete: *1968*

Grantland Rice - *(1880–1954) sportswriter*
Play ball! Means something more than runs
  Or pitches thudding into gloves!
  Remember through the summer suns
This is the game your country loves.

Frank Robinson - *Baltimore Orioles*
Close don't count in baseball. Close only counts in horseshoes and hand grenades.

Will Rogers - *(1879–1935) humorist*
I've never seen a baseball game I didn't like.

George H. Sage - *(b 1929) writer*
It is a well-established fact that baseball was the first professional sport to appeal to the masses: *1970*

Howard Senzel
Why this baseball? Why not Greek tragedies or symphonies? Why not economics, history or philosophy?

George Bernard Shaw - *(1856–1950) Irish playwright & novelist*
Baseball has the great advantage over cricket of being sooner ended. It combines the best features of that primitive form of cricket known as Tip-and-Run with those of lawn tennis, Puss-in-the-corner and Handel's Messiah.

J. G. Taylor Spink
Baseball is the great American success story. It is, moreover, a great common ground on which bartenders and bishops, clergymen and bosses, bankers and laborers meet with true equality and understanding. The game has proved in everyday language that democracy works.

Robert Steen - *British writer*
You remember baseball? A sort of razzamatazz rounders, played by rowdy rough-necks,

wielding oversize clubs and oversized tennis balls.

Tom Stoppard - *(b 1937) British playwright*
I don't think I can be expected to take seriously a game which takes less than three days to reach its conclusion: *1984*

Fred Trueman - *(b 1931) British cricketer*
The under-privileged people of the Americas play some strange game with a bat which looks like an overgrown rolling pin.

BATTING

Anon
Batting around at night doesn't help you hit home runs in the daytime.

Baseball is the only place in life where a sacrifice is appreciated.

Henry 'Hank' Aaron - *(b 1934) Atlanta Braves*
It took me seventeen years to get three thousand hits. I did it in one afternoon on the golf course.

Throwing a fastball by Hank Aaron is like trying to sneak the sunrise past a rooster:
  Curt Simmons – Philadelphia Phillies

Johnny Bench - *(b 1947) Cincinnati Reds*
Slumps are like a soft bed – they're easy to get into and hard to get out of.

George Brett - *Kansas City Royals*
He could get good wood on an aspirin: *Jim Frey*

He hits better than any white man I've seen. As a matter of fact, Brett hits so good he hits like a black man: *Al Oliver*

If God had him no balls and two strikes, George Brett would still get a hit: *Steve Palermo*

Rod Carew - *(b 1945) California Angels & Minnesota Twins*
The only guy I know who can go four for three:
  Alan Bannister

Ty Cobb - *(1886–1961) Detroit Tigers*
Every great batter works on the theory that the

pitcher is more afraid of him than he is of the pitcher.

Joe DiMaggio – *(b 1914) New York Yankees*
There's no skill involved. Just go up there and swing at the ball.

A ball player's got to be hungry to become a big leaguer. That's why no boy from a rich family ever made the big leagues.

On his marriage to Marilyn Monroe
It's no fun being married to an electric light.

I don't know if it's good for baseball but it sure beats the hell out of rooming with Phil Rizzuto!: *'Yogi' Berra – Yankees*

On the break-up of the marriage – It proves that no man can be a success in two national pastimes: *Oscar Levant – humorist*

On Marilyn Monroe's marriage to him – Why marry a ballplayer when you can have the whole team?: *Mae West – actress*

George Foster – *Cincinnati Reds*
I don't know why people like the home run so much. A home run is over as soon as it starts . . . wham, bam, thank you ma'am. The triple is the most exciting play of the game. A triple is like meeting a woman who excites you, spending the evening talking and getting more excited, then taking her home. It drags on and on. You're never sure how it's going to turn out.

Josh Gibson – *(1911–47) Negro League player*
A homer a day will boost my pay.

He can do everything. He hits the ball a mile. And he catches so easy he might as well be in a rocking chair. Throws like a rifle. His name – Josh Gibson: *Walter Johnson – Senators*

Dick Gregory – *comedian*
Baseball is very big with my people. It figures. It's the only time we can get to shake a bat at a white man without starting a riot.

Ken Harrelson – *Kansas City Royals & Boston Red Sox*
Baseball is the only sport I know that when

you're on offense, the other team controls the ball.

Zander Hollander – *sports editor & writer*
RBI's [Runs Batted In] are the lifeblood of the offense.

Reggie Jackson – *(b 1946) New York Yankees & Oakland Athletics*
Fans don't boo nobodies: 1975

If I played in New York, they'd name a candy bar after me.

After he arrived in the 'Big Apple' – I didn't come to New York to be a star; I brought my star with me.

This team, it all flows from me. I've got to keep it all going. I'm the straw that stirs the drink. It all comes back to me.

On the legal wheeling & dealing in the sport – The way things are going the faces on next year's bubble gum cards will be lawyers.

He's a chocolate hot-dog:
Dock Ellis – Pittsburgh Pirates

There isn't enough mustard in the world to cover Reggie Jackson:
Darrold Knowles – Yankees

The advantage of playing in New York is in getting to watch Reggie Jackson play every day. And the disadvantage is in getting to watch Reggie Jackson play every day:
Graig Nettles – Yankees

Fred Lynn – *Baltimore Orioles & Boston Red Sox*
I never saw anybody with mediocre ability become a star through more batting practice. Either you have natural ability or you don't.

Garry Maddox – *Philadelphia Phillies*
Garry Maddox has turned his life around. He used to be depressed and miserable. Now he's miserable and depressed:
Harry Kalas – Phillies' announcer

The earth is two-thirds covered by water, and the other one-third is covered by Garry

Maddox: *Ralph Kiner – Pirates' announcer*

Don Mattingly – *(b 1961) New York Yankees*
If Don Mattingly isn't the American League
MVP [Most Valuable Player], nothing is kosher
in China: *Phil Rizzuto – Yankees' announcer*

Willie Mays – *(b 1931) San Francisco Giants*
When I'm not hittin', I ain't hittin' nobody. But
when I'm hittin', I hit anybody.

I played the game the same every time –
because I was playing for the fans, not for me.
It's their game.

I believed when I went on that field that I was
on stage.

To watch Willie Mays play was to watch
Rembrandt paint or Caruso sing: *Anon*

Willie Mays can help a team just by riding on
the bus with them:
Charlie Grimm – Chicago Cubs

He could go 0 for 4 and beat you:
Reggie Jackson – New York Yankees

I'm not sure what the hell charisma is, but I get
the feeling it's Willie Mays:
Ted Kluszewski – Cincinnati Reds

They invented the All-Star game for Willie
Mays: *Ted Williams – Boston Red Sox*

Kevin Mitchell – *San Francisco Giants*
You've got to swing that bat; only the mailman
walks: *1989*

Stan 'The Man' Musial – *(b 1920) St Louis
Cardinals*
The best way to pitch to Musial was to walk
him and try and pick him off first base:
Joe Garagiola – Pirates & TV commentator

John W. Raper – *(1870–1950) journalist*
Hit the ball over the fence and you can take
your time going around the bases.

Jackie Robinson – *(1919–72) Brooklyn Dodgers*
*To his wife, before becoming the first black player in
the Major Leagues* – If you come down to Ebbets
Field today, you won't have any trouble

recognizing me. My number is 42: *1946*

Like a few, very few athletes, Jackie Robinson
did not merely play at centre stage. He was
centre stage, and wherever he walked, centre
stage moved with him: *Roger Kahn*

Pete Rose – *(b 1941) Cincinnati Reds &
Philadelphia Phillies*
I don't believe in ever knocking your sport or
knocking another player in my sport, because if
you knock a player in your sport, you hurt your
sport.

I would walk through hell in a gasoline suit to
keep playing baseball.

His suggested epitaph – Here lies the man who
could hit forever.

If anybody plays harder than Pete Rose, he's
gotta be an outpatient: *Tug McGraw – Phillies*

George 'Babe' Ruth – *(1895–1948) Baltimore
Orioles & New York Yankees*
I guess I just liked the game.

I swing as hard as I can and I try to swing
through the ball. In boxing, your fist usually
stops when you hit a man, but it's possible to
hit so hard that your fist doesn't stop. I try to
follow through the same way. It's a gift.

All I can tell 'em is pick a good one and sock it.
I get back to the dug-out and they ask me what
it was I hit and I tell 'em I don't know except it
looked good.

The fans would rather see me hit one homer to
right, than three doubles to left.

If I hit a home run every time I bat they think
I'm all right. If I don't, they think they can call
me anything they like.

I only have one superstition. I make sure to
touch all the bases when I hit a home run.

A home run is the best medicine in the world.

I was listed as incorrigible, and I guess I was.

During Grantland Rice's radio show, referring to the

Duke of Wellington's famous remark – 'Duke'
Ellington said the Battle of Waterloo was won
on the playing fields of Elkton.
[*Elkton was where 'Babe' got married!*]

The origin of the nickname – Here comes Jack
with his new babe:
Anon Orioles coach to owner Jack Dunn

For almost two decades he battered fences with
such regularity that baseball's basic structure
was eventually pounded into a different shape:
Lee Allen

I don't room with 'Babe' Ruth, I room with his
suitcase: *Ping Bodie – Yankees*

The Ruth is mighty and shall prevail:
Heywood Broun

He was a parade all by himself, a burst of
dazzle and jingle: *Jimmy Cannon – sportswriter*

'Babe' Ruth wasn't born – the sonofabitch fell
from a tree: *Joe Dugan – Yankees*

The door opened and it was God himself who
walked into the room, straight from his
glittering throne, God dressed in a camel's hair
polo coat and flat camel's hair cap. God with a
flat nose and little piggy eyes, a big grin, and fat
cigar, sticking out of the side of it:
Paul Gallico – writer

A more determined athlete than George
Herman Ruth never lived: *Paul Gallico*

Some twenty years ago I stopped talking about
the 'Babe' for the simple reason that I realized
that those who had never seen him didn't
believe me: *Tommy Holmes – sportswriter*

He was the greatest crowd pleaser of all time:
Waite Hoyt – Red Sox & Yankees

'Babe' Ruth was great, I was just lucky:
Reggie Jackson – Yankees

He was always the leader of the pack – a King
of Diamonds, an Ace pitcher and always
looking for the Grand Slam home run:
Colin M. Jarman – British sportswriter

With vim and verve,
He walloped the curve,
From Texas to Duluth.
Which is no mean task,
And I rise to ask –
Was there ever a guy like Ruth?:   *John Kieran*

'Babe' Ruth and Old Jack Dempsey,
Both Sultans of Swat,
One hits where the other people are,
The other where they're not:
John Lardner – sportswriter

Who is this 'Babe' Ruth? And what does she
do?:   *George Bernard Shaw – Irish playwright*

I chased the balls that Ruth hit:
'Casey' Stengel – Yankees

A rabbit didn't have to think to know what to
do to dodge a dog. The same kind of instinct
told 'Babe' Ruth what to do and where to be:
Sammy Vick – Yankees

George Scott – *Boston Red Sox*
When you're hitting the ball, it comes at you
like a grapefruit. When you're not, it looks like
a black-eyed pea.

'Casey' Stengel – *(1891–1975) New York
Yankees*
I was such a dangerous hitter, I even got
intentional walks in batting practice.

Ability is the art of getting credit for all the
home runs somebody else hits.

Ted Williams – *(b 1918) Boston Red Sox*
I get paid for playing left field and for hitting
that baseball. I am not a participant in a
popularity contest: *1954*

I've found that you don't need to wear a neck-
tie if you can hit.

On his retirement – Now Boston knows how
England felt when it lost India:
Ed Linn – sportswriter (1961)

Dick Young – *sportswriter*
There is something uniquely American about
hitting one out of the park.

FIELDING

Anon
If you don't succeed at first, try second base.

Bud Abbott *(1958-1974)* **& Lou Costello**
(1906-59) – comedians
Let's see who we have on the bags – We have
Who's on first, What's on second, I Don't
Know's on third. . . : *Who's On First?*

Tom Boswell – *sportswriter*
Fielding is treated with knee-jerk disdain in the
baseball community. 'Gloveman' is not a
description, but a pejorative.

America responds to a gloveman who learns to
hit the same way it does to a blonde bombshell
who publishes a volume of poetry.

Defense is baseball's visible poetry and its
invisible virtue.

Behind the plate, the catcher looks like a
beached crustacean; at bat, he seems denuded
as a moulting lobster, shorn of authority
without his equipment.

Cesar Cedeno – *(b 1951) Houston Astros*
The nice thing about Cesar Cedeno is that he
can play all three outfield positions – at the
same time: *Gene Mauch – manager*

Roberto Clemente – *(1934-72) Pittsburgh
Pirates*
Most of what I know about style I learned from
Roberto Clemente:
John Sayles - film maker & novelist

Roberto Clemente was Manolete in a Pirates'
uniform, an elegant adventurer who should
have played right field with a cape:
John Schulian - sportswriter

Robert W. Creamer – *sportswriter*
The small boy does not know that the best
third baseman in baseball is human; that he
fights with his wife, worries about bills and
occasionally swears at the bat-boy. All the
small boy does know is that the third baseman
is his hero, and a hero does the right thing,
always right.

Joe DiMaggio – *(b 1914) New York Yankees*
The test of an outfielder's catch comes when he
has to go against the fence to make a catch.

The phrase 'off with the crack of the bat', while
romantic, is really meaningless since the
outfielder should be in motion long before he
hears the sound of the ball meeting the bat.

An outfielder who followed a fly ball with a deft
serenity as though his progress had been
plotted by a choreographer concerned only with
the defeat of awkwardness:
Jimmy Cannon – sportswriter

Bob Gibson – *St Louis Cardinals*
A great catch is just like watching girls go by –
the last one you saw is always the prettiest.

Tommy Henrich – *New York Yankees*
Catching a fly ball is a pleasure but knowing
what to do with it after you catch it is a
business: *1976*

Willie Mays – *(b 1931) San Francisco Giants*
Willie Mays and his glove – where triples go to
die: *Fresco Thompson – Dodgers executive*

George Bernard Shaw – *(1856-1950) Irish
playwright & novelist*
There is no reason why the infield should not
try to put the batter off his stride at the critical
moment, by neatly-timed disparagements of his
wife's fidelity and his mother's respectability.

Ozzie Smith – *St Louis Cardinals*
On the back of Ozzie Smith's uniform should
be the word 'SHAZAM'. Instead of '1' his
number should be '8', but turned sideways,
because the possibilities it brings to his
position are almost infinite:
Tom Boswell – sportswriter

You feel Ozzie Smith could field a ground ball
while juggling three oranges and get the guy
out without dropping one:
Jim Murray – sportswriter

'Casey' Stengel – *(1891-1975) Yankees &
Mets manager*
A double play gives you two twenty-sevenths of
a ball game.

On the Mets choosing a catcher as first choice in the draft – You have to have a catcher, because if you don't, you're likely to have a lot of passed balls.

Jeff Torborg – *LA Dodgers & California Angels*
Almost every catcher goes through a phase during which he can throw perfectly to second base, but, with men on base, he can't throw the ball back to the pitcher.

There must be a reason we're the only ones facing the other way?

Bob Uecker – *Milwaukee Brewers catcher*
Autobiography – Catcher in the wry: *1982*

Claudell Washington – *New York Yankees*
Claudell Washington plays the outfield like he's trying to catch grenades:
                              Reggie Jackson – Yankees

Jerry Weinstein – *coach*
Catchers have to do two things supremely well – handle pitchers and discourage stealers: *1981*

MANAGERS & OWNERS

Anon
You give the coach the horses, and they can make any coach look good.

Lawrence 'Yogi' Berra – *(b 1925) New York Yankees*
So I'm ugly. So what? I never saw anyone hit with his face.

You can't think and hit at the same time.

If the people don't want to come out to the park, nobody's going to stop them.

On a player he had just traded – He made too many wrong mistakes.

His philosophy on managing – You can observe a lot just by watching.

When a $25 cheque he received for a radio interview with sportscaster Jack Buck was made payable to 'The Bearer' – How long have you known me, Jack? How could you spell my name like that?

On 'Yogi Berra Night' in St Louis – I want to thank everybody who made this night necessary.

On being asked if he knew Ernest Hemingway, the writer – I don't think so. What paper does he write for?

Rocky Bridges – *Minor League manager*
There are three things the average man thinks he can do better than anybody else; build a fire, run a hotel and manage a baseball team.

Rocky chews tobacco because the chewing gum industry wants no part of him:
                              Don Rickles – comedian

Alvin Dark – *San Francisco Giants & New York Yankees*
If you're looking for job security, drive a mail truck. Managers always get fired.

Leo Durocher – *(b 1906) Brooklyn Dodgers*
There are only five things you can do in baseball – run, throw, catch, hit, and hit with power.

How can the manager exert discipline? What is he going to do to a guy with a million dollar contract – fine him?

Leo Durocher made me a star:
                              Willie Mays – Giants

Leo Durocher is a man with an infinite capacity for immediately making a bad thing worse: *Branch Rickey – Dodgers*

Charlie O. Finley – *Oakland Athletics*
My middle initial stands for 'Owner'!
[*The 'O' actually stands for Oscar*]

Prospects are a dime a dozen.

If a manager of mine ever said someone was indispensable, I'd fire him.

His motto – Sweat + Sacrifice = Success.

We had a common bond on the A's; everybody hated Charlie Finley:
                              Reggie Jackson – Athletics & Yankees

He is so cold-blooded, he ought to make anti-
freeze adverts: *Reggie Jackson*

Finley is a self-made man who worships his
creator: *Jim Murray – sportswriter*

Tommy LaSorda – *LA Dodgers*
Managing is like holding a dove in your hand.
Squeeze too hard and you kill it; not hard
enough and it flies away.

Nobody had to tell Richard Burton he was a
great actor. Nobody has to tell Frank Sinatra he
is a great singer. Nobody has to tell Robert
Wagner he's handsome. Nobody has to tell me
I'm a good manager: *1989*

When you say you're a Padre, people ask when
did you become a parent. When you say you're
a Cardinal, they tell you to work hard because
the next step is Pope. But when you say you're
a Dodger, everybody knows you're in the Major
Leagues.

You could plant two thousand rows of corn
with the fertilizer LaSorda spreads around:
Joe Garagiola – TV commentator

Cornelius 'Conny Mack' McGillycuddy –
(1862-1956) Oakland Athletics
Any minute, any day, some player may break a
long standing record. That's one of the
fascinations about the game – the unexpected
surprise.

His suggested epitaph – He loved his God, his
home, his country, his fellow man, and
baseball.

Billy Martin – *New York Yankees*
*On Reggie Jackson [player] & George Steinbrenner
[owner]* – The two of them deserve each other.
One's a born liar, the other's convicted.

You wouldn't hold up Billy Martin to your sons
as an example of what kind of person you'd
want them to be, except as an example of how
to win: *Anon*

If Billy Martin wins, he can take the credit; but
if he loses, he'll have to take the blame:
George Steinbrenner – Yankees owner

John McGraw – *New York Giants*
With my team I am an absolute Czar.

In playing or managing, the game of ball is only
fun for me when I'm out in front and winning. I
don't care a bag of peanuts for the rest of the
game.

It was an important part of McGraw's great
capacity for leadership that he would take the
kids out of the coal mines and out of the wheat
fields and make them walk and talk and chatter
and play ball with the look of eagles:
Heywood Broun – humorist

I have seen McGraw go on to ball fields where
he is as welcome as a man with the black
smallpox: *Christy Mathewson – Giants*

What I learned from McGraw I used with all
my teams. They're still playing with a round
ball, a round bat, and nine guys on each side:
'Casey' Stengel – Yankees & Mets

Wesley 'Branch' Rickey – *(1881-1965)*
Brooklyn Dodgers
Trade a player a year too early, rather than a
year too late.

George Steinbrenner – *New York Yankees*
They say I'm tough to work for. Well I am, but
I'm not trying to win any popularity contest. I
know only one way, and that is to work my butt
off and demand everybody else do the same.

Baseball is show business. How do you think
we average thirty-two thousand a game here?
We've got stars, that's how.

You measure the value of a ball-player by how
many fannies he puts in the seats.

The ideal example of the American capitalist
who saw himself as a romantic hero:
Tom Boswell – sportswriter

A first-and-ten capitalist in a bunt-and-run
world: *Tom Boswell*

Football is an adrenalin game. Baseball is a
sport of properly balanced metabolism.
Steinbrenner hasn't a clue as to the difference:
Tom Boswell

If Steinbrenner says 'Jump in a lake', he thinks you're supposed to: *Catfish Hunter - Yankees*

George understands me. He's a business man. Billy Martin doesn't understand that. He's only a baseball manager: *Reggie Jackson - Yankees*

Steinbrenner has one of the most expensive toys in the world and what he does is manipulate people. He won't let anybody relax. He throws fear into everybody. He makes the players fear for their jobs. That's his theory and it works: *Tony Kubek - TV commentator*

There are two things that George Steinbrenner doesn't know about – baseball and weight control: *Graig Nettles - Yankees*

It's a good thing Babe Ruth isn't still here. If he was, George would have him bat seventh and say he's overweight: *Graig Nettles*

Charles 'Casey' Stengel - *(1891-1975)*
Yankees & Mets
The secret of managing a ball club is to keep the five guys who hate you away from the five who are undecided.

I don't play cards. I don't play golf. I don't go to the pictures. All that's left is baseball.

What's the use of asking a man to execute if he can't execute?

There's three things you can do in a baseball game – you can win, you can lose, or it can rain.

They say you can't do it, but sometimes it doesn't always work.

All right, line up alphabetically according to your height.

On the Yankees – I'll tell you what I think of our prospects. I think we've got the world by the ears, and we're not letting go.

The Mets has come along slow, but fast!

I love signing autographs. I'll sign anything, but veal cutlets. My ball-point pen slips on veal cutlets.

On his triumphs – I couldn't have done half of it without the players.

He's a dandy ball-player, except for one thing – it's from his shoulders down: *Anon*

If Casey Stengel were alive today, he'd be spinning in his grave:
Ralph Kiner - Mets announcer

He can talk all day and all night, and on any kind of track, wet or dry: *John Lardner*

He spoke in a non-stop style that became known as Stengelese – a kind of circuitous doubletalk laced with ambiguous antecedents, dangling participles, a lack of proper names, and a liberal use of adjectives. He would clinch points by saying with finality, 'You could look it up!': *New York Times epitaph (1975)*

He walked on a pair of legs that resembled a pair of parentheses: *'Red' Smith - sportswriter*

Bill Veeck - *(1914-86) St Louis Browns & Chicago White Sox*
I have discovered, in twenty years of moving around a ballpark, that the knowledge of the game is usually in inverse proportion to the price of the seats.

Baseball is a kind of surety in a changing world.

Baseball is the only game left for people. To play basketball, you have to be 7' 6". To play football, you have to be the same width.

Baseball is almost the only orderly thing in a very unorderly world. If you get three strikes, even the best lawyer in the world can't get you off.

I want the fans to know that the White Sox management will scheme, connive, steal, and do everything possible to win the Championship pennant, except pay increased salaries.

Earl Weaver - *(b 1930) Baltimore Orioles*
The secret to managing is to get the guy up there you want.

Baseball is pitching, three-run homers and fundamentals.

Philip Wrigley - *(1894-1977) Chicago Cubs owner & chewing gum magnate*
Baseball is too much of a sport to be called a business, and too much of a business to be called a sport.

PITCHING

Rex Barney - *(b 1924) Brooklyn Dodgers*
He would be the league's best pitcher if the plate were high and outside: *Bob Cooke*

Robert 'Bo' Belinsky - *(b 1936) Los Angeles Angels*
My only regret in life is that I can't sit in the stands and watch me pitch.

Vida Blue - *Oakland Athletics*
Our best shot against him was ball four, and he never threw it all night:
Earl Weaver - Orioles manager

Jim Bouton - *(b 1939) New York Yankees & TV sportscaster*
You spend a good piece of your life gripping a baseball and in the end it turns out that it was the other way around all the time.

On making a comeback, aged 38 - This winter I'm working out every day, throwing at a wall. I'm 11 and 0 against the wall.

Rupert Brooke - *(1887-1915) British poet*
There is excitement in the game, but little beauty except the long-limbed pitcher. In his efforts to combine speed, mystery, and curve, he gets into attitudes of a very novel and fantastic, but quite obvious beauty.

Steve Carlton - *(b 1944) Philadelphia Phillies*
Sometimes I used to hit Steve Carlton like I used to hit Koufax, and that's like drinking coffee with a fork. Did you ever try that?:
Willie Stargell - Pirates

Alvin Dark - *San Francisco Giants & New York Yankees manager*
A pitcher who throws at a batter and deliberately tries to hit him is a Communist.

Jay 'Dizzy' Dean - *(1911-74) St Louis Cardinals & sportscaster*
I may not have been the greatest pitcher ever,
but I was amongst 'em.

The good Lord was good to me. He gave me a strong body, a strong right arm and a weak mind.

After a doctor had told him the extent of an injury – Fractured! Hell! My damn toe's broken.

If you can do it, it ain't braggin'.

I ain't what I used to be, but who the hell is?

Some people who don't say 'ain't', ain't eating.

It don't make no difference how you say it, just say it in a way that makes sense. Did you ever meet anybody in your life who didn't know what 'ain't' means?

During a TV commentary – He slud into second. *After his grammar had been pointed out* – What should I have said – Sludded?

Where do folks get off criticising my grammar? I only went up to the second grade, and if I'd gone up to the third, I'd a passed my Old Man.

Old Diz knows the King's English. And not only that. I also know the Queen is English.

He realized the American Dream at a time when most Americans had abandoned it. The country wanted entertainment more than it wanted inspiration, and he filled the need: *Anon*

X-rays of Dean's head show nothing:
Newspaper headline

The only way you can get along with newspapermen is to be like Dizzy Dean. Say something one minute, and something different the next: *Hank Greenberg - Tigers*

Don Drysdale - *LA Dodgers*
Drysdale's idea of a waste pitch is a strike:
Jim Brosnan - Reds

Leo Durocher - *(b 1906) Brooklyn Dodgers manager*
You don't save a pitcher until tomorrow. Tomorrow it may rain.

'Rapid Rob' Feller – *Cleveland Indians*
On how to hit him – Go up and hit what you see.
And if you don't see anything, come on back:
Bucky Harris – Washington Senators manager

Rollie Fingers – *Oakland Athletics relief pitcher*
What they start, I finish.

Rollie Fingers has 35 saves and has a better
record than John the Baptist:
Lon Simmons – sportscaster

Bob Gibson – *St Louis Cardinals*
Bob Gibson is the luckiest pitcher I ever saw.
He always pitches when the other team doesn't
score any runs: *Tim McCarver*

Gibson pitches as though he is double-parked:
Vin Scully – TV commentator

Vernon 'Lefty' Gomez – *New York Yankees*
On his declining speed – I'm throwing just as
hard as I ever did. The ball's just not getting
there as fast.

When Neil Armstrong first set foot on the
moon, he and all the space scientists were
puzzled by an unidentifiable white object. I
knew immediately what it was. That was a
home run hit off me in 1937 by Jimmie Foxx.

Reporter – As a pitcher, what is your greatest
asset?
Gomez – Fast outfielders!

Robert 'Lefty' Grove – *(1900–75) Oakland
Athletics & Boston Red Sox*
'Lefty' Grove could throw a lamb chop past a
wolf: *Arthur 'Bugs' Baer*

Luke Hamlin – *Brooklyn Dodgers*
'Hot Potato' Hamlin is so wild, if he fell off
Brooklyn Bridge, he would not hit the water:
Tom Meany – sportswriter

Orel Hershiser – *LA Dodgers*
Hershiser is the only Major League player to
have two consecutive pronouns in his surname:
Roger Angell – sportswriter

Steve Hovley – *Seattle Pilots*
To a pitcher a base hit is the perfect example of
negative feedback.

Walter Johnson – *Washington Senators*
You can't hit what you can't see:
Ping Bodie – Yankees

He's got a gun concealed about his person.
They can't tell me he throws them balls with
his arm: *Ring Lardner – humorist*

Knuckleball
There are two theories on hitting the
knuckleball. Unfortunately, neither of them
work: *Charlie Lau – batting coach*

The way to catch a knuckleball is to wait until
the ball stops rolling and then pick it up:
Bob Uecker – Milwaukee Brewers catcher

Sandy Koufax – *(b 1935) LA Dodgers*
Pitching is the art of instilling fear by making a
man flinch.

I became a good pitcher when I stopped trying
to make the batsmen miss the ball and started
trying to make them hit it.

It is almost painful to watch. For Koufax,
instead of merely overpowering hitters as some
fastball throwers do, appears to dismantle
them, taking away first one then another of
their carefully developed offensive weapons and
judgements, and leaving them only with the
conviction that they are victims of a total
mismatch: *Roger Angell*

On his 25–5 season in 1963 – I can see how he
won twenty-five games. What I don't
understand is how he lost five:
'Yogi' Berra – Yankees

When they operated on my arm, I asked them
to put in a Koufax fastball. They did. But it was
a Mrs Koufax fastball: *Tommy John – Yankees*

Sandy Koufax's fastball was so fast, some
batters would start to swing as he was on his
way to the mound: *Jim Murray*

Bill 'The Spaceman' Lee – *Montreal Expos*
You have two hemispheres in your brain – a
left and a right side. The left side controls the
right side of your body and the right controls
the left half. It's a fact. Therefore, left-handers
are the only people in their right minds.

Fred Lynn – *California Angels & Boston Red Sox*
We hitters are facing monsters weighing 230lbs, with arms as long as a pro basketballer's. They throw rockets.

Christopher 'Christy' Mathewson – *(1880–1925) New York Giants*
A pitcher's speed is worth nothing if he cannot put the ball where he wants to.

Plaque on his 'Hall of Fame' bust – Matty was master of all.

There ain't nobody else in the world that can stick a ball as near where they want to stick it as he can. I ain't tryin' to make you believe that he don't never fail to pitch where he's aimin' at. If he done that, he wouldn't be here; he'd be workin' agin' the angels in St Peter's League:
Ring Lardner

Mathewson pitched against Cincinnati yesterday. Another way of putting it is that Cincinnati lost a game of baseball. The first statement means the same as the second:
Damon Runyon

Stu Miller – *San Francisco Giants*
Miller has three speeds – slow, slower and slowest:
Anon

To hit Stu Miller, a batter needs the patience of a guy waiting for his wife to get dressed:
Jim Murray

Phil Niekro – *Atlanta Braves*
Trying to hit Phil Niekro is like trying to eat jelly with chopsticks: *Bobby Murcer – Yankees*

Leroy 'Satchel' Paige – *(1906–82) St Louis Browns & Cleveland Indians*
It got so I could nip frosting off a cake with my fastball.

Throw strikes – Home plate don't move.

J. Richard – *(b 1950) Houston Astros*
I don't know how fast I am throwing, 'cause I haven't run alongside one of my fastballs yet.

Nolan Ryan – *(b 1947) California Angels & Houston Astros*

Nolan Ryan is pitching much better now that he has his curve ball straightened out:
Joe Garagiola – TV commentator

Tom Seaver – *New York Mets & Yankees*
As a pitcher, I feel I'm creating something. Pitching itself is not enjoyable while you're doing it. Pitching is work. I don't enjoy it until I can stand back and look at what I've created. That is something.

Blind people come to the park, just to hear Tom Seaver pitch: *Reggie Jackson – Yankees*

Warren Spahn – *Atlanta Braves*
Hitting is timing; pitching is upsetting timing.

Henry A. Thomas – *coach*
Every pitcher is a creature of habit: *1980*

Luis Tiant – *Boston Red Sox*
He comes from everywhere except between his legs: *Curt Gowdy*

Luis Tiant is the Fred Astaire of baseball:
Reggie Jackson – Yankees

Fernando Valenzuela – *(b 1960) LA Dodgers*
The man whose name sounds like a mailing address in the Lower Andes: *Tom Boswell*

Watching Fernando Valenzuela force himself into a Dodger uniform is like seeing Kate Smith struggling to fit into a pair of Brooke Shield's designer jeans: *H. G. Reza*

Arthur Vance – *(1891–1961) Brooklyn Dodgers*
'Dazzy' Vance could throw a cream puff through a battleship: *Johnny Frederick – Dodgers*

Bob Veale – *Pittsburgh Pirates*
Good pitching will beat good batting, any time, and vice versa.

Early Wynn – *Cleveland Indians*
I don't like losing a ball game any more than a salesman likes losing a sale. I've a right to knock down anybody holding a bat.

When asked if he'd throw 'at' his grandmother – Only if she was crowding the plate!

RUNNING

Anon
It takes longer to run from second to third, than first to second, because there is a short stop in the middle.

A conservative is like a player trying to steal second while keeping his foot on first.

James 'Cool Papa' Bell – *Negro League player*
He was so fast he could get out of bed, turn out the lights across the room, and be back in bed under the covers before the lights went out:
Josh Gibson

'Cool Papa' Bell was so fast, one time he hit a line drive right back past my ear. I turned round and saw the ball hit his ass sliding into second: *'Satchel' Paige – Browns*

Ty Cobb – *(1886–1961) Detroit Tigers*
The baseline belongs to me.

Cobb lived off the field as though he wished to live forever. He lived on the field as though it was his last day: *Branch Rickey – Dodgers*

Phil Linz – *New York Yankees*
I don't know why, but I can run faster in tight pants.

Willie Mays – *(b 1931) San Francisco Giants*
Seeing him drift across a base and then sink into full speed, I noticed all at once how much he resembles a marvellous skier in mid-turn down some steep pitch of fine powder. Nobody like him: *Roger Angell*

Leroy 'Satchel' Paige – *(1906–82) St Louis Browns*
Don't look back, something may be gaining on you.

Phil Rizzuto – *(b 1918) New York Yankees*
They still can't steal first base.

Ozzie Smith – *St Louis Cardinals*
Ozzie Smith is an international jewel thief, masquerading as a baseball player; he could steal second and third in a black tie:
Tom Boswell

Maury Wills – *LA Dodgers*
At third, it's 'Be safe'. At second base, I concentrate on one thing, 'Be careful'. At first, it's 'Be daring'.

There's no such thing as an unimportant stolen base.

My instructions for preventing Wills from stealing are simple. Don't let him get on base:
Fred Hutchinson – Reds

STATISTICS

Anon
Baseball is an island of activity amidst a sea of statistics.

Jim Bouton – *(b 1939) New York Yankees & TV sportscaster*
Statistics are about as interesting as first base coaches.

Bobby Bragan – *Atlanta Braves pitcher & sportswriter*
On baseball statistics – Say you were standing with one foot in the oven and one foot in an ice bucket. According to the percentage people, you should be perfectly comfortable: *1963*

John M. Culkin
I don't think baseball could survive without all the statistical appurtenances involved in calculating pitching, hitting and fielding percentages. Some people could do without the games as long as they got the box scores.

Arthur Daley – *(1904–74) sportswriter*
A baseball fan has the digestive apparatus of a billy goat. He can – and does – devour any set of diamond statistics with insatiable appetite and then nuzzle hungrily for more.

Jim Kaat – *Minnesota Twins pitcher*
As I get older, I think more about the Hall of Fame. My stats are of Hall of Fame calibre, but my career has been one of obscurity. I know that. I've been a workhorse, not a Seattle Slew. I hope there's a place in there for a nag like me.

Ralph Kiner – *Pittsburgh Pirates announcer*
The Pirates won eight of their 102 losses against the Mets last year.

William O. McGeehan – *(1879–1933) editor*
I am quite sure that statistics will show that the
greatest number of successes have been scored
by those who have led moderately dirty lives.

Ben Mondor – *President of Pawtucket Red Sox*
It is the symmetry that is so perfect. Five feet,
even two feet more or less between bases and
baseball would be quite different.

Jim Wohlford – *Milwaukee Brewers*
Ninety per cent of this game is half-mental.

UMPIRES & RULES

Anon
Pity the woman who marries a baseball umpire
and has to have a man around the house who is
always right.

Umpires have got to be stupid to begin with or
they wouldn't take the job. Even when they're
right, they're wrong. Would you want your
daughter to marry one?:
American League manager

Robert Benchley – *(1889–1945) humorist*
Eighteen men play a game and eighteen
thousand watch them, and yet those who play
are the only ones who have any official
direction in the matter of rules and regulations.
The eighteen thousand are allowed to run wild.

Jim Brosnan – *Cincinnati Reds & St Louis
Cardinals*
Umpires are most vigorous when defending
their miscalls.

Nestor Chylak – *umpire*
They expect an umpire to be perfect on opening
day and to improve as the season goes on.

Larry Goetz – *umpire*
In a way, an umpire is like a woman. He makes
quick decisions, never reverses them, and
doesn't think you're safe when you're out: *1955*

Doug Harvey – *umpire*
When I'm right, no one remembers. When I am
wrong, no one forgets.

Tim Hurst – *umpire*
Why do I like baseball? The pay is good, it
keeps you out in the fresh air and sunshine, and
you can't beat the hours.

Ken Kaiser – *umpire*
We're always like the first cop at the scene of
the crime. We see people when they're on their
worst behaviour.

Ron Luciano – *umpire*
We're four men controlling forty thousand
people most of whom aren't so sure they want
to be controlled.

Managers holler for three reasons – they think
we erred, they're trying to keep a player from
being ejected, and, most frequently, they're
temporarily insane.

Autobiography – The Umpire Strikes Back!

General Douglas MacArthur – *(1880–1964)*
It is wonderful to be here, to be able to hear the
baseball against the bat, ball against glove, and
be able to boo the umpire.

Bob McKenty
The Umpire has the awesome power
To send a grown man to the shower.
  Yet cannot, in the aftermath,
Coerce his kids to take a bath.

Time Magazine
Ideally, the umpire should combine the
integrity of a Supreme Court Justice, the
physical agility of an acrobat, the endurance of
Job and the imperturbility of Buddha.

Harry Wendelstadt – *umpire*
Baseball regards umpires as a necessary evil. If
they could play games without umpires, I'm
sure the majority would vote to do so.

YOUTH

'Yogi' Berra – *(b 1925) New York Yankees*
I think Little League is wonderful. It keeps the
kids out of the house.

Rocky Bridges – *Minor League manager*
I think Little League is all right: it keeps the
parents off the street: *1964*

Bob Lemon – *New York Yankees manager*

Baseball was made for kids, and grown-ups only screw it up.

Tug McGraw - *Philadelphia Phillies*
Kids should practice autographing baseballs.

This skill is often overlooked in Little League.

Earl Wilson - *writer*
For parents of a Little Leaguer, a baseball game is a nervous breakdown divided into innings.

BASKETBALL

Pete Axthelm - *TV commentator & writer*
The game is simple , but its simple motions swirl into intricate patterns, its variations become almost endless, its brief soaring moments merge into a fascinating dance.

Bill Bradley - *(b 1943) New York Knicks*
An exceptional player is simply one point of a five-pointed star. Great individual players may earn dollars for the owner just as a sideshow does for a circus, but stardom is if anything a deterrent in the pursuit of a championship.

Teams develop when talent and personalities mesh.

Wilt 'The Stilt' Chamberlain - *(b 1936) Golden State Warriors & LA Lakers*
If I were given a change of life, I'd like to see how it would be to live as a mere six-footer.

Nobody roots for Goliath: 1967

Chick Davies - *sportswriter*
I'd rather play a pin-ball machine than watch a basketball game. You can score the same number of points.

Darryl Dawkins - *Philadelphia 76ers*
I'm six foot eleven. My birthday covers three days.

Julius Erving - *(b 1950) New Jersey Nets & Philadelphia 76ers*
I put the most pressure on myself because of my ambitions to be the best basketball player ever. What happens around me can't put any more pressure on me than that.

I'm a utility man. I do a little of everything. All right - so I do a 'lot' of everything: 1976

The thing about Julius Erving is that you know he is going to the basket, you just never know how: *Bobby Jones (1976)*

Bill Fitch - *coach*
On a losing run - Sometimes you wake up in the morning and wish your parents had never met.

Marv Harshman - *coach*
On drafting players from college - Quick guys get tired; big guys don't shrink.

Neil Isaacs & Dick Motta - *coaches*
The thinking parts of basketball, in actual play, are like combining the lightning attack and response of an epee duel with finding the optional solutions to a sequence of variable algebraic-geometric problems.

Earvin 'Magic' Johnson - *(b 1959) LA Lakers*
When he has to score or wants to score, he can will the ball into the basket:
Jud Heathcote - Michigan State University coach

The Lakers without Earvin would be like Camelot without Merlin: *Colin M. Jarman*

Don't talk about Magic. He's so special you can't compare anyone to him. If 10 is the limit for a point guard, then Magic gets 20:
Dan Nelson - Warriors coach

On a basketball court he is one of ten - he is also one of a kind. He slices the heart out of an opposition, as surely as if he had a scalpel:
Art Spander

He should change his name from Magic to 'Mystifying': *Mychal Thompson - Lakers*

He throws the ball behind his back, waves to

the girls, has fun. But he's also a thug, barging into the boards, knocking people over. Maybe that's why he's Magic. Because now you see him, now you don't:

Paul Westhead – Lakers coach

Gene Klein – *Seattle Supersonics owner*
On tactics – The first person to touch the ball shoots it. Either that or the coach carefully diagrams a 'set play' and then the first person to touch it shoots it.

John Kolver – *Chicago Bulls owner*
After 13 years I still love basketball, and I'm even starting to enjoy it: *1985*

Larner & Nicholson – *screen writers*
Basketball is staying in after school in your underwear: *Drive He Said (1970)*

Abe Lemmons – *Oklahoma City University coach*
We can alley but we haven't the oop!

James Michener – *(b 1907) writer*
It has been basketball which has shown the most conspicuous explosion of black talent.

Ogden Nash – *(1902–71) poet & humorist*
Basketball, a game which won't be fit for people until they set the basket umbilicus-high and return the giraffes to the zoo.

Jack Ramsay
The game is five men playing as one.

Pat Riley – *LA Lakers coach*
We have total discipline in the Lakers' locker room. It's yes sir, and no sir. 'Yes sir, Kareem'. 'No sir, Magic'.

On the sidelines Pat Riley may look like he's waiting for his car to be brought round; he is, underneath that cool, unwrinkled exterior, a man possessed: *Diane K. Shah (1988)*

Lee Rose – *coach*
I would like to deny the statement that I think basketball is a matter of life and death. I feel it is much more important than that.

Russell Sherman – *concert pianist*
Basketball is an ongoing tension between style and efficiency.

Art Spander – *sportswriter*
Basketball has so much show-boating you'd think it was invented by Jerome Kern.

Paul Westhead – *LA Lakers coach*
If Shakespeare had been in pro basketball he never would have had time to write his soliloquies. He would always have been on a plane between Phoenix and Kansas City.

John Wooden – *(b 1910) UCLA coach*
There's no way you can have consistent success without players. No one can win without material. But not everyone can win with material: *1972*

BILLIARDS

Charles Cotton – *(1630–87) poet & translator*
Billiards, this most genteel, cleanly and ingenious game: *1674*

Alfred E. Crawley – *(1869–1924) social anthropologist*
The billiard table is the paradise of the ball:
                   1913

Steve Davis – *(b 1957) snooker player*
Billiards is very similar to snooker, except there are only three balls and no one watches it: *1988*

William S. Gilbert – *(1836–1911) dramatist & lyricist*
The billard sharp whom any one catches,
    His doom's extremely hard –
He's made to dwell,
    In a dungeon cell,
On a spot that's always barred.
        And there he plays extravagant matches,
            In fitless finger stalls,
        On a cloth untrue,
With a twisted cue,
And elliptical billiard balls.

Edward V. Lucas – *(1868-1938) novelist &*
poet
A man who wants to play billiards must have
no other ambition – billiards is all.

Herbert Spencer – *(1820-1903) philosopher &*
scientist

To an opponent – A certain dexterity in games of
skill argues a well-balanced mind, but such
dexterity as you have shown is evidence, I fear,
of a misspent youth.
[*Often misquoted as* – To play billiards (snooker/
pool) well is a sign of a misspent youth]

BOARD GAMES

BACKGAMMON

Anon
If thou wisheth to win at backgammon, take a
raven's heart, dry it in a spot on which the sun
doth not shine, crush, then rub it on the dice:
Icelandic manuscript

Douglas Jerrold – *(1803-57) playwright &*
humorist
The only athletic sport I mastered was
backgammon.

Terence 'Spike' Milligan – *(b 1918) comedian*
I always thought Backgammon was a side of
bacon.

CHESS

International Rule Book
Chess is a game in the playing of which there is
no element of chance.

Proverbs
There are rare beauties in chess.

Chess is a sea in which a gnat may drink and
an elephant may bathe: *Indian*

There are many moves, but only one mate:
Soviet

Woody Allen – *(b 1935) US actor & director*
I failed to make the chess team, because of my
height.

Frank Betts – *poet*
Knight nor Bishop can resist
The pawns of this antagonist.
Whose countenance is dark with mist.

The game goes on and will not wait
Caesar is gripped in a deadly strait –
What if the pawns should give checkmate?:
The Pawns

Mikhail M. Botvinik – *Russian 3 times world
champion [1948-63]*
When I ceased to experience chess hunger, I
always played without drive.

Robert Browning – *(1812-89) poet*
We call the chess-board white – we call it black.

Robert Burton – *(1577-1640) churchman &*
writer
Chess is a game too troublesome for some
men's braines, too testy full of anxiety, all out
as bad as study; besides, it is a cholericke game,
and very offensive to him that looseth the
Mate.

Henry J. Byron – *(1834-84) playwright*
Life's too short for chess: *Our Boys (1874)*

Raymond Chandler – *(1888-1959) US
novelist*
As elaborate a waste of human intelligence as
you can find outside an advertising agency.

Earl of Chatfield – *(1873-1967)*
Chess is a wooden or ivory allegory.

Geoffrey Chaucer – *(1340-1400) poet*
They dancen and they play at ches and tables.

G. K. Chesterton – *(1874-1936) novelist &*
poet
Poets do not go mad; but chess players do.

Marcel Duchamp – *(1887-1968) French/US*

artist
Chess can be described as the movement of
pieces eating one another: *1969*

When you play a game of chess, it is like
designing something or constructing some
mechanism of some kind by which you win or
lose.

Bobby Fischer – *(b 1943) US world champion
[1972-5]*
There was something that didn't turn me on
about games like Chinese Chequers. I like to
watch my opponent's egos crumble.

If I win a tournament, I win by myself. I do the
playing, no-one helps me.

All I want to do, ever, is play chess.

I add status to any tournament.

On the 1972 World Championships v Boris Spassky
– It will probably be the great sports event in
history. Bigger than the Frazier-Ali fight. It's
really the free world against the lying, cheating,
hypocritical Russians.

Chess is like playing a concert. That's where
it's at. Some day I'm going to dress for a show,
. . . I mean a game, like Tom Jones or Liberace:
1976

Chess is better than romance.

Fischer is socially evasive rather than hostile,
likely to greet even an old friend as if he were
expecting a subpoena: *Anon*

Finally, the USA produces its greatest chess
genius, and he turns out to be another stubborn
boy: *Chess Life magazine*

Bobby Fischer is a chess phenomenon, it is
true, but is also a social illiterate, a political
simpleton, a cultural ignoramus, and an
emotional baby: *Mary Kenny – journalist*

It's hard to describe this Fischer aura.
Relentless, monomaniacal and pitiless; it is the
aura of a killer:
Harold Schonberg – US writer (1972)

On offering him an extra £50,000 to face Spassky –
If you aren't afraid of Spassky, then I have
removed the element of money:
Jim Slater – financier (1972)

There has never been a chess master in the
history of the game as consistently aggressive as
Fischer: *David Spanier*

Edward Fitzgerald – *(1809–83) translator*
'Tis all a chequer board of nights and days,
Where destiny with men for pieces plays;
Hither and thither, and mates, and slays:
The Rubaiyat of Omar Khayyam (1859)

Thomas Fuller – *(1608–1681) clergyman*
When a man's house is on fire, it's time to
break off chess.

Paul Fussell – *(b 1924) US humorist*
Chess is seldom found above the upper-middle
class; it's too hard.

Henry Hartshorne – *(b 1823) US scientific
writer*
Chess is a game in which no other approaches
it in the scope afforded, by the number and
variety of powers of the pieces, for skill and
foresight, involving the faculties of memory and
conception, especially to a large degree.

Eliot Hearst
Many outsiders regard the chessmaster as a
kind of superman.

Chessmasters as well as chess computers
deserve less reverence than the public accords
them.

Durrell Huff
There are far, far more permissible moves in a
chess game than there are electrons in the
universe: *1959*

Thomas H. Huxley – *(1825–1895) teacher &
biologist*
The chess-board is the world; the pieces are the
phenomena of the universe; the rules are what
we call the laws of Nature. The player on the
other side is hidden from us. We know that his
play is always fair, just and patient. But also we
know, to our cost, that he never overlooks a
mistake, or makes the smallest allowance for

ignorance: *Lay Sermons, Addresses & Reviews*

Colin M. Jarman - *(b 1958) sportswriter*
Mixed chess is the ultimate mating game: *1988*

Randall Jarrell - *(1914-65) US poet & critic*
She looked at me the way you'd look at a chess-man if it made its own move.

Viktor Korchnoi - *Russian Grandmaster*
If a chess player believes in miracles, he can sometimes perform them.

Karpov beat me unfairly. It was the struggle of the State against the individual: *1979*

Emanuel Lasker - *German world champion [1894-1921]*
Chess has been represented, or misrepresented, as a game. By some ardent enthusiasts, chess has been elevated into a science or art. It is neither, but its principle characteristic seems to be - what human nature mostly delights in - a fight.

Vladimir Lenin - *(1870-1924) Russian communist leader*
Chess is the gymnasium of the mind.

Robert Lowell - *(b 1917) US poet*
I have a few peripheral friends, here and there, who are non-chess players: *The Winner*

Lord Macaulay - *(1800-59) poet*
Soon fades the spell, soon comes the night;
Say will it not be then the same,
    Whether we played the black or white,
Whether we won or lost the game?

Mencius - *(372-289 BC) Chinese philosopher*
Chess-playing is but a small art, yet without the whole mind being given, a man cannot succeed at it.

Moses Mendelsson - *(1729-86) German philosopher*
For a game it is too serious, for seriousness too much of a game.

Thomas Middleton - *(1570-1627) dramatist*
I know the knights walke in this game too well, hee maye skip over mee, and where am I then?: *1624*

A. A. Milne - *(1882-1956) dramatist and humorist*
It is impossible to win gracefully at chess. No man has yet said 'Mate!' in a voice which failed to sound to his opponents bitter, boastful and malicious.

Paul Morphy - *US world champion [1858-62]*
Chess has been and never can be aught but a recreation. It should not be indulged in to the detriment of other and more serious advocations.

Christophe Opoix - *(1745-1840) French author*
In a game of chess, we see illustrated the game of life and its vicissitudes - success and failure.

George Bernard Shaw - *(1856-1950) Irish dramatist & critic*
Chess is a foolish expedient for making idle people believe they are doing something clever, when they are only wasting their time.

Savelly Tarkatower - *(1887-1956) Russian Grandmaster*
The mistakes are all waiting to be made.

DOMINOES

Anon
Dominoes is a very childish sport and could have nothing but the novelty to recommend it to grown ups: *1810*

Steuart Emery - *(b 1891) US writer*
For real harmony, the sort that is divine. I'll take the animated dominoes.

Oscar Wilde - *(1854-1900) Irish dramatist & humorist*
I'm afraid I play no outdoor games at all, except dominoes. I have sometimes played dominoes outside a French cafe.

DRAUGHTS

John Palsgrave - *(1480-1554) grammarian*
He that looketh on seeth many draughts that the player considereth nothing at all: *1529*

BOBSLEIGH

The Cresta Run – *St Moritz, Switzerland*
As Mecca is to the Mohammedan, as St Peter's
is to the Catholic, so is the Cresta Run to the
tobogganer: *E. Benson*

Because there is only one Cresta Run, the sport
cannot hope to be so internationally
representative as lugeing:
Lord Brabazon of Tara

Tony Nash – *Olympic 2-man bobsleigh champion
[1964]*
Bobsleigh bears certain similarities to rowing.
It teaches the same kind of team cohesion.
Every man has to pull together.

BODY-BUILDING

Sayings
No pain – No gain.
[*Echoes of Adlai Stevenson's acceptance speech at
the 1952 Democratic Convention* – There are no
gains without pain]

Charles Atlas – *(1894–1972) US physical
culturist*
Advertising slogan – You too can have a body
like mine!

The Barbarian Brothers – *US body-building
duo*
There is no such thing as over-training. There
is only under-eating, under-sleeping and failure
of will.

Jasmine Birtles – *writer*
It is difficult to respect a sport that has 'posing'
as part of its jargon: *1975*

Bob Fitzsimmons – *world light-heavyweight
boxing champion [1897]*
A muscle-bound man is worse than a skin-
bound horse.

David Hunn – *sportswriter*
Body-builders do not throw their weight
around – they flaunt it.

Martial – *(42–102) Latin epigrammist*
Why do strong arms fatigue themselves with
silly dumb-bells? Trenching a vineyard is
worthier exercise for men.

Kenneth Robinson – *writer*
The whole point of this so-called body-building,
I gather, is to get rid of the attractive flesh on
the surface and to display all the working bits
underneath: *1983*

Arnold Schwarzennegger – *six times Mr
Olympia & actor*
Motto – Pain means progress.

Posing is a performing art: *1975*

The muscle-man with heart – and pectorals – of
gold: *Jack Kroll – US film critic*

Seneca – *(4 BC–65 AD) Roman philosopher &
playwright*
It is foolish and quite unfitting for an educated
man to spend all his time on acquiring bulging
muscles, a thick neck and mighty lungs. The
large amounts they are compelled to eat make
them dull-witted.

BOWLING

CROWN GREEN

Tony Allcock - *world Indoor bowling champion [1986-7]*
On Crown Green bowlers playing Lawn bowls -
It's like a street-fighter conforming to the
Marquis of Queensberry rules: *1986*

George T. Burrows - *sports journalist*
With all its appeal to strength and sheer
vitality, the crown green game fails to approach
the rink style from the viewpoint of artistry:
                                                 1931

For pure bowling, the northerner's game takes
pride of place; for the finer elements of bowl
play, calling for generalship and ability to rise
to the solving of a hundred difficult problems,
the rink game is unsurpassed: *1931*

James Hartley - *writer*
It can scarcely be claimed that rink bowling
calls for the exercise of the same skill as crown
green bowling. Rink players are confined to the
same piece of land throughout their game, the
crown green style calls for incessant change:
                                                 1922

James A. Manson - *(1851-1921) poet*
The utmost that can be urged in favour of
crown green is that it yields a sporting though
not scientific game: *1912*

Gwyn Morris - *President of the Crown Green
Bowling Association*
The element of chance adds greatly to the
interest in many sports and is certainly present
in the bustling, vigorous, thriving crown green
game: *1986*

LAWN

Anon
Rules observed, a man may play his game
On bowling greens -
Or thro' the world with fame: *c 1815*

Naught can rival bowles for sport save a good

ale and a comely wench.

There is more to bowls than the mere playing
of it.

Peter Brimble - *English Indoor champion [1963]*
He is the Joe Davis of Indoor bowls:
                                 Arthur Sweeney (1966)

Elizabeth Barrett Browning - *(1806-61) poet*
Bowling greens of poets are fresher than the
world's highways.

David Bryant - *(b 1931) world champion [1966 & 1980]*
I'm not an athlete, more a gymnast and golfer,
soldered together.

In golf, if you play a good shot the other chap
has to match it; he can't do anything about
your ball. In darts, if a chap makes a good
score, then the other fellow has to match it. He
can't do anything about what you've thrown,
can't alter it. And in snooker you can do
something when you get to the table. In bowls,
you can bowl three good ones and the fellow
who hasn't can all of a sudden wipe out all the
good you've done with one bowl and score
several shots.

Soccer men can work off all their heat and
adrenalin by charging about kicking things.
Cricketers can either bowl a bumper or start
swiping at every ball that comes down. We have
to rely on nothing else than concentration and
self-discipline.

The Don Bradman of bowls: *Anon*

I have seen David Bryant referred to as the
'Don Bradman of bowls'. I would rather in a
way call him its W. G. Grace. Grace was the
first cricketer to become a household name.
Bryant is the first bowler to be admitted to that
exclusive club: *Gordon Allan (1983)*

No sport has had more diligent student of its subtleties, a greater exponent of its skill, or a better ambassador: *Gordon Allan (1983)*

He stood upright, sighted the target in that firing position that thrills spectators across the world and delivered an impeccable wood at a speed that would have taken your foot clean off at the ankle: *David Hunn (1981)*

He is at his best when on the ropes:
Donald Newby (1982)

The man is a complete professional, one who seems to regard each loss merely as a preparation for his next game:
Patrick Sullivan (1984)

It would hardly be fair to describe Bryant as a bowling machine: *Arthur Sweeney (1966)*

Bowling Magazine
Bowling is a sober game. The ruffianism of football, the effeminacy of tennis, the manliness of cricket and the buoyancy of baseball give way to a stateliness and gracefulness not met in no other sport: *1908*

British Rural Sports
It is a very quiet game and calculated rather for the steady old gentleman than for his racketty son: *1861*

George T. Burrows - *sports journalist*
The thirty-five to forty yards of slow trundle to the jack is the soul of the game: *1915*

Bowls is the only perfect recreation and the only pure game so far invented by man! At what other sport do men persevere so resolutely to achieve just nothing? *1915*

Canadian Handbook
Bowls is a quiet and philosophical amusement which depends for its success entirely on a thorough realisation that nothing happens in it, any more than in real life, exactly according to scientific calculation: *1902*

Bowls are built with a bias, and so for that matter are many of the players: *1902*

Herbert Collings - *journalist*

We are too prone to treat the old green as something that does not matter very much. We do not grasp the fact that we have in our midst a priceless treasure that cannot be matched in any other country in the world.

Country Contentment
A man shall find great art in chusing out his ground, and for his sport the chusing of the bowle is the greatest cunning: *1615*

Sidney Daryl - *writer*
Bowls is a very nice game for ladies, and nothing can be more picturesque than to see the dear creatures doing their best to cut cousin Tom, Dick or Harry out his advantageously near position to the jack: *1868*

Humphrey J. Dingley - *author*
There is nothing complicated in the game, and the exertion necessary is not half that of lawn tennis: *1893*

Sir Francis Drake - *(1540–96) Elizabethan sea captain & explorer*
When his game of bowls was interrupted by news that the Spanish Armada had been sighted – There is plenty of time to win this game, and to thrash the Spaniards too: *Attrib. (1588)*

John Earle - *(1601–65) writer*
A bowling green is a place where three things are thrown away besides the bowls – time, money and curses: *1628*

Dr John W. Fisher - *player & author*
Bowling looks so simple; you only throw one thing at another: *1948*

Girls Realm
Bowls – a graceful game for girls: *1902*

Count Grammont - *courtier & wit of Charles II*
The places where it is practised are charming, delicious walks called bowling greens, which are little square grass plots where the turf is almost as smooth and level as the cloth of a billiard table.

Matthew Green - *(1696–1737) civil servant & poet*
To cure the mind's wrong bias, spleen

Some recommend the bowling green;
Some hilly walks, all, exercise
Fling a stone, the giant dies,
Laugh and all be well.

Frederick W. Hackwood - *sportswriter*
As a pastime it appeals more perhaps to the
sober and sedate than to the super-abundant
energies of youth: *1907*

Ronnie Harper - *writer*
A game of remorse and unpredictability; a game
of skill and a game of chance; a game of joy and
a game of frustration; a game of dry throats and
sweaty palms: *1979*

Alfred Haynes - *writer*
Bowls has never been a prerogative of the male
sex: *1972*

Colin M. Jarman - *(b 1958) sportswriter*
A game of bowls can never be tied because
there are just so many ends: *1988*

Bowls without its Jack is like the Sun without
its Ray: *1988*

C. M. Jones - *journalist*
Stiffness is an occupational hazard as far as
bowls players are concerned: *1972*

The ultimate test always comes in competition
on green.

Arthur Knowling
One cannot say Arthur Knowling bowls his
woods, he decants them: *C. M. Jones*

Daniel Leslie - *Scottish green-layer*
A bowling green is the place par excellence,
where the motto of the French republic –
Freedom, Equality, Fraternity – can be most
readily realised: *1907*

Manual of Playing Bowls
No other game is so provocative of genial
mirth, nor more conducive to sociality and
good fellowship: *1864*

Geoffrey Nicholson - *writer*
There is something in the elaborate etiquette of
bowls, the snatches of conversation between
opponents, the applauding of each other's good

woods, which inhibits public displays of
temperament: *1985*

Robert Recorde - *(1510–58) mathematician*
A little altering of one side, maketh the bowl to
run biasse waies: *1556*

William Shakespeare *(1564–1616)*
playwright
Nay sometimes, like to a bowl upon a subtle
ground, I have tumbled past the throw:
Coriolanus

What I have lost today at bowls I'll win tonight
of him: *Cymbelline*

When I kissed the jack, upon an up-cast to be
hit away: *Cymbelline*

Challenge her to bowl – I fear to much rubbing:
Love's Labours Lost

Well, forward, forward! Thus the bowl should
run, and not unluckily against the bias:
Taming of the Shrew

If it be not too rough for some that know little
but bowling, it will please plentifully:
Winter's Tale

Horace Smith - *(1779–1849) humorist*
It is not every rogue that, like a bowl, can gain
his object the better by deviating it from the
straight line: *c 1812*

Tobias Smollett - *(1721–71) novelist*
He that plays at Bowls will sometimes meet
with Rubbers: *1762*

William Strode - *(1602–45) poet*
The fairest casts are those
That owe no thanks to fortune's giddy sway;
Such honest men good bowlers are whose
On true bias cutts the way: *1663*

John Taylor - *(1580–1653) 'The Water Poet'*
Bias, the philosopher, was the first bowler and
ever since, the most part of bowles do in
memory of their original weare his badge of
remembrance and very dutifully hold bias: *1630*

Touches and Rubs
In the handling of the shapely polished spheres

there is pleasure to the touch; the very poetry
of motion is the course of the bowl to the jack:
1893

Bowling, as an outdoor pastime, is the most
truly recreative, combining the minimum of
mental and physical effort with the maximum
of recuperative energy: *1893*

Elsie Walters – *President of the EWBA*
If John McEnroe turned up we'd throw him
out. We like polite people in bowls: *1985*

Charles Wigg – *President of Worthing Bowls
Club*
It takes fifteen or sixteen seconds for the wood
to end on the jack and there are not many
sports where you have to wait so long to see the
result: *1985*

TEN-PIN

Anon
An hundred Knightes truly tolde,
Shall play with bowles in alleys colde:
The Squyer of Low Degree (1475)

Bowling is the quietest sport in the world,
because you can hear a pin drop.

Good bowlers have time to spare.

Thomas Dekker – *(1572–1632) dramatist*
I live, like those that keep bowling alleys, by the
sins of the people.

George du Maurier – *(1834–96) novelist*
Life ain't all beer and skittles, more's the pity.

Stephen Gosson – *(1554–1624) ecclesiastic &
writer*
Common bowling alleys are privey mothes that
eat up the credit of many idle citizens: *1579*

Martin Mull – *US humorist*
Having a family is like having a bowling alley
installed in your brain.

Dick Ritger – *US winner of 20 Professional
Bowling Association titles*
Too many times a pro bowler is classed with
the average fun bowler. That's equating a touch
football game with the Super Bowl: *1979*

BOXING

ANCIENT

Antyllus – *(c 200–300) Greek physician*
The shadow boxer must use not only his hands,
but also his legs, sometimes as if he were
jumping, at other times as if he were kicking.

Euripides – *(480–406 BC) Greek playwright*
The fight is a feeble affair when you have only
one hand.

Seneca – *(4 BC–65 AD) Roman philosopher &
playwright*
An athlete cannot bring true courage to his
fights unless he has sometimes been beaten
black and blue. The fighter who has seen his
own blood, whose teeth have been rattled by a
blow from his opponent, who has not lost his
spirit even when hurled about the ring, who,

every time he has been knocked down, has got
to his feet again more pugnacious than ever,
this is the man who faces his next fight with
confidence.

If the body can be brought by training to
endure the blows of opponent after opponent,
to face the sun blazing down on the burning
sand of the ring, and to last out all day,
dripping with its own blood, how much more
easily could the soul be strengthened to endure
the blows of fate without flinching, and rise
again after being thrown and trampled on.

Think of all the blows which athletes receive on
their faces and indeed all over their bodies. Yet,
they put up with all this pain because they long

for fame. And they do not face it merely because they are fighting, but so that they may be able to fight; for their very training involves pain.

Socrates - *(469–399 BC) Greek teacher*
Do you not suppose that a single boxer who is perfect in his art would easily be a match for two or more well-to-do gentlemen who are not boxers?

BARE-KNUCKLE

Anon
To box, or not to box, that is the question,
Whether it is nobler in the mind to suffer
The stings and goadings of a well-tweak'd nose,
Or to take heart with Humphries or Mendoza:
1792

George Borrow - *(1803–81) author*
Let no one sneer at the bruisers of England. What were the gladiators of Rome or the bull-fighters of Spain, in its palmiest days, compared to England's prize-fighters?: *Lavengro*

Lord Byron - *(1788–1824) poet*
'Twas blow for blow, disputing inch for inch,
For one would not retreat, not t'other flinch.

Dan Donnelly - *19th century bare-knuckle champion*
He died at last, from forty-seven
Tumblers of punch he drank one even';
Overthrown by punch, unharmed by fist,
He died, unbeaten pugilist: *Epitaph*

Jeffery J. Farnol - *(1878–1952) novelist*
We boast a science sprung from manly pride,
Linked with true courage and to health allied.
A noble pastime, void of vain pretense,
That fine, old English art of self-defense.

'Gentleman' John Jackson - *(d 1845) bare-knuckle champion*
He was so strong that he could write his name with an eighty-four pound weight dangling from his little finger:
Denzil Batchelor – US writer (1954)

And men unpractised in exchanging knocks,
Must go to Jackson, ere they dare box:
Lord Byron

Samuel Johnson - *(1709–84) lexicographer*
I should be sorry to see prize-fighting go out. Every art should be preserved, and the art of self-defence is surely important.

Sir Henry Newbolt - *(1862–1938) poet*
To set the cause above renown,
To love the game beyond the prize,
To honour while you strike him down,
The foe that comes with fearless eyes: *1898*

John H. Reynolds - *(1794–1852) poet*
I've watched the seconds pat and nurse
Their man; and seen him put to bed;
With twenty guineas in his purse,
And not an eye within his head.

William Shakespeare - *(1564–1616) playwright*
The glove which I have given him for a favour,
May haply purchase him a box o' the ear:
Henry V

Give him a box o' the ear, and that will make
'em red again: *Henry VI*

Richard Steele - *(1672–1719) founder of Tatler magazine*
On a prize-fight – There is something in Nature very unaccountable on such occasions, when we see the people take certain gratification on beholding these encounters. Is it cruelty that administers this sort of delight? Or is it a pleasure which is taken in the exercise of pity?

MODERN

GENERAL

Anon
Marriage is like a boxing card. The preliminaries are frequently better than the main event.

You've heard about the bees and the honey? The lightweights do the work and the heavies get the money.

Sayings
Kill the body and the head will follow.

Fight to the finish.

Shadow box till your shadow gets tired.

They'll all go if you hit them right.

Jab and weave.

When in doubt – Stick the left out.

They never come back.

Styles make fights.

BRITISH

Nigel Benn 'The Dark Destroyer' – *middleweight*
I don't want to fight no Mexican road-sweepers, no more: *1988*

I get worried when a guy goes down, in case he doesn't get up – for me to hit him again.

A cruiserweight is a boxer too heavy to fight the 'Dark Destroyer':
            Colin M. Jarman – sportswriter (1988)

Jack Bodell – *heavyweight*
I had offers to come back, but I wasn't going to get any better. I wanted to take care of myself – it's no use being the richest corpse in the graveyard.

Frank Bruno – *heavyweight*
I didn't want to go round mugging old ladies or robbing banks. So I took up boxing.

It's surely more honourable to fight for a living than to be fighting in the streets.

My aim is to become another Diego Maradona – the man with the golden fist.

Perhaps we Brits don't deserve the heavyweight title. If we deserve Frank Bruno, we are doing well enough: *Hugh McIlvanney – sportswriter*

Stephen Brunt – *writer*
Boxing is a world of ethnic and racial stereotypes, truisms that are too often true; white fighters can't move their heads and therefore catch too many blows; blacks are slick and speedy; Mexicans are always tough with lots of heart; Koreans raw and gritty; the poor

British tend to stand up straight and take it on the chops, bleeding almost before the opening bell.

Joe Bugner – *heavyweight*
On taking a punch – It's like a woman concentrating on intricate sewing. If she pricked her finger she'd hardly notice it and just carry on.

Britain has no time for winners for successes like me. To become popular there you have to be a loser, like Henry Cooper when he lost to Ali and me: *1984*

Before his last fight – Frank Bruno says I'm chicken. Well, you can tell him that I've come home to roost: *1988*

Everybody thinks the whole thing is a huge laugh. But I can assure you that when it gets down to business there's nothing funny about seeing your husband beaten senseless:
                                               Marlene Bugner

I don't know what impressive is, but Joe was impressive tonight: *Marlene Bugner*

Joe Bugner was like a volcano that never erupted: *Henry Cooper*

After the media accused him of not trying against Muhammad Ali – Get me Jesus Christ, I'll fight him tomorrow!
Hugh McIlvanney – Joe, you're only saying that because you know He's got bad hands!

Harry Carpenter – *TV commentator*
They said it would last two rounds – they were half wrong, it lasted four.

Charlie Magri has to do well against this unknown Mexican who comes from a famous family of five boxing brothers.

Know what I mean, Harry?:   *Frank Bruno*

John Conteh – *world light-heavyweight champion [1974]*
Boxing was a quick way out of being poor. I hadn't time for a five-year apprenticeship and no one was going to send me to Hollywood.

Boxing was never a sport to me. It was a deadly game. It was a path I was forced to follow.

When I go into a ring I never know for certain that I'm coming back.

My working-class instincts had begun to tell me that I was being exploited. I felt the top men in boxing were in the meat business and I was the meat in the middle of the sandwich.

He has a neck built like a stately home staircase: *Tom Davies*

Henry Cooper – *(b 1934) heavyweight*
Boxers are the most docile men in sport.

Boxers need somewhere to fight, that is why we have this square we call a ring.

The boxing public generally are a blood-thirsty lot. They like to see a good hard fight, and if there's plenty of gore and snot flying around they love it.

You don't feel a bad cut. What tells you it's a bad one is when you feel the warm blood dripping on your body.

You are there to win at all costs. It's the killer instinct. If I saw a man with a cut eye I didn't think, 'Oh dear, what a terrible eye'. I said, 'Good! Wallop! Take that! Take that!'

Baroness Summerskill – Mr Cooper, have you looked in the mirror lately and seen the state of your nose?
Henry Cooper – Well, Madam, have you looked in the mirror and seen the state of your nose? Boxing is my excuse. What's yours?

On why he quit his greengrocer's business – His potatoes kept getting cut eyes:
Reg Gutteridge – TV commentator

Terry Downes – *world middleweight champion [1961]*
On being asked, by a female reporter, if he watched his opponent's eyes or gloves – His gloves, dear. I've never been hit by an eye in my life!

Terry Downes' face looked as if he had slept on it: *Michael Parkinson – TV presenter*

Jim Driscoll – *featherweight*
A scrupulously fair boxer is badly handicapped in a clinch.

Mickey Duff – *manager & matchmaker*
A lot of boxing promoters couldn't match the cheeks of their buttocks: *1972*

Boxing is unrehearsed entertainment, and you're never sure what you're going to get.

Hands were made for hitting people.

Richard Dunn – *heavyweight*
Before he fought Muhammad Ali – Richard's not over-awed by this Ali. Why, we've got far too many of those black chat merchants back home in Bradford. He's right used to seeing them dance up and down Westgate with their tambourines every Saturday:
Jimmy Devanney – trainer (1976)

Chris Finnegan – *Olympic middleweight champion [1968]*
I know it's said I can't punch, but you should see me putting the cat out at night.

Bob Fitzsimmons – *(1862–1917) world light-heavy & heavyweight champion [1897]*
Before losing his title to James J. Jeffries – The harder they are the heavier they fall: *1899*
[*As Jeffries was much larger than Fitzsimmons this is frequently misquoted as* – The bigger they come the harder they fall]

John F. Gilbey – *writer*
Glamour and fighting seldom marry. Fighting is a rough trade and is as distant from Hollywood sets as Tierra del Fuego.

Herol 'Bomber' Graham – *middleweight*
I would like to retire with my brains still intact.

He has turned defensive boxing into a poetic art. Trouble is, nobody ever knocked anybody out with a poem: *Eddie Shaw – trainer*

Lloyd Honeyghan – *world welterweight champion [1986]*
When he lost his title to Jorge Vaca [Mexico] after an accidental clash of heads – That's cricket. You get these sort of things in boxing:
Frank Bruno (1987)

Doug Ibbottson – *sportswriter*
Cynics might observe that there appears to be a greater affinity between villains and boxing than any other sport – except, possibly, horse-racing.

Colin M. Jarman – *(b 1958) sportswriter*
Boxing is described as a 'noble art' because the winner is usually the first to draw blood on the canvas: *1988*

A well attended boxer has more time than his opponent – he always has a few more seconds:
1988

In recent years the number of weight categories has grown, due to the addition of the prefix 'Super'. In future years, we may see fighters challenging for their ninth or tenth division title in the Super-ficial, Super-fluous and Super-numary categories: *1988*

Brian London – *heavyweight*
Brian London possesses the most unbeautiful face – it looks as if it, at one time, fell apart and was re-assembled by a drunken mechanic:
Michael Parkinson – TV presenter

Lord Lonsdale – *founder of the Lonsdale Belt*
I have always considered that boxing really combines all the finest and highest inclinations of a man – activity, endurance, science, temper, and, last, but not least, presence of mind.

Barry McGuigan – *world featherweight champion [1985]*
Why he became a boxer – I can't be a poet and I can't tell stories.

It's not the size of the dog in the fight that counts, but the size of the fight in the dog.

If they said I had to defend my title against Mahatma Gandhi I would fight him: *1985*

Barry fights for money. Amateurs fight for Ireland. Barry is a professional.
Pat McGuigan – father

Barry McGuigan has the lot. Nice lookin'; a wife; a child – and a dad who can sing 'Danny Boy' in tune: *Dr Ferdie Pacheco*

I saw that kid some time ago. He was special, gifted, a born fighter. He has strength that surprises his body structure: *Sylvester Stallone*

Field-Marshal Montgomery – *(1887–1976) military leader*
There is nothing bellicose about boxing. It is fully in keeping with the principles of the United Nations Organisation: *1948*

Dame Edith Summerskill – *(1902–80) MP*
Prize-fighting is still accepted as a display worthy of civilised people, despite the fact that all those connected with it are fully aware it caters to their latent sadistic interests.

Unlike promoters, the average spectator at a boxing bout, knows little about the psychology of man, nor has he given any serious thought to the primitive impulses involved: *1956*

Lord [Thomas J.] Taylor of Gryfe – *(b 1912)*
Speech to the House of Lords – Among the boxing fraternity there is an adage – first the timing goes, then the legs, then the mind, and then the friends. That is the history of many people who thought boxing an easy way to riches: *1981*

Randolph Turpin – *world middleweight champion [1951]*
Randolph Turpin does everything wrong – right: *Sugar Ray Robinson*

Billy Walker – *heavyweight*
In pro boxing, let's face it, the name of the game is how much you make – not how many honours won. Billy Walker was the most successful flop in history:
Reg Gutteridge – TV commentator

Jim Watt – *world lightweight champion [1979]*
Suggested epitaph – You can stop counting, I'm not getting up.

Bruce Woodcock – *heavyweight*
Sleep came as it must come to all British heavyweights, midway in the fifth round:
'Red' Smith – US sportswriter

WORLD

Muhammad Ali [Cassius Clay] - *(b 1942)*
world heavyweight champion [1964]
Archie Moore has been living off the fat of the
land,
I'm here to give him his pension plan.
When you come to the fight, don't block the
aisle or door;
'Cause you're all going home after round
four: *1963*

This is the legend of Cassius Clay.
The most beautiful fighter in the world today.
He talks a great deal and brags indeed
Of a muscular punch that's incredible in speed.
This brash young boxer is something to see
And the heavyweight championship is his
destiny: *1963*

Here I predict Sonny Liston's
dismemberment,
I'll hit him so hard, he'll forget where
October–November went: *1964*

Nature is a mysterious thing. It is just like me.
Sometimes I wonder when a big fist comes
crashing by and at the last moment I just move
my head the smallest bit and the punch comes
so close I can feel the wind, but it misses me.
How do I know at the last minute to move just
enough? How do I know which way to move?

They say when you get hit and hurt bad you
see the 'Black Lights' – the black lights of
unconsciousness. But I don't know nothing
about that. I've had twenty-eight fights and
twenty-eight wins. I ain't never been stopped:
                                                  1967

The man who will whip me will be fast, strong
and hasn't been born yet.

I am an astronaut of boxing. Joe Louis and Jack
Dempsey were just jet pilots.

You know why I talk like no fighter ever did
before, no athlete of any kind, black or white?
There's two reasons. One's for business, that's
the side I expose. The other is the real me.

When you're as great as I am, it's hard to be
humble.

When my title was taken away, Boxing died:
                                                  1971

Before his first fight with Frazier –
Joe's gonna come out smokin',
And I won't be jokin'.
I'm gonna be a peckin' and a pokin',
Pouring water on his smokin'.
This might shock and amaze ya,
But Ali will destroy Joe Frazier!:   *1971*

Before the rematch with Frazier –
Now Ali lands with a right, what a beautiful
swing,
And the punch lifts Frazier clean out of the
ring.
Joe Frazier's still rising, but the referee wears a
frown,
For he can't start counting till Frazier comes
down.
Now Joe Frazier disappears from view,
The crowd is getting frantic
But our radar stations have picked him up,
He's somewhere over the Atlantic!
Who would have thought, when they came to
the fight,
That they would have witnessed
The launching of a coloured satellite: *1974*

Before the showdown with Frazier in Manila –
It's gonna be a thrilla, a chilla, and a killa,
When I get the gorilla in Manila: *1975*

Boxing was the only way I could get rich. But if
I could, I'd have been a great doctor or
something like that.

I'm not only a great boxer, I'm a genius. I ain't
just a dumb negro boxer. I'm a great writer,
too.

People don't realise what they had till it's gone.
Like President Kennedy – nobody like him.
The Beatles, there will never be anything like
them. My man – Elvis. I was the Elvis of
boxing.

Hitting hard don't mean nothing if you don't
find nothing to hit.

Because a boxer gets hurt, should they stop
boxing? That would be crazy – more people die
in the bath: *1984*

I can't believe some of the things I did. Can't believe it. Saying I was the greatest and the beautifullest and I was gonna whup this guy and that guy, saying I'm pretty, I can't be beat, I'm the King. I see myself on TV and can't believe it.

On the biggest change since he retired – Johnny Carson [chat show host] don't call me any more.

Before going into hospital, suffering from Parkinson Syndrome – People say I talk so slow today. That's no surprise. I calculate I've taken 29,000 punches, but I earned $7m and I saved half of it. I may talk slow, but my mind is okay.

General Gowan of Nigeria – I used to do some boxing.
Ali – What did you box? Apples or oranges?

Isaac Stern [violinist] – You might say we're in the same business – we both earn a living with our hands.
Ali – You must be good. There isn't a mark on you.

Publicity poster – ALI v FOREMAN: From the Slave-ship to the Championship: *1974*

He stings like a bee, but lives like a W.A.S.P:
Eamonn Andrews

I could announce tomorrow that Ali will walk across the Hudson River and charge $20 admission and there would be 20,000 down there to see him. Half would be rooting for him to do it, the other half would be rooting for him to sink: *Teddy Brenner – promoter*

The first man at his weight to fight with his legs:
Georges Carpentier – French light-heavyweight

A slave in private life, a King in public – this is the life that every black champion has had to lead – until the coming of Muhammad Ali:
Eldridge Cleaver – writer (1965)

He was quickly dubbed the 'Louisville Lip', as he drummed up business with a tongue that was even quicker than his fists: *Henry Cooper*

He's not only a lousy fighter, he's a bad actor. Louis or Marciano could have whipped him by telephone: *Dan Digilio (1965)*

Put him in a ring, even it if's only in the gym, and you're seeing him. That's him at his happiest: *Angelo Dundee – trainer*

His career goes beyond boxing, it's history:
Angelo Dundee

Ali wouldn't have hit Louis on the bum with a handful of rice:
Tommy Farr – British heavyweight

When you have spilled and tasted another man's blood, and smelled his sweat, and made a million dollars, you don't hate him: *Joe Frazier*

Sometimes, we make great fighters out to be more than they really are. Joe Louis was a brilliant fighter, the epitome of a heavyweight, but he had no personality. Outside the ring, Jack Dempsey was a nice, tough, simple guy; that's all. But Ali was extraordinary. He was boxing's premier fighter and its best actor, as well: *Bill Gallo*

Every time Ali dances for another million, I think of good boxers who starved:
John F. Gilbey – British writer

Like Peter Pan, he seemed forever young, but he was in a sport where men grow old before their time: *Thomas Hauser – writer*

After God created Clay he broke the mould:
Colin M. Jarman – British sportswriter (1988)

He's not only a champion of boxing, he's a champion of justice, peace and human dignity:
Coretta King – wife of
Martin Luther King (1967)

Because of Muhammad Ali, I never had to start at the bottom and work my way up. I started at the top, doing world title fights:
Don King – promoter

A fighter better known for the size of his mouth than his potency in the ring:
Herbert Kretzmer – British critic (1963)

Two blacks on a 15 bus,
Ali for King, their quid pro quo:
'He may be quick – but is he strong?'
'Is Ali strong? – O daddy-O.
When that Muhammad pats your cheek
    It breaks your little toe!'
                    Chris Logue – British writer & poet

Ali – Joe, you really think you coulda whup me?
Louis – When I was champion, I went on a
bum-of-the-month tour.
Ali – You saying I'm a bum?
Louis – You woulda been on the tour!

The Prince of Ego: *Norman Mailer (1971)*

For Ali to compose a few words of real poetry
would be equal to an intellectual throwing a
punch: *Norman Mailer*

Working, apparently, on the premise that there
was something obscene about being hit, he
boxed with his head back and drew it further
back when attacked, like the kid who is shy of
punches in a street fight, because he had a
waist that was more supple than the average
fighter's neck, he was able to box with his arms
low, surveying the fighter in front of him,
avoiding punches by the speed of his feet and
the reflexes of his waist: *Norman Mailer*

He is a fighter who stands for something, and
that's the mark of a fighter. He doesn't stand
neutral. He's a rights fighter also, like me. The
man who stands neutral stands for nothing:
                    Archie Moore – heavyweight

He was like God with a custard pie up his
sleeve: *Joseph O'Brian*

His position in life depends upon winning. His
looks depend upon his not getting beaten. He
purposely walks the plank to the very end while
somebody's sawing it off, and fortunately, he
has the ability to do it: *Dr Ferdie Pacheco*

When it comes to Bally-hoo, he made Barnum
and Bailey look like non-starters and he had the
incandescent quality of the real star which
would have made him world famous, even if his
gift was knitting not fighting:
                    Michael Parkinson

Ali wasn't just a symbol of emerging black
pride, he was a source of it:
                    John Schulian – sportswriter

Did they expect that, after twenty-four years of
being slugged in the head, Ali could be gainfully
employed as a systems analyst? Plainly, it was
boxing that did it, and just as plainly, the man
stuck around the game too long: *Fraser Scott*

No black boxer ever had a better shot at full
colour-blind acceptance by the white
community. None had less of the ghetto or the
cotton-field about him: *Wilfred Sheed – writer*

People talk about Joe Louis, but Muhammad
Ali was the greatest heavyweight of all. Look at
Louis against Billy Conn. Louis couldn't deal
with footwork. And if Louis had hit Ali, no man
ever had the punch to keep Ali down:
                    Emanuel Steward

I think they shouldn't base the security of
boxing on what happened to Ali. Anybody who
starts at twelve and finishes at forty is bound to
have some problems:
                    Pinklon Thomas – heavyweight

Idi Amin – *(b 1925) Ugandan President &
heavyweight*
I am still heavyweight champion of Uganda.
Nobody is willing to fight me.
[*He won the title in 1951*]

Ray Arcel – *manager & trainer*
Boxing goes through stages. I've seen it grow
and deteriorate, grow and deteriorate, but it
will always be there.

There's no time out in boxing. So you've got to
be perfect. You must know what you're doing
in there. If you make a mistake in the ring you
wake up looking at the lights.

Ring sense is an art, a gift from God that flows
out of a fighter like a great painting flows out of
an artist, or a great book flows out of an author.

Bob Arum – *promoter*
I like to outwit an opponent. I like to get
something done cleverly but not by stealing.
Stealing makes me very uncomfortable.

I'm a business man. Two guys fighting in a ring, that has nothing to do with me. Fighters bore me.

There ain't nobody as bad as Bob Arum. That New York city Jew lawyer will make you hate city folks, Jews, and lawyers in the same day:
'Tex' Cobb – heavyweight

I like to do business with a handshake, but if you make the mistake of doing business with Bob Arum, you get it in writing:
Cus D'Amato – trainer

Bob Arum is one of the worst people in the western hemisphere. I don't know the eastern hemisphere very well, but I suspect he'd be one of the worst people there too, if he went:
Cus D'Amato

When Bob Arum pats you on the back, he's just looking for a spot to stick the knife:
Cus D'Amato

Someone once said Bob Arum is his own worst enemy. Not while I'm alive he isn't:
Cus D'Amato

I'll shake hands with Bob Arum, but I'll take my ring off first:
Mickey Duff – British promoter

The trouble with suing Bob Arum is that you have to stand in the line: *Jim Jacobs – manager*

When Arum is totting up the millions his ventures are likely to amass, zeros tend to be floated in the air as casually as smoke rings and they often disappear almost as suddenly when the actual accounting has to be done:
Hugh McIlvanney

One of the Ph.D Liars in the world is Bob Arum: *Dr Ferdie Pacheco – trainer*

Bob Arum is happy to completely base his life on misrepresentation. He is the biggest liar I have ever met: *Jose Sulaiman – President of the World Boxing Council*

I was talking with Bob Arum. He told me something, and I said 'But Bob, yesterday you told me the exact opposite.' 'I know,' Arum answered, 'Today, I'm telling the truth, yesterday I was lying.': *Bob Waters – sportscaster*

Bob Arum & Don King – *rival promoters*
On King's similarity to Arum – There can't be two Bob Arums, God couldn't make the same mistake twice: *Cus D'Amato*

King and Arum are alike. One's black and one's white. That's the only difference: *Mickey Duff*

Bob Arum is my greatest foe and nemesis, completely devoid of principle, a despicable and unconscionable cad – the master of all evil:
Don King

There was only one tune and if you didn't dance to Bob Arum's music, you didn't dance. I just brought another tune to town. Where he had Bach and Brahms, I brought rhythm and blues to give them an opportunity to go in another direction: *Don King*

Me and Bob Arum are reasonable men when it comes to money. We take our separate bags of money to separate banks and then it's, 'You're a sonofabitch' and 'You're a sonofabitch', but we're both two rich sonsofbitches: *Don King*

Max Baer – *world heavyweight champion [1934]*
After being knocked-out early by Joe Louis – Sure I quit. He hit me 18 times while I was in the act of falling that last time. I don't want to be cutting up paper dolls for a living. Besides, I got a wife and family to think about. If anyone wants to see the execution of Max Baer he's gotta pay more than $25 for a ringside seat!:
1935

Last words – to the hotel operator who asked if he wanted the house doctor – No, get me a people doctor.

Denzil Batchelor – *writer*
There have been champions who hated the game and animated punch-bags who could not get enough of it: *1947*

Boxers are as various as finger-prints; no two are alike: *1947*

David Belasco – *(1859–1931) theatre producer*
Boxing is show-business with blood.

Trevor Berbick – *Canadian world heavyweight champion [1986]*
What does awkward mean? Awkward is when a fighter can't hit you with his punches or put you away, so he calls you awkward.

Ronald Bergan – *writer*
The boxer is a round peg in a square ring, manipulated by others for profit.

Teddy Brenner – *Madison Square Gardens' President*
If you're a boxing promoter, you go into town and there are fifty managers begging you to use their fighters. You say 'maybe', but you can only use ten. And later when you don't use the others, someone calls you a liar.

A. A. Brill – *psychoanalyst*
Prize-fighters are direct descendants of pure sadism: *1949*

Those who witness a prize-fight soon observe that the whole audience actually 'participate' in the fight: *1949*

Drew 'Bundini' Brown – *Ali's trainer*
  Float like a butterfly, sting like a bee.
His hands can't hit what his eyes can't see.

'Bundini' Brown has a face like Stan Laurel, except black:
Ian Wooldridge – British sportswriter

Freddie Brown – *Roberto Duran's trainer*
This is the greatest of all sports. They don't play around with no substitutes in boxing, like they do in baseball or basketball or football. If a boxer gets a busted rib, he stays in there with it or he is a loser.

Hector 'Macho' Camacho – *Puerto Rican world super-featherweight champion [1983]*
There's only one man who can bring boxing alive, only one charismatic fighter out there, only one with all the flash and all the tools. Me – the 'Macho' man!

Camacho, he's a pest. He's a mosquito. You either ignore a pest or you swat it:
Ray Mancini – super-featherweight

Hector Camacho's great dream is to someday die in his own arms:
Irving Rudd – fight publicist

Dr Edwin Campbell
I think the most brutal thing about boxing is the seven o'clock weigh-in.

Primo Carnera – *Italian world heavyweight champion [1933]*
During the 1934 fight in which he lost his title to Max Baer –
Grantland Rice – The big fellow sure can take it.
Heywood Broun – Yes, but he doesn't know what to do with it!

Georges Carpentier – *French world light-heavyweight champion [1920]*
There are more ways of stopping punches than there are of delivering them.

Attack is only one half of the art of boxing.

Gil Clancy – *Gerry Cooney's manager*
I personally think that every young man in the United States should put on a pair of boxing gloves and learn how to box. Too many people today are afraid of a challenge.

Randall 'Tex' Cobb – *heavyweight*
All I want to do is hit somebody in the mouth. It's a whole lot easier than working for a living.

You've got to realize that everybody in this game is a liar and thief at one level or another.

If you screw up in tennis, it's 15-love. If you screw up in boxing, it's your ass.

I was once knocked out by a Mexican bantamweight – six of my pals were swinging him around by his heels at the time.

Cobb's head must have been carved out of Mount Rushmore and he certainly has a chin of granite: *Howard Cosell – commentator (1982)*

Gerrie Coetzee – *South African world heavyweight champion [1983]*
Out of all the fighters that I have developed, clothed, financed, Gerrie Coetzee is the only one who had the decency to say 'Thanks':
Don King – promoter

Gerry Cooney – *heavyweight*
When you go in the ring with Gerry Cooney, he puts marks on you. If you are in there with him for three minutes, you look like you have been in there three hours: *Gil Clancy – manager*

I'd love to fight Gerry Cooney. But I have my price – 25 cents and a loose woman: *'Tex' Cobb*

The world's going to fall in love with Gerry Cooney. There will be America, Apple Pie, Wheaties, and Gerry Cooney:
Dennis Rappaport – trainer

Gerry Cooney has the good looks and the charm of an Irish tenor, the humility and graciousness of a Victorian maiden:
Dennis Rappaport

James J. Corbett – *world heavyweight champion [1892]*
To become a champion, fight one more round:
1954

Eugene Corri – *referee*
Boxing is a game for men, and only men: *1915*

Howard Cosell – *(b 1920) TV commentator*
During the one-sided Holmes v Cobb title fight – I can't believe this referee. It is outrageous. He is constructing an advertisement for the abolition of the very sport he is part of: *1982*

After the Holmes v Cobb fight he quit commentating on boxing – I have walked away from it. I am past the point where I want to be part of it. I don't want to be party to the hypocrisy, the sleaziness. I'm worn out by it: *1982*

Boxing once had appeal to me. It was the romantic appeal of a way out of the ghetto, and I've always had great unwavering respect for men who fight for a living: *1982*

I now find the whole subject of professional boxing disgusting. Except for the fighters, you're talking about human scum, nothing more: *1982*

On Cosell's 'retirement' after the Holmes v Cobb fight – I can do my sport no greater service than this: *'Tex' Cobb*

Saying that Cosell quit boxing because it's sleazy is like saying Nixon quit politics because it's crooked: *Paul Gereffi*

John Cottrell – *British sportswriter*
The world heavyweight champion has always been expected to be part superman, part statesman, a paragon of all that is regarded as good and wholesome in America: *1967*

Cus D'Amato – *trainer of Patterson & Tyson*
Fear is an asset to a fighter. It makes him move faster, be quicker and more alert. Heroes and cowards feel exactly the same fear. Heroes just react to it differently.

Boxing is a contest of will and skill, with the will generally overcoming the skill, unless the skill of one man is much greater than the skill of the other.

His influence on boxing style was greater than Ernest Hemingway's impact on young American writers: *Norman Mailer – novelist*

He was a man of high moral integrity. Therefore, in this business, he was perceived as an eccentric: *Dr Ferdie Pacheco*

Guy Deghy – *writer*
If professional boxing is morally indefensible, so are zoos and circuses and those TV games that play strip-tease with human dignity: *1956*

Jack Dempsey – *(1895–1983) world heavyweight champion [1919]*
After being knocked out by Gene Tunney – Honey, I forgot to duck: *1926*

Tall men come down to my height when I hit them in the body.

He hits like an epileptic pile-driver:
Harry C. Witwert

Wilfrid Diamond – *(b 1931) writer*
The heavyweight championship of the world never dropped into anybody's lap. It's on the top of a hill, and a mighty steep, slippery hill.

The fight racket may be good for those at the top, but for the rank and file it is a heart-breaking, as well as a bodybreaking, business.

Angelo Dundee - *trainer of Ali & Leonard*
When you're working with a fighter, you're a surgeon, an engineer and a psychologist.

If you take the endurance of a tennis player, the courage of a racing driver, the sensibility of an actor, the continued discipline of a long distance runner, and mix those ingredients, you are on the way to knowing what it takes to be a professional boxer.

Boxers are highly trained athletes, tuned up to a degree not known in other sports. They ply their trade alone, and there is nowhere to hide. It is a marriage of top physical conditioning with unrelenting bravery.

To me, boxing is a very tough sport, but a ring is not the Roman Coliseum, and boxers aren't gladiators who must fight to the death.

Stillman's Gym [New York] was to boxers like Harvard Law School is to lawyers. A university where you competed against your peers under the scrutiny and tutelage of astute and knowledgeable coaches. Attending the place didn't guarantee success, but it certainly helped.

Roberto Duran - *Panamanian multi-world champion*
I'm not God - but I am something similar.

The only time Duran is serious is when he's sleeping or when he's fighting:
Freddie Brown - trainer

Duran reminded me of a bull rhino battling his way out of the bush, a grinding, rather than chilling puncher, who seemed to resent the inhibiting presence of a referee:
Reg Gutteridge - British commentator

Nat Fleischer - *founder & editor of The Ring magazine*
Like a game of chess, boxing, when properly followed, is a sport of wits.

Three of the blackest evils in boxing, other than the control of boxers by unsavoury characters, are fouls, mismatches and odorous decisions.

Boxing is definitely here to stay, no matter what the general attitude of those male grandmothers and young men of the nincompoop class who want to see its demise:
1965

The most insidious and dangerous enemies of boxing have not been foes from without, but the terrible breakers-down on the inside. The most serious threats to boxing always have come from within.

If *The Ring* is the 'Bible of Boxing', then boxing needs a New Testament:
Teddy Brenner - promoter

Frank 'The Animal' Fletcher - *middleweight*
I hate to say it, but it's true - I only like it better when the pain comes.

George Foreman - *world heavyweight champion [1973]*
I'm world heavyweight champion. I consider myself a citizen of the whole world.

Boxing is the sport to which all other sports aspire.

Boxing will never end. People will get tired of professional football and basketball. They're just watered down boxing, anyway.

A boxer never sees the big one that hits him.

Foreman can knock down an oak tree, but oak trees don't move:
Angelo Dundee - trainer (1974)

Bob Foster - *world light-heavyweight champion [1968]*
When you're in there with Foster it's like having a loaded gun pointed at your head. One wrong move and the lights go out:
Chris Finnegan - British light-heavyweight (1972)

Joe Frazier - *world heavyweight champion [1970]*
I don't want to knock my opponent out. I want to hit him, stay away, and watch him hurt. I want his heart.

I like to hit guys and see their knees tremble. I like to feel my strength and go for broke.

I never feel any pity for any man I beat. But, I respect any man who signs that contract to fight me, because he knows I'm gonna go out there to take him out: *1971*

Before their first meeting – He's so ugly they ought to donate his face to the World Wildlife Fund: *Muhammad Ali (1971)*

To Frazier's son, Marvis, after fighting his father for the third time – Your father is a great man and a great fighter. Never forget that. I have nothing bad to say about Joe Frazier. Without him I couldn't be who I am and without me he couldn't be who he is. We've been a pretty good team for four, five years: *Muhammad Ali (1975)*

Marvis Frazier – *heavyweight*
I just visualise fighting as a sport, no worse than football, no worse than basketball. I believe it's the public that makes the sport as brutal as it is. David slew Goliath. Look at Samson. Look at Moses and the Hebrew boys. All those guys were warriors.

Eddie Futch – *Joe Frazier's trainer*
On futile comebacks – There are certain things you can't get back, like the elastic in your socks.

'Two Ton' Tony Galento – *heavyweight*
I was a clean fighter; I always took a bath before the fight.

Paul Gallico – *(1897–1976) journalist & founder of the Golden Gloves tournament*
Prize-fighting and boxing are stupid, senseless, unappetising, inefficient and one hundred per cent useless.

Charlie Goldman – *Marciano's manager*
If you get a good idea for your fighter, like a different move or something, tell your fighter in a way that will make him believe he really thought of it himself. That way, he'll make the move naturally, without worrying about if he is doing it right.

Rocky Graziano – *world middleweight champion [1947]*
On winning the title – Hey, Ma your bad boy did good!: *1947*

I wouldn't recommend fighting any more because it's a tough business and it's a million to one shot if you make it. When you're playing football you got 26 guys on your side. When you're playing baseball you got twenty-whatever guys on your side, basketball you got a gang of guys on your side. When you're in the ring you're all alone, baby, and there's a guy throwing punches at you.

It's a terrible sport, but it's a sport. The fight for survival is in the fight.

Man in street – Would you like to join the Jehovah's Witnesses?
Graziano – I didn't see nothing!

Marvelous Marvin Hagler – *(b 1954) world middleweight champion [1980]*
I am a fighter who walks, talks, and thinks fighting, but I try not to look like it.

If they cut my bald head open, they will find one big boxing glove. That's all I am. I live it.

When I see blood, I become a bull.

On his shaven head – With four sisters about the house, I could never get my hands on a comb.

Before his fight against Leonard – I'm not sure you can get a fair shake in Las Vegas, I mean, they've got very bad judges there, and it's a town where they'll bet on which cockroach will get across the sidewalk first: *1987*

After his disputed loss, on points, to Leonard – You've got to remember this is a gambling city. Anywhere else in the world I think I would have got the decision: *1987*

For most of my life, nobody listened to what I had to say. Now, wherever I am, everyone pushes and shoves, trying to get close so they can hear me.

You got three strikes against you, kid – you're black, you're a southpaw and you can fight: *Joe Frazier*

I always knew I wouldn't be fully content with my life until I fought Marvin: *Sugar Ray Leonard (1986)*

Thomas Hauser – *writer*
A referee's decision as to whether or not to stop a fight is an enormous responsibility. The wrong decision can kill a career if a fight is stopped too early. The wrong decision can kill a fighter if it's stopped too late: *Black Lights*

Thomas 'The Hit Man' Hearns – *(b 1958) multi-weight world champion*
The ring – that's where I conduct my business. And my business is beating up people.

Ernest Hemingway – *(1898-1961) novelist*
My writing is nothing, my boxing is everything.

Life itself is the most savage left-hooker of all; but after that comes Charley White of Chicago.

Eugene Henderson – *referee & writer*
Woe betide the boxer who does not use his brains for defensive work, but uses his skull instead.

Boxing as a science stands on the most elementary basis – the stance.

Loser's mother – If you're a boxing referee, I'm the Queen of England!
Henderson – Excuse me, Your Majesty, but I have to get back to the dressing room!

Larry Holmes – *(b 1949) world heavyweight champion [1978]*
I'm an executive boxer, not ordinary like Gerry Cooney. He ain't no Great White Hope. He's the Great White Hype: *1982*

All fighters are prostitutes and all promoters are pimps.

Getting hit hard doesn't really hurt. It's more like someone taking your picture. You see a flash, and then suddenly everything is groggy, but you recover.

It's hard being black. You ever been black? I was black once – when I was poor.

Before fighting Carl Williams – People say that Larry Holmes is picking stiffs. I have a right to after 17 years. Every fight doesn't have to be a war.

On Marciano's record – If I wanted to break the record, I could go over to England and break it in a week.

Larry has the dexterity to put both his feet in his mouth: *Larry Merchant – TV sportscaster*

Bob Hope – *(b 1903) comedian*
I was called 'Rembrandt' Hope in my boxing days, because I spent so much time on the canvas.

Francis 'Kin' Hubbard – *(b 1868) humorist*
I'll bet th' hardest thing 'bout prize fightin' is pickin' up yer teeth with a boxin' glove on.

Jack Hurley – *promoter*
Looking at a fighter who can't punch is like kissing your mother-in-law.

Putting a fighter in the business world is like putting silk stockings on a pig.

Autobiography – 'Don't call me honest, you'll ruin me.'

Jim Jacobs – *manager of Benitez & Tyson*
The cardinal rule of managing is never put your fighter in a match you don't think he can win.

Ingemar Johansson – *Swedish world heavyweight champion [1959]*
A leviathan with a strangler's hands and a smile like the beam of a lighthouse:
Louis T. Stanley – sportswriter

Mike Jones – *trainer & manager of Basilio & Costello*
Boxing is beautiful – the purest sport in the world.

To understand boxing, you have to understand tradition and what it takes to get inside a ring.

You have to grasp the reality of smashed faces and pain, and understand how they can be part of something courageous, exciting and beautiful.

Boxing means more to me than dollars and cents. It's my life. How many people get to make their fantasies come true?

You can knock promoters; you can knock trainers, managers, even fighters. But don't knock boxing. It's the best sport there is, and anyone who's ever been involved will tell you it's an honour to be associated with boxing.

Fight managers travel so much we get ground lag.

A fight manager by trade, Mike Jones is as decent as the business allows. In an environment where most people have allies, he has friends: *Thomas Hauser – writer*

Michael Katz – *sportswriter*
Anything seems to go in a business in which larceny is sometimes mistaken for charm, and cheating for cleverness.

Don 'Only in America' King – *(b 1932)*
promoter
Only in America could a Don King happen.
[*Hence his nickname*]

On his 'time' before boxing – Intellectually, I went into jail with a peashooter and came out armed with a nuclear bomb. I made time serve me, rather than me serve time.

There's only one rule anyone connected with boxing must keep in mind – everything you hear in boxing is a lie.

Martin Luther King took us to the mountain top; I want to take us to the bank. I'm fighting the Civil War. I'm fighting the poverty war.

You can see me. My name's on everything. This ain't no No-Name Productions. It's Don King Productions. I perform.

I am accused of being impartially prejudiced.

There has only been three great promoters in this century – P. T. Barnum, Michael Todd and me.

People just don't like me for the same reason they didn't like Muhammad Ali. We're the wrong kind of nigger. We're not quiet. We stand up to be counted.

I am the promoter. First, there was the prophet

Isaiah. Then, Nostradamus. Then, P. T. Barnum and Buffalo Bill – and then me!

I was the man who turned colossal into super-colossal.

People are my most important asset. Faith in the Supreme Being, trust, credibility and performance are the things that have brought me to the top.

You must be able to deal with the fact that you have racism out there. A white fighter is platinum gold if he can fight.

On an FBI investigation into his finances – They went down the list of every known charge conceivable to man – racketeering, skimming, kickback, ticket scalping, fixing fights, pre-ordaining fights, vitiating officals, corrupting judges, all the way down to laundering money. Everything, but the Lindbergh baby.

Whenever you do business with Don King, you can never lose sight of the fact that he's smarter than you are: *Anon*

Don King is like everybody else in boxing. He's a liar, a thief, a murderer and a racketeer. And a con man: *'Tex' Cobb – heavyweight*

Don King is one of the great humanitarians of our time. He has risen above that great term, prejudice. He has screwed everybody he has ever been around. Hog, dog, or frog, it don't matter to Don. If you got a quarter, he wants the first 26 cents: *'Tex' Cobb*

My complaint is that Jose Sulaiman [WBC] is not happy his friend Don King is the biggest promoter in boxing. Sulaiman will only be happy when Don King is the 'only' promoter in boxing: *Mickey Duff – British promoter*

I told him that if God needed a PR man he'll send an earthquake or a hurricane along:
George Foreman – heavyweight (1979)

Don King is a liar and a thief, the greediest bastard I've ever known:
Rich Giachetti – Holmes' manager

The man's so insecure he goes around wearing

his hair like a fucking idiot, so people will recognise him: *Rich Giachetti*

The man's greatest asset is that he was born black, because the fighters are black. He knows them. He knows how to rile them, how to sweet talk them. He'll say and do whatever it takes to win them over: *Rich Giachetti*

If I was a fighter and needed a promoter, who would I take? Don King. The man is the best. Don King delivers: *Rich Giachetti*

If you stay in a room with Don King for an hour, he'll con you into anything. That's why I talk to him over the phone. So I can hang up:
Larry Holmes – heavyweight

His unashamed 'Hi Mom!' camera-hogging makes Fatima Whitbread look like a Carmelite:
Frank Keating – British sportswriter

Don King is a man who wants to swallow mountains, walk on water and sleep on clouds:
Mark Kram – sportswriter

Don King is the best snake-oil salesman I ever met. The absolute best:
Butch Lewis – Michael Spinks' manager

On King being previously awarded the 'Keys to the City' of Scranton, Philadelphia – Since then, we've changed the locks:
James McNulty – Mayor of Scranton

He couldn't turn lemon into lemonade:
George Plimpton – writer

Don King dresses like a pimp and speechifies like a store- front preacher:
John Schulian – sportswriter

I don't like Don King. I don't trust Don King. I don't need Don King. I want nothing to do with Don King: *Michael Spinks*

When Don King promotes Michael Jackson, he wants to overshadow even Michael Jackson:
Jose Sulaiman

I tried to stay away from King. You can't do it. It's like staying away from taxes; sooner or later he will get you: *Pinklon Thomas – heavyweight*

Mark Kram – *sportswriter*
Boxing promoters have seldom been easy on the eyes or ears. There has always been a flaccid pulp quality about their presence, and often it seems that, if one tried to reach out and grab whatever it is they represent, there would be only air or at best a gummy substance. They view words like loyalty, character and honour as cave animals look upon sunlight.

Jake LaMotta – *world middleweight champion [1949]*
If you want a fancy dan, that I wasn't. What's that got to do with fighting?

Me and Jake LaMotta grew up in the same neighbourhood. You wanna know how popular Jake was? When we played hide and seek, nobody ever looked for LaMotta:
Rocky Graziano – middleweight

Jake LaMotta and I fought six times. We almost got married: *Sugar Ray Robinson – middleweight*

LaMotta couldn't punch at all but he was tough, kept coming. He wore you out. You couldn't miss him. You'd throw a punch backwards, you'd hit him. You'd throw it under his legs, you'd hit him. He was tough:
Fritzie Zivic – welterweight

'Sugar' Ray Leonard – *(b 1956) multi-weight world champion*
After winning Olympic gold – I'm finished. I've fought my last fight. My journey has ended. My dream is fulfilled: *1976*

We're all endowed with certain God-given talents. Mine happens to be punching people in the head.

Boxing is more than a sport, it's a skill.

In the ring your fists are like little snakes that strike before you can tell them to.

In the ring I can feel that halo over my head turn into those two little horns.

The first thing I do when a fight is over is to run to the mirror to see what damage has been done.

Every day I feel like quitting. Every time in fact that somebody hits me. But every time I hit it is a thousand dollars: *1980*

On retirement – A fighter never knows when it's the last bell. He doesn't want to face that.

After an operation on a detached retina – I ought to get a card printed up that I can hand out that says 'The eye's okay'.

Before returning to the ring – I'm not concerned about another injury to my eye, or the threat of blindness. That's what made me a champion. We assume the risks. That's what makes a great champion. We care, but you can't let that be a burden to you.

If 'Sugar' Ray Leonard had weighed a few stone heavier, he could have fought as a heavyweight against John Tate and Ron Lyle:
Colin M. Jarman – British sportswriter (1988)

I told him that if he didn't quit I'd break all his fingers: *Juanita Leonard – wife (1982)*

Ray is not just an accomplished boxer – he's an accomplished human being. He's not a wise ass. There are boxing people who mistake intelligence for wise assery:
Mike Trainer – adviser

Ray Leonard is the kind of guy who's always looking at the edge of the cliff, fascinated as to how close to the edge he can get to it. He hasn't gotten to the edge yet: *Mike Trainer*

Butch Lewis – *Michael Spinks' manager*
On the fee offered for the Spinks v De Leon fight – CBS were offering beer money for a champagne fight.

On the Spinks v Tyson fight – You can't negotiate with Butch. You ever try to negotiate with an earthquake?: *Jim Jacobs – manager*

It's like we're two guys who met in the Army and have spent the last ten years in the same fox-hole. We look to one another to cover each other's back: *Michael Spinks*

I'd rather starve before I'd sell Butch out:
Michael Spinks

Sonny Liston – *(1932–71) world heavyweight champion [1962]*
I couldn't pass judgement on no one. I haven't been perfect myself.

A prize-fight is like a cowboy movie. There has to be a good guy and a bad guy. People pay their money to see me lose. Only, in my cowboy movie, the bad guy always wins.

After his fight with Patterson was switched to the Windy City – Don't matter where the fight is. My punches are just as hard in Chicago as in New York.

On choosing referees – It don't matter as long as he can count up to ten.

On Cassius Clay – That young pup? What do you want . . . to get me arrested for murder?:
1963

On life after losing the title to Clay – Even the push button elevators don't stop for me now:
1965

On his pre-boxing mob employment – Boxing gave Sonny Liston the opportunity to meet big-time hoodlums instead of small ones:
Jimmy Cannon – sportswriter

He's so ugly, that when he cries the tears run down the back of his head: *Cassius Clay (1964)*

If Sonny liked you, he could be very friendly. The trouble was he didn't like too many people:
Cus D'Amato

We don't want to meet this geezer Liston walking down the street let alone in a ring:
Jim Wicks – British trainer & manager

Konrad Lorenz – *(b 1903) Austrian behavioural psychologist*
Few lapses of self-control are punished as immediately and severely as loss of temper during a boxing bout.

Joe Louis – *(1914–81) world heavyweight champion [1937]*
Once that bell rings you're on your own. It's just you and the other guy.

There's no such thing as a natural boxer. A natural dancer has to practice hard. A natural painter has to paint all the time. Even a natural fool has to work at it.

Nobody gets hurt, but the customer.

Before he knocked out Billy Conn in the 13th – He can run, but he can't hide: *1941*

After being chewed out by a truck driver, he was asked why he hadn't decked the offender – If somebody was to insult Caruso, would he sing the guy an aria?

On his death – Joe Louis was my inspiration. I idolize him. I just give lip service to being the greatest. He was the greatest:
Muhammad Ali (1981)

On facing 'The Brown Bomber' – I looked across the ring and realised I wanted to go home:
Max Baer (1935)

On being hit by Louis – It's like someone jammed an electric light bulb in your face, and busted it. I thought half my head was blowed off:
James J. Braddock – heavyweight

And again – When he knocked me down I could have stayed there for three weeks:
James J. Braddock

Joe Louis was a credit to his race – the human race: *Jimmy Cannon – sportswriter*

He was a big lean copper spring, tightened and retightened through weeks of training, until he was one pregnant package of coiled venom:
Bob Considine – journalist

Joe Louis was always a clean fighter in a dirty game: *Wilfrid Diamond – writer*

I've only to read his name again and my nose starts to bleed again:
Tommy Farr – British heavyweight

Before fighting Louis – I'll moider the bum:
Tony 'Two-Ton' Galento (1939)

His fists were weapons that seemed to fire automatically. Fighting Joe Louis in his prime

was like staying in the casino too long. Eventually, you were going to lose:
Thomas Hauser

The most beautiful fighting machine I have ever seen: *Ernest Hemingway*

Rabbit say to the bee, 'What make you sting so deep?'
The bee say, 'I sting like Joe and rock 'em to sleep!':
Richard Wright – 'The Ballad of Joe Louis' (1942)

John Lovesey – *British sportswriter*
Soviet boxing, at its best, is clearly a game of chess with muscles.

Norman Mailer – *(b 1923) novelist*
The closer a heavyweight comes to the championship, the more natural it is for him to be a little insane, secretly insane, for the heavyweight champion of the world is either the toughest man in the world or he is not, but there is the real possibility he is. It is like being the big toe of God: *1971*

Boxing is not violence, it's a conversation, an exchange between two men who talk to each other with their hands instead of their voices; hitting at the ear, the nose, the mouth, the belly, instead of hitting at each other's minds. When a man fights in the ring, he is not expressing brutality. He expresses a complex, subtle nature like that of a true intellectual, a real aristocrat. With his fists a pugilist transforms violence into something noble and disciplined. It's a real triumph of the spirit.

Ray 'Boom-Boom' Mancini – *world lightweight champion [1982]*
If bullshit was poetry, Boom Boom's last name would be Shakespeare: *Dennis Rappaport*

Rocky Marciano – *(1923–69) world heavyweight champion [1952]*
I was a strong guy who trained hard but I didn't have the talent of, say, Sugar Ray Robinson.

It doesn't do any good to hit a guy if you don't hurt him.

When you become heavyweight champion,

something comes between you and other people, even your family. Everybody stands back a little, not because of anything you do but because of what you are.

After being roughed up in San Francisco – He didn't foul deliberately; it was the way he fought. Mind you, he was a bit deaf when it came to hearing the bell:
                    Don Cockell – British heavyweight (1955)

Two things about Marciano's career to date stand out like a couple of black eyes at a church supper – he has a punch and a manager. Mighty potent is the punch, and mighty shrewd was the manager: *Wilfrid Diamond*

Rocky Marciano doesn't need a shillelagh - he had one built into each hand: *Wilfrid Diamond*

On his lack of natural talent – They all look better than Rocky when they're doing their job. But they don't look so good on the canvas:
                    Charlie Goldman – trainer

Marciano didn't know enough boxing to know what a feint was, he never tried to outguess you – he just kept trying to knock your brains out:
                    Archie Moore – heavyweight

Saoul Mamby – *world super-lightweight champion [1980]*
On managers – Never have so few taken so much from so many.

Harry Markson – *promoter*
Boxing is replete with instances of potential delinquents who were 'straightened out'.

Boxing is a sport that symbolizes democracy in action.

'Ageless' Archie Moore – *(b 1913) world light-heavyweight champion [1952]*
On his durable career – I lasted because I learned to keep my head out of the way of blows. I could take a punch, but it's better to evade them, I say.

Boxing is syllables. You learn them one by one.

What I do is philosophy.

There's only one Moore. He's the Einstein of boxing: *Tony Anthony – light-heavyweight*

Willie Pastrano – *world light-heavyweight champion [1963]*
I look at ordinary people in their suits, them with no scars, and I'm different. I don't fit in with them. I'm where everybody's got scar tissue on their eyes and got noses like saddles. I go to conventions of old fighters like me and I see the scar tissue and all them flat noses and it's beautiful. Galento, Giardello, LaMotta, Carmen Basilio. They talk like me, like they got rocks in their throats. Beautiful.

Floyd Patterson – *(b 1935) world heavyweight champion [1956]*
I don't like to see blood. It's different when I bleed, that doesn't worry me because I can't see it.

I was never knocked out. I've been unconscious, but it's always been on my feet.

On being knocked down – You don't feel a thing. Honest. No pain at all. Sometimes I've gone down and it feels sweet as hell, like it must be the other guy falling, not you yourself. In a way it's a very lovable feeling.

After losing his title to Sweden's Ingemar Johansson – Losing a championship is bad enough, but losing it to a foreigner was even worse.

Vinnie Pazienza – *world lightweight champion [1987]*
On how he finished an opponent – His legs turned to spaghetti, and I was all over him like the sauce.

On the Pazienza v Greg Haugen fight at Providence, Rhode Island, June 1987
Because this is a title fight, I can have four people in the corner and I'll have an extra cut man. I'll also have an extra stool, one for Vinnie to sit on, and the other to throw at him if he doesn't listen to me: *Lou Duva – trainer*

He's a loud-mouth punk. He's running around saying he draws 15,000 people in Rhode Island. Big deal. You can get 10,000 people out there to watch the tide come in: *Greg Haugen*

You can't get better than this side of homicide:
Ferdie Pacheco – TV commentator

After winning on points despite suffering a broken nose – He could've broken my nose five times and I could've fought him with one arm and a couple of toes missing. I won this fight on guts. I told you I'd fight my heart out and I did:
Vinnie Pazienza
[*Haugen won the re-match eight months later, in Atlantic City*]

Willie Pep – *world featherweight champion [1946]*
I had the bravest manager in the world – he didn't care who I fought.

They call Ray Robinson the best fighter pound for pound. I'm the best fighter, ounce for ounce.

Greeting an old adversary – Lay down, so I can recognise you.

Dr R. Ravina
Years ago, the science of evasion and passing was stressed, nowadays the public wants offensive action to the utmost without regard to the blows received.

Sugar Ray Robinson – *(1920–89) world middleweight champion [1951]*
Unless you've been in the ring when the noise is for you, there's no way you'll ever know what it's like.

Fighting, to me, seems barbaric. It seems to me like the barbarous days when men fought in a pit and people threw money down to them. I don't really like it. I enjoy out-thinking another man and out-manoeuvring him, but I still don't like to fight.

I loved boxing. Every time I hear someone say 'pound for pound', it's the most wonderful feeling in the world. I can't say anymore.

You always say, 'I'll quit when I start to slide', and then one morning you wake up and realize you've done slid.

How he got his nickname – This Robinson is as sweet as sugar:
Jack Case – writer

I fought Sugar Ray Robinson so many times that I'm lucky I didn't get diabetes:
Jake LaMotta – middleweight

I'd like to introduce a man who is a legacy in his own lifetime:
Dennis Rappaport

Damon Runyon – *(1884–1946) journalist & writer*
A fight manager may have a lightweight champion of the world, but he will get more heated up about some sausage who scarcely knows how to hold his hands up, if he is a heavyweight.

Budd Schulberg – *(b 1914) writer*
So what happens – this bum Wilson gets the title shot – outdoors in a ball-park! And what do I get – a couple of bucks and a one-way ticket to Palookaville:
On the Waterfront

Prize-fighting is the one escape-hatch to fame and fortune and respectability for the child forsaken.

John Schulian – *sportswriter*
Honesty is not a criterion for membership in the promoter's lodge. It may even be grounds for expulsion.

Earnie Shavers – *heavyweight*
There's excitement when I fight because I'm a hitter. And that's what the fans really want to see, a guy getting his block knocked off. It sounds bad but that's what it's all about.

Anybody can hit as hard as Earnie Shavers. The thing that makes Earnie Shavers so significant is that Earnie Shavers is gonna hit you that hard every single time he lays leather on you:
'Tex' Cobb – heavyweight

Holmes doesn't hit as hard as Shavers. Nobody hits like Shavers. If anybody hit harder than Shavers, I'd shoot him:
'Tex' Cobb

He hit me, man, and knocked me face down on the canvas. I was in the land of make-believe. I heard saxophones, trombones. I saw little blue rats, and they were all smoking cigars and drinking whisky:
James 'Quick' Tillis – heavyweight

George Bernard Shaw - *(1856-1950) Irish playwright*
If I ever act as a referee in an American glove fight I shall demand at least an equal share of the gate money and cinema rights with the rival champions, and I shall have to work just as hard and get no glory by it: *1921*

Abe Simon - *heavyweight*
There's a whole lot of difference between pain and damage. The bruises from punches are like icebergs. You see only a small part of the damage on the surface.

Leon Spinks - *world heavyweight champion [1978]*
Before fighting Muhammad Ali for the title - I got to fight to do my job, but I can't wait to get out of the ring. I don't enjoy hitting nobody: *1978*

After beating Ali - I am not the Greatest, I am the latest: *1978*

After losing a re-match to Ali - To experience the agony of defeat makes you stronger. It's like taking one step back and two steps forward. To experience the agony of defeat makes you appreciate the experience of winning. That's what makes a champion. *1978*

I'm always into a positive black image. Whenever Leon Spinks fights I always pray, 'Dear Lord, please don't let them interview Leon on TV': *Arsenio Hall - comedian*

After the Ali re-match - They're selling video cassettes of the Ali v Spinks fight for $89.95. Hell, for that money Spinks will come to your house: *Dr Ferdie Pacheco*

When Leon became champ, it was like taking a man off the street and making him President: *Sam Solomon - trainer*

On his brother's fall from glory - What Leon went through was like a rush through the Twilight Zone: *Michael Spinks*

Michael Spinks - *world light-heavy & heavyweight champion*
It's a life threat. I'm telling you, what I do for a living can be terrifying.

Teofilio Stevenson - *Cuban Olympic heavyweight champion [1972]*
I don't like professional boxing. And I don't like the way professional fighters are handled. I want to be an athlete and that would not be allowed if I turned professional.

Professional boxing treats a fighter like a commodity to be bought and sold and discarded when he is no longer of use.

You don't see his right hand. All of a sudden it is there - on your chin:
Peter Hussing - Canadian amateur (1972)

John L. Sullivan - *(1858-1918) world heavyweight champion [1882]*
When going into the ring I have always had it in mind that I would be the conqueror. That has always been my disposition.

I will not fight a Negro. I never have, and I never will: *1892*

I believe in having a little fight in most everything except funerals. Anything that ain't got some fighting in it is like a funeral and I don't like funerals.

After losing to James Corbett - The old pitcher went to the well once too often, but I'm glad the championship remains in America: *1892*

When Sullivan struck me, I thought a telegraph pole had been shoved against me:
Paddy Ryan - heavyweight (1882)

Sullivan found prize-fighting a mean, ill-assorted pastime, half rough-and-tumble wrestling, half eye-gouging, hip and knee street fighting, and he left it a modern sport:
William V. Shannon

Robert Teague
Boxing is the opportunity for the low man on the ethnic totem pole.

Mike Trainer - *adviser to Sugar Ray Leonard*
In boxing, you're not entitled to a bad day. A tennis player gets smoked by a guy not even in the top 100, and life goes on. In boxing, you're only as good as your last performance. In that situation, you're probably inclined to be more

careful than you should be.

Lee Trevino – *(b 1939) golfer*
If I'd been born within walking distance of a gym, I wouldn't mind betting I'd be welterweight champion of the world today.

Tony 'TNT' Tubbs – *world heavyweight champion [1985]*
After losing his crown to Tim Witherspoon – There ain't no excuses in the game of boxing: *1986*

Gene Tunney – *(1897-1978) world heavyweight champion [1926]*
A boxing match is two men on public exhibition, paid to beat each other to the floor, unconscious or helpless.

In human endeavour, the most important thing is not so much the realization of the goal; the effort of the chase is worth more to the hunter than the actual capture. I cherish my crown. But my greatest thrills came not in winning it, but my climb to the top. Now that goal has been reached, it is just another incident in my boxing career.

Mike Tyson – *world heavyweight champion [1986]*
The nature of my business is to hurt people.

Sometimes I wonder what would happen if I fought myself. I think it would be a one-round KO. If I was fighting myself, I know I could take my best punch. No, make that two rounds. I would knock myself out in two rounds.

There's nothing I ever saw that can compare with a heavyweight championship. It's the idea that you never know what is going to happen. When you go to a comedy show, you know you're going to laugh. When you go to a horror show, you know you're going to be scared. When you go to a fight and you root for somebody and he loses, you leave crying and emotionally drained. It's the idea of not knowing.

I always try to catch them right on the tip of the nose because I try to push the bone into the brain.

He fights like you stole something from him or said something nasty about his family:
Mike Acri – *promoter*

To say Tyson is predictable is rather like saying a runaway truck is predictable; you know it is going to career straight down the hill towards you, so where is the problem? All you have to do is stop it!:   *Simon Barnes* – *British sportswriter*

I'd rather live on a street corner in Texas than climb into the ring with that man Tyson:
O. T. Davis – *heavyweight*

I don't know how you slow Mike Tyson down. He's young, maybe he'll find himself a girlfriend: *Angelo Dundee* – *trainer & TV commentator (1986)*

Tyson hit me on top of the head in the first round and it felt like my neck went down to my belly button: *Mike Jameson*

On the brevity of his fights – Mike's like a Gershwin or Beethoven. You go for the quality of the performance, not the longevity of it:
Don King – *promoter (1989)*

Everything he's got has 'goodnight' written all over it: *Mills Lane* – *referee*

Victor Valle – *trainer*
Fighters are like beautiful women – too many times they break your heart.

Jersey Joe Walcott – *world heavyweight champion [1951]*
Abolishing boxing is like abolishing the Police department.

Jess Willard – *world heavyweight champion [1915]*
Against Jack Dempsey – Jess Willard was staggering around like a farmer's wife in the old days of Peruna and Dr Pierce's Golden Remedy: *Arthur Baer* – *sportswriter (1919)*

WBC & WBA – *world boxing authorities*
I see myself as a hard-working man. I do the best that I can like everyone else who cares about what he does. I love boxing, so I'm a salesman for boxing. I love the WBC, so I'm a salesman for the WBC: *Don King* – *promoter*

Two nickel and dime outfits, the WBC and WBA, run their fights to their own aggrandizement and the detriment of the sport:
Pat Putnam – sportswriter

Boxing is run by a little fat Mexican dictator and a group of corrupt Panamanians:
Bert Sugar – sportswriter

Fritzie Zivic – *world welterweight champion [1940]*
I never lost a fight on a foul in my life. I'd give 'em the head, choke 'em, hit 'em in the balls, but I'd never gouge their eyes, because I didn't want 'em to do that to me.

I never in my life used the thumb. You're fighting, not playing a piano in there.

Being remembered as a dirty fighter is not the best of compliments, but then again, we have our own set of values.

Kids today think that laces are for tying up the gloves!

BULLFIGHTING

Anon
What I like best about bullfighting is the big money and the small bulls: *Matador*

Garcia Baquero – *Spanish writer*
What is being attempted is not simply to kill the bull in any way possible, but to do so according to certain rules which demand that it be carried out in a requisite time and by a determined method.

Homer Casteel – *writer*
The mistake most people make about the bullfight is that they assume it is a contest between the man and the bull. It is not. It is a contest within the man himself. He pits his bravery and his training, which dictates he must plant his feet and pass the horns as closely past his body as possible, against the innate human impulse to get the hell out:
Running of the Bulls (1953)

Rafael Campos de Espana – *Spanish writer*
In the bullfight the Spaniard has found the most perfect expression for defining his human quality.

'El Cordobes' [Manuel Benitez] – *(b 1936) Spanish matador*
El Cordobes seemed to know about as much about bullfighting as he did about the rules of cricket: *El Pipo – manager*

Ernest Hemingway – *(1898–1961) US*
novelist
Bullfighting is worthless without rivalry. But with two great bullfighters it becomes a deadly rivalry: *The Dangerous Summer*

Bullfighting is the only art in which the artist is in danger of death and in which the degree of brilliance in the performance is left to the fighter's honour.

Bullfighting is not a sport. It was never supposed to be. It is a tragedy. A very great tragedy. The tragedy is the death of the bull.

Bullfighting is an exceedingly dangerous occupation. It is a good deal like Grand Opera for the really great matadors, except they run the chance of being killed every time they cannot hit a high C.

Colin M. Jarman – *(b 1958) sportswriter*
Bullfighting is as close to sport as the Earth is to the Sun: *1988*

Federico Garcia Lorca – *(1898–1936) Spanish poet & dramatist*
Spain is the only country where death is the national spectacle.

John Marks – *writer & critic*
Bullfighting is not a cruel sport, but a cruel method of achieving plastic beauty:
To the Bullfight again (1966)

El Pipo – *El Cordobes' manager*
Art you can get in the Prado. In the bull-ring you want something else. In the bull-ring one thing interests me; it's a kid who can excite a crowd. Show me a kid who can make a crowd's hair stand up in the bull-ring, and I'll show you a kid who can make money as a matador.

Arthur Rubinstein – *(b 1889) Polish/US concert pianist*
A concert is like a bullfight – the moment of truth.

CANOEING

Proverbs
Paddle one's own canoe.

Ivars Simanis – *USSR*
Canoe Slalom racing is a bit like chess; the straightest path is by no means always the quickest.

CARDS & DICE

Anon
Cards and dice are the Devil's books and bones.

Francis Bacon – *(1561–1626) poet & statesman*
Dice and cards may sometimes be used for recreation when field sports cannot be had.

Henry Ward Beecher – *(1813–87) US clergyman & editor*
Gambling with cards, or dice, or stocks is all one thing – it is getting money without giving an equivalent for it.

Joan Collins – *(b 1933) actress*
She has the assurance of someone dealing herself a fifth ace in a card game with children:
Louis T. Stanley – sportswriter

David Garrick – *(1717–79) actor*
Shake off the shackles of this tyrant vice,
Hear other calls than those of card and dice.

John Locke – *(1632–1704) philosopher*
As to cards and dice, I think the safest and best way is never to learn to play upon them, and so to be incapacitated for those dangerous temptations and encroaching waters of time.

Jack Richardson
Whenever dice are thrown or cards shuffled the Dark Ages get another turn on this planet.

CARDS

GENERAL

Proverbs
Lucky at cards, unlucky in love.

A card which never appears neither wins or loses: *Brazilian*

Cards are the Bible of 52 leaves: *Dutch*

Cards are the devil's prayer book: *German*

Similes
As honest a man as any is in cards with the Kings taken out: *Anon*

As calm as a good player with a Royal Flush: *Arthur Reeve*

As dark as a club flush: *H. C. Witwert*

Francis Bacon – *(1561–1626) poet & statesman*
There can be that can pack the cards, and yet cannot play well: *Of Cunning*

Lord Birkenhead [Frederick E. Smith] –

(1872-1930) MP & lawyer
I do not, more than another man, mind being cheated at cards; but I find it a little nauseating if my opponent then publicly ascribes his success to the partnership of the most high.

Nicholas Breton - *(1545-1626) poet*
There is no pack of cards, without the knave:
1600

Thomas Brown - *(1663-1704) poet*
However all flattery apart,
You've played your Cards with wondrous Art:
1702

Robert Burton - *(1577-1640) churchman & writer*
They turned up trumps, before the Cards were shuffled: 1621

Miguel de Cervantes - *(1547-1616) Spanish novelist & poet*
What I say is, patience, and shuffle the cards.

As much is lost by a card too many, as a card too few.

Anton Chekov - *(1860-1904) Russian novelist*
If the Prince of Monaco has a roulette table, surely convicts may play cards.

William Cowper - *(1731-1800) poet*
With spot quadrangular of diamond form,
Ensanguined hearts, clubs of typical strife,
And spades, the emblem of untimely graves.

Finlay Peter Dunne - *(1867-1936) US humorist*
Trust everybody, but cut the cards.

A man's idea of a card game is war - cool, devastating and pitiless. A lady's idea of it is a combination of larceny, embezzlement and burglary.

Eugene Field - *(1850-1895) US critic*
Last night Mr Creston Clarke played King Lear at the Tabor Grand. All through the five acts of the Shakespearian tragedy he played the King as though under the premonition that someone was about to play the Ace.

David Garrick - *(1717-79) actor*

Cards were at first for benefits designed,
Sent to amuse not to enslave the mind.

Baltasaar Gracian - *(1601-58) priest & writer*
A cunning gamester never plays the card which his adversary expects, and far less that which he desires.

Texas Guinan - *(1884-1933) US nightclub owner & entertainer.*
A guy who'd cheat on his wife would cheat at cards.

John Hay - *(1838-1905)*
True luck consists not in holding the best of cards at the table; luckiest he who knows just when to rise and go home.

Friedrich Hebbel - *(1813-63) German dramatist*
With someone who holds nothing but trumps, it is impossible to play cards.

Edmond Hoyle - *(1672-1769) card authority & historian*
When in doubt, win the trick.

Samuel Johnson - *(1709-84) lexicographer*
I am sorry I have not learned to play at cards. It is very useful in life: it generates kindness and consolidates society.

Charles Lamb - *(1775-1834) essayist*
They do not play at cards, but only play at playing at them.

H.T. Leslie
The game of life is not so much in holding a good hand as playing a poor hand well.

Jawaharlal Nehru - *(1889-1964) Indian political leader*
Life is a game of cards. The hand that is dealt you represents determinism; the way you play it is free will.

Anne N. Royall - *(1769-1854) US author & traveller*
Cards subject you to bad company and bad hours. Which is worse?

William Shakespeare - *(1564-1616) playwright*

The most patient man in loss, the most coldest
that ever turned up the ace: *Cymbelline*

'Bishop' Arnold Snyder - *founder of 'First
Church of Blackjack'*
Onward Blackjack soldiers. Counting down the
deck
    Never be a loser. You can win your bet.
    You can Beat the Dealer. Leave him in
disgrace
You can make the pit boss wish he'd never seen
your face.

Learn ye to count the cards and thou shalt take
from Caesar the chips that are Caesar's: *1981*
[*Caesar in this instance being Caesar's Palace in
Las Vegas*]

Jonathan Swift - *(1667-1745) poet & satirist*
I must complain the cards are ill shuffled till I
have a good hand.

Sophie Tucker - *(1884-1966) US actress*
I've cut out smoking and drinking, all I have
left is gin rummy – they can't take that away
from me: *1944*

Oscar Wilde - *(1854-1900) Irish dramatist &
humorist*
One should always play fairly when one has the
winning cards.

BRIDGE

Anon
Bridge, because of its tendency to encourage
prolonged smoking and its deadly immobility is
probably the most dangerous game played in
England now: *Anon doctor*

Arthur C. Benson - *(1862-1925) master at
Eton*
Bridge I regard as only one degree better than
absolutely vacuous conversation, which is
certainly the most fatiguing thing in the world.

Don Herold - *US humorist*
I say, let's banish bridge. Let's find some
pleasant way of being miserable together.

Joe Laurie Jr - *US comedian*
If you play bridge badly you make your partner
suffer; but if you play bridge very badly you

make everybody suffer.

W. Somerset Maugham - *(1874-1965)
novelist & playwright*
I hate people who play bridge as though they
were at a funeral and knew their feet were
getting wet: *1921*

Anne H. Shaw - *(1847-1919) suffragette*
When the human passions are ebbing, bridge
takes their place.

Ruth M.Teague - *US writer*
Bridge is a social but not very sociable game –
that is, if you take it seriously, as most bridge
players do: *Ladies Home Journal*

POKER

Sayings
Read them and weep.

Proverbs
A Smith and Wesson beats four aces: *American*

Never do card tricks with the boys you play
poker with: *American*

Ambrose Bierce - *(1842-1914) US journalist
& poet*
A miracle is an act or event out of the order of
nature and unaccountable, as beating a normal
hand of four kings and an ace, with four aces
and a king: *1906*

Arthur Brisbane - *(1864-1936) US editor*
There is enough energy wasted in poker to
make a hundred thousand successful men every
year.

Al Jolson - *(1886-1950) US jazz singer &
actor*
In Hollywood, I played poker with the film
magnates. I played for about a minute because
they regard ten thousand dollars as tissue
paper.
[*Jolson died while playing a hand of Gin Rummy*]

George S. Kaufman - *(1889-1961) US
humorist & playwright*
Playing stud poker at the National Press Club
was what hardened my character.

He had integrity, George did. You never had to watch him when he was dealing:
Harpo Marx - US comedian

Hilde Spiel - *(b 1911) US author*
Malice is like a game of poker; you wouldn't play it with anyone who is manifestly inferior to you.

Tennessee Williams - *(1911-83) US playwright*
Poker shouldn't be played in a house with women.

WHIST

Edmond Hoyle - *(1762-1769) card authority & historian*
Troy owes to Homer what Whist owes to Hoyle: *Lord Byron*

The Humour of Whist
    Who will believe that a man could ever exist
Who spent near half an age, in studying whist?
    Grow grey with calculation, labour hard,
As if life's business center'd in a card.

Charles Lamb - *(1775-1834) essayist*
A clear fire, a clean hearth, and the rigour of the game: *Whist*

DICE

Anon
Spotted like a pair of dice.

Proverbs
The devil is in the dice.

The best throw of the dice, is to throw them away.

Dicing, drabbing and drinking bring men to distractions.

Dicing, drabbing and drinking are the three d's to destruction.

Similes
About as much chance as a nickel in a two-bit crap game: *Ray Cohen*

St Augustine - *(354-430) Church father &*

philosopher.
The devil invented dice.

Lord Byron - *(1788-1824) poet*
Whose game was empires,
And whose stakes were thrones;
Whose table was earth,
    Whose dice were human bones.

Confucius - *(551-497 BC) Chinese philosopher*
He that is afraid to throw the dice, will never throw a six.

Albert Einstein - *(1879-1955) German/Swiss/US physicist*
His reaction to the Quantum Theory - God does not play dice.
[*Also attributed as* - I cannot believe that God plays dice with the cosmos]

Samuel Foote - *(1720-77) playwright & actor*
Death and dice level all distinctions.

Lord E. Herbert of Cherbury - *(1583-1648) soldier & philosopher*
Is the die cast, must at this one throw all thou hast gained be lost?: *1634*

Douglas Jerrold - *(1803-57) playwright & humorist*
I never hear the rattling of dice that it does not sound to me like the funeral bell of the whole family.

Plato - *(428-347 BC) Greek philosopher*
The best partner for dice-playing is not just a man, but a good dice player.

Plutarch - *(50-120) Greek biographer*
Mercury once played dice with the moon.

Alexander Pope - *(1688-1744) poet*
How, sir! Not damn the sharper, but the dice.

William Shakespeare - *(1564-1616) playwright*
It is lost at dice, what ancient honour won.

This is the ape of form, monsieur nice,
That when he plays at tables, chides the dice:
Love's Labours Lost

He won it of me with false dice:
Much Ado About Nothing

Sophocles - *(495-406 BC) Greek dramatist*
A wise player ought to accept his throws, and
score them, not bewail his luck.

Oscar Wilde - *(1854-1900) Irish dramatist &
humorist*
And once or twice,
To throw the dice
  Is a gentleman's game.
But he does not win,
  Who plays with sin,
In the secret House of Shame.

CLIMBING

Anon
The toughest form of mountain climbing is
climbing out of a rut.

Proverbs
Mountaineers are always freemen.

Who never climbs high never fell low.

Hasty climbers have sudden falls: *German*

Marie Blake - *poet*
I will exchange a city for a sunset,
The tramp of legions for a wind's wild cry,
And all the braggard thrusts of steel triumphant
  For one far summit, blue against the sky.

William Blake - *(1757-1827) poet*
Great things are done when men and
  mountains meet;
This is not done by jostling in the street: *1808*

Walter Bonatti - *French writer*
Mountaineering - struggle, adventure,
romance, escapism, sport.

Chris Bonnington - *mountaineer*
Climbing is not actually doing something
dangerous, dangerously; the elation comes from
being in what seems an extremely dangerous
situation when literally your life is in your
hands: *1981*

John Cleare - *(b 1936) photographer & writer*
Rock-climbing is the art of climbing a steep
rock. At its most aesthetic it has been likened to
ballet in a vertical idiom.

The blind suppression of justified fear makes

heroes, but vastly reduces a climber's life
expectancy.

Rene Daumal - *French writer*
One climbs, one sees, one sees no longer but
one has seen. There is an art of conducting
oneself in the lower regions by the memory of
what one saw higher up. When one can no
longer see one can at least know.

George Finch - *writer*
Mountaineering is a game second only to the
greatest and best of man's games - life: *1927*

Brendan Francis - *writer*
Whether a man's lust for big-breasted women is
a hunger for mountains or his hunger for
mountains is a lust for big-breasted women is a
moot question.

William Howitt - *(1792-1879) writer &
traveller*
Whoever has not ascended mountains, knows
little of the beauties of nature.

Colin M. Jarman - *(b 1958) sportswriter*
Climbing a mountain because 'it is there', is
comparable to eating horse manure because 'it
is organic':   *1988*

George Mallory - *(1886-1924) mountaineer*
On why he climbs - Because it is there: *1923*

Arthur Marshall - *(1910-89) journalist &
author*
Climb every mountain, ford every burn,
Suffer a thrombosis, end up in an urn.

Albert Mummery

The true mountaineer is a wanderer: *1893*

Friedrich Nietzsche – *(1844–1900) German philosopher & poet*
A few hours mountain climbing turn a rascal and a scout into two pretty similar creatures. Fatigue is the shortest way to Equality and Fraternity – and, in the end, Liberty will surrender to sleep.

Eddie Quinn
The only thing on the level is mountain climbing.

Andre Roche
Mount Everest is very easy to climb, only just a little too high: *1953*

Mickey Rooney – *US actor*
Mickey Rooney's favourite exercise is climbing tall people: *Phyllis Diller –US comedienne*

Count Henry Russell – *(b 1834)*
To climb with a friend is a pleasure; to climb alone is an education.

Olive Risley Seward – *US author*
Mountaineers are always frugal and brave; as well as lovers of freedom.

Francis S. Smythe – *(1900–49) mountaineer*
A full appreciation of mountains is not to be experienced by merely looking; that is why men climb: *1930*

Stanley Snaith – *(1903–76) writer & librarian*
Mountain climbing is a sport. It is not practised for rewards, for fame, or even primarily for scientific purposes. Like any other sport, it has its own reward. A swimmer does not plunge into the seas at Dover because he thinks that it is the easiest or safest way of reaching France. The fox hunter is not chasing his dinner. Sport is independent of results. It is a personal thing. To the mountaineer, it is not merely the attainment of the summit that counts, but the exercise of craft, knowledge, nerve and sinew in achieving that goal.

Richard Taylor – *(1781–1858) printer & journalist*
The mountaineer excels in size the inhabitant of the plain.

Sherpa Tensing – *Nepalese mountaineer*
On Everest's summit – We've done the bugger!:   *1953*

James R. Ullman – *(1907–71) US novelist*
A man climbs because he needs to climb, because that is why he is made. Rock and ice and the great blue canopy of the sky are not all that he finds upon the mountain-tops. He learns what his legs are for, what his lungs are for, what the wise men of old meant by 'refreshment of the spirit'.

E. A. Wedderburn – *writer*
Sporting mountaineering requires that the skill of the party be nicely matched against the defences of the route. If it is too easy, it is not sport; if it is too hard, it is not pleasure: *1954*

Mountaineering is something more than healthy exercise; it is a sport, and a great one: *1954*

Edward Whymper – *(1840–1911) wood engraver & alpinist*
When a man who is not a born mountaineer gets upon the side of a mountain, he speedily finds out that walking is not an art: *1880*

William Wordsworth – *(1770–1850) poet*
Thou wears't upon thy forehead clear
The freedom of a mountaineer: *1803*

Geoffrey Winthrop Young – *(b 1876) writer*
The hills are the opponents with whom we compete, not other climbers.

CRICKET

PLAYERS

MCC & COUNTY

Harry Altham – *Surrey, Hampshire & President of the MCC [1959–60]*
The basic background is the plain fact that cricket is not a natural game: we walk, we run, we write, we drive, we ride 'full chested', but cricket whether batting, bowling or fielding must be played sideways: *1963*

Les Ames – *(1905–1990) Kent*
Years lost in early life are irrecoverable, particularly where cricket is concerned.

L.E.G. Ames
Was good at games
But when batting at cricket
He was always L.E.G. before wicket: *James Moss*

Trevor Bailey – *(b 1923) Essex*
Cricket is a situation game. When the situation is dead, the game is dead.

Seeing Trevor Bailey prepare for a session in the field was like a lecture in anatomy:
Ray East – Essex

Ken Barrington – *(1930–81) Surrey*
Whenever I see Ken Barrington coming to the wicket, I imagine the Union Jack fluttering behind him: *Wally Grout – Australia*

Alec Bedser – *(b 1918) Surrey, England & MCC selector*
I didn't need anyone to motivate me. Playing for England was all I needed.

Remember selectors don't make cricketers, the system produces them – for better or worse.

Ian Botham – *(b 1955) Somerset & Worcestershire*
Cricket may be a game to some, but not to me. It's not just a game, it's my living. I give everything I've got and when I'm doing that I know I am liable to lose my temper.

You have got to make every batsman wonder 'What's he going to bowl me now?'

Cricket is full of theorists who can ruin your game in no time.

There is more to life than cricket.

Ian did so much in so short a time that his few inevitable setbacks were doubly disappointing:
Alec Bedser

I don't know what it is, but I take stuff from him I'd clip other guys in the ear for:
Mike Brearley – England captain

Bonny Botham my oh me
Hit the ball at ten to three
Didn't come down 'til after tea: *Jeff Cloves*

He would probably not fit the bill as the schoolboy's vision of the dedicated superstar:
Graham Gooch

He plays a net as if he is on Weston-super-Mare beach and the tide is coming in fast:
Frank Keating – sportswriter

This fellow is the most over-rated player I have ever seen. He looks too heavy, and the way he's been bowling out here, he wouldn't burst a paper bag: *Harold Larwood*

Ian Botham has achieved so much because he is courageous enough to risk looking an idiot. He allows himself to explore the extreme limits of his talents rather than settling for a safe mediocrity: *Vic Marks – Somerset*

His whole-heartedness leads to triumphs and troubles, to success and scrapes, for it is not balanced by a shrewd appreciation of public relations nor by a tolerance of rudeness or criticism: *Peter Roebuck – Somerset*

Whether hunting, shooting, fishing, kicking, bowling or drinking, Ian resembles a baron of the wild, medieval days: *Peter Roebuck*

He has put more backsides on seats than any other English player: *Bob Taylor*

As a 'Pom', he'd make a great Aussie:
Jeff Thomson – Australia

He couldn't bowl a hoop downhill:
Fred Trueman

A guerrilla fighter impatient of discipline:
Graeme Wright

Denis Compton – *(b 1918) Middlesex*
Recorded centuries leave no trace,
On memory of that timeless grace: *John Arlott*

I wouldn't say I coached him, but I didn't mess him up: *George Fenner – head coach at Lord's*

If my mother hadn't thrown my football boots on the fire, I might have become as famous as Denis Compton: *Sir Len Hutton*

Enjoyment, given and felt, is the chief thing about Compton's batting; it is a clear-flowing stream, a breath of half-holiday among work days: *R. C. Robertson-Glasgow*

He was the only player to call his partner for a run and wish him good luck at the same time:
John Warr – Middlesex

Denis Compton, as one of the greatest artists the game has known, made a strangely plebeian start, by being born in Hendon. He should, in light of future events, have been borne down from Valhalla, on a silver cloud:
World of Cricket

Denis Compton & Bill Edrich – *Middlesex & England opening batsmen*
Compton and Edrich go together in English cricket, like Gilbert and Sullivan go together in English Opera: *R. C. Robertson-Glasgow*

Compton and Edrich are of that happy philosophy which keeps failure in its place by laughter, like boys who fall on an ice slide and rush back to try it again:
R. C. Robertson-Glasgow

Colin Cowdrey – *(b 1932) Kent*
The dot-ball has become the Holy Grail.

I don't mind if I'm not as good as my father, as long as I'm good enough: *Chris Cowdrey*

Ted Dexter – *(b 1935) Sussex*
When I see a young man who has an expensive and pretty hair-do, I have doubts as to his ability to reach Test standard.

On his omission from the touring party – A child of six, who's played one season's cricket on the lawn with his mother, could surely have seen Dexter's genius: *Anon*

No English cricketer bred since the war has so captured the imagination of those inside, outside and far from the boundary ropes of our big cricket grounds than Ted Dexter:
Wisden (1961)

Phil Edmonds – *(b 1951) Middlesex*
On being asked what he looked forward to most upon returning from a long tour of India – A dry fart!

Bill Edrich – *(b 1922) Middlesex*
Hard-wicket cricket is like chess – there is no element of chance in it, and only those who perfect themselves survive: *1948*

Charles B. Fry – *(1872–1956) Sussex*
I have a notion that the cricket of the nineties and early nineteen hundreds was more amusing to watch, but I am not sour that the game of today is not more difficult to play: *1939*

David Gower – *(b 1957) Leicestershire*
I tend to look for my runs using the wrong shot at the wrong time. My instincts are to hit the ball on the up. I like, as much as the spectator, to see the ball disappearing at a high rate of knots.

Learning that the England selectors were concerned over his lack of assertive captaincy – What do they expect me to do? Walk around in a T-shirt with 'I'm in charge' on it?: *1986*

Gower, looking frail, with a half-sleeve shirt clinging closely to a not very substantial physique: *John Arlott – commentator*

David Gower has that thoroughbred walk, which marks him an athlete of distinction, before the pavilion gate is ten yards behind him: *Henry Blofeld - commentator*

He has the slight, angular figure of a fine athlete. When he walks his feet appear hardly to bruise the grass: *Henry Blofeld*

Perhaps Gower will eventually realise cricket's not always about champagne. It's a bread and butter game: *Brian Brain*

It's difficult to be more laid back without being actually comatose: *Frances Edmonds*

The words 'laid-back' fit as snugly around his blond curls as a halo: *Peter Hayter*

David Gower makes batting look as easy as drinking tea: *Sir Len Hutton*

Within his blond, curly hair and juvenile appearance Gower seemed to step out of the now defunct pages of *Boys' Own* paper: *E. W. Swanton - sportswriter*

W. G. Grace - *(1848-1915) Gloucestershire*
A cricketer's life is a life of splendid freedom, healthy effort, endless variety, and delightful fellowship: *1988*

Leaving the ball alone never won matches.

I don't like defensive shots, you can only get threes.

There is no crisis in cricket, there is only the next ball.

I cannot remember when I began to play cricket. Respect for the truth prevents me from saying I played the first year of my existence, but I have little hesitation in declaring that I handled a bat and ball before the end of my second.

I have very seldom met with a cricketer of eminence who did not impress upon his tailor the momentous importance of comfortably fitting clothes: *1890*

On a big innings - I did not feel anything. I had too much to do to watch the bowling and see how the fieldsmen were moved about to think of anything.

Maxim for batting first after winning the toss - Let's be getting at them before they get at us.

His personality was such that it is remembered by those who played with him to the exclusion of his actual performance: *John Arlott*

Dr W. G. Grace,
Had hair all over his face.
Lord! How all the people cheered,
When a ball got lost in his beard:
E. C. Bentley

He orchestrated the folk music of cricket:
Sir Neville Cardus

The bat is as the sonnet is, but small,
Yet with it batsmen, a stout hearted band,
Waged ceaseless, changing conflict with ball;
Till Grace arose and in his mighty hand,
The thing became a sceptre, which he wields,
Unchallenged yet, Lord of the playing fields:
Edmund B. V. Christian

He has one of the dirtiest necks I have kept wicket behind: *Viscount Cobham*

He was just a great big schoolboy in everything he did: *Bernard Darwin*

To W. G., cricket being a game was a vehicle for a practical rough and tumble humour:
Bernard Darwin

He dab 'em, but seldom; but when he dab 'em, he do dab 'em for four: *C. B. Fry - Sussex*

He did, positively, block balls for four:
C. B. Fry

None of the English cricketers could waltz like W. G. Grace: *C. B. Fry*

He was not a graceful bat and he was not ungraceful, just powerfully efficient: *C. B. Fry*

He might not have had the shots of Bradman, not the flowing strokes of Hammond, but he had a shot for every ball. No shouldering arms to a ball for him: *Major J. Gillman*

No monument, no portrait, no book can adequately represent either the vitality of W.G., or his superb skill in the game he loved:
Lord Hawke - Yorkshire

May the death of no other cricketer who has taken part in great matches be like his:
Arthur Haygarth

Had Grace been born in ancient Greece, the Iliad would have been a different book:
The Bishop of Hereford

It was by modern scientific methods, that this pre-Victorian lifted cricket from a more or less casual pastime into the national institution which it rapidly became: *C. L. R. James*

Like all truly great men, he bestrides two ages:
C. L. R. James

He revolutionised cricket. He turned it from an accomplishment into a science, he turned a one-stringed instrument into a many chorded lyre: *Jubilee Book of Cricket*

Lawn mowers and W. G. Grace made the 1860's and 1870's a golden age for batsmen:
Teresa McLean

W. G. Grace has had the whole world as his stage, and his friends are as numerous as pebbles on the seashores: *W. Methven-Brownlee*

He has drained the language of eulogy and it is no use applying superlatives to him any more:
Pall Mall Gazette

The Australian came down like a wolf on the fold,
   The Mary'bone Cracks for a trifle were bowled;
   Our Grace before dinner was very soon done,
And Our Grace after dinner did not get a run:
Punch (1878)

In playing a ball, Mr Grace puts every muscle into it, from the sole of his foot to the crown of his head: *Lord Charles Russell*

I puts the ball where I likes it, and that beggar, he puts it where he likes it: *Jemmy Shaw*

W. G. Grace was by no conceivable standard a good man. He was a cheat on and off the cricket field: *Sir C. P. Snow*

All his life he was facing the next ball:
A. A. Thompson

Only those who played with and against him could have appreciated his true greatness and his impact on the game: *Sir Pelham Warner*

W. G. Grace's position has for years been an anomalous one, but 'nice customs curtsy to Kings' and the work he has done in popularising cricket outweighs a hundredfold every other consideration: *Wisden*

Tony Greig - *(b 1946) Sussex*
There's only one head bigger than Tony Greig's and that's Birkenhead: *Fred Trueman*

J. B. 'Jack' Hobbs - *(1909-63) Surrey*
I didn't think of playing for England or anything like that, but it seemed to me the best way I could make a decent living.

No one else ever batted with more consummate skill than his, which was based on an infallible sympathy with the bowled ball: *John Arlott*

A snick by Jack Hobbs is a sort of disturbance of a cosmic orderliness: *Sir Neville Cardus*

Jack Hobbs - The bridge between the Classic and Modern periods: *J. L. Carr*

It were impossible to fault him:
Wilfred Rhodes - Yorkshire

Jack Hobbs could have scored thousands more runs, but he often was content to throw his wicket away when he had reached his hundred and give someone else a chance: *Wilfred Rhodes*

John Jameson - *(b 1941) Warwickshire*
John Jameson is expressionless and big. Big in the way they used to describe barrel chested; which means that he looks as if he is permanently holding his breath: *Clive Taylor*

Gilbert Jessop - *(1874-1955) Gloucestershire*
To get down to hard facts, cricket matches are now won by runs not style.

Innovations invariably are suspect, and in no quarter more so than the cricket world.

There was a young fresher called Jessop,
Who was pitching it less up and less up.
'Till one of the pros,
Got a blow on the nose,
And said, 'Inside a helmet I'll dress up':
Anon Cambridge student

If you imagine Clive Lloyd as being small, white, and right-handed, then you've got Gilbert Jessop: *Anon*

Peter May – *(b 1929) Surrey*
Peter May was a cricketer of sensitive nature who could be as hard as nails on the field without ever slipping from the peak of sportsmanship: *Richie Benaud*

Colin Milburn – *(1941-90) Northamptonshire*
Colin Milburn is as untidy as an unmade bed, as devastating as a hand grenade: *Clive Taylor*

Derek Randall – *(b 1951) Nottinghamshire*
It's a marvellous thing to play for England. You get a few quid, it's nice for the family, and you wear three lions on your chest.

Prince Ranjitsinhji – *(1872-1933) Sussex*
It is very important for a man who wishes to have a good season to take regular exercise.

John Snow – *(b 1941) Sussex*
I believe cricket to be the finest game there is to play. A game embracing the individual challenge of one against one inside the framework of a team where eleven men are against eleven, each with his own specific role to play, but always mindful of the interests of the other ten he plays for and against.

A. G. Steel – *(1858-1914) Lancashire*
Cricket, to maintain its hold on the national character, must be eager, quick and full of action. Today it is the reverse: *1900*

David Steele – *(b 1941) Northamptonshire*
With his greying hair and glasses David Steele is an unlikely athletic hero and I think this is partly the reason the English public took to him: *John Snow – Sussex*

David Steele – a bank clerk going to war:
Clive Taylor – sportswriter

Sir Pelham 'Plum' Warner – *(1873-1963)*
Middlesex
Cricket is the greatest game that the wit of man has yet devised.

Peter Willey – *(b 1949) Northamptonshire*
I am, of course, a great Willey supporter:
Trevor Bailey – commentator

Frank Woolley – *(1886-1954) Kent*
One thinks of him as a butterfly in a city street on a summer's day: *Sir Neville Cardus*

When Frank Woolley got out, it seemed as if the sun had set: *Sir Neville Cardus*

To have watched him, close up instead of from the ringside, I count as a privilege:
Sir Len Hutton

The most graceful of the efficient, and the most efficient of the graceful: *Ian Peebles*

He was easy to watch, difficult to bowl to, and impossible to write about. When you bowled there weren't enough fielders; when you wrote about him there weren't enough words:
R. C. Robertson-Glasgow

On Woolley's omission from the England Test team
– The greatest crime since the crucifixion:
Gerry Weighell

He made the game look so untidy:
Bill Woodfull – Australia

I cannot ever recall him in a defensive role. His defence was invariably counter-attack:
R. E. S. Wyatt – Warwickshire

YORKSHIRE

Anon
A strong Yorkshire means a strong England:
Traditional

Arthur Booth – *(1902-74)*
If you have not talked cricket with Arthur Booth, it is almost true to say you did not know the real game: *Leslie Deakin*

Small, almost frail in physique, Arthur Booth was a giant in all other respects: *Leslie Deakin*

To the uninitiated, Arthur Booth was a little man who once won a championship for Yorkshire; to the initiated, he was a prophet, spiritual architect and adviser: *Leslie Deakin*

After Booth had been run out twice in one match – Arthur Booth is a slow bowler, and on the evidence of this match the characteristic would appear to apply equally to his running:
J. M. Kilburn – sportswriter

Bill Bowes – *(b 1908)*
If you mention the word cricket, Yorkshire must come in. Cricket and Yorkshire go together.

I'll admit bowlers are not often over-generous to batsmen, but the real generosity in a cricketer is generosity to his successors, or possible successors.

A Yorkshire cricketer is one born within the sound of Bill Bowes: *Michael Carey*

Geoffrey Boycott – *(b 1940)*
Test Matches are won by long innings, not brief hard-hitting ones, however spectacular they may seem.

I reckon that if I bat for a day and a half and make a big score, that is half the battle.

There is more to cricket than batting all day and scoring plenty of runs: *1975*

I have always thought, that if I keep my form, and played long enough, the runs would look after themselves.

I never intend to get out. It's always a tragedy for me when I do. I feel sick inside.

After a barrage of bouncers left him with a black eye – I've heard of fellows getting $3 million for going three rounds with Muhammad Ali – I think I will be writing to the Test and County Cricket Board: *1978*

To David Gower – If I could add your shots to my brain, I would be an incredible player.

On W. G. Grace – Unless I'm crackers or something, I've scored a bloody sight more runs than that bearded old bugger.

Telegram to Boycott after he had taken an age to score fifty at Perth – You have done for Australian cricket what the Boston Strangler did for door-to-door salesmen: *Jack Birney*

It really is extraordinary how anything to do with him is inflated out of all proportion:
Mike Brearley

Boycott and controversy have shared the longest opening partnership in the game.
Terry Brindle – sportswriter

His centuries are an act of will: *Terry Brindle*

Boycott builds an innings, brick by brick, cementing each stroke to the next with the extraordinary power of concentration which frustrates good bowling and intimidates poor:
Terry Brindle

His character and performance are indivisible; more than any player he has been judged in terms of personality: *Terry Brindle*

He took his cricket very much to heart. It was the breath of life to him to succeed: *Brian Close*

Geoff Boycott is enough of an enigma to puzzle the sphinx: *David Gower*

Geoff Boycott has the uncanny knack of being where fast bowlers aren't: *Tony Greig*

The tragedy of Geoff Boycott is that his batting was always going to entitle him to a place in cricket's Hall of Fame: *Don Mosey*

He goes out there on the cricket square and doesn't give a bugger what the critics are saying. He just gets his head down and bats. He's a good 'un: *Harvey Smith – Yorkshireman*

I hope that Geoff Boycott will be remembered for more than an indigestible mass of statistics, however impressive: *Mike Stevenson*

He is a real tiger who hates bowlers as much as I hate batsmen: *Fred Trueman*

It's impossible to speak to him for half an hour before an innings. Even while he is having lunch, he's concentrating on how many runs he is going to score: *Fred Trueman*

Boycott's idea of bliss might be to bat all night, having batted all day: *John Woodcock*

Sir Neville Cardus – *(1899–1975) writer*
The Yorkshireman's intolerance of an enemy's prowess is simply the measure of the Yorkshireman's pride in his county's genius for cricket: *1924*

Brian Close – *(b 1931)*
Without in any way sounding melodramatic about it, it is no exaggeration to say I would have died for Yorkshire. I suppose once or twice I nearly did.

John Hampshire – *(b 1941)*
John Hampshire was as popularly gregarious as Geoff Boycott was introvertedly solitary:
Don Mosey

George Hirst *(1871–1954)* **& Wilfred Rhodes** *(1877–1973)*
Hirst to Rhodes, when England needed 15 runs to beat Australia with one wicket left – We'll get them in singles, Wilfrid: *Attrib. 1902*
[*Hirst then scored 13 singles off 14 strokes*]

Rhodes' comments on this episode – That is all someone's imagination and the 'We'll get them in singles' is ridiculous. After all, if we could have got four fours it would have been just the same and over much quicker: *1902*

Sir Len Hutton – *(b 1916)*
From the very earliest days I can recall, I have loved the feel of a cricket bat.

In an England cricket eleven, the flesh may be of the South, but the bone is of the North, and the backbone is Yorkshire.

We shake hands on t'first morning and say 'How do?' Then we say nowt for three days, but 'How's that?': *Roy Kilner – Yorkshire*

In a county that regards itself as special, Len Hutton was very, very special: *Don Mosey*

His bat was part of his nervous system:
Harold Pinter – playwright

Hutton – the perfectionist – ruthless, powerful, a piece of cricket out of the top drawer:
Gordon Ross – sportswriter

Yorkshire were 232 all out. Hutton ill. No! I'm sorry, Hutton 111:
John Snagge – radio commentator

Don Mosey – *writer & commentator*
A Yorkshire team without a left-arm slow bowler would be like an army without its general, a jockey without a horse, a fish without chips.

Emmott Robinson – *(1883–1969)*
I imagine that the Lord one day gathered together a heap of Yorkshire clay and breathed life into it and said 'Emmott Robinson, go and bowl at the pavilion end for Yorkshire':
Sir Neville Cardus

Emmott Robinson shambled about the field with his trousers loose. You were getting ready to see them fall down altogether when he would remember them in time: *Sir Neville Cardus*

Herbert Sutcliffe – *(1894–1978)*
He often had to live above his technical income. He had, remember, to keep up with the Hobbses and Hammonds. His wasn't a triumph of skill only. It was a finer triumph of character, application and will-power:
Sir Neville Cardus

He sets himself the highest available standard of batting and deportment. If he is bowled he appears to regard the event less as a human misfortune than some temporary, and reprehensible, lapse of natural laws. There has been a blunder, to which he is unwillingly privy and liable: *R. C. Robertson-Glasgow*

Fred Trueman – *(b 1931) fast bowler*
To a boy's parents in those days, a Yorkshire cap was as good as one for England.

People started calling me 'Fiery' because 'Fiery' rhymes with Fred, just like 'Typhoon' rhymes with Tyson.

They set me up as an untameable northern savage who ate broken glass and infant batsmen for breakfast.

I have never believed in making life easier for batsmen.

If there is any game in the world that attracts the half-baked theorist more than cricket I have yet to hear of it.

No one will argue that the greatest English batsmen of modern times have been Hutton, May and Compton. As a fast bowler, it's been my job to try and find chinks in their armour. And, despite their gifts, they were there to be found.

Billy Ibadulla had more edges than a broken piss-pot.
[*Applied to many other luckless batsmen to have faced Trueman*]

After the Rev. David Sheppard had dropped a catch off his bowling in the slips - You might keep your eyes shut when you're praying, Vicar, but I wish you'd keep 'em open when I'm bowling:
1963

After the ball Raman Subba Row had dropped off Trueman's bowling had gone for four -
Subba Row - I'm sorry about that, it might have been better if I had kept my legs together.
Trueman - Aye, it's a pity your mother didn't!

Suggested title for his autobiography - 'The definitive volume on the finest bloody fast bowler that ever drew breath.'

Henry Irving never made greater impact with a stage entrance than Freddie Trueman in a pub:
John Hampshire

Tell me, Fred, have you ever bowled a ball which merely went straight?: *Richard Hutton*

Trueman's cricket drew response from both student and the simple spectator. His bowling gave satisfaction through its vigour and by its sophistication. Greatness was in him and it was not obscured: *J. M. Kilburn*

Without rival, the ripest, the richest, the rip-roaringest individual performer on cricket's stage: *A. A. Thompson*

Cricket and the Anglo-Saxon tongue have been enriched by his presence: *John Warr*

When Fred reached his 307 wickets he said afterwards that anyone who passed him would be very tired. Well, you can tell him I'm not:
Bob Willis (1984)

Eddie Wainwright - *(1865-1919)*
Prayer before playing a Roses match - Oh God, if you're on our side, then we'll win. If you're on their side, then they'll win. But, please, please God, just stay out of the way for the next three days, so as we can thrash 'em.

Ernie Wise - *(b 1925) comedian*
The only qualification a man needs to become a first-class cricketer is Yorkshire blood in his veins.

ABROAD

Alfred Shaw - *(1842-1907) Nottinghamshire*
Cricket education is of a much higher type in the colonies now; so high, in fact, that I am afraid they are the masters and we the pupils:
1877

AUSTRALIA

Simon Barnes - *British sportswriter*
The traditional dress of the Australian cricketer is the baggy green cap on the head and the chip on the shoulder. Both are ritualistically assumed.

Richie Benaud - *(b 1930) Test captain & TV commentator*
Batting is a major trial before an eleven-man jury.

Richie Benaud is like a Scotsman, saving his breath to cool his porridge. He lets the picture speak for itself, like the true artist, he always leaves you wanting more - sometimes, you even wonder if he is still there:
Tony Brace - sportswriter

Benaud's criticisms, like those of Brearley, are never spiteful or unkind, he obviously recalls

that he, too, bowled the odd long hop or
dropped an occasional catch: *Tony Brace*

He simply says 'out' with the grisly finality of
the hangman: *Tony Brace*

A leg cutter is a delivery which batsmen play
and miss at outside off-stump when Richie
Benaud is commentating:
Vic Marks – Somerset & writer

Benaud has always had the will to challenge the
bowler. In fact, he has both as a batsman and
captain waged unceasing war against stodge:
A. G. Moyes

David Boon – *(b 1960)*
I can visualise David Boon on a sheep farm in
Tasmania, sipping lager on the verandah, the
ideal temperament for dealing with fast
bowlers: *Sir Len Hutton*

Allan Border – *(b 1955)*
There is a possibility that your ability as a
player may well be analysed by future
generations on your one-day statistics. That's
the day I dread most: *1985*

Allan Border has not so much a style as a *modus
operandi*: *John Woodcock – British sportswriter*

Sir Donald Bradman – *(b 1908)*
Every ball is for me the first ball, whether my
score is 0 or 200, and I never visualize the
possibility of anybody getting me out.

It's a constant battle, one man against another.
I try to hit the bowler and he to beat me.

After being bowled for a duck in his last Test innings
– It's hard to bat with tears in your eyes:
1948

Twenty years of cricket do not seem to have
taught Bradman the real British Empire
meaning of the word: *Anon*

I didn't get Bradman's autograph, but he trod
on my toe, though:
Anon Sussex schoolboy (1948)

Figures can lie, but in cricket taken in the large,
they tell the truth, and in his case defy all

argument: *Harry Altham – MCC President*

I love to play against him, and that goes for all
my players, because he is such a great
sportsman and a thorough gentleman:
Lala Armanath – India (1948)

People say 'Oh, but he hasn't the charm of
McCabe, or the mercury of Macartney, or the
dignity of Hammond'; the objection is a little
unintelligent, as though a lion were criticized
for lacking the delicacy of the gazelle, the
worrying tenacity of the terrier and the
disdainful elegance of a swan or camel:
Sir Neville Cardus

He's the brain and the vertebra of Australian
cricket, government and executive:
Sir Neville Cardus

You might have thought they lost their life
savings in a crash; apparently Bradman losing a
wicket without scoring was almost as big a
debacle: *Denis Compton*

He pities none. If he can make any bowler look
foolish, he will do it: *Learie Constantine*

You have to mother a cricket team. Bradman is
no mother. He is too brilliantly individual:
Alan Fairfax

Three possessions lie nearest to the true
Sydneyite's heart; our 'arbour, our bridge, and
our Bradman – and maybe I have placed them
in the wrong order. When there is cricket about
Bradman becomes number one:
Bruce Harris (1933)

He spoilt the game – he got too many runs:
Jack Hobbs

Millions who had not a notion of an off-break
or a square cut, knew him only as the
International Bogeyman of cricket:
Margaret Hughes

He is like a robot. Runs come to him as if they
were being manufactured by a slow, but
infinitely efficient machine: *James A. Joyce*

Don Bradman was enclosed in a legend that
grew bigger daily, like a gigantic indestructible

crystal: *Philip Larkin*

I didn't get on with him as a man. We had nothing in common. But, as a batsman, captain and tactician, he had no equal:
Keith Miller - Australia

There are those who say that he cannot get any better, but when a genius or phenomenon of this nature crops up, there is no telling what he may do: *Frank Mitchell (1930)*

He is an ornament to his country:
The Observer (1931)

There's nothing new to say about Bradman, any more than there is about Moiseiwitsch, or the Tower of London:
R. C. Robertson-Glasgow

No one ever laughed at Bradman. He was no laughing matter: *R. C. Robertson-Glasgow*

I have known him for many, many years, and no one I can think of has equalled him as a player, as a thinker, or as a citizen. He's an astonishing man: *Walter Robins*

Sir Donald Bradman
Would have been a very glad man
If his Test average had been .06 more
Than 99.94: *T.N.E. Smith*

Do not assume that young Bradman is a batsman without delicacy of touch. I have seen him score many hundreds, in his many thousands of runs, by strokes of a delicacy which a billiardist might envy:
Geoffrey Tebbutt

There's no ruddy best ball to bowl to 'The Don': *Bill Voce*

Sir Neville Cardus - *(1889-1975) British writer*
The Australian temper is at bottom grim, it is as though the hot sun has dried up his nature:
1934

Ian Chappell - *(b 1943)*
A cricketer of effect rather than the graces:
John Arlott

Ted Dexter - *(b 1935) Sussex*
Australians can, and do, quite readily and often in my experience, throw off all their 180 years of civilized nationhood; they gaily revive every prejudice they ever knew, whether to do with accent, class consciousness or even the original convict complex, and sally forth into battle with a dedication which would not disgrace the most committed of the world's political agitators: *1972*

Clarrie Grimmett - *(1891-1980)*
Clarrie Grimmett thought a full toss was the worst form of cricket vandalism and the long hop a legacy from pre-historic days when barbarians rolled boulders towards the enemy:
Arthur Mailey - Australia

Taking a cricket ball away from Clarrie Grimmett during a match was like taking a bone from a dog: *R. S. Whitington*

Lord Harris - *(1851-1932) Kent*
They are capital winners out here; but I am afraid I cannot apply the same adjective to them as losers: *1879*

Neil Harvey - *(b 1928)*
You get intoxicated with the champagne of a Neil Harvey innings: *Sir Neville Cardus*

Margaret Hughes - *British writer*
When the Australians come to England, people here tend to lose their sense of proportion about the game.

Harold Larwood - *(b 1904) Nottinghamshire*
A cricket tour in Australia would be the most delightful period in one's life, if one was deaf.

Dennis Lillee - *(b 1949)*
Dennis Lillee is wearing a voluminous nightshirt which would have room for another man, if he could get into the trousers:
John Arlott

Are you aware, Sir, that the last time I saw anything like that on a top-lip, the whole herd had to be destroyed: *Eric Morecambe*

Ashes to ashes, dust to dust –
If Thomson don't get ya, Lillee must:
Sydney Telegraph (1975)

Arthur MacLean - *(b 1946)*
Arthur MacLean was very lordly, a man born to rule, to dictate, and to wear the imperial robe: *Sir Neville Cardus*

Arthur Mailey - *(1886–1967)*
After figures of 64–0–362–4, when Victoria scored a record 1,107 runs – If that chap in the brown derby hat at the back of the grandstand had held his catches, I'd have had them out days ago: *1926*

On the same game – Very few chances were given, but I think a chap in a tweed coat dropped Jack Ryder [295] near the shilling stand: *1926*

And still on the same game – It was rather a pity that Ellis got out at 1,107, because I was just striking a length: *1926*

In international cricket a player should be made to fight for everything he gets on the field in gratitude for all the things he gets for nothing off the field.

Did I find Test tours too strenuous? The very question is sacrilegious.

The contrast between the civilian life of the ordinary Australian cricketer and his existence as a touring Test player is fantastic. I cannot think of one of my contemporaries who was fabulous enough to live at a decent hotel or travel a hundred miles in luxury.

Sign outside his Sydney butcher's shop – I used to bowl tripe, then I wrote it, now I sell it.

Hostess – Aren't you going to dance, Mr Mailey?
Mailey – No Ma'am, I'm a little stiff from bowling.
Hostess – Oh really, so that's where you come from!

If Arthur Mailey was not cricket's greatest bowler, he was its greatest philosopher:
                                    Ben Travers

Greg Matthews
Cricket is indescribable. How do you describe an orgasm?

Keith Miller - *(b 1919)*
His strokes are lordly and pedigreed, his attitude to cricket is almost as obsolete as chivalry: *Sir Neville Cardus*

A young eagle among crows and daws:
                                    Sir Neville Cardus

I always felt I was number one enemy as far as Keith Miller's concerned, when he had the ball in his hand: *Sir Len Hutton*

There's always action when Keith Miller is on the field, and very often when he's off it:
                                    Norman Yardley

If you hit Keith Miller for four, he stands there and claps, and says 'Jolly good shot'. But, you know perfectly well that as he walks back and grabs the ball, throwing back his hair, that he's certainly going to let you have it when you get the next one: *Norman Yardley*

M. A. Noble – *(1873–1940)*
They say onlookers see most of the game. But not always. The batsman at the other end sees more.

Kerry Packer – *World Series Cricket founder*
Remember, with these speedsters bowling at 95 mph – Cricket can kill!:   *TV advert (1977)*

World Series Cricket was 'not cricket', it was show-biz: *William J. Baker*

The more Americanised cricket here becomes, the easier England will find it to defeat Australia – and the less like an Ashes series it will be: *Scyld Berry*

Kerry Packer did for cricket what Frank Whittle did for air travel:
                                    Colin M. Jarman – British sportswriter

The most dangerous act in the entertainment business these days is not balancing on the high wire nor even putting a head in a lion's mouth. It is, without doubt, batting in Kerry Packer's flying circus: *Tony Lewis (1979)*

Bill Ponsford – *(b 1900)*
Because Bradman will always be remembered is no reason why Ponsford should be neglected;

when the sun rises it is a mistake to forget the moon: *R. C. Robertson-Glasgow*

Ian Redpath – *(b 1941)*
Ian Redpath is everything most Australians are not – a model of batting: *Ray Illingworth*

Barry Richards – *(b 1945) South Africa*
The only time an Australian walks is when his car runs out of petrol: *1980*

F. R. Spofforth – *(1853-1926)*
Spofforth was the Australian of Australians, a stark man that let in with him the coldest blast of antagonism that ever blew over a June field: *Sir Neville Cardus*

Victor Trumper – *(1877-1915)*
Victor Trumper had the greatest charm and two strokes for every ball: *Charles B. Fry*

Compared to Victor Trumper, I was a cab-horse to a Derby winner: *Arthur MacLean*

Glenn Turner – *(b 1947) New Zealand*
The Australians have different standards and ways of expressing themselves – and swearing has been part of their approach on the field: *1983*

R. S. Whitington – *(b 1912) writer & lawyer*
Australians are notorious gamblers, and it probably has been an urge for adventure, combined with a natural partiality and prowess for attack, that lies at the core of the Australian way of cricket: *1972*

Bill Woodfull – *(1897-1965)*
Bill Woodfull was a great gentleman, a fine citizen and an ornament to the game of cricket: *Sir Don Bradman*

INDIA

Bishen Bedi – *(b 1946)*
A great clock-maker would have been proud to have set Bedi in motion – a mechanism finely balanced, cogs rolling silently and hands sweeping in smooth arcs across the face: *Tony Lewis*

The Nawab of Pataudi – *(b 1941)*
In the country of the blind, the one-eyed man is king. But in the keen-eyed world of cricket, a fellow with just one good eye and a bit, has to settle for something less than the perfection he once sought. Lucky me, despite this I have been able to play the game all over the world in the company of giants.

NEW ZEALAND

Ewan Chatfield – *(b 1950)*
After he had run out Derek Randall, while backing up – Just remember one thing, son, you've already been killed once on a cricket field!: *Ian Botham*

Richard Hadlee – *(b 1951)*
At Test level, the batsman is there to be tested.

What I try to do is think aggression. Think smooth. When I know I've got rhythm, I know also I'm going to be dangerous.

Being a professional cricketer isn't a normal way of life.

On playing against Hadlee in a Test match – It was like batting against the World XI at one end, and Ilford Second XI at the other: *Graham Gooch (1987)*

Glenn Turner
During a Test match against England, he was dealt a painful blow to the 'box' by the fifth delivery of an over – Turner looks a bit shaky and unsteady, but I think he's going to bat on – one ball left!: *Brian Johnston – commentator*

PAKISTAN

Javed Miandad – *(b 1957)*
Miandad stokes up his batteries on upsetting the opposition: *Rodney Marsh*

If I was given the choice of watching any batsman in the world, I would plump for Javed Miandad: *Ben Travers*

Mudassar Nazar – *(b 1956)*
A dark horse with a golden arm: *Trevor Bailey*

SOUTH AFRICA

Graeme Pollock – *(b 1944)*

I believe in cricketing terms Graeme Pollock was a sadist: *Eddie Barlow*

Fielding was not Graeme Pollock's pleasure. He would not lower himself to bowl and appeared bored unless a bat was in his hand: *Eddie Barlow*

I should like to be around when he bats again: *Sir Don Bradman*

WEST INDIES

Sir Neville Cardus - *(1889-1975) British writer*
The first vision that comes to mind as we think of West Indies cricket is of joyful noise, a bat flailing the air, the ball whizzing here, there, everywhere, stumps flying, shining black faces and mouths laughing white-toothed, like melons: *1966*

Lord Learie Constantine - *(1902-71)*
I never wanted to make a hundred. Who wants to make a hundred anyway? When I first went in, my immediate objective was to hit the ball to each of the four corners of the field. After that, I tried not to be repetitive.

Tony Cozier - *writer & commentator*
West Indian cricketers crave the padding grace and striking power of a panther.

Joel Garner - *(b 1952)*
They should cut him off at the knees to make him bowl at a normal height: *Geoff Boycott*

Michael Holding - *(b 1954)*
A perfect running specimen, but I don't go to a Test to see running; if I wished to see that I would go to Crystal Palace to see Coe and Ovett: *Jack Fingleton*

C. L. R. James - *writer*
What do they know of cricket who only know of cricket?

Rohan Kanhai - *(b 1935)*
When I bat my whole make up urges me to destroy the opposition as quickly as possible and once you are on top to never let up. I've never been one for second-best - that is why I never want fours, I want sixes: *1966*

I have never doubted my batting ability from the day I could hold a piece of wood between two small grimy hands.

Once I've got the fielders with their tongues hanging out I aim to run them into the ground: *1966*

Sobers came close to being the best batsman, but he was the greatest cricketer ever, and he could do just anything. But as a batsman Kanhai was just a little better: *Sunil Gavaskar*

For years I believed Sobers was the greatest of living batsmen. But who could have foreseen that Kanhai would hit Test bowlers in Australia as if they were league bowlers in Scotland?: *C. L. R. James*

Lord Kitchener - *calypso singer*
On beating England for the first time in the second Test, 1950 -
Yardley tried his best,
But Goddard won the Test,
With those little pals of mine,
Ramadhin and Valentine:
[Yardley & Goddard were the two opposing captains]

Clive Lloyd - *(b 1944)*
In the first World Cup final - Lloyd hits him high away over mid-wicket for four, a stroke of a man knocking a thistle top with a walking stick: *John Arlott - British commentator*

Clive Lloyd doesn't accumulate runs, he butchers them: *Peter Lever - Lancashire*

Whoever it was that described Clive Lloyd as a 'great, gangling, begoggled super-cat', must (temporarily at least) have been inspired: *Mike Stevenson*

J. B. Priestley - *(1894-1984) British novelist & playwright*
England is not ruined because sinewy brown men from a distant colony sometimes hit a ball further and oftener than our men do.

Sonny Ramadhin - *(b 1929)*
Facing Sonny Ramadhin was like trying to face a 'boonch' of confetti: *Anon Derbyshire batsman*

Viv Richards – *(b 1952)*
A right-handed Clive Lloyd: *Brian Close*

Sir Gary Sobers – *(b 1936)*
It's a game for which a player needs all the physical assets of every other sport. It needs stamina, speed, strength, agility, a keen eye, a strong character, individual initiative, team spirit, cool judgement and fast reflexes. Many other sports and games need one or more of these, but not all of them: *1967*

Gary Sobers was unsurpassed as an all-rounder, he always played cricket the way the Gods intended – absolutely straight, absolutely hard, but never with malice: *Trevor Bailey*

He carries himself with a gangling sort of movement which is not graceful to the eye – until the ball is on him. Then, he becomes all curves, lissom yet concentrated:
Sir Neville Cardus

His immense power is lightened by a rhythm which has in it as little obvious propulsion as a movement of music by Mozart:
Sir Neville Cardus

Gary Sobers never had a nickname, he was always called Gary or the 'King': *Pat Pocock*

BATTING

Anon
A cricket bat is an instrument that looks like a baseball bat run over by a steam-roller:
Canadian newspaper

Kingsley Amis – *(b 1922) novelist*
Nervous? I felt more and more like a man going in to bat in his first Test match with the score at nineteen for three.

John Arlott – *(b 1914) writer & commentator*
The big hit – for six – is the most companionable of cricketing acts.

Ken Barrington – *(1930–81) Surrey*
When you're playing well, you don't think about anything and run-making comes naturally. When you're out of form, you're conscious of needing to do things right, so you have to think first and act second. To make

runs under these conditions is mighty difficult.

Geoffrey Boycott – *(b 1940) Yorkshire*
Boycott batted under the premise that "slow and sure wins the race'. His tactics for winning the Indy 500 would have been to slip a council dust-cart into second gear:
Colin M. Jarman – sportswriter

Sir Don Bradman – *(b 1908) Australia*
There is probably a greater premium on temperament for a batsman than for any other player in any branch of sport.

Bradman is the greatest batsman of his day, not because he can make better strokes than others, but because he has a wonderful cricket mentality, and a wonderful control of his own emotions and his powers:
Dr Eric Barbour (1934)

On and on and on, he seemed to go, batting into cricket eternity: *Jack Fingleton*

I wish I could have used my bat like Don. He's a gem of a batsman. How he must enjoy getting his runs: *C. B. Fry*

What mystifies bowlers when Bradman is batting is the unerring certainty with which he sends the bad ball to the boundary:
G. C. Macartney

Like W. G. Grace, he has changed the conception of first class batting, opening avenues hitherto untrodden, suggesting possibilities till now unsuspected:
R. C. Robertson-Glasgow

About his batting, there was no style for style's sake. His aim was the making of runs, and he made them in staggering and ceaseless profusion: *R. C. Robertson-Glasgow*

At the crease he was master; the bowler, the servant: *Wisden*

Ian Chappell – *(b 1943) Australia*
At the crease my attitude towards three bouncers an over has been that if I'm playing well enough, three bouncers an over should be worth twelve runs to me.

Denis Compton – *(b 1918) Middlesex*
The increased weights of bats has contributed
to our weakness in hooking. The shot demands
speed of stroke and timing. How much simpler
it is to swat a fly with a rolled up newspaper
than with a telephone directory: *1978*

Colin Cowdrey – *(b 1932) Kent*
The cover drive is the most beautiful stroke in
batsmanship. Does that throw any light on why
I am a self-admitted lover of all things British
and traditional?

Walter Hammond – *(1903-65) Gloucestershire*
Every career has an ignition point somewhere,
and in my case, it was not watching a giant
batting, but merely watching a giant walking
out to bat: *Colin Cowdrey (1976)*

Whenever I saw Wally Hammond batting, I felt
sorry for the ball: *Sir Len Hutton*

Hammond's batting placed him as an equal of
those who created the glory of the golden age:
A. A. Thomson – sportswriter

Norman de Mesquita – *radio commentator*
57 runs needed by Hampshire in 11 overs and it
doesn't need a calculator to tell us that the run
rate required is 5.1818 recurring.

Ted Dexter – *(b 1935) Sussex*
There are many cries for batsmen to get behind
the ball, but how can you hit the ball hard if
you are behind it?

Unlike tennis players who enjoy a knock-up on
court, the Test batsman, even after net
practice, is still forced to use the first few overs
in the middle as a warm-up: *1976*

Charles B. Fry – *(1872-1956) Sussex*
If one hit the ball in an unexpected direction to
the on side, intentionally or otherwise, one
apologised to the bowler: *1891*

W. G. Grace – *(1848-1915) Gloucestershire*
Before W. G. batsmen did not know what to
make of batting: *Prince Ranjitsinhji*

He revolutionised batting. He turned it from an
accomplishment to a science, he turned its
many narrow straight channels into one great
winding river: *Prince Ranjitsinhji*

Maurice Leyland – *(1900-67) Yorkshire*
None of us likes the ball up round our ears, but
some of us shows it less than others.

Majid Khan – *(b 1946) Pakistan*
You don't need footwork in batting, just hands
and eyes.

Viv Richards – *(b 1952) West Indies*
Dominating a fast bowler is a joy – one of the
best parts of batting.

Peter Roebuck – *(b 1956) Somerset*
He who strokes the ball with loving care is a
gentleman. He who studies it with hawk eyes is
a worried man. He who blocks fast bowlers and
belts spinners is a wise man.

Fred Titmus – *(b 1932) Middlesex*
During a mid-wicket conference in a Test match –
Ken Barrington – Let's cut out some of the quick
singles.
Fred Titmus – OK! We'll cut out yours, Ken.

Frank Woolley – *(1886-1954) Kent*
When I am batting, I am the attack.

As the afternoon softened, Woolley's batting
seemed to take on the changing light as the heat
cooled and the shadows began to come over the
green: *Sir Neville Cardus*

His off-drives are like a white owl flying:
Sir Neville Cardus

A glorious upstanding batsman of free-flowing
beauty of execution: *Ronald Mason*

BOWLING

GENERAL

Anon
I don't mind you getting the rabbits, but that
bugger had myxomatosis.

H. M. Herman – *writer*
Bowling is the most important thing in the
game. It's the brainiest part of cricket: *1937*

J. M.Kilburn – *sportswriter*

Bowlers tend to become cricketing heroes for what they do, as distinct from how they do it:
1975

A. E. Knight – *(1872-1946) Leicestershire & writer*
Bowling which does not get men out, like batting which brings no runs to the score, is an art abused:
1906

Arthur Mailey – *(1886-1967) Australia*
The last bowler they knighted was Sir Francis Drake.

If I ever bowled a maiden over, it's not my fault.

Ian Peebles – *(1908-80) Middlesex & writer*
The bowler is a mere delicate plant, less certain to rear, and shorter lived than the batsman:
1953

Alfred Shaw – *(1842-1907) Nottinghamshire*
His last request – Bury me twenty-two yards from Arthur [Shrewsbury], so I can send him down a ball, now and then:
1907
[*The two friends were buried twenty-seven yards apart – to take account of Alfred's five yard run-up*]

FAST

Sidney F. Barnes – *(1873-1967) Warwickshire & Lancashire*
If you wanted to score runs off S. F. Barnes, you had to score off good bowling:
Learie Constantine – West Indies

Alec Bedser – *(b 1918) Surrey*
To be fit is one thing, strong another. You have to be strong to bowl.

Scyld Berry – *sportswriter*
England's pace bowlers are making the helmet go out of fashion:
1981

Geoff Boycott – *(b 1940) Yorkshire*
On facing the 'quicks' – To have some idea what it's like, stand in the outside lane of a motorway, get your mate to drive his car at you at 95 mph and wait until he's 12 yards away, before you decide which way to jump:
1989

Ian Chappell – *(b 1943) Australia*

To me a fast bowler is like a wild animal. If he smells fear, he will be after you twice as hard.

Brian Close – *(b 1931) Yorkshire*
Fast bowlers are bully boys – they can dish it out, but they can't take it.

Norman Cowans – *(b 1961) Middlesex*
He should remember what happened to Graham Dilley, who started off as a genuinely quick bowler. Then, they started stuffing 'line and length' into his ear, and now he has Dennis Lillee's action with Denis Thatcher's pace:
Geoff Boycott (1982)

Joel Garner – *(b 1952) West Indies*
I find it more satisfying to bowl batsmen out than scare them out.

W. G. Grace – *(1848-1915) Gloucestershire*
The faster they bowl, the better I like them.

He killed fast bowling; for years they were almost too afraid to bowl within his reach:
Anon

A. B. Hollowood – *writer*
Fast bowlers enjoy bad light, and never have any difficulty in picking out the shape of the stumps or the batsman's skull.

Colin M. Jarman – *(b 1958) sportswriter*
In baseball, pitchers who spit on the ball are ejected from the game, whereas fast bowlers in cricket spit on the ball as a shining example:
1988

Kevin Jarvis – *(b 1953) Kent & Gloucestershire*
If I could bowl at myself, I would be very keen. It would be an amputation job to get the ball out of my hand:
1985

Lambert Jeffries
If a fast bowler is allowed to strike a batsman on the head with the ball, why shouldn't the batsman be allowed to retaliate by giving the bowler a crack on the head with his bat?

A. E. Knight – *(1872-1946) Leicestershire & writer*
Fast bowling, unlike slow, has not to trust to deceptive arts:
1906

Charles Kortright - *(1871–1952) Essex*
There's a great deal of satisfaction in hulking a stump out of the ground with a fast one, which a slow one doesn't often do.

Harold Larwood - *(b 1904) Nottinghamshire*
I never bowled to injure a man. Frighten them, intimidate them - yes.

Maurice Leyland - *(1900–67) Yorkshire*
None of us likes fast bowling, but some of us don't let on.

Dennis Lillee - *(b 1949) Australia*
I bowl bouncers for one reason and that is to hit the batsman and thus intimidate him.

Ray Lindwall - *(b 1921) Australia*
There's no sitting duck like a scared duck.

Michael Parkinson - *(b 1935) TV presenter & writer*
I am not saying that it is necessary for a fast bowler to be a homicidal maniac, but it certainly helps.

Mike Procter - *(b 1946) South Africa*
Mike Procter bowls at a hundred miles an hour, from extra cover, off the wrong foot:
David Green - Gloucestershire

John Snow - *(b 1941) Sussex*
A fast bowler who doesn't get results has no future.

Brian Statham - *(b 1930) Lancashire*
If I want to get fit for bowling, I do a lot of bowling.

On opening with Statham - It felt like having Menuhin playing second fiddle to my lead:
Frank Tyson

Jeff Thomson - *(b 1950) Australia*
Broken marriages, conflicts of loyalty, the problems of everyday life fall away as one faces up to Thomson: *Mike Brearley*

Fred Trueman - *(b 1931) Yorkshire*
If the odd bouncer helped break their concentration – and that is what I was trying to break, not their skulls – then, I considered it to be a fair weapon.

To be a great fast bowler, you need a big heart and a big bottom.

The difference between a fast bowler and a good fast bowler is not extra muscle, but extra brains.

Never simply a cricketer. He was purely, in method, mind and heart, a fast bowler:
John Arlott

Fast bowlers are a breed apart, and Fred Trueman was apart from the breed:
Denis Compton

Frank Tyson - *(b 1930) Northamptonshire*
To those who have bowled quick, really quick, there is no comparable feeling in the world.

To bowl fast is to revel in the glad animal action.

Bob Willis - *(b 1949) Warwickshire*
It's part of a fast bowler's job to be aggressive. He's got to have 'devil'. He doesn't want to see the batsman injured, but he wants to tickle his ribs with a fast one.

On his long run-up - I don't go that far on my holidays: *Anon*

BODYLINE

Warwick Armstrong - *(1879–1947) Australia*
Had Bradman been built with more backbone, it is possible the bodyline story might have been different.

Jack Fingleton - *(1908–81) Australia*
The Don had two views of bouncers – one when they were bowled against him and the other when bowled by his side with no fear of retaliation: *1946*

C. L. R. James - *West Indian writer*
Body-line was not an incident, it was not an accident, it was not a temporary aberration. It was the violence and ferocity of our age expressing itself in cricket: *1963*

Douglas Jardine - *(1900–58) Surrey*
To me the term is meaningless. What is the body line?

[*Jardine, as England captain, was the instigator of leg-theory – dubbed 'bodyline'*]

Harold Larwood – *(b 1904) Nottinghamshire*
Bodyline was devised to stifle Bradman's batting genius. They said I was a 'killer with the ball', without taking into account that Bradman, with the bat, was the greatest killer of all: *1965*

SLOW

David Acfield – *(b 1947) Essex*
When you're an off-spinner there's not much point glaring at a batsman. If I glared at Viv Richards he'd just hit me even further: *1982*

Trevor Bailey – *(b 1923) Essex*
The first time you face up to a googly, you're going to be in trouble if you've never faced one before.

A. P. 'Tich' Freeman – *(1888–1965) Kent*
If 'Tich' Freeman could see the state of English slow bowling he'd turn in his grave:
Colin M. Jarman – sportswriter

Lord Home – *(b 1903) statesman*
My wife had an uncle who could never walk down the nave of his abbey without wondering whether it would take spin: *1982*

Allan Lamb – *(b 1954) Northamptonshire*
When a spinner comes on, your eyes go round like dollar signs on a fruit machine. Everyone wants to hit him because they can't smash the fast bowler.

Arthur Milton – *(b 1928) Gloucestershire*
Spinning – it's all a matter of inches; those between your ears.

Bill O'Reilly – *(b 1905) Australia*
O'Reilly's googly was harder to spot than a soda-fountain in the bush: *Colin McCool*

Abdul Qadir – *Pakistan*
Leg-spinners are such an amazingly contrasting group of individuals and Qadir very much fits that mould: *Intikhab Alam*

Fred Trueman – *(b 1931) Yorkshire*
Spinners have an advantage over fast bowlers

because they can go on until they qualify for old age pension.

Derek Underwood – *(b 1945) Kent*
The face of a choirboy, the demeanour of a civil servant and the ruthlessness of a rat-catcher:
Geoff Boycott

Derek Underwood is one of the larger gold nuggets on the cricket scene: *Robin Marlar*

Hedley Verity – *(1905–43) Yorkshire*
To dismiss a modest side on a turning wicket was to him no more than the routine of a bank cashier completing a single balance:
J. M. Kilburn – sportswriter

FIELDING

OUTFIELDERS

Benson & Miles
Whereas cricket is often called a trinity of games, of which one member is fielding, fielding itself, though regarded as a single occupation, involves a multitude of arts and, too often, a multitude of sins: *1903*

Lord Learie Constantine – *(1902–71) West Indies*
Learie Constantine wanted to field all the time, everywhere, and there were many moments when he appeared to be doing just that:
J. M. Kilburn

W. G. Grace – *(1848–1915) Gloucestershire*
On missing a ball in the outfield – It's the ground; it's too far away.

Percy Holmes – *(1886–1971) Yorkshire*
It is worth padding many miles, with a nail in your boot, to see Percy Holmes in the field:
R. Edwards

Colin M. Jarman – *(b 1958) sportswriter*
Extra-cover is a premium rather than a policy in the Refuge Assurance League.

Rohan Kanhai – *(b 1935) West Indies*
After he caught Bobby Simpson at leg-slip – He moved like a black mamba, famished after hibernation, on sighting its first prey:
Jack Fingleton – Australia

Edward V. Lucas – *(1868–1938)*
Give me the fieldsman whose eyes never stray
from me,
 Eager to clutch me, a roebuck in pace;
 Perish the unalert, perish the 'buttery',
Perish the laggard I strip in the race.

Christopher Martin-Jenkins – *radio*
commentator
It is extremely cold here. The England fielders
are keeping their hands in their pockets
between balls.

Ian Peebles – *(1908–80) Middlesex & writer*
Good fielding will do as much to compensate
for dull bowling and batting as bad fielding will
do to mar fine play.

Derek Randall – *(b 1951) Nottinghamshire*
Derek Randall stretched like Nureyev for a one-
handed catch: *Scyld Berry – sportswriter*

When we first married Derek used to throw tea
cups behind his back and catch them. That's
one way he got out of doing the washing up:
 Liz Randall

Prince Ranjitsinhji – *(1872–1933) Sussex*
Fielding is the only branch of the game in
which, if one tries hard enough, one can be sure
of success: *1897*

Mickey Stewart – *(b 1932) Surrey*
Mickey Stewart stood closer at silly mid-on
than I would ever think fair to ask: *Jim Laker*

To stand at Mickey Stewart's 'pick-pocketing'
distance at short-leg, needs more than a safe
pair of hands, quick reflexes and a stout heart;
it demands complete faith in his bowlers:
 Wisden

J.Tunnicliffe – *(1866–1948) Yorkshire*
Tunnicliffe was the best slip fielder of the
century, a long giant with a reach into infinity:
 Sir Neville Cardus

Norman Yardley – *(b 1915) Northamptonshire*
A remarkable catch by Yardley, especially as
the ball quite literally rolled along the ground
towards him: *Mike Denness*

WICKET-KEEPERS

J. T. Kellet-Kirtley
Admirers joked that he squatted with his face
so close to the bails so he could flick them off
with his moustache: *Clive Crickmer*

Alan Knott – *(b 1946) Kent*
Small, pokey, alert as a cat . . . as alive to
possibilities of misadventure as a boy playing
French cricket on a bumpy lawn:
 John Thicknesse – sportswriter

Rod Marsh – *(b 1947) Australia*
I made it very plain to my fielders that I set the
standard, and if any of them didn't reach it, I
let them know I wasn't happy about it.

C. B. Ponsonby – *Worcestershire*
A wicket-keeper who is on his toes is likely to
overbalance: *1920*

Bob Taylor – *(b 1941) Derbyshire*
Of all the good and bad repercussions of the
Packer revolution the happiest was that this
perfect craftsman and ideal sportsman suddenly
acquired a status which his exceptional ability
warranted: *Christopher Martin-Jenkins*

CAPTAINCY & TACTICS

R. L. Arrowsmith – *sportswriter & historian*
Cricket is a game in which attack and defence
need to be nicely balanced, but with a tendency
to attack. It is often right for one side to attack
and the other to defend; often right for both
sides to attack. What can never be right is for
both sides to defend.

Trevor Bailey – *(b 1923) Essex*
No captain with all the hindsight in the world
can predict how the wicket is going to play.

S. F. Barnes – *(1873–1967) Yorkshire*
There's only one captain of a side, when I'm
bowling – me!

Richie Benaud – *(b 1930) Australia*
The hallmark of a great captain is the ability to
win the toss, at the right time.

Sir Don Bradman – *(b 1908) Australia*
A captain must always make his decision before

he knows what will happen. The critic usually bases his statements on what has happened and thus takes no risk: *1950*

Mike Brearley - *(b 1942) Middlesex*
The captain of a county cricket side is, all at once, managing director, union leader, and pit-face worker.

The county side with a good captain has no urgent need for a manager, while no manager, however brilliant, can make up for a bad captain.

It is easier for a football manager to play God, to read the riot act to the players, because he does not have to perform himself. Sales managers don't sell, foremen don't hump bricks. All cricket captains bat and field, and some bowl. We receive repeated intimations of our own infallibility: *1985*

Mike Brearley is the bloke with the degree in life: *Rodney Hogg - Australia*

Tony Brown - *(b 1942) Gloucestershire*
The great skill in modern cricket is getting a side out that wants to stay in.

Ian Chappell - *(b 1943) Australia*
Playing against a team with Ian Chappell as captain turns a cricket match into gang warfare: *Mike Brearley*

Brian Close - *(b 1931) Yorkshire*
The greatest disaster in my life was when I lost the captaincy of England.

Ted Dexter - *(b 1935) Sussex*
Dexter finds himself steering England with a dubious wheel: *Sir Neville Cardus*

J. W. H. T. Douglas - *(1882-1930) Essex*
From Douglas' captaincy no idea ever emerged: *C. B. Fry*

Phil Edmonds - *(b 1941) Middlesex*
On a meddling non-captain - Phil Edmonds needs two more field changes to get his 1,000 for the season: *Jim Laker - commentator*

Tony Greig - *(b 1946) Sussex*
Tony Greig was the first England player I

remember actively indulging in gamesmanship: *Bob Taylor*

Lord Hawke - *(1860-1938) Yorkshire*
Pray God no professional may ever captain England.

Rachael Heyhoe-Flint - *(b 1939) England ladies captain*
After being dropped from the England captaincy - As one door closes another slams in your face.

J. B. 'Jack' Hobbs - *(1882-1963) Surrey*
Although Jack did have the honour of captaining England, he felt at the time like the best man who was asked to become a bigamist because the groom failed to appear: *Arthur Mailey*

Sir Len Hutton - *(b 1916) Yorkshire*
A Test match rubber played under Hutton's captaincy became a business undertaking with its principal satisfactions represented by the dividends paid. Hutton did not expect his players to enjoy their Test matches until the scoreboard showed victory: *J. M. Kilburn*

Doug Ibbotson - *sportswriter*
As harrowing experiences go there can't be much to choose between the Australian cricket captaincy and social work on skid row.

Ray Illingworth - *(b 1932) Yorkshire*
If he can get 100 per cent performance out of the other ten, a captain is worth his place.

Doug Insole - *(b 1926) Essex*
A captain's role - A PR officer, agricultural consultant, psychiatrist, accountant, nursemaid and diplomat.

The player who stands at fine leg and occasionally refrains from admiring the female talent just long enough to castigate his captain for not changing the bowling is not recognisable when the onus of decisive action falls on him.

John Invererity - *(b 1944) Australia*
A team functions best when the captain takes a high profile and calls the shots.

Peter May - *(b 1929) Surrey*
Peter May is a cavalier batsman and a

roundhead captain:
                    A. A. Thompson - sportswriter

John Nyren - *sportswriter*
Any device or excuse is legitimate that may
delay the game and the strikers thus become
cold and inactive.

Prince Ranjitsinhji - *(1872-1933) Sussex*
An organism must have a central principle to
make it efficient, and a captain ought to be this
central principle to his side: *1897*

Peter Roebuck - *(b 1956) Somerset*
Captaincy seems to involve half-hearing
conversations which you'd rather not hear at
all: *1984*

Derek Underwood - *(b 1945) Kent*
Why do so many players want to be captain?

UMPIRES

Anon
Some mark the strokes upon the shaven spray,
And others umpires stand whom all obey.

Each at his wicket, near at hand,
Propped on his staff, the umpires stand.

John Arlott - *(b 1914) writer & commentator*
The umpire signals a bye with the air of a
weary stork.

It is rather suitable for umpires to dress like
dentists, since one of their tasks is to draw
stumps.

Harold 'Dickie' Bird - *(b 1933)*
Umpire Bird, having a wonderful time,
signalling everything in the world, including
stopping traffic coming on from behind:
                    John Arlott - commentator

My only complaint with 'Dickie' Bird is that he
requires a degree of certainty that is almost
neurotic; like the man who has to keep going to
the front door to make certain that he's locked
it: *Mike Brearley*

Sir Don Bradman - *(b 1908) Australia*
Good umpires are vital enough to the success of
any sport, but in cricket one decision can decide

the fate of a Test match.

Sir Neville Cardus - *(1889-1975) writer*
The umpire is the law of cricket, image of the
noble constitution of the best of games.

What a great country this would be if every
man, whatever his station, concentrated half as
much on the smallest detail of his work, as an
umpire is compelled to do, from high noon to
dewy evening.

The umpire at cricket is like the geyser in the
bathroom; we cannot do without it, yet we
notice it only when it is out of order.

Pauline Chase - *US actress*
At her first [and possibly last] game of cricket -
What are the butchers for?

Edmund B. V. Christian - *(1864-1938)*
solicitor & poet
    Shall I never storm or swear,
Just because the umpire's fair?
    If he will not favour me,
What care I how fair he be?

David Constant - *(b 1941)*
It can be a thankless task. Few people come up
to you and say, 'Well umpired', whereas a
cricketer who's performed well that day can be
the centre of attraction. Everybody likes to be
praised, but an umpire has to stand apart from
the back-slapping.

W. G. Grace - *(1848-1915) Gloucestershire*
Australia has always lacked good umpires.

On being given out by an umpire - They haven't
come to see you umpiring, they have come to
see me bat.

George Parr - *(1826-91) Nottinghamshire*
When you play in a match, be sure not to forget
to pay a little attention to the umpire. First of
all, inquire after his health, then say what a fine
player his father was, and finally present him
with a brace of birds or rabbits. This will give
you confidence and you will probably do well.

'Quid' [Robert A. Fitzgerald] - *writer*
An umpire should be a man. They are for the
most part old women: *Jerks In From Square Leg*

When a cricketer no longer had nerve, eye or sinew left, then he was put out to grass as an umpire.

In no department of the game has so little progress been made as in that part which is summed up in the little word 'umpire'.

Alec Skelding - *(1886-1960) Leicestershire & writer*
Most of the time he stands to be shot at;
An immobile creature, for mankind to pot at:
1930

Katherine Whitehorn - *writer*
I cannot for the life of me see why the umpires, the only two people on a cricket field who are not going to get grass stains on their knees, are the only two people allowed to wear dark trousers.

GROUNDS & WICKETS

John Arlott - *(b 1914) writer & commentator*
He pats the pitch like an old lady with an umbrella.

Sir Don Bradman - *(b 1908) Australia*
To be truthful, I would prefer to see all matches played on dry wickets. It would be a fairer test of skill for both sides:
1950

B. R. Ellis
Nor sweeter music in the world is found,
Than that upon an England cricket ground:
1935

Fred Gale [Old Buffer] - *(1823-1904) writer*
The wicket reminded me of a middle-aged gentleman's head of hair when the middle-aged gentleman, to conceal the baldness of his crown, applies a pair of wet brushes to some favourite long locks and brushes them across the top of his head:
1868

Sir Len Hutton - *(b 1916) Yorkshire*
Pitches are like wives, you can never tell how they're going to turn out:
1954

Lord's Cricket Ground
The only respect in which the pitch resembled a billiard table was the pockets:
Harry Altham - MCC President

Lord's cricket is cricket straight out of Debrett:
Sir Neville Cardus

The general atmosphere of Lord's is more like that of a prayer meeting than a ball game. It could be, of course, everybody is simply praying for the English team:
Alistair Cooke - writer

To sit at Lord's watching a Test match equates with my requirements for heaven:
John Drinkwater

Lord's, it's a magical word to me, the 'open sesame' to a lifetime of happiness:
Margaret Hughes - writer

This Centenary Lord's Test is an unique occasion - a repeat of Melbourne 1977:
Jim Laker - commentator

The ghosts of the giants of other days stalk in the shadows of every Test match ground, but they always seem to be less ethereal or abstract at Lord's:
Arthur Mailey - Australia

The risk of being lynched at Lord's is a very small one:
Lord Winterton

Arthur Mailey - *(1886-1967) Australia*
I shudder at the cold, gloomy picture of Lord's or Melbourne's 'Bull Ring' after play is ended. The man who wrote 'The song is over but the melody lingers on' never, I'll warrant, played cricket on either of these grounds.

Michael Parkinson - *(b 1935) TV presenter & writer*
Not long ago, Harvey-Walker, the Derbyshire batsman, announced his opinion of a brutal wicket at Buxton by striding to the middle and handing his false teeth to the square-leg umpire.

Sydney Cricket Ground
Sydney Cricket Ground, with its baroque architecture and domed pavilions, is the Grand Opera house of the game:
Ian Wooldridge

Trent Bridge
Before a Test match - There has been a heavy fall of rain here at Trent Bridge, fortunately it didn't touch the ground:
BBC Radio Three spokesman

At Trent Bridge, it is always four o'clock in the afternoon and 300–2: *Sir Neville Cardus*

The County Ground, Worcester
Music and cricket are inseparable when I think of Worcester: *Sir Neville Cardus*

VILLAGE CRICKET

Adrian Allington – *writer*
I would rather see the whole village dead at my feet than a man bowling in braces: *1984*

John Arlott – *(b 1914) writer & commentator*
Villagers do not think village cricket is funny: *1981*

Ian Peebles – *(1908–80) Middlesex & writer*
Real old-fashioned village cricket is a serious matter for the villager and immense fun for the visitor: *1953*

George M. Trevelyan – *(1876–1962) historian*
Village cricket spread fast through the land. In those days, before it became scientific, cricket was the best game in the world to watch – each ball a potential crisis: *1946*

MEDIA

John Arlott – *(b 1914) writer & commentator*
Cricket, like the novel, is great when it presents men in the round, when it shows the salty quality of human nature: *1953*

All cricketers are cricketers, none the less so for not being 'first-class', which is no more than a statistical distinction.

On his scorer – Bill Frindall has done a bit of mental arithmetic with a calculator.

I don't go in for statistics, but that's history.

Gower passes Boycott, who's got his helmet underneath his arms, like a knight at arms, 'alone and palely loitering'.

Butcher drops his head, both hands behind his back and looks sheepishly down the wicket like a small boy caught stealing jam.

During the first World Cup final – They've scored off the last fifteen balls – now difficult not only to bowl a maiden over, but apparently a maiden delivery: *1975*

They might have given him that hundred, like laying your hand down at bridge when you've got a Grand Slam.

Commenting on the appearance of a streaker [or as Arlott called him, a freaker!] – Very shapely, and it's masculine. Fine performance, but what will they do about finding his swimming trunks?

John Arlott has been that rarity; a man respected by players as much as the public – somehow his presence made you feel cricket was in good hands: *Brian Brain*

He sounds like Uncle Tom Cobleigh reading Neville Cardus to the Indians: *Dylan Thomas*

What seems to me to make Arlott the best cricket commentator and perhaps the best sports commentator I have ever heard is the way he combines manner with matter: *Brian Glanville*

Sir Neville Cardus – *(1889–1975) writer*
Where the English language is unspoken there can be no real cricket.

The day was warm and the wicket still so beautiful that the bowlers might well have watered it with tears: *1934*

Since around about 1960, cricket, in the organised form in which it is presented to the public, has been changed so much that W. G. Grace would not know it was cricket at all.

Our cricket, like that of all boys that ever lived or ever shall live, was quick with the spirit of hero-worship.

There is one great similarity between music and cricket. There are slow movements in each.

If a cricketer's mind and every nerve are awake, and all his wits, there can be no dullness, whether the scorers are active or not.

I can take no interest in any cricketer if I have to look to the scoreboard for a clue to the meaning of his existence at the wicket: *1961*

There ought to be some other means of reckoning quality in this the best of games; the scoreboard is an ass.

Like the British constitution, cricket was not made, it has grown.

To go to a cricket match for nothing but cricket, is as though a man were to go into an inn for nothing but a drink.

J. A. Dixon
It takes a long time to become recognised in big cricket, and just as long to be dropped.

Brian Johnston – *commentator*
The bowler's Holding, the batsman's Willey:
England v West Indies (1976)

The latest news is that Warr's declared:
Middlesex v Sussex

You've come over at a very appropriate time; Ray Illingworth has just relieved himself at the pavilion end: *Grace Road, Leicester*

Fred Titmus has two short legs, one of them square.

There's a small crowd here to watch this important game, in fact I would say there are more cars than people:
Northants v Worcestershire

Neil Harvey's at slip, with his legs wide apart, waiting for a tickle: *Australia v England*

J. M. Kilburn – *sportswriter*
The ultimate prosperity of first class cricket must be based upon the merits of first class cricket: *1975*

Cricket is a team game of individual encounters.

Cricket shares with Cleopatra the charm of infinite variety.

Cricketing days remembered are coloured by the weather.

Overthrows are outside the necessities of cricket, but sometimes they do augment the enjoyment of the game.

Overthrows have a dubious standing in the accountancy of cricket.

When 'it isn't cricket' has become an anachronism and a smear, cricket will be close to its deathbed: *1971*

Teresa McLean – *sportswriter*
The first law of cricket nostalgia is that today's cricket is never as good as yesterday's.

Robin Marlar – *(b 1931) Sussex & writer*
Cricket dimensions will always defy the metric system – that Roman legacy to Europe: *1979*

Ian Peebles – *(1908-80) Middlesex & writer*
Having attracted good material, cricket seems to enhance it, and is as good a form of democracy as exists in the world of sport: *1977*

Sporting Times
On the birth of the 'Ashes' –
In Affectionate Remembrance
of
ENGLISH CRICKET
WHICH DIED AT THE OVAL
on
29th AUGUST 1882
Deeply lamented by a large circle of sorrowing friends and acquaintances.
R. I. P.
The body will be cremated and the ashes taken to Australia
September 1882

E. W. Swanton – *(b 1907) Middlesex & sportswriter*
Cricket is one of the saner relaxations of a weary world.

Allen Synge – *sportswriter*
Behind the pomp and majesty of our summer game, there has always been a basic uneasiness:
1974

LITERARY & OTHER

Anon
Life is simply a cricket match, with temptation as the bowler.

The rudiments of sciences in bowling may be found;
For 'tis in vain to think to bowl,
'Til you first know the ground.
No stings of remorse hurt the cricketer's mind,
To innocent animals never unkind.
The guiltless his doctrine is ever to spare,
Averse to the hunting or killing the hare:
19th Century

He played his cricket on the heath,
The pitch was full of bumps.
A fast ball hit him in the teeth,
The dentist drew the stumps.

I bowl'd, I struck, I caught, I stopp'd;
Sure life's a game of cricket.
I block'd with care, with caution popp'd;
Yet death has hit my wicket:
The Salisbury Cricketer

Lady Baldwin [Lucy Ridsdale] - *England ladies*
The crack of bat against ball amid that humming and buzzing of summer sound is still to me a note of pure joy that raised haunting memories of friends and happy days: *1930*

J. M. Barrie - *(1860-1937) Scottish novelist & dramatist*
I bowl so slow that if after I have delivered the ball and don't like the look of it, I can run after it and bring it back.

Hilaire Belloc - *(1870-1953) poet*
I wish you'd speak to Mary, Nurse,
She's really getting worse and worse.
Just now when Tommy gave her out,
She cried and then began to pout.
And then she tried to take the ball,
Although she cannot bowl at all.
And now she's standing on the pitch,
The miserable little bitch!

Lewis Carroll - *(1823-98) writer*
I once delivered a simple ball, which I was told, had it gone far enough, would have been considered a wide.

Marvin Cohen - *writer*
Is there life after cricket?: *Strangers Gallery*

I like to think about time and I like cricket. The two likings are possibly not inconsistent.

Earl of Derby - *(1865-1948)*
To play cricket is synonymous with running straight: *1926*

Duke of Dorset - *politician*
What is human life but a game of cricket?: *1777*

He firmly stands with bat upright
And strikes with his athletic might
Sends forth the ball across the mead
And scores six notches for the deed.

Gavin Ewart - *(b 1916) poet*
Watching cricket is habit-forming, it can
    become habitual,
    It's a kind of long-lasting white-robed ritual.
    And until recently it's been a male
    prerogative,
Played by big hairy bowlers and blacksmiths
    who were slogative: *Not Quite Cricket*

Leslie Frewin - *writer & poet*
And when time bowls me out – as time bowls
    all
(The canny lob you thought you might have
    seen),
I'll seek Valhalla's field of bat and ball;
I'll seek Valhalla's verdant village green.

***Gentleman's* magazine**
Cricket is certainly a very innocent and wholesome exercise, yet it may be absurd, if either great or little people make it their business: *1743*

Thomas Hood - *(1799-1845) poet & humorist*
Of all games or sports, cricket appears to be the most trying to the temper, for a player cannot lose his wicket without being put out: *1830*

Ernest W. Hornung - *(1866-1921) novelist*
Cricket like everything else, is good enough sport until you discover a better:
Raffles - The Amateur Cracksman

Alfred E. Housman - *(1859-1936) poet*
Now in Maytime to the wicket
Out I march with bat and pad;
See the son of grief at cricket
   Trying to be glad: *1896*

Thomas Hughes - *(1822-96) novelist*
Cricket - it's more than a game. It's an
institution: *Tom Brown's Schooldays*

Samuel Johnson - *(1709-84) lexicographer*
A sport in which contenders drive a ball with
sticks or bats in opposition to each other.

Brian Jones - *poet*
These players like white legends of themselves,
step soundless onto May green.

Rudyard Kipling - *(1865-1936) writer*
Casting a ball at three straight sticks and
defending the same with a fourth.

Andrew Lang - *(1844-1912) Scottish writer*
   If the wild bowler thinks he bowls,
Or if the batsman thinks he's bowled,
They know not, poor misguided souls,
   They too shall perish unconsoled.
I am the batsman and the bat,
   I am the bowler and the ball,
The umpire, the pavilion cat,
The roller, the pitch, and stumps, and all.

There is no talk, none so witty and brilliant,
that is so good as cricket talk, when memory
sharpens memory, and the dead live again –
and the old happy days of burned-out June
revive. We shall not see them again. We lament
that lost lightness; 'for no man under the sun
lives twice, outliving his day', and the day of
the cricketer is brief: *1893*

James Love - *(1722-74) comedian*
Hail Cricket! Glorious, manly, British game!
First of all Sports! Be first alike in Fame!:
                                    Cricket (1740)

Groucho Marx - *(1895-1977) US comedian*
On seeing a game at Lord's - When's the game
itself going to begin?

On a peculiar bowling action - He approaches the
wicket like Groucho Marx chasing a pretty
waitress: *John Arlott - commentator*

Mr Punch's Book Of Sport
The most remarkable instance of a hybrid
animal is the cricket bat: *1906*

The British 'Sphere of Influence' – the cricket
ball: *1906*

Nancy Mitford - *(b 1904) author*
Who would think that a little bit of leather, and
two pieces of wood, had such a delightful and
delighting power!:   *1924*

Thomas Moult - *writer*
Cricket is an ancient pastime; it ripened
sweetly, it has endured nobly: *1935*

Cricket in action is as honest today as the
timber from which its bats are made: *1935*

Frank Muir - *(b 1920) writer & broadcaster*
I am to cricket what Dame Sybil Thorndike is
to non-ferrous welding: *1972*

Sir Henry Newbolt - *(1862-1938) poet*
There's a breathless hush in the Close tonight –
Ten to make and the match to win –
   A bumping pitch and a blinding light,
An hour to play and the last man in.

   This they all with a joyful mind,
Bear through life like a torch inflame.
And falling, fling to the lost behind –
'Play up! Play up! And play the game!'

George Orwell - *(1903-50) novelist & critic*
Cricket is a game full of forlorn hopes and
sudden dramatic changes of fortune and its
rules are so ill-defined that their interpretation
is partly an ethical business: *1944*

J. B. Priestley - *(1894-1984) novelist &
playwright*
It is hard to tell where MCC ends and the
Church of England begins.

Punch magazine
First World War cartoon caption –
When the Kaiser plays what isn't cricket,
   God help the Hun who takes his wicket.

Rev James Pycroft - *(1813-95) writer*
The pest of the cricket field is the man who
bores you about his average; and looks blue

even at the success of his own party. If
unsuccessful, in batting or fielding, he 'shuts
up' – the wretch concentrated all in self.

Tim Rice – *lyricist*
It would be extremely difficult for me to choose
between singing Elvis Presley songs and scoring
a century for England, but I think I would
choose a century for England: *1981*

George Bernard Shaw – *(1856–1950) Irish
dramatist*
When asked what he thought of the Test – What
are they testing?

H. Silver
The average mania is as fatal to cricket as trade
unions are to commerce: *1882*

Alfred Lord Tennyson – *(1809–1892) Poet
Laureate*
Cricket, however, has more in it than mere
efficiency. There is something called the spirit
of cricket, which cannot be denied: *1950*

Francis Thompson – *(1859–1907) poet*
Wake! For the ruddy ball has taken flight
   That scatters the slow wicket of the night;
And the swift batsman of the dawn has driven,
   Against the star-spiked rails, a fiery smite.

For the field is full of shades as I near the
shadowy coast,
   And a ghostly batsman plays to the bowling
of a ghost.

Time magazine
Watching cricket is easy. All anyone needs is a
deckchair, a pipe or knitting, and a week off
from the office.

Peter Ustinov – *(b 1921) actor & writer*
I have always imagined cricket as a game
invented by roughnecks in a moment of
idleness by casually throwing an unexploded
bomb at one another. The game was observed
by some officer with a twisted and ingenious
mind who devoted his life to inventing
impossible rules for it.

Evelyn Waugh – *(1903–66) author*
With a thorough knowledge of the Bible,
Shakespeare and Wisden, you cannot go far
wrong.

Rev Cotton of Winchester
   Assist all ye muses and join to rehearse,
In old English sport, never praised yet in verse.
   'Tis cricket I sing, of illustrious fame,
   No nation e'er boasted so noble a game:
          1770

CROQUET

Anon
Hurlingham rules – Croquet: *graffiti*

W. H. Auden – *(1907–73) poet*
For the clear voice suddenly singing,
   High up in the convent wall,
The scent of elder bushes,
   The sporting prints in the hall.
The Croquet matches in summer,
   The handshake, the cough, the kiss,
There is always a wicked secret,
   A private reason for this: *Twelve Songs*

Veronica Carlisle – *player*
Some people say that croquet players can never

have a friendly game, but that's not true.

Croquet Association
As the sport needs a high degree of skill and
intelligence, it is not, therefore, going to attract
the lower income groups.

Graphic
Croquet has a wonderful hold, it is even more
popular than golf and suits equally the active
older lady or the dashing girl: *1903*

John Jacques – *(b 1795) innovator & equipment
manufacturer*
The history of croquet is peculiar, it found its

way into the world without any acknowledged parentage, and immediately won a popularity which has almost revolutionised an outdoor social life: *c 1850*

When Croquet sprang to benefit the earth;
   What happy garden gave the pastime birth?
What cunning craftsman carved its graceful tools?
   Whose oral teachings fixed its equal rules?
Sing Jacques, then, apostle of the game!:
                                        Anon (1860)

Henry Pollack – *writer*
I do not think I know anything of the game of croquet which is worth communicating: *1870*

Punch magazine
Mysterious Croquet, like 'my little star', of infancy, I wonder what you are?:   *1864*

   Whoever will play Croquet, must first see,
The ground well chosen and the ground should
   be.
   A paradox wherein your sophists revel,
At once a lively ground and a clear level: *1864*

Captain Mayne Reid – *(1818-83) Anglo-Irish novelist*

Praise the sports of the land
And water, each one –
The bath by the beach, or the yacht on the sea –
But of all the sweet pleasures
Known under the sun;
   A good game of Croquet's the sweetest to me:
                                        1863

Richard Rothwell – *Secretary of the Croquet Association*
I took to wearing shorts at tournaments to improve the image of the game – to show that it wasn't just a collection of old women of both sexes playing: *1955*

John W. Solomon – *10 times Open Champion [1953–68]*
To peg out, or not to peg out – that is the question: *1966*

Alexander Woollcott – *(1887-1943) US critic and writer*
It is no game for the soft of sinew and the gentle of spirit. The higher and dirtier croquet can use the guile of a cobra and the inhumanity of a boa constrictor.

My doctor forbids me to play, unless I win.

CURLING

Anon
Lawn bowls on ice.

Proverbs
Nae curlers like the clergy: *Scottish*

Henry Adamson – *(d 1639) Scottish reader*
   His hats, his hoods, his bones,
His allay bowles, and curling stones.
   The sacred game to celebrat,
Which to the Gods are consecrat.

Robert Burns – *(1759-96) Scottish poet*
   The sun had clos'd the winter day,
The Curlers quat their roaring play.

When winter muffles up his cloak,
   And binds the mire like a rock,

Then to the loch,
The Curlers flock.

Colin M. Jarman – *(b 1958) sportswriter*
Curling is a game where everything goes straight: *1988*

A female curling team is a group of sporting ladies with large besoms: *1988*

Rev John Kerr – *(d 1907) Chaplain of the Royal Grand Caledonian Curling Club*
Choice of stones is almost as important as choice of a wife. It must not be done lightly or inadvisably.

Ladies do not curl – on ice.

It is the broom that wins the battle.

George McIndoe - *Scottish poet*
He's a the curle! – the game is ended,
And that is all that was intended: *1805*

Dr Alex Penecuik - *(1652–1722) Scottish poet*
To curle on the ice, does greatly please,
  Being a manly Scottish exercise;
It clears the Brains, stirs up the Native Heat,
  And gives a gallant appetite for Meat: *1715*

Allan Ramsey - *(1686–1758) Scottish poet*
Frae northern mountains clad with snaw,
  Where whistling winds incessant blaw,
In time now where the curling stane

Slides murmuring o'er the icy plain.

From ice with pleasure he can brush the snow
And run rejoicing with his curling throw:
                                         1724

John Struthers - *(1776–1853) poet*
Frequent meanwhile the curlers' roar
  Rolls round the meadows icy shore,
As tee-drawn shots the smooth lead fill,
  Out ports wick'd with hair-breadth skill: *1811*

Robin Welsh
There are keen golfers, keen shinty players,
keen anglers. But only curlers are 'Keen, Keen':
                                         1969

CYCLING

Anon
Whoop la, out of the way
We come with lightning speed,
There's nothing like the rattling gait
Of the flying velocipede.

J. Else - *writer*
The first cycle race probably took place as soon
as the second bicycle was completed:
                      The A–Z of Cycling (1978)

Doug Ibbotson - *sportswriter*
Talking of saddles; the first impression on
climbing aboard is that it is slightly less
comfortable than sitting astride a meat cleaver.

Geoffrey Nicholson - *sportswriter*
A fast car is a fast car whoever is at the wheel,
which isn't to deny the driver's contribution.
But, on a bike, the cyclist is both the driver and
the engine.

Tommy Simpson - *(d 1967)*
Final words after collapsing in the Tour de France –
Put me back on my bike: *1967*

Tour de France
The Tour de France is a totally different ball-
game from English cycle-riding:
                            Sidney Bennett

The Tour de France is different each year, but
always based upon the same two principles –
tradition and solvency – and the same four
landmarks: the Alps, the Pyrenees, the Massif
Central and Paris: *Geoffrey Nicholson*

The Tour de France – all those bicycles roaring
through the countryside:
                  Andy Peebles – disc jockey

DARTS

Eric Bristow - *England*
When I finally retire from darts, I would like to
leave the sort of record that future champions
are always struggling to match. Great players

from other sports have done much the same
thing and that's what I would like to achieve in
darts.

If his dad had taken him to Sunday school instead of down the pub, it would have been better for all of us: *Tony Brown*

If Eric Bristow was at Cape Canaveral, he'd take off before the rocket:
Sid Waddell - TV commentator

Tony Brown - *England*
If you give your opponent one dart at a double, you must expect to lose.

Learning to count and knowing your shots is more than half the battle to become a good darts player. It is, perhaps, the equivalent of putting the white ball where you want in snooker.

Tony Brown attacks his opponents the same way Desperate Dan attacks cow-pie:
Sid Waddell

Keith Deller - *England*
Winning the Embassy [World Championships] was perhaps the next best thing that could happen to me; next to playing for Ipswich Town: *1983*

Bobby George - *England*
If I drop a few games, so what? I never mind about losing. People are getting shot up and dying. In the great scheme of things, darts isn't really that important.

If I could wear a flashing light on my head I would, but the rules of darts say you can't wear headgear.

Tony Green - *TV commentator*
There's only one word for that - Magic Darts!

Hattie Hayridge - *comedienne*

I was watching sumo wrestling on the television for two hours before I realised it was darts:
1989

Danny Pollock
Double-top is needed I have just one shot,
My dart is radar-guided as it hits the spot.
Seb Coe eat your heart out, 'cause you could be like me.
Smoking fags and drinking beer and tasting sweet victory.

Leighton Rees - *Wales*
A good darts player who can count can always beat a brilliant player who can't.

Jocky Wilson - *Scotland*
I have been described as fat, boozy, and toothless. That's pretty accurate, I guess.

He is 16 stain
Of fat and pain,
When he steps up to the oche.
When he throws the spears,
You can hear the cheers,
For Fife's wee hero, Jocky: *Bill Hill*

He naething wins, wha never ventures,
World Champion, Jock - withoot yer dentures:
Angus McIntyre

After being blanked by Wilson in 14 minutes - It was like trying to stop a train with a fishing-rod: *Terry O'Dea*

Jocky Wilson is the pride of Kirkcaldy in Scotland. He is no Robert Redford and he is built like a long succession of talented Scottish 'engine-room' forwards: *Radio Times (1981)*

Jocky Wilson has the psychology of a claymore:
Sid Waddell

DOGS

Dame Juliana Berners - *(1343-1443) prioress*
If you will have a good sike*,
Of which there a few like,
He must be headed like a snake,
Necked like a drake,

Backed like a beam,
Sided like a bream,
Tailed like a rat,
And footed like a cat.
[*A sike is a greyhound]

Geoffrey Chaucer - *(1340-1400) poet*
Greihounds he hadde as swift as fowl of flight:
Canterbury Tales

'Bud' Flanagan - *music hall comedian*
No dog can go as fast as the money you bet on him.

Phil Read - *trainer*
Greyhounds are pure carnivores. When they chase the hare at a race, it's not for fun: they literally want to tear it to pieces: *1980*

Sir Walter Scott - *(1771-1832) Scottish novelist & poet*
Remember'st thou my greyhounds true?
    O'er holt or hill there never flew.
From slip or leash there never sprang,
More fleet of foot, more sure of fang.

Two dogs of black St Hubert's breed

Unmatched for courage, breath or speed.

William Shakespeare - *(1564-1616) playwright*
I see you stand like greyhounds in the slips,
Straining upon the start. The game's afoot;
Follow your spirit: and, upon this charge,
Cry - God for Harry! England! and St George!:
Henry V

Thy wit is as quick as the greyhound's mouth,
it catches: *Much Ado About Nothing*

Lucentio slipp'd me like his greyhound,
Which runs himself, and catches for his master:
The Taming of the Shrew

Keith Waterhouse - *writer & critic*
And now, here are the results of the Sheepdog Trials. All the Sheepdogs were found not guilty.

EQUESTRIAN

Anon
Riding is the art of keeping a horse between yourself and the ground.

There are two important rules in horse-riding. The first is to mount the horse. The second is to stay mounted.

Here's to the bundle of sentient nerves with the heart of a woman, the eye of a gazelle, the courage of a gladiator, and the proud obedience of a soldier - The Horse!:   *Toast*

Proverbs
A horse that will not carry a saddle must have no oats.

Behind the horseman sits care.

A running horse is an open grave.

If two men ride a horse, one must ride behind.

One cannot shoe a running horse: *Dutch*

Leonard Bacon - *(1887-1954) US poet &*

critic
Men will keep going on their nerve or their head,
    But you cannot ride a horse when he's dead.

Badminton Horse Trials
Badminton is to horse trials what Lord's is to cricket: *Sheila Wilcox*

Dame Juliana Berners - *(1343-1443) prioress*
    Her fifteen qualities of a horse –
Of a man; bolde, proude, and hardy;
Of a woman; fayr-breasted, fayr of heere, and
    easy to leape upon;
Of a fox; a fayr taylle, short eeres, with a good
    trotte;
Of a haare; a grete eye, a dry hede, and well
    runnynge;
Of an ass: a bigge chin, a flatte legge, and a
    good hoof.

John Betjeman - *(1906-84) Poet Laureate*
    It's awf'lly bad luck on Diana,
Her ponies have swallowed their bits;
She fished down their throats with a spanner

And frightened them all into fits:

Hunter Trials

Bible
A horse is a vain thing for safety:

Psalms 33:17

Rita Mae Brown - *(b 1944) social activist &*
writer
If the world were a logical place, men would
ride side-saddle.

Lord Byron - *(1788-1824) poet*
So that his horse, or charger, hunter, hack;
Knew that he had a rider on his back.

William Cavendish - *(1592-1676) Duke of*
Newcastle
Sitting is but one thing in horsemanship and
there are thousands of things in the art. I never
knew in my life a good horseman thrown, but I
have known many presumptuous, ignorant
fellows get falls, for it is a mistake as ridiculous
as it is common to take sitting fast on
horseback for the whole art of horsemanship.

Miguel de Cervantes - *(1547-1616) Spanish*
novelist
The seat on a horse makes gentlemen of some
and grooms of others.

Geoffrey Chaucer - *(1340-1400) poet*
Full many a dauntie horse had he in stable:

Canterbury Tales

John Clark
A good horse oft needs a good spur.

Benjamin Franklin - *(1706-90) US*
statesman & philosopher
For want of a shoe, the horse was lost;
For want of a horse, the rider was lost.

Thomas Fuller - *(1654-1734) physician*
A good horse should be seldom spurred.

Harewood Horse Trials Programme
In the ever-increasing standard of modern
competition, the athlete, be he human or
equine, is forced to specialise in his own
particular sport, often even in his own branch
of that particular sport, but unlike the majority
of competitions, the Three Day Horse Trials

search out the 'complete' horse and the
'complete' horseman - the all-rounders: *1959*

George Herbert - *(1593-1633) poet*
Good horses make short miles.

When one is on horseback, he knows all things.

A good rider on a good horse is as much above
himself and others as the world can make him.

Rachel Hunt - *three-day eventer*
The main thing is that the horse must have
confidence in you: *1987*

Stephen Leacock - *(1869-1944) Canadian*
humorist & scientist
There are no handles to a horse: *1910*

Hugh McIlvanney - *sportswriter*
Gold medals aren't given out with the oats and
the bran in three-day eventing: *1984*

Thomas Malory - *(1408-71) poet*
He rides sure that never fell.

The Manual of Horsemanship
Riding at its simplest is a means of transport.
At its most developed, it is one of the supreme
partnerships that exist between man and
animal: *1950*

Ogden Nash - *(1902-71) US poet & humorist*
Equestriennes prefer to jump
    Onto horses pillow-plump.
Equestriennes will never ride
    As other people do, astride.
    They like to balance on one foot,
And wherever they get, they won't stay put.

Pliny the Younger - *(62-113) Latin literist*
You have to set spurs to a willing horse.

William Shakespeare - *(1564-1616)*
playwright
That horse his mettle from his rider takes:

A Lover's Complaint

Round-hoof'd, short-jointed, fetlocks shag
    and long,
Broad breast, full eye, small head and nostril
    wide
High crest, short ears, straight legs and passing

strong,
Thin mane, thick tail, broad buttock, tender
  hide:
Look what a horse should have he did not lack,
Save a proud rider on so proud a back:
Venus and Adonis

George Bernard Shaw - *(1856-1950) Irish
playwright*
Go anywhere in England where there are
natural, wholesome, contented and really nice
English people; and what do you always find?
That the stables are the real centre of the
house.

There are two classes in good society in
England; the equestrian classes and the
neurotic classes.

Harvey Smith - *(b 1938) show jumper*
The American horses know the fences like the
back of their hand.

Title of Autobiography - V is for Victory.

When I asked Harvey Smith to choose a book
to take to the desert island, he laughed and said
he had never read a book in his life:
Roy Plomley - Desert Island Discs presenter

On one of his horses, Sanyo Music Centre - You
might have imagined that Harvey was mounted
on a piece of stereo equipment, but Sanyo
Music Centre is in fact a living creature with
no provision for the electronic reproduction of
sound: *Clive James (1981)*

Robert S. Surtees - *(1803-64) sportswriter*
There is no secret so close as that between a
rider and his horse.

Philip Walsh - *writer*
Horses are like children, they'll learn
something bad quicker than they'll learn
something good: *1979*

George John Whyte-Melville - *(1821-78)
novelist*
A rider unequalled - a sportsman complete,
A rum fellow to follow, a bad one to beat.

Now, in riding for himself, a man preserves his
confidence till he is in the air. Should he be
luckless enough to light in a chasm, he has at
least the advantage of not being frightened to
death in advance; and I am convinced that all
the extraordinary leaps on record have thus
been made by these forward horsemen, who,
trusting Dame Fortune implicitly, find that she
nearly always pulls them through.

FENCING

Colin M. Jarman - *(b 1958) sportswriter*
The first point - wins!

Albert Manley - *writer*
Experienced fencers occasionally spend a few
minutes giving pointers to beginners:
Complete Fencing (1979)

William Shakespeare - *(1564-1616)
playwright*
He will fence with his own shadow:
Merchant of Venice

Gillian Sheen - *coach*
To be successful in any sport from soccer to
horse-racing, from gliding to golf, needs brains
as well as physical skill; neither is much use
without the other; and I think fencing
demonstrates this more fully than any other
sport: *1958*

Valentina Sidorova -*Russian world foil
champion [1977/78]*
Fencing is like playing chess with a sword in
your hand!: *1975*

FOOTBALL

PLAYERS

Anon
A bad football team is like an old bra – no cups and little support.

We beat them five-nothing, and they were lucky to score nothing.

When at thy gate my weary feet I turn,
  The gates of paradise are open wide,
  At Goodison, I know a man can learn,
Rapture more rich than Anfield can provide:
Everton fan

Supporters
Against Wimbledon – Here one goes, here one goes, here one goes: *Cambridge United fans*

Ossie Ardiles – *(b 1952) Argentina & Spurs*
If you're confident, you're always totally different to the player that's lacking confidence.

  Ossie's going to Wembley.
His knees have gone all trembly:
Chas & Dave – Ossie's Dream (1981)

Eddie Bailey – *(b 1925) Spurs*
Neat as a privet, busy as a one-man band, alert as a boarding house cat, and elusive as a dog in a fair: *John Arlott*

Sergei Baltacha – *USSR & Ipswich*
In Russia we play the ball first. In England, there are times when it is the man who is played first. But I am learning: *1989*

Alan Ball – *(b 1945) Everton*
I'm not a believer in luck, although I do believe you need it.

Autobiography – It's all about a Ball

Franz Beckenbauer – *West Germany, Bayern Munich & New York Cosmos*
Tell the Kraut to get his ass up front. We don't pay a million dollars for a guy to hang around in defense: *Cosmos Executive*

Colin Bell – *(b 1946) Manchester City*
Colin Bell did the work of two men, as if he had an extra lung: *Jimmy Greaves – Spurs*

George Best – *(b 1946) Manchester United*
I don't want to be an ordinary player: *1972*

Most of the things I have done are my own fault, so I can't feel guilty about them.

I'd have to be superman to do some of the things I'm supposed to have done. I've been in six different places at six different times.

People always say I shouldn't be burning the candle at both ends. Maybe because they don't have a big enough candle.

When he's boozing, he's the most deplorable, obnoxious, sarcastic, ignorant, horrible piece of rubbish: *Angie Best (1982)*

He had ice in his veins, warmth in his heart, and timing and balance in his feet:
Danny Blanchflower

We had problems with the wee feller, but I prefer to remember his genius:
Sir Matt Busby – Manchester United manager

With a gun to my head, I would concede that George Best was the greatest player of my time, when it came to flair and mind-boggling invention: *Jimmy Greaves*

He became a cult of youth, a new folk hero, a living James Dean, who was a rebel with a cause: *Geoffrey Green – sportswriter (1985)*

He was a son of instinct rather than logic:
Geoffrey Green

Some monopolies arise through the possession of land containing particular minerals, spa water or a desirable location. Other monopolies may reflect freakish ability – Maria Callas' voice or George Best's feet: *B. J. McCormick*

The only thing I have in common with George Best is that we come from the same place, play for the same club, and were discovered by the same man:
Norman Whiteside - Manchester United & Northern Ireland

Danny Blanchflower - *(b 1926) Spurs*
I love soccer because it is vital and fluid, and free from the little legal barriers that frustrate the rest of our everyday activities.

The great fallacy is that the game is first and last about winning. It's nothing of the kind. The game is about glory. It's about doing things in style, with a flourish, about going out and beating the other lot, not waiting for them to die of boredom: *1972*

The FA Cup Final is a great occasion, but only until ten minutes to three o'clock. Then the players come on and ruin the whole thing.

On Northern Ireland's World Cup tactics - We try to equalize before the others have scored: *1958*

Stan Bowles - *(b 1948) Crewe & QPR*
If Stan could pass a betting shop like he can pass a ball he'd have no worries at all:
Ernie Tagg - Crewe manager

Trevor Brooking - *(b 1948) West Ham*
On playing non-league football - You drop your shoulder and move round a defender only to discover he didn't read your first dummy. So you crash straight into him and he comes away with the ball: *1985*

Trevor Brooking floats like a butterfly and stings like one too:
Brian Clough - Nottingham Forest manager (1981)

Horatio 'Raich' Carter - *(b 1913) Sunderland*
It was said of Whistler (probably by himself) that he mixed paint with brains. So Raich Carter does with his football:
H. D. 'Donny' Davies - sportswriter

I never saw Raich under pressure. He carried empty space around with him like an umbrella:
Willie Watson - Sunderland

John Charles - *(b 1931) Swansea City*
John Charles is a giant who can leap and sprint and shoot, and shake off opponents as a dog shakes water off its back: *H.D. 'Donny' Davies*

Bobby Charlton - *(b 1937) Manchester United*
Some folks tell me that we professional players are soccer slaves. Well, if this is slavery, give me a life sentence: *1960*

I wish I could play music and talk the way I play football.

They know on the Continent that European football without the English is like a hot dog without mustard: *1988*

Old Trafford is the 'Theatre of Dreams'.

Bobby Charlton almost rivals Churchill as the best known Briton of all the 20th century. Britain never had a greater sporting ambassador: *Jimmy Greaves*

Bobby Charlton - the dashing leader of the line on a white charger, releasing rockets from the edge of the area that go home like a clap of thunder and lift the opposing net as if a gale had struck it: *Geoffrey Green*

The persistent complaint I have heard made against Bobby Charlton is that he avoids the fury of the game, where the hacking and elbowing are fiercest. This is like dismissing Dickens from the world's literature greats because he never went to gaol for throwing bricks at politicians: *Arthur Hopcraft (1968)*

Jack Charlton - *(b 1935) Leeds United*
Soccer is a man's game, not an outing for namby-pambies.

Allan Clarke - *(b 1946) Leeds United*
You don't think in this game.

Charlie Cooke - *(b 1942) Chelsea*
When Cookie sold you a dummy, you had to pay to get back into the ground: *Jim Baxter*

Warney Cresswell - *Everton*
Good goalkeepers never make great saves.

Garth Crooks - *(b 1958) Spurs, Charlton &*

President of the PFA
Football's football; if it weren't the case it wouldn't be the game it was.

Maggie [Thatcher] isn't the only one with Crooks at No. 11:   *Spurs fans' banner (1981)*

Johan Cruyff - *Holland*
The failure to understand the physical and mental strains on a professional is behind the widely held belief that footballers are stupid:
1973

Johann Cruyff at the age of 35 added a whole new meaning to the word 'Anno Domini':
Archie MacPherson

Kenny Dalglish - *(b 1951) Celtic & Liverpool*
Kenny Dalglish has about as much personality as a tennis racket: *Mike Channon*

Kenny Dalglish is the sort of player who is so unique: *Bob Wilson*

Derek Dougan - *(b 1938) Wolves*
People keep talking about Total Football, all I know about is Total petrol.

Eamonn Dunphy - *Millwall & writer*
When they sign a new player who plays your position it's not funny.

Duncan Edwards - *(1936–58) Manchester United*
The Kohinoor Diamond amongst our Crown Jewels: *Jimmy Murphy - Manchester United assistant manager*

Tom Finney - *(b 1922) Preston North End*
Tom Finney was the first gentleman of football:
Jimmy Greaves

Trevor Francis - *Birmingham, Nottingham Forest & Sampdoria*
In England a lot of fouls are bad timing, people going for the ball late; but in Italy it is just a blatant 'Thou shalt not pass' attitude.

Paul Gascoigne - *(b 1967) Newcastle & Spurs*
He is accused of being arrogant, unable to cope with the press, and a boozer. Sounds like he's got a chance to me: *George Best*

George Best without brains:
Stan Seymour - Newcastle Chairman

He's like the golfer who's got all the shots. The question is - how good is he at selecting which shot and when?:   *Howard Wilkinson (1988)*

Jimmy Greaves - *(b 1940) Spurs*
I was born with a natural gift for sticking the ball into the net, and wasn't interested in doing much else.

Work-rate hardly existed in my vocabulary.

Goals obsess me. I like scoring. They satisfy me.

Football is the game of adventure.

Football tactics are rapidly becoming as complicated as the chemical formula for splitting the atom: *1963*

Banner at a European Cup game - The world Greaves for Benfica tonight.

Where scoring goals was concerned, he was a Picasso: *Clive Allen - Spurs*

Jimmy Greaves is the complete professional who rates his 'bitsy' goals just as important as his classic ones. As he says, 'They don't bother to describe them in the record books. They just count them.':   *Paul Gardner*

He was the Fagin of the penalty area; the arch-pickpocket of goals: *Geoffrey Green*

When he slipped the ball into goal it was like someone closing the door of a Rolls-Royce:
Geoffrey Green

He'll shoot about two seconds before I've even thought about it: *Johnny Haynes*

Ruud Gullit - *Holland*
If I'd wanted to be an individual, I'd have taken up tennis.

If all else fails, you could wait for the first corner and tie his dreadlocks to the goal-post:
Vinny Jones

He has everything, apart from a short-back-
and-sides: *John Toshack (1988)*

Glenn Hoddle - *(b 1957) Spurs & Monaco*
Bobby Robson must decide what he wants for
the European Championships. If he wants to
play English-style, I will not be in the side; if he
wants inspiration, I'll be there: *1988*

People in England forget that playing football is
not just about running fast, hitting the ball as
far as you can and jumping as high as possible.
For many, constructive and creative play are of
little consequence: *1988*

For me the ball is a diamond. If you have a
diamond, you don't get rid of it, you offer it:
1988

Football's about ninety minutes on the day; it's
about tomorrows really.

On his becoming a born-again Christian - I hear
Glenn has found God. That must have been
one hell of a pass!: *Jasper Carrot - comedian*

You can scare Hoddle out of a match and you
couldn't depend on him to bring you a cup of
tea if you were dying: *Tommy Smith - Liverpool*

Jim Holton - *(b 1951) Manchester United*
Six foot two, eyes of blue,
Big Jim Holton's after you: *United fans (1973)*

We put bells on a football so he would know
where it was. We had complaints from Morris
Dancers saying he was kicking them all over
the place:
Tommy Docherty - Manchester United manager

A one-man grappling iron:
David Meek - sportswriter

As centre halves go, Jim Holton is a bony,
booted, gangling threat who patrols in defence
with the soft tread of an elephant's rumba:
Julie Welch - writer

Geoff Hurst - *(b 1941) West Ham United*
Geoff Hurst had a hammer in his left boot and
good left feet are like bricks of gold:
Jimmy Greaves

Geoff Hurst may have proved that in football
this is the age of the common man, just so long
as he can do something as uncommon as
scoring three goals in a World Cup Final:
Hugh McIlvanney - sportswriter (1966)

Pat Jennings - *(b 1945) Spurs & Arsenal*
Pat Jennings clapped his hand round the ball
like banging a piece of toast:
Barry Davies - TV commentator

Somewhere in there, the grace of a ballet
dancer joins with the strength of an SAS
squaddie, the dignity of an ancient king, the
nerve of a bomb disposal officer:
Eamonn Dunphy - Millwall & writer

Pat Jennings' hands are so large, from his
thumb to his fingertips is a foot:
Steve Ryder - TV presenter

If Pat Jennings had been available on that
memorable occasion when the Romans met the
Etruscans, Horatius surely would have had to
be satisfied with a seat on the substitute's
bench: *Eric Todd - sportswriter*

Kevin Keegan - *(b 1951) Liverpool, Hamburg
& Southampton*
The coach means a lot, but it's the players who
play.

Jesus saves - but Keegan scores on the
rebound: *Graffiti on religious poster*

To call Keegan a superstar is stretching a point.
He's been very, very lucky, an average player
who came into the game when it was short of
personalities. He's not fit to lace my boots as a
player: *George Best*

Keegan is not fit to lace George Best's drinks:
John Roberts - sportswriter

He is the Julie Andrews of football:
Duncan McKenzie

Denis Law - *(b 1940) Manchester United*
And when he's hurtling for the goal,
    I know he's got to score.
Defences may stop normal men -
They can't stop Denis Law: *Gareth Owen*

Denis Law could dance on egg-shells:
Bill Shankly - Liverpool manager

Gary Lineker - *(b 1960) Everton, Barcelona &*
Spurs
In response to Emlyn Hughes and Mike Channon's
World Cup comments on ITV - Conjugate the
verb 'done great': I done great. He done great.
We done great. They done great. The boy
Lineker done great:
Letter to The Guardian (1986)

Mick Lyons - *(b 1940) Everton*
If there wasn't such a thing as football, we'd all
be frustrated footballers.

Wilf Mannion - *Middlesborough*
Wilf Mannion was Mozartian in his exquisite
workmanship, with a style so graceful, and so
courtly, that he would not be out of place if he
played in a lace ruffle:
H. D. 'Donny' Davies - sportswriter

Diego Maradona - *Argentina*
On his record transfer from Barcelona to Napoli -
£6.9 million is a large loaf to be throwing away
before a ball's been kicked:
Jimmy Greaves

I don't think there is anyone bigger or smaller
than Maradona: *Kevin Keegan*

The best one-footed player since Puskas:
Sir Stanley Matthews

Rodney Marsh - *QPR*
Most people are in a factory from nine till five.
Their job may be to turn out 263 little circles.
At the end of the week they're three short and
somebody has a go at them. On Saturday
afternoons they deserve something to go and
shout about: *1969*

Take away Match of the Day and all the
hangers-on and it's all very empty and lonely
being a footballer: *1971*

Soccer in England is a grey game, played on
grey days, by grey people: *1979*

Rodney Marsh was a magician with a ball at his
feet: *Jimmy Greaves*

Sir Stanley Matthews - *(b 1915) Blackpool*
Playing Stanley Matthews is like playing a
ghost: *John Carey*

Stanley Matthews & Stan Mortensen -
Blackpool
The last player to score a hat-trick in an FA
Cup final was Stan Mortensen. He even had a
final named after him - The Matthews Final:
Lawrie McMenemy

If Matthews dominates a match, calling up the
thunder on the wings for all to admire,
Mortensen is the lightning that strikes
immediately after: *Alan Ross - sportswriter*

Steve McMahon - *(b 1961) Liverpool*
I'd kick my own brother if necessary. That's
what being a professional is all about: *1988*

Mirandinha - *Brazil & Newcastle United*
We've got Mirandinha
He's not from Argentina
He's from Brazil
And he's effing, effing brill:
Newcastle United supporters

Pele - *(b 1940) Brazil*
I was born for soccer, just as Beethoven was
born for music.

Football is the ultimate in team sport, and no
individual can win a game by himself. Pele is a
famous name, but Pele made his goals because
another player passed to him at the proper
time.

A penalty is a cowardly way to score.

Martin Peters - *(b 1943) West Ham United*
Martin Peters is ten years ahead of his time:
Alf Ramsey - England manager (1968)

Martin Peters? He's the one who's ten years
ahead of his time, so we've got to wait for him
to come good: *Malcolm Allison - Manchester City*
manager (1970)

Kevin Ratcliffe - *(b 1960) Everton*
Over short distances Kevin is unbeatable - the
Carl Lewis of Goodison:
Andy Gray - Everton (1986)

Graham Roberts – *(b 1959) Spurs, Glasgow Rangers & Chelsea*
Football's a game of skill. We kick them a bit and they kick us a bit.

On his transfer to Glasgow Rangers – Graham has kicked a few in England, now he can go and kick some in Scotland:
David Pleat – Spurs manager (1986)

Bryan Robson – *(b 1957) Manchester United*
It's a fantastic job – to be paid for what you enjoy doing.

Ian Rush – *(b 1961) Liverpool*
As quick as a needle: *Ron Jones – commentator*

On Rush's appearance as a substitute – It's like Bradman coming out to bat with 500 already on the board: *Charlton fan (1988)*

Ian St John – *(b 1938) Liverpool*
Poster on wall – What would you do if Jesus returned among us?
Graffiti – Move St John to inside left!

Peter Shilton – *(b 1949) Southampton & Derby*
You've got to believe that you're going to win and I believe that we'll win the World Cup until the final whistle blows and we're knocked out: *1986*

If you stand still, there is only one way for you to go, and that's backwards.

Graeme Souness – *(b 1953) Liverpool*
If Graeme Souness was a chocolate drop, he'd eat himself: *Archie Gemmill*

Tommy Smith with a Rolls-Royce engine:
John Roberts – sportswriter (1984)

Gary Stevens – *(b 1962) Spurs* **& Gary Stevens** – *(b 1963) Everton*
During the Mexico World Cup finals – Two Gary Stevens; there's only two Gary Stevens:
England supporters (1986)

Nobby Stiles – *Manchester United*
Nobby Stiles a dirty player? No, he's never hurt anyone. Mind you, he's frightened a few!:
Sir Matt Busby – Manchester United manager

Ray Wilkins – *Manchester United*
He can't run, he can't tackle and he can't head the ball. The only time he goes forward is to toss the coin: *Tommy Docherty*

Ron Yeats – *Liverpool*
On his 'big' signing – Ron Yeats is a colossus – come and walk round him:
Bill Shankly – Liverpool manager (1961)

With him at centre-half, we could play Arthur Askey in goal: *Bill Shankly (1962)*

MANAGERS

Anon
Football is a simple game made unnecessarily complicated by managers.

Malcolm Allison – *Manchester City*
You're not a real manager unless you've been sacked.

No player of real talent should play in the back four: *1975*

John Bond – *(b 1932) Manchester City*
I promise results, not promises.

History, as John Bond would agree, is all about todays and not about yesterdays:
Brian Moore – TV commentator

Matt Busby – *Manchester United*
Matt Busby is a symbol of everything that is best in our national game:
Sir Harold Wilson (1978)

Brian Clough – *(b 1935) Derby County & Nottingham Forest*
If a fox is completely brilliant he finds a hole and hides. If he's discovered, he's dug up and thrown to the hounds. But, a football manager hasn't even got a hole to hide in.

I am not equipped to manage successfully without Peter Taylor. I am the shop window and he is the goods in the back.

I happen to believe that God gave us grass for various reasons – for cows to eat and give us milk and for football to be played on. A ball looks at its best when it's brushing blades of grass around the world. I don't believe that football was designed to be played in the clouds.

Football hooligans? Well, there are ninety-two club chairmen for a start: *1980*

There's a seven man board at Derby, and I wouldn't give you twopence for five of them.

When the FA get in their stride, they make the Mafia look like kindergarten material.

I shout my opinion. I yell my contempt. I mean every word of it. But when you talk like that you are a target. I've got to be a winner or they'll cut me to shreds.

If the African nations ever succeeded in their plan for one British team in the World Cup, I'd vote Tory. I ask you, a load of spear-throwers trying to dictate our role in world football:
1987

He is a kind of Rolls-Royce communist:
Malcolm Allison (1973)

Tommy Docherty - *(b 1928) much travelled manager*
Preston? They're one of my old clubs. But then most of them are. I've had more clubs than Jack Nicklaus: *1979*

If you have the ball, you should have ten attackers. Only when the other side has it should you have ten defenders.

Some teams are so negative they could be sponsored by Kodak.

The ideal board of directors should be made up of three men – two dead and one dying: *1977*

Altrincham are the Manchester United of non-league soccer: *1987*

Robert Maxwell has just bought Brighton and Hove Albion, and he's furious to find it is only one club: *1988*

On a fellow coach – He's not so much a coach as a hearse.

On Aston Villa chairman Doug Ellis – He said he was right behind me, so I told him I'd rather have him in front where I could see him.

On Manchester City [the Light Blues] – There are three types of Oxo cubes. Light brown for chicken stock, dark brown for beef stock, and light blue for laughing stock.

On 'long ball' tactics – Football wasn't meant to be run by two linesmen and air traffic control:
1988

On 'The Doc's move to Australia – He's gone 200 years too late: *Anon manager (1981)*

His knowledge of what goes on outside football is so restricted that he couldn't understand why he kept getting into trouble for parking on double yellow lines. He thought they were a new form of street decoration:
Catherine Lockley – daughter (1981)

All this talk about Docherty not being fit to run a football club is rubbish. That's exactly what he's fit for: *Clive Thomas – referee (1979)*

John Greig – *Glasgow Rangers*
Football's not like an electric light, you can't just flick the button and change from slow to quick.

Geoffrey Green – *sportswriter*
Managers are as expendable as the leaves of autumn.

Ron Greenwood– *West Ham United & England*
Football is a simple game. The hard part is making it look simple.

Francesco Gross – *Juventus*
The game has lost some of its beauty in gaining speed. Today the rhythm is rock; it used to be like the tango.

Gordon Lee – *Everton*
Even when you are dead, you must never allow yourself just to lie down and be buried.

This game's not all about stars and flair. Stars are just those little things that glimmer in the sky at night and flares are those things that stick on the bottom of your trousers.

Ally MacLeod – *Scotland*
I think Ally MacLeod believes tactics are a new kind of peppermint:
Anon Scottish international (1978)

Peter McWilliams – *Middlesborough*
In the office, the streets, the theatre, there's no escape from football, and that's no good for a worrying man. I have reached the limit, I'm going fishing.

Joe Mercer – *Manchester City*
There are some things wrong with clubs, with managers, with administrators, with Pressmen, with referees. The only thing with which there is nothing wrong is the game itself.

Terry Neill – *(b 1942) Spurs*
I'm not superstitious or anything like that, but I'll just hope that we'll play our best and put it in the lap of the Gods.

I read in the newspapers that Terry Neill says he'll put the joy back in Tottenham's football. What's he going to do – give them bloody banjos?:
Eddie Bailey – former Spurs assistant (1974)

Bill Nicholson – *(b 1919) Spurs*
I remember as a kid, we used to kick a ball about; a little rubber ball, about the size of a coconut. You learned something about ball-control with those. Today's kids insist on a full-size plastic ball – and it's almost impossible to mis-kick one of them:
1974

Michael Parkinson – *(b 1935) TV presenter & writer*
Sky-diving apart, I can think of no other occupation with more inherent risks than that of managing a football team.

Sir Alf Ramsey – *(b 1920) Ipswich & England*
After Ipswich had won the League Championship – I feel like jumping over the moon:
1962
[*A possible precursor to the old football adage of sick as a parrot and over the moon?*]

As a manager, Alf Ramsey is like a good chicken farmer. If a hen doesn't lay, a good chicken farmer wrings its neck:
Jackie Milburn

There is no substitute for skill, but the manager's job is usually to find one. Alf Ramsey obviously found one:
George Raynor (1966)

Don Revie MBE – *Leeds United & England*
When I went to Buckingham Palace, I collected the award on behalf of Leeds United.

Don Revie's appointment as England manager was a classic example of poacher turned game-keeper:
Alan Hardaker – Football League secretary

Bobby Robson – *(b 1933) Fulham, Ipswich & England*
The first ninety minutes are the most important.

We shall be as positive as we can, and look to pick up a point:
1989

On the suicide of property tycoon Sir Eric Miller, the chairman who sacked him at Fulham – Shows how he reacted to pressure doesn't it?:
1981

His natural expression is that of a man who fears he might have left the gas on:
David Lacey – sportswriter

Bill Shankly – *(1913–81) Liverpool*
We murdered them 0–0.

We're not mechanical, we're methodical.

If you're in the penalty area and aren't sure what to do with the ball, just stick it in the net, and we'll discuss your options afterwards.

I don't drop players – I make changes.

This city has two great teams – Liverpool and Liverpool reserves.

If Everton were playing down at the bottom of my garden, I'd draw the curtains.

When I've got nothing better to do, I look *down* the league table to see how Everton are getting along.

Of course I didn't take my wife to see Rochdale as an anniversary present. It was her birthday.

Would I have got married during the football season? And, anyway, it wasn't Rochdale, it was Rochdale reserves.

On the delayed announcement of his team line-up before a European Cup game – I'm not giving away any secrets like that to Milan. If I had my way, I wouldn't even tell them the time of the kick-off.

Shanks died of a broken heart after seeing Liverpool go on to greater success without him:
Johnny Giles

A man who even sees red in his dreams, and flies in imagination with the Liver bird:
Geoffrey Green

Shanks is past it. These days he's letting the left-half take his own throw-ins:
Joe Mercer (1974)

George Smith – *Portsmouth*
Look at it! Look at it! It's round and it's still. It can't move an inch until someone touches it, so don't talk to me about the run of the ball.

We all like to win, but soccer is just a game. I would have been a darned sight more worried sitting in that space capsule coming back from the moon. Now those boys really had something to worry about.

A talk with George Smith is like having a sauna bath - you come out feeling clean and refreshed because it opens the pores of your mind:
Frank Taylor

Alec Stock – *Fulham*
Recently my coach underwent a course on attacking football run by the FA. He didn't see a goal scored all week: *1973*

Terry Venables – *(b 1943) Barcelona & Spurs*
If history is going to repeat itself, I should think we can expect the same thing again.

Certain people are for me, certain people are pro me.

I felt a lump in my throat as the ball went in.

CHAIRMEN

Gilbert Blades – *Lincoln City*
It wasn't so much the death threats or the vandalism, but when you sit with your family in the Directors' Box and hear a couple of thousand chanting, 'Gilbert Blades is a wanker!' then you feel it's time to resign: *1983*

Ernie Clay – *Fulham*
The Super League idea has about as much chance of getting through as there is of Arthur Scargill admitting he needs a wig: *1982*

The Cobbold family – *Norwich City*
Of course we're going to continue in Europe. How else can we get our duty-free cigarettes?:
John Cobbold (1973)

You ask what constitutes a crisis here. Well, if we ran out of white wine in the boardroom:
Patrick Cobbold (1982)

Jimmy Guthrie – *Chairman of the Football & Trainers' Association*
After whisky, footballers have been the favourite and most expensive export from Scotland to England.

MEDIA

John Arlott – *(b 1914) writer & commentator*
Football can be no more than a minor corner of any balanced life. Within that corner, however, it can be roundly satisfying.

N. J. Dixon – *sportswriter*
Just before the end O'Donnell banged a fierce shot against the underside of the crossbar and an eagle-eyed linesman announced that a goal had been scored. Arsenal could hardly have been more indignant had they been told the goal counted four, that Preston had won the match, the championship, the FA Cup, the Doggetts Coat and Badge, and the Open Championship, and that the Arsenal team would have to carry their bags to the station:
Manchester Guardian (c 1930)

Geoffrey Green – *sportswriter*
Poor Fulham, with no real method up front, resembled a fire engine hurrying to the wrong fire.

Di Stefano was manufactured on earth, Pele was made in Heaven.

Rachael Heyhoe-Flint – *(b 1939) England Ladies cricket captain*
On her new job, as PR officer, with a struggling Wolves team – It's a bit like joining the Titanic in mid-voyage: 1985

Jimmy Hill – *(b 1928) TV presenter*
What makes this game so delightful is that when both teams get the ball they are attacking their opponents' goal.

Peter Jones – *(1930–90) radio commentator*
Sporting Lisbon in their green and white hoops, looking like a team of zebras.

Peter Lorenzo – *TV commentator*
Harlow Town are in their infancy compared to other giant-killing giants.

Hodge scored for Forest after only twenty-two seconds, totally against the run of play.

Desmond Lynam – *(b 1942) TV sports presenter*
Chesterfield 1, Chester 1. Another score draw there in that local derby.

Roger McGough – *Liverpool poet*
I'd be bisexual if I had time for sex 'Cos it's Goodison one week and Anfield the next: *'Footy poem'*

Arthur Marshall – *(1910–89) journalist & author*
I would have thought that the knowledge that you are going to be leapt upon by half-a-dozen congratulatory, but sweaty team-mates would be inducement not to score a goal.

Archie MacPherson – *TV commentator*
Queen's Park v Forfar; you can't get more romantic than that.

Brian Moore – *TV commentator*
The news from Guadalajara, where the temperature is 96 degrees, is that Falcao is warming up.

The European Cup is seventeen pounds of silver and it's worth its weight in gold.

John Motson – *TV commentator*
The World Cup – truly an international event.

Jim Murray – *US sportswriter*
Soccer is a game in which everyone does a lot of running around. Twenty-one guys stand around and one guy does a tap dance with the ball. It's about as exciting as Tristan and Isolde: 1967

Alan Parry – *TV commentator*
With the last kick of the game, Bobby MacDonald scored a header.

Mike Royko – *US sportswriter*
When you talk about international soccer competition you are talking about mayhem, mauling and stomping. First they announce the final score, then they give you the body count: 1988

Percy Rudd – *writer*
The time has come, the Walrus said, To talk of football pools, Of fixture lists and copyright, Of clever men and fools: *News Chronicle*

LITERARY

Anon
And sometimes football for the men, To try their strength ten against ten: *An Almanac (1696)*

Lord Baden-Powell – *(1857–1941) founder of the Boy Scout movement*
Football, in itself, is a grand game for developing a lad physically and also morally, for he learns to play with good temper and unselfishness, to play in his place and 'play the game', and these are the best of training for any game of life. But it is a vicious game when it draws crowds of lads away from playing the game themselves to be merely onlookers at a few paid performers: *Scouting for Boys (1908)*

Badminton magazine
The artisan differs from the public school man in two important points, he plays to win at all costs and, from the nature of his associations, he steps onto the football field in better training: 1896

Alexander Barclay - *(1475-1552) Scottish poet*
The sturdy plowman, lustie, strong and bold,
Overcometh the winter with driving the foote-
ball,
Forgetting labour and many a grievous fall:
1508

Anthony Burgess - *writer*
Five days shalt thou labour, as the Bible says.
The seventh day is the Lord thy God's. The
sixth day is for football.

Charterhouse school song
I challenge all the men alive
To say they e'er were gladder,
Than boys all striving,
Who should kick most wind out of the bladder:
1794

Geoffrey Chaucer - *(1343-1400) poet*
One rolls along a football to his foes.

Sir William Davenant - *(1606-68) poet & playwright*
Methinks I am stopt by one of your heroic
games, call'd football, which I conceive not very
conveniently civil in the streets, especially in such
irregular and narrow roads as Crooked Lane.

Charles Edwardes - *(1865-1928) writer*
Football is a far more effectual arouser of the
unregenerate passions of mankind than either a
political gathering or a race meeting:
The New Football Mania (1892)

Sir Thomas Elyot - *(1499-1546) diplomat & writer*
Footballe was a pastime to be utterly objected
by all noble men, the game giving no pleasure,
but beastlie furie and violence.

Robert Greene - *(1558-92) dramatist*
Within thy cap 'tis thou shalt weare my glove,
at football sport, thou shalt my champion be:
1587

Elizabeth Hogg - *writer*
Miry gladiators whose sole purpose in life is to
position a surrogate head between two poles:
1979

Alfred E. Housman - *(1859-1936) poet*

Twice a week the winter through
Here I stood to keep the goal:
Football then was fighting sorrow
For the young man's soul:
A Shropshire Lad

Francois Misson - *(1650-1722) French travel writer*
In winter football is a useful and charming
exercise. It is a leather ball about as big as one's
head, filled with wind. This kick'd about from
one to t'other end in the streets, by him that
can get it, and that is all the art of it:
Memoirs of Travels in England (1697)

L. E. Mongiardino
Never on the football field,
To the foreman shall we yield.
Never shall we cravens be,
Cravens ne'er win victory.

Thomas Naogeorgus - *(1511-63) poet*
To play they go, to casting of the stone,
To runne or shoote.
To toss the light and windy ball aloft
With hand or foote.

Norman Nicholson - *poet*
Red-headed footballer, four-foot tall,
Chalking his goal on the back-yard wall.

George Orwell - *(1903-50) writer & critic*
During the between-war years the football
pools did more than any one thing to make life
bearable for the unemployed.

Samuel Pepys - *(1633-1703) diarist*
The streets were full of footballs:
2 January 1665

J. B. Priestley - *(1894-1984) playwright*
To say that men paid their shillings to watch
twenty-two hirelings kick a ball is merely to say
that a violin is wood and catgut, that Hamlet is
so much paper and ink.

Frederic Raphael - *(b 1931) US novelist & playwright*
As soon as soccer became the so-called
'national sport', the whole idea of a game that
was played for its own sake among people who
understood each other went by the board: *1973*

Vidal Sassoon – *hair stylist*
Soccer has elements of both ballet and chess:
1979

Sir Walter Scott – *(1771–1832) Scottish poet & dramatist*
Then strips lads and to it, though sharp be
the weather,
And if, by mischance, you should happen to
fall,
There are worse things in life than a tumble on
the heather,
And life is itself but a game at football.

Scottish Athletic Journal
That Association Football is becoming
notorious for scenes and disgraceful exhibitions
of ruffianism. The rabble will soon make it
impossible for law-abiding citizens to attend
matches: *1887*

William Shakespeare – *(1564–1616) playwright*
Am I so round with you as you with me.
That like a football you do spurn me thus?:
Comedy of Errors

Your base foot-ball player: *King Lear*

James Shirley – *(1596–1666) poet*
Your Lordship, may make one at foot-ball, 'tis
all the sport now-a-days: *1633*

Sir Philip Sidney – *(1554–86) poet & statesman*
A tyme there is for all,
My mother often sayes,
When she, with skirt tuck't very high,
With girls at football playes.

Phillip Stubbes – *(1555–91) puritan*
For as concerning football playing. I protest
unto you it may be rather called a friendlie
kinde of fyghte than a play or recreation, a
bloody or murmuring practise than a fellowly
sporte or pastime.

John Webster – *(1580–1625) dramatist*
Like a wild Irish, I'll nere thinke thee dead.
'Till I can play at football with thy head:
The White Devil

Oscar Wilde – *(1854–1900) Irish dramatist & humorist*
Football is all very well as a game for rough
girls, but it is hardly suitable for delicate boys.

GOLF

GENERAL

Anon
The true definition of a golfer is one who
shouts 'Fore', takes five, and puts down a three.

A golf ball is a small object that remains on the
tee while a perspiring citizen fans it vigorously
with a large club.

An amateur golfer is a man who moves heaven
and earth whilst playing golf.

A golf player is someone who can drive 70 miles
an hour in heavy traffic with perfect ease; but
blows up on a two foot putt if somebody
coughs.

A Scotsman is the only golfer not trying to hit
the ball out of sight.

The average suburbanite either putters around
the house or the golf course.

The difference between learning to play golf
and learning to drive a car is that in golf you
never hit anything.

A well-adjusted man is one who can play golf as
if it were a game.

The real test of golf – and life – is not keeping
out of the rough, but getting out after we are in.

A sports encyclopaedia says there are 300 kinds
of games played with balls. There are more
than that played with golf balls alone.

Your bad days at golf are not at all serious to your fellow players. If anything, each of your bad shots builds the other fellow's ego.

Few people carry a heavy burden farther than a golf caddie.

When you are playing golf, nothing counts like your opponent.

When ground rules permit a golfer to improve his lie, he can either move his ball or change the story about his score.

Golf is a lot of walking, broken up by disappointment and bad arithmetic.

Golf liars have one advantage over fishing liars – they don't have to show anything to prove it.

Nothing handicaps you so much in golf as honesty.

In golf the ball usually lies poorly, but the player well.

Any golfer can be devout on a rainy Sunday.

A Jewish golfer plays orthodox golf – he never drives on Saturday.

Old golfers never die – they simply lose their drive.

Proverbs
All is fair in love and golf: *American*

Sayings
It'll take three damn good shots to get up in two today: *Old caddie's saying*

Traditional
Oh! The dirty little pill
Went rolling down the hill
And rolled right into a bunker.
From there to the green,
I took thirteen,
And then, by God, I sunk her!

PROFESSIONAL

BRITISH

Henry Cotton
I firmly believe that baseball, with its horizontal throwing and batting action, is the best preparation if one thinks of other sports as good training for golf.

Henry Cotton wore Savile Row clothes and silk monogrammed shirts. He drove a large motor car, which he had a tendency to park opposite a sign saying 'No parking':
Henry Longhurst – commentator

W. J. Cox
If you could putt as straight as you drive, you would hole a hell of a lot more putts.

Nick Faldo
He has developed the best swing since Tarzan:
Colin M. Jarman – sportswriter (1988)

Tony Jacklin – *(b 1944)*
I know of no recreation which is a better character builder than golf.

John Jacobs
One reason why golf can become such a difficult game is simply because there are so many different ways of playing it correctly; and the one secret, for any golfer striving to improve, is to decide first which is his or her own correct way.

Ernest Jones – *coach*
Those who think in terms of golf being a science, have unfortunately tried to part from each other the arms, head, shoulders, body, hips and legs. They turn a golfer into a worm cut into bits, with each part wriggling in every-which-way direction – this is 'paralysis by analysis'.

Andra Kirkaldy
You cannot play scratch golf, or better, till you are as full of confidence as an egg is full of meat.

Golf is played as muckle by the heid as by the hand.

To be a great golfer is all very well, but to play the game for the love of it and the good out of it – that's the main thing.

Willy Park Jr
Golf is a fickle game, and must be wooed to be won.

Edward Ray
Golf is a fascinating game. It has taken me nearly forty years to discover that I can't play it!

Harry Vardon
No matter what happens, keep on hitting the ball.

He proves, as no other man does, that golf is an art. The game is a pure joy to him, he makes every shot in such an effortless way:
Andra Kirkaldy

Ian Woosnam
On his anonymity and lack of inches – Perhaps if I dyed my hair peroxide blonde and called myself the 'Great White Tadpole' that would help?:
1978

WORLD
[*US unless otherwise stated*]

Isao Aoki – *Japan*
Eric Sykes – What do you think of my tee shot?
Isao Aoki – Very nice, but sleeves a little long!

Tommy Armour
Golf is an awkward set of bodily contortions designed to produce a graceful result.

Paul Azinger
After finishing second in the British Open – Don't worry about me, it'll make me a better player next year: *1987*

Azinger is wearing an all-black outfit – black jumper, blue trousers, white shoes, and a pink tea cosy: *Renton Laidlaw – British commentator*

Severiano Ballesteros – *(b 1957) Spain*
I have nothing to prove in golf and I do not regret not having as much culture as other people. I shall learn my own way through life.

In the United States, I'm lucky; in Europe, I'm good.

I don't like doctors. They are like golfers. Every one has a different answer to your problem.

On winning the German Open – I played golf today the way Franz Beckenbauer played football for West Germany. Close to perfect:
1988

He was one of the best looking young men in sport. He didn't fall into the blonde-and-boring category of young Americans all trying to look like Johnny Miller: *Ed Barner – manager*

He's a gorilla off the tee. He's out of control, certainly, but that goes with being young:
Billy Casper (1975)

On Seve's US Masters triumph – He was like a Ferrari and made us all look like Chevrolets:
Tom Kite (1980)

He goes after a golf course the way a lion goes after a zebra: *Jim Murray – sportswriter*

Unless his putting stroke deserts him, Seve should become the richest Spaniard since Queen Isabella: *Jim Murray (1976)*

Frank Beard
I've won ten tournaments, and I'd gladly give up any five of those titles to win the Masters. If pressed, I'd probably be willing to give up all ten. That's how much the Masters means.

Homero Blancas
The way I putted, I must've been reading the greens in Spanish and putting them in English:
1970

Gay Brewer
Sounds like a fag winemaker from Modesto:
Jimmy Demaret

Billy Casper Jr
Golfers are the greatest worriers in the world of sports. In fast-action sports, like football, baseball, or tennis, there is little time to worry compared to the time a golfer has on his hands between shots.

Ray Floyd
On winning the US Open – I finally got me an Open. I don't think my career would have been complete without an Open: *1986*

Hubert Green
Ninety-five percent of putts which finish short don't go in.

Hubert Green was so ugly when he was a baby, that his mother tied a pork chop around his neck to get the dog to play with him:
Larry Ziegler

Walter Hagen – *(1892–1969)*
Amateurs are always short.

Dave Hill
Nothing compares to the thrill of hitting golf shots. That's it. That's all I want to do. I don't care about major titles. I don't care about publicity. I don't care if anybody remembers me or not. When I die, they can throw me in a pine box and forget me: *1970*

Ben Hogan – *(b 1912)*
When you played Hogan, he never walked for the left or right of the fairway, he walked down the centre of the fairway. He never missed a shot: *Roberto de Vicenzo – Argentina*

Ben has probably hit more good shots and fewer bad shots than any man in history:
Jack Nicklaus

Ben Hogan was the greatest striker of the ball that ever existed, and although he was never a great putter he still won tournaments by the length of a street: *Chris Plumridge*

Nobody ever covered the flag like Ben Hogan:
Gene Sarazen

In a game like cricket, every bad shot you hit, you are liable to get out, whereas it is possible to play golf, and in fact win, by hitting an awful lot of bad shots if somehow you make up for them with spectacular recoveries or fantastic putting. But Hogan would play a whole tournament, sometimes for four days, without a single bad shot: *Peter Thompson – Australia*

Hale S. Irwin

When asked what his middle initial stood for – Sometimes it stands for Stupid, sometimes it stands for Smart.

Robert T. 'Bobby' Jones – *(1902–71)*
I admit that eighteen holes constitutes a round of golf. But since this came about by accident rather than design, the fact supplies no reason why eighteen holes should be accepted as an adequate test in important competition.

One reason golf is such an exasperating game is that a thing learned is so easily forgotten and we find ourselves struggling year after year with faults we had discovered and corrected time and time again.

To my knowledge, I have never taken a golf tournament casually. It did not make sense to me to travel 3000 miles for a 'lark'. It is nothing new or original to say that golf is played one stroke at a time. But it took me many years to realise it.

There are two distinct types of golf. Golf – the plain variety – is the most delightful of games, an enjoyable, companionable pastime; tournament golf is thrilling, heart-breaking, terribly hard work – a lot of fun when you are young with nothing much on your mind, but fiercely punishing in the end.

Never should I knowingly discourage any man from trying to learn to swing a golf club correctly, for I think the game is well worth whatever effort one may make towards this end.

Bobby Jones stands to the ball, as if engaged in conversation: *Anon*

What we talk about here is not the hero as golfer, but that something Americans hungered for; the best performer in the world who was also the hero as human being, the gentle, wholly self-sufficient male:
Alistair Cooke – writer

An uncomplicated man, who simply stands up and gives it one:
Henry Longhurst – British commentator

The flavour of the Masters reflects the personality of Robert Tyre Jones Jnr, and Bob

has always epitomised the best in golf:
Gene Sarazen

Herman Keiser
It's no fun to watch me play. In fact, it's
painful: *1946*

Tom Kite
Golf is not like tennis, or basketball, or football,
where you can control your opponent. With
golf you cannot control your opponent: *1986*

Bernard Langer - *West Germany*
There's no word for it; the Germans don't have
'yips'.

Tony Lema
Where else can a man advance on pure and
simple ability, where only scores, not office
politics, or friends in the right places count?

A good teaching professional can teach a young
man to hit a golf ball with a stick pretty near
perfectly every time. But how do you teach that
man to hit that tiny ball with a long whippy
stick when 15,000 people are jammed around
him like a crowd at a six-alarm fire, and a
quarter of a million dollars is riding on the next
shot that he hits?

Bobby Locke
Bobby Locke was a golfer with an amazingly
even temperament. He did everything quietly
and in slow-motion:
Peter Thompson - Australia

Mark McNulty - *Zimbabwe*
After shooting 59 in the German Open - It's every
golfer's dream to break 60 and I've got a watch
to prove it: *1985*

Dave Marr
At my first Masters, I got the feeling that if I
didn't play well, I wouldn't go to heaven.

Steve Melnyk
On his first pro tour - I'm surprised that a lot of
the pros don't seem more intelligent than they
do about anything other than golf: *1969*

Cary Middlecoff
A golf game doesn't end until the last putt
drops.

Johnny Miller
The best thing that ever happened to me was
coming second in the 1971 Masters. I couldn't
have coped if I had won.

You've got to turn yourself into a material as
soft as putty, and then just sort of slop the
clubhead through. You'll hit much farther and
with less effort.

Jack Nicklaus - *(b 1940)*
Golf is not and never has been a fair game.

Putting is the least manly thing in golf, and
therefore, when a player gets older and he does
not win as much, he blames it on his putting.
He does not want to admit that his power may
be leaving him.

I'll be honest about it, I want to win more than
Bobby Jones. That's what you play for - to
separate yourself from the crowd: *1971*

After winning his sixth US Masters, aged 46 - It
would be the smartest thing to quit now. But
I'm not that smart: *1986*

Book title - Jack on my Back:
Andrea Angela - caddie

I'm not fit to lace Jack Nicklaus' shoes:
Hubert Green

I like the idea of playing with Nicklaus. Jack
plays golf just the way I'd like to:
Steve Melnyk (1970)

When Nicklaus plays well he wins, when he
plays badly he comes second. When he's
playing terribly, he's third: *Johnny Miller*

It's one thing to beat the young guys, but when
you beat Jack Nicklaus on national television, it
is real sweet: *Johnny Miller (1983)*

*After Nicklaus had won the 1962 US Open, from
five strokes back, Arnold Palmer warned* - Now
that the Big Bear's out of the cage, everybody
better run for cover.
To which Nicklaus replied - I'm hungry as a bear.
But I'm gonna slim down and go for gold.
[*And so the legend of the Golden Bear was born*]

Greg Norman ['The Great White Shark'] – *Australia*
I owe a lot to my parents – especially my mother and father.

Commenting on 'fishy tales' that Norman went shark shooting – I don't mind playing golf with Greg Norman, but I'll be damned if I'll go swimming with him: *Lee Trevino*

Mac O'Grady
One minute the sword [putter] is making you king, the next it is lacerating you.

Arnold Palmer – *(b 1929)*
Golf is deceptively simple, endlessly complicated. A child can play it well and a grown man can never master it. It is almost a science, yet it is a puzzle with no answer.

Golfers today learn to hit hard and long before they learn any other aspect of the game.

On being asked if his play-off loss in the 1966 US Open was similar to two previous play-off losses in 1962 & 1963 – It was pretty damn similar – I lost all three!: *1966*

Palmer lashes into the ball with such explosive force that he almost falls off the tee after his follow-through. The word 'caution' is not in his vocabulary: *Billy Casper (1967)*

If ever I needed an eight foot putt, and everything I owned depended on it, I would want Arnold Palmer to putt for me: *Bobby Jones*

Arnold Palmer is going to be a great player. When he hits the ball the earth shakes: *Gene Littler (1954)*

Palmer has a deep affection for golf courses, a love of them, if you like. He wants courses to fight back at him and considers them gallant opponents: *Mark McCormack – managing agent*

Being paired with Arnold Palmer is like a two-shot penalty: *John Schlee (1973)*

Palmer hitched up his baggy pants and turned golf into a game of 'Hit it hard, go find it and hit it hard again': *John Schulian – sportswriter*

Arnold Palmer was everyone's hero, a common guy who hitched his pants and let his shirt-tail flap in the breeze, a man who came from behind to win: *Lee Trevino*

Arnie would go for the flag from the middle of an alligator's back: *Lee Trevino*

'Deacon' Palmer – *Arnold's father*
90 per cent of golf is played from the shoulders up.

Calvin Peete
Who wants to chase a little ball around under the hot sun?

Gary Player – *(b 1935) South Africa*
I'm an athlete, I can go 72 holes in a day if I have to.

Where did the ball go? There must be a hole in this green!

It's funny, but the more I practice, the luckier I become.

The average weekend golfer is far too greedy.

Chi-Chi Rodriguez – *Puerto Rico*
The last time I played Augusta, I was listed as a foreign player. Then they found out that Puerto Rico was part of the United States.

The Masters' green coat plays castanets with your knees.

I'm playing like Tarzan – and scoring like Jane.

I once hit a drive 500 yards. On a par three hole. I had a three wood coming back.

On his 120lb physique – Some people say that golf pros are athletes. How the hell can you call me an athlete?

Gene Sarazen – *(b 1902)*
The fellows today play too much golf. They burn themselves out. And on their tombstones it says: 'Here lies a millionaire. The downhill putts got him': *1970*

If a player hasn't got a good grip – he has two chances; slim and none.

After beating Hagen in a World Challenge match despite suffering from appendicitis – A sick appendix is not as difficult to deal with as a five-foot putt: 1922

Gene Sarazen just tears the ball through the wind as if it did not exist:
Bernard Darwin – British writer

The boldness of Gene Sarazen's play leaves him no middle ground. He has to go for the flag: *Bobby Jones*

Horton Smith
Too much is done with too little thought, it must be mind over putter.

Sam Snead – *(b 1912)*
The only reason I ever played golf in the first place was so I could afford to hunt and fish.

To baseball player Ted Williams – If you hit a 'foul ball' in golf you have to go and play it.

Sam Snead did to the tee-shot what Roger Bannister did to the four-minute mile:
Byron Nelson

Like classic plays and symphonies, Sam Snead doesn't just belong to a generation. His mark will be left on golf for an eternity:
Peter Thompson – Australia

Craig 'The Walrus' Stadler
I wish they would start talking about the quality of my golf, not my wardrobe; print my score, not my measurements.

Payne Stewart
Payne Stewart has developed an infinite capacity for self- destruction: *Ben Wright*

Dick Stockton
Everyone complains about his own putting, but Dick Stockton doesn't know how dangerously he's living when he moans. He's such a great putter, someday someone's gonna hit him in the head with a club: *Dan Sikes*

Walter Travis
I always visualise my putting stroke as an attempt to drive an imaginary tack into the back of a ball.

Lee Trevino – *(b 1939)*
Golf isn't just my business, it's my hobby.

I'm hitting the driver so good, I gotta dial the operator for long distance after I hit it.

I am not saying my golf game went bad, but if I grew tomatoes they'd come up sliced.

They say I'm famous for my delicate chip shots. Sure, when I hit 'em right, they land, just so, like a butterfly with sore feet.

I've stopped practising, I've stopped worrying and I've got a new wife who travels with me. If I get any happier, I've got to be in heaven.

I swing the way I used to swing, but the ball is going in a different direction.

I really appreciate Lee Trevino Drive, it's the only street in El Paso I can spell.

There are two things that don't last long – dogs that chase cars and pros that putt for pars.

They say, 'Trevino is wondering whether to play a five- or six-iron to the green', when all the time I'm gazing at some broad in the third row of the gallery, wondering where my wife is.

After winning the US Open – Yesterday, I was a poor Mexican. From now on I'm going to be a rich Spaniard: 1968

On what he might do with his $30,000 prize-money – I may buy the Alamo and give it back to Mexico.

After seeing the Alamo – I'm not going to buy this place, it doesn't have any inside plumbing.

Caddies are a breed of their own. If you shoot a 66, they'll say, 'Man, we shot a 66!' But go out and shoot 77 and they'll say, 'Hell, he shot a 77!'

On Herman Mitchell [his heavyweight caddie] – I always know which side a putt will break, it slopes towards the side of the green Herman is standing.

I was twenty before I realised that Manual

Labour wasn't a Mexican.

If my IQ had been two points lower, I'd have been a plant somewhere.

He has the gift, unusual among top sportsmen, for the bon mot, and his delivery is that of an ace comedian:

John Ballantine – British writer (1970)

Roberto de Vicenzo – *Argentina*
If everybody play safe, your chances will be the same as everybody else's. You must play different. You must forget everybody else and hit the ball.

I learn English from American pros, that is why I speak so bad. I call it PGA English.

Lanny Wadkins
Put a pin in the middle of a lake and Lanny Wadkins will still 'attack' it: *John Mahaffey*

Tom Watson – *(b 1949)*
British galleries understand the game, and are very respectful. In my opinion, it's the last civilised country left in the world: *1983*

My golf swing is like ironing a shirt. You get one side smoothed out, turn it over and there is a big wrinkle on the other side. You iron that side, turn it over and there's another wrinkle:

1987

Tom Weiskopf
Golf has never been and never will be the most important part of my life.

I'm the Ilie Nastase of golf. If golf didn't have a player like me it would be a dreary sport.

Bert Yancey
Everything before the Masters is just shadow-boxing, I never feel like playing golf until I get there: *1970*

WOMEN
[*US unless otherwise stated*]

Joanne Carner
After finishing second in the US Women's Open, after being 115th after the first round – I did something by climbing over 113 golfers. The only trouble is there were 114 ahead of me:

1983

Henry Cotton – *Great Britain*
Golf to my mind is a game for the ladies to enjoy. I think that when it becomes a job they have to want to win very badly and, as a result, they can become tough, even bitchy.

Nancy Lopez
Her looks are just perfect for the part. Arnold Palmer was attractive and virile. Nancy Lopez is attractive and vibrant:

Frank Deford – sportswriter

It's not just that Nancy Lopez is pretty, it's that she is pretty in everything she does:

Betsy Rawls

Marley Spearman
Practice, with all its intrinsic disciplines, is a wonderful part of the sport. You can give yourself so much more than just a good round of golf.

Jan Stephenson
After winning the US Women's Open – Maybe people will stop thinking of me only as a sex symbol and realise I can really play golf: *1983*

Louise Suggs
If a woman can walk, she can play golf.

Mildred 'Babe' Zaharias – *(1914–56)*
It was not too unusual for me to get tee-shots of 280–300 yards or more. The other women did not slug the ball that way. In women's golf today you've got to have that distance. You've got to be a slugger as well as a swinger.

On her driving style – I just loosen my girdle and let 'er rip.

COURSES

Augusta, Georgia
Augusta is the only course I know where you choke when you come in the gate:

Lionel Herbert

There is no tougher course than Augusta when your game starts to go: *Tony Jacklin*

On designing the Augusta course – Two things were essential. First, there must be a way around for those unwilling to attempt the carry; and, second there must be a definite reward awaiting the man who makes it. Without the alternative route the situation is unfair. Without the reward it is meaningless:

Bobby Jones

On the opening of the Augusta course – I hope it is perfect, for it is both easy and tough; there isn't a hole out there that can't be birdied if you just think; there isn't one that can't be bogeyed if you stop thinking: *Bobby Jones*

Augusta is just not my kind of course. With my game, I can't play there. They can invite me all they want, but I'm not going there any more:

Lee Trevino (1969)

Chaska, USA
After the US Open – All you need is eighty acres of corn and some cows: *Dave Hill (1970)*

Jean Giradoux – *(1882–1944) French dramatist & diplomat*
A golf course is the epitome of all that is purely transitory in the universe, a space not to dwell in, but to get over as quickly as possible: *1933*

Bobby Jones – *USA*
Golf is a game that is played on a five inch course – the distance between the ears.

Royal Dornoch, Scotland
Remember the maxim for all you are worth, If you scuff with your iron, you put back the turf: *Sign*

Royal St George's, Kent
Playing Royal St George's is like trying to read the mind of a beautiful woman. It can be difficult but never onerous. It is for reading, not bashing. You can be in the soup at St George's, but it is delicious: *William Deedes*

St Andrew's, Scotland
I could take out of my life everything except my experiences at St Andrew's and I would still have a rich, full life. *Bobby Jones*

There are three British Opens – the one played in Scotland, the one played in England, and the one played at St Andrew's: *Jack Nicklaus*

One can feel so lonely at St Andrew's missing a putt: *Jack Nicklaus*

Gene Sarazen – *(b1902) USA*
When someone tells me his new course measures more than 7,000 yards, it is usually said with the pride of a new father, as if distance, or wasting of land, is something to boast about.

Sir Walter Simpson – *writer*
The vital thing about a hole is that it should either be more difficult than it looks or look more difficult than it is. It must never be what it looks.

Sir Osbert Sitwell – *(1892–1969) poet*
A golf course outside a big town serves an excellent purpose in that it segregates, as though a concentration camp, all the idle and idiot well-to-do.

Troon, Scotland
Someone once said that nobody 'murders' Troon. The way I played in the Open they couldn't even arrest me for second degree manslaughter: *Lee Trevino (1973)*

MEDIA

Peter Alliss – *TV commentator*
All games are silly, but golf, if you look at it dispassionately, goes to extremes.

You couldn't really find two more completely different personalities than these two – Tom Watson and Brian Barnes – one the complete golf professional, the other the complete professional golfer.

O. K. Bovard – *US editor*
Golf is 'Cow-pasture pool'.

Arthur Daley – *(1904–74) US sportswriter*
Golf is like a love affair. If you don't take it seriously, it's no fun; if you do take it seriously, it breaks your heart.

Bernard Darwin – *sportswriter*
Golf is not a funeral, though both can be very sad affairs.

No castles tower higher and more glittering in the air than golfing castles.

Peter Dobereiner - *(b 1925) sportswriter*
Acquiring a new set of golf clubs is rather like getting married. The honeymoon is wonderful, but how things go after that depend on whether the courtship has properly tested the true compatibility of partners.

Dan Jenkins - *US sportswriter*
The devoted golfer is an anguished soul who has learned a lot about putting, just as an avalanche victim has learned about snow:
1962

Frank Keating - *(b 1937) sportswriter*
Golf - indeed all sport - retains an eye-lowered reverence, a religious solemnity, when the hushed talk gets round to Augusta's green jacket.

Andra Kirkaldy
What golf-writers call 'temperament' - I just call common-sense.

Henry Longhurst - *MP, journalist & TV commentator*
A golf shot entails merely hitting a half-volley straight back to the bowler without giving a catch.

Angus MacVicar - *sportswriter*
Where would the excitement be in life or golf, without the factor of luck?

Golf is a game in which you are alone with your creator.

Paul O'Neill - *US sportswriter*
Golf is essentially an exercise in masochism conducted outdoors:
1962

Grantland Rice - *(1880-1954) US sportswriter*
Golf gives you an insight into human nature. Your own as well as your opponents.

Sports Illustrated - *US magazine*
If the weather is too hot for a flannel jacket, it is too hot for golf:
Editorial (1901)

AMATEUR

Captain Beefheart - *US musician*
Earth - God's golf ball.

John Betjeman - *(1904-84) Poet Laureate*
Now they lie in centuries of sand, beside the church. Less pitiable are they than the corpse of a large golfer only four weeks dead.

Al Boliska - *US humorist*
Have you ever noticed what golf spells backwards?

Patrick Campbell - *writer*
My back swing off the first tee had put him in mind of an elderly woman of dubious morals trying to struggle out of a dress too tight around the shoulders.

Of all the tools in a golfer's sack, none is as personal to him as the putter.

James Cantlie - *(1851-1926) Scottish physician & writer*
The game of golf fulfills the axioms laid down for a perfect exercise - a walk with an object:
Physical Efficiency (1906)

G. K. Chesterton - *(1874-1936) novelist*
I regard golf as an expensive way of playing marbles.

Winston Churchill - *(1874-1965) Prime Minister*
An ineffectual attempt to direct an uncontrollable sphere into an inaccessible hole with instruments ill-adapted to the purpose.

Henry Cooper - *(b 1934) heavyweight boxer*
Funny game golf, especially the way I play it.

Harry L. 'Bing' Crosby - *(1904-77) US singer*
I never sing on the golf course - that would be too conspicuous. At golf, I only allow myself to whistle:
1976

His last words - That was a great game of golf:
1977

John Cunningham
Golf is a game in which a ball - one and half

inches in diameter – is placed on a ball – 8,000 miles in diameter. The object being to hit the small ball, but not the larger.

Frank Dane – *US comedian*
Work is the thing that interferes with golf.

G. R. Devereaux
Don't sound the 'l' in golf; speak of it as goff, not gauff.

Bill Duncan
Don't trust little putts until you've sunk 'em;
De mortis nil nisi . . . is all bunkum.

Aubrey 'Abba' Eban – *(b 1921) Israeli diplomat*
Golf has given me an understanding of the futility of life.

Farmer's Almanac
If you can't break 85, you have no business on the golf course. If you can break 85, you probably have no business: *1966*

B. C. Forbes – *epigrammist*
Golf is an ideal diversion, but a ruinous disease.

Michael Green – *writer*
If you can drive further with a putter than a wood, then by all means do so.

The number of shots taken by an opponent who is out of sight is equal to the square root of the sum of the number of curses heard plus the number of swishes.

George Greenwood – *(1881–1953) civil servant*
Golf is the most skilful of all games; it has baffled mankind for centuries and because of its inherent qualities and subtleties, will continue to do so for all-time.

Nubar Gulbenkian – *(1896–1972) philanthropist*
It is more satisfying to be a bad player at golf. The worse you play, the better you remember the occasional good shot: *1972*

Joachim Heinrich
A golf cart is a method of transporting clubs, that has one advantage – it can't count.

John Hogben
It seems that the most reticent of men on other subjects no sooner takes to golf than eloquence descends on him.

Bob Hope – *(b 1903) US comedian*
If you watch a game, it's fun. If you play it, it's recreation. If you work at it, it's golf.

If I'm on the course and lightning starts, I get inside fast. If God wants to play through, let him.

Horizons magazine
Golfers blame fate for other accidents, but feel personally responsible for a hole in one.

George Houghton – *cartoonist*
The hardest thing to learn about golf is keeping quiet about it.

Colin Ingleby-McKenzie – *Hampshire cricket captain*
Golf is a game to be played between cricket and death.

Samuel Johnson – *(1709–84) lexicographer*
A game in which you claim the privileges of age, and retain the playthings of childhood.

Michael 'Air' Jordan – *(b 1963) US basketball player*
I never thought I'd play golf, I thought it was a sissy game.
[*He now plays off a handicap of 5*]

Joe Laurie Jnr – *US humorist*
Magellan went round the world in 1512 – which isn't too many strokes when you consider the distance.

Stephen Leacock – *(1869–1944) Canadian humorist & scientist*
Golf may be played on Sunday, not being a game within the view of the Law, but being a form of moral effort.

Joe E. Lewis – *(b 1926) US comedian*
I play in the low 80's, if it's any hotter than that, I won't play.

Eric Linklater – *(1899–1974) Scottish novelist*
All I have against it is, that it takes you so far

from the clubhouse.

Arnold Lunn – *(1888-1974) author*
If the golfer's object was merely to sink the ball in the hole, he could walk around the course with a bag of golf balls and drop each one in.

Robert Lynd – *(1879-1949) Anglo-Irish essayist*
It is almost impossible to remember how tragic a place this world is when one is playing golf.

Charles MacDonald – *(1855-1939) Scottish writer*
When you come to play golf ye maun hae a heid!

Norman Mair
Given that he understands the game, customs and courtesies, the bad player can play with acceptance alongside the good, because golf so lends itself to handicapping.

Arthur Marshall – *(1910–89) journalist & author*
Golf – Hockey at the halt: *1985*

Groucho Marx – *(1895-1977) US comedian*
When asked if he would like to play Hamlet - Not unless he gives me a stroke a hole.

Thomas Mathison – *poet*
On Fame's triumphant wings his name shall sour
Till Time shall end, or Golfing be no more:
                                    The Goff (1763)

Henry L. Mencken – *(1880–1956) US journalist & critic*
If I had my way, any man guilty of golf would be ineligible for any office of trust in the United States.

A. A. Milne – *(1882-1956) writer*
Golf is so popular simply because it is the best game in the world at which to be bad.

Frank Muir – *(b 1920) writer & broadcaster*
Any golfer whose ball hits a seagull shall be said to have scored a 'birdie'.

Ogden Nash – *(1902-71) US poet & humorist*
The wretched golfer, divot-bound.
Persists in dreams of the perfect round.

And that is why I wander alone,
From tee to green to tee.
For every golfer I've ever known,
Is too good or too bad for me.

The gallery sways like a primitive throng at a ceremony pagan.
And murmurs the names of its ancient gods,
      Ouimet and Jones and Hagen.
The swirls around the gods of today an argumentative chorus;
Can Player match muscle with Nicklaus?
      Can Palmer give weight to Boros?

Geoffrey Nunn
I took up golf for the exercise and all I keep getting is holes-in-one.

Allan Robertson
Stick in, my little mannie, ye'll be a gowfer yet.

Robert Robinson – *(b 1927) TV presenter & writer*
You hit the ball and if it doesn't go far enough you just hit it again, and if that doesn't work, you hit it again, and so on.

Will Rogers – *(1879-1935) US comedian*
Income tax has made more liars out of the American people than golf.

Bertrand Russell – *(1872-1970) philosopher*
The place of the father in the modern suburban family is a very small one, particularly if he plays golf, which he usually does.

George Bernard Shaw – *(1856-1950) Irish playwright & novelist*
Men trifle with their business and their politics, but never trifle with their games. They cannot pretend that they have won when they have lost, nor made a magnificent drive when they foozled it.

The sight of the little children carrying the golf clubs of tourists as a preparation for the life to come.

Sir Walter Simpson – *writer*
A game in which each player has a small hard ball of his own, which he strikes with a stick, with the intention of putting into a hole. Abstractly, he wishes to do this with as few

blows as possible, concretely in fewer than his opponent: *c 1880*

Golf should be a game of real adventure as against an examination of stroke production. It should combine a pleasant form of physical vigour with the problems of the chess-board.

Excessive golf dwarfs the intellect.

Putting becomes attractive in proportion to the skill acquired in it.

Bernard Suits – *essayist*
A good golf swing is simply useless in any other human pursuit.

Freddie Tait
Match-play's the thing; stroke play is no more than rifle shooting.

Mark Twain – *(1835-1910) US novelist*
Golf is a good walk spoiled.

Ira Wallach – *(b 1913) US writer*
Statistics indicate that, as a result of overwork, modern executives are dropping like flies on the nation's golf courses.

H. G. Wells – *(1866-1946) novelist*
The uglier a man's legs are the better he plays golf. It's almost a law.

Robin Williams – *US comedian*
Golf is a game where white men can dress up as black pimps and get away with it: *1986*

P.G. Wodehouse – *(1881-1975) novelist & humorist*
You can't play a really hot game unless you're so miserable that you don't worry over your shots.

Statisticians estimate that crime among good golfers is lower than in any class of community except possibly bishops.

The least thing upset him on the links. He missed short putts because of the uproar of butterflies in the adjoining meadows.

William Wordsworth – *(1770-1850) poet*
Golf is a day spent in a round of strenuous idleness.

GYMNASTICS

Anon
There are certain sports where physical perfection is transferred to a different level into art, the art of eurythmic movement, an art related to ballet. Gymnastics is such a sport.

John Atkinson
Gymnastics is the only true sport. The rest are just Mickey Mouse games. To develop a perfect human body, and have absolute control over its function, then to train it to perform acts that require courage, skill and grace. What could be more basically fine than that?

Adrianne Blue – *writer*
Olga Korbut invented Killer Gymnastics. Nadia Comaneci perfected it.

Nadia Comaneci – *(b 1962) Rumanian multi-Olympic champion [1976 & 1980]*
I was born that way, it was myself. I was gifted, that's all.

Gymnastics does put a young girl at risk – it can cause damage to a developing body.

Suzanne Dando – *British champion [1980]*
Gymnastics is enjoyable until you reach the top level.

Sho Fukushima – *Japan*
We have a centuries-old tradition in the martial arts, in self discipline in physical activity based upon physical strength – that is today expressed in gymnastics.

Arnold Haskel – *writer & dance instructor*
The difference between dancing and acrobatics lies not so much in technique as in state of mind: *1938*

Olga Korbut - *Russian multi-Olympic champion [1972]*
If there had not been a thing as gymnastics, I would have had to invent it because I feel at one with the sport.

Yun Lou - *Chinese Olympic gold medallist [1984]*
On scoring a low 9.20 on the pommel horse - Suit too big. Grabbed pants instead of pommel:
1984

William Meade - *US men's coach*
The mind is perhaps one of the greatest factors in gymnastics; if one cannot control his mind, he can't control his body:
1980

Ron Pickering - *TV commentator*
See that tremendous flexibility of her ankles; they really are an extension of her legs.

Pauline Prestidge - *national gymnastics coach*
The handstand is the gymnast's lifeline: *1978*

Yuriy Titov - *Russian world champion [1962]*
I love gymnastics because I love to fly.

Ian Wooldridge - *sportswriter*
On the Soviet system - I longed to see a gymnasium in Russia where somebody laughed. I longed to see schoolboys sky-larking and fat girls with pigtails doing something hopelessly badly. I longed to see someone dropping in after school for an hour's enjoyment.

HOCKEY

Badminton magazine
The most odious of all games for a woman: *1900*

Mildred Barnes
Hockey is a reaching game: *1969*

Colin M. Jarman - *(b 1958) sportswriter*
Unlike its colder cousin Ice Hockey, modern Field Hockey is played on 'terra firma' - a Latin phrase meaning 'artificial turf': *1988*

HORSE RACING

FLAT

Anon
All the best jockeys are on the ground giving advice to those mounted.

Proverbs
A fool can train a race-horse, but two wise men can't.

Nobody every committed suicide who had a good two-year-old in the barn.

Eddie Arcaro - *(b 1916) US jockey*
My riding career was fired with an ambition to be in the front end as often as possible.

Sir Abe Bailey - *South African politician*
I do not say that all those who go racing are

rogues and vagabonds, but I do say that all rogues and vagabonds seem to go racing.

Jeffrey Bernard - *writer*
You will never see a pretty unattached girl on a racecourse. But you will often see positive gangs of rather unpretty ones. They are the owners or owners' wives.

Racing is really an alfresco drinking club that moves location from day to day.

Robert Benchley - *(1889-1945) US humorist*
At American horse-races I can see the horses at least start. At English horse-races, I never can see the horses at all.

John Betjeman - *(1906-84) Poet Laureate*
Leathery breeches, spreading stables,

Shining saddles left behind,
To the down the spring of horses,
Moving out of sight and mind.

Rintoul Booth - *writer*
Thoroughbreds are superior horses which sneer
at other horses who are not in their 'Who's
Who' - the General Stud Book. Their
telephone numbers are always ex-directory.
They often gather for major social events such
as Ascot when they study one another's clothes
and general turn-out: *1975*

Denise Bourdot - *(b 1952) US jockey*
I don't ride to beat the boys, just to win: *1975*

Maurice Camacho - *US jockey*
Racing is about everybody having a chance:
1985

Viscount Castlerosse [Valentine Browne]
- *(1891-1943) Irish gossip columnist*
How amusing racing would be if it were not for
the horses. They take people's minds off
conversation.

Steve Cauthen - *US jockey*
In this game, you're only as good as your last
ride - just like many think horses are only as
good as their last run: *1981*

I like the horses to pick the bit up. When they
run, they run.

The horse is such a beautiful animal. When
you're on him, in control of him, moving with
him, it is a beautiful feeling.

Even on horseback, where he does his job
better than anyone of his age ever thought of
doing, there is no swagger in Steve Cauthen:
Pete Axthelm - US sportswriter

Cauthen is not just a rider of winners, but a
maker of a horse:
Richard Baerlein - sportswriter

They say Steve Cauthen is 18 and comes from
the Bluegrass country, but I don't believe them
- he's 103 and comes from another planet:
Laz Bazzera - US trainer (1978)

Henry Cecil - *trainer*

I don't suppose God cares very much if you get
done in a race at Wolverhampton.

Fred Darling - *jockey*
Fred Darling was a genius. He would walk
down the yard at night with his little stick
under his arm and all the horses would stand to
attention: *Sir Gordon Richards*

Edgar Degas - *(1834-1917) French artist*
When somebody sells one of my paintings, I feel
as a horse must feel when the beautiful cup is
given to the jockey.

It is doubtful if he could convey the difference
between a two-year-old or three-year-old or
even a stallion, or indeed visualize two horses
fighting out a finish, but when it comes to the
flavour of a false start, or jockeys collecting
their mounts for a race, he was a master:
Oliver Beckett (1982)

Pat Eddery- *jockey*
Autobiography - Pat on the Back

The Epsom Derby
You've got no chance with a race like the
Derby - the bastards are all trying:
Anon head lad (1979)

The Epsom Derby - the blue ribbon of the
track: *Benjamin Disraeli - Prime Minister*

I never rode a Derby that wasn't a bit like a
polo match, only with more horses:
Jack Leach - jockey

On being the first lady to ride in the Derby - As we
ride, the air is blue with all sorts of language:
Joanna Morgan (1979)

The Derby is a national day out for aristocrats
and artisans, gypsies and generals, viscounts
and villains: *Tim Nelligan (1979)*

On his first Derby success, aged 18 - Why all the
fuss? After all, the Derby is just another race!:
Lester Piggott (1954)

It is vulgar to win the Derby two years running:
Lord Weinstock - owner

I won't be happy until a horse owned by a

working man's club wins the Derby:
Lord Wigg - Jockey Club Chairman

It has always been a mystery to me why our
best race should be run on our worst
racecourse: *Julian Wilson - TV presenter*

'Bud' Flanagan - *music hall comedian*
I'm getting to be so big on the turf they are
calling me the 'Aga Cohen'.

Susan Gallier - *stable girl for Clive Brittain*
Forget the Cossacks and the Comanches; the
greatest horsemen in the world are the
Newmarket stable lads: *1988*

Samuel Goldwyn - *(1882-1974) US movie
producer*
My horse was in the lead, coming down the
home stretch, but the caddie fell off.

Clive Graham
The form book should be written in Braille for
the benefit of the stewards.

Gilbet Harding - *(1907-60) broadcaster*
I have no intention of watching undersized
Englishmen perched on horses with matchstick
legs race along courses planned to amuse Nell
Gwynn.

Al Hatiml - *(d 998) Arabian scholar*
Horses win the race not so much by their
vigour, as by the impulse of their riders.

Ernie Hide - *jockey*
Winning a race is ninety-five per cent being on
the best horse in the race: *1975*

Oliver Wendell Holmes Sr - *(1809-94) US
professor*
Every New England deacon ought to see Derby
day to learn what sort of a world he lives in.

Illustrated Sporting and Dramatic News
Horse-racing would not be the exciting
diversion it is unless the horses were, as they
are, bred for the purpose. A match between a
couple of dray horses would have little interest,
except perhaps for the horses involved: *1980*

John Henry - *US Eclipse horse of the year [1981
& 1984]*

John Henry was no prize. He was back at the
knee, ungainly in appearance and had a
disposition to rival Dennis the Menace:
Mel Snowdon - US trainer (1982)

James Lawton - *sportswriter*
Racing is not a place where praise gushes.
Tribute is a rivulet which only gathers force
down the years: *1980*

Jack Leach - *jockey*
A real racehorse should have a head like a lady
and a behind like a cook.

Horses are like people, most of them are fairly
normal.

Doug Marks - *trainer*
I have been everything in racing except a horse.

John Masefield - *(1879-1967) poet*
I have seen flowers come out in stony places,
    And kind things done by men with ugly faces,
And the Gold Cup won by the worst horse at
the races.

Sheikh Mohammed - *first owner to win £1
million in a season [1985]*
Everything has its price - there is no horse that
is priceless.

Of course, I want my horse to win, but if he
can't then I want my brother's to come first.

On his favourite jockey - The one who wins most
races for me.

Robert Morley - *(b 1908) actor and owner*
Racing is like fishing; it's the one that gets
away that fascinates and intrigues: *1975*

I didn't know I had such a valuable horse until
I heard the auctioneer describe him.

Wolfgang A. Mozart - *(1756-91) Austrian
classical music composer*
When I think of a good melodist I think of a
fine race-horse.

Vincent O'Brien - *Irish trainer*
A horse is like a car. He has only got a certain
mileage. The difficulty is to discover the
amount of that mileage.

Ovid – *(43 BC-17 AD) Roman poet*
The valiant horse races best, at the barriers fall,
when he has others to follow and o'er pass.

Competition makes a horse race.

The spirited horse, which will of its own accord
strive to win the race, will run more swiftly if
encouraged.

Samuel Pepys – *(1633-1703) diarist*
This day there is a great throng to Banstead
Downs upon a great horse-race.

Lester Piggott – *(b 1935) jockey*
I still get a kick out of every ride, every winner.
All horses, every race is different. The
challenge is to get it right.

People ask me why I ride with my bottom in
the air. Well, I've got to put it somewhere.

Provided you enjoy it, it gets easier as you get
older.

Good trainers are good to ride for. Bad trainers
make good horses bad. The best trainers make
the easy look easy.

I always dreamt of being a millionaire and a
racing driver.
*[He earned the money and also received ten speeding
tickets in a ten year period]*

Jeremy Tree [trainer] – I've got to speak to my
old school, Lester, and tell them all I know
about racing. What should I tell them?
Lester Piggott – Tell 'em you have got the flu!

On his deafness – The only thing I need to hear
are the horses' hooves behind me.

They say that Lester is mean, but that isn't
true – he's twice as mean as they say. They say
that he's difficult to get along with and that's
not true either – he's impossible. They also say
that he's a great jockey, but that's certainly not
true – he's the best the world will ever see and
the word great doesn't do him justice: *Anon*

Lester's a lovely bloke – he is surrounded by
this mystique and everyone wants to keep it
that way: *Willie Carson*

If I ever won a million on the pools, I'd ring up
Lester and ask him to invest it for me:
Pat Eddery

He gives the impression that if he rode facing
backwards, he would still win the races that
count: *John Hislop – sportswriter (1980)*

He has a face like a well-kept grave:
Jack Leach – jockey

There should be a law against Lester Piggott:
Darrell McHargue– US jockey

Knowing just how far the rules of racing can be
bent was part of Lester's job, a part, I guess,
which gave him special pleasure:
[Lord] John Oaksey – TV presenter

In a perfect world, I would have Lester ride for
me in all the big races, but in none of the
Trials: *Vincent O'Brien (1977)*

The real charm of having Lester ride for you is
that it gets him off the other fellow's horse:
Vincent O'Brien

He relishes every crisp fiver like some rare
jewel, for money is his staff of life and he ekes it
out as sparingly as a man faced with fifty years
of unpensionable retirement:
Bill Rickaby – cousin & jockey

Watch him in the paddock, landing cat-like, not
lumpy on a horse's back:
Brough Scott – TV commentator

Make the journey down to the starting stalls
and see his mastery of what is the most
explosive athletic moment in the whole
landscape of sport: *Brough Scott*

With other jockeys you can have a joke or laugh
about a girl in the morning paper. Not Lester.
You can only ask him questions like 'Do you
ride that two-year-old at Chester next week?':
Bill Williamson – jockey

Jenny Pitman – *National Hunt trainer*
Flat racing? No thanks. They're like battery
hens – if they don't lay so many eggs they've
had their chips.

Sir Gordon Richards – *jockey*
Mother always told me my day was coming, but I never realised I'd end up being the shortest knight of the year.

In my life I have had four 'greats' – Abernant, Petite Etoile, Crepello and Sir Gordon Richards: *Noel Murless – trainer (1975)*

Robert Robinson – *(b 1927) TV presenter & writer*
While horses are walking you can't tell the difference between me and Nimrod; it's when they start going a bit faster that the fraudulence of my boots and breeches becomes apparent.

'Saki' [H. H. Munro] – *(1870–1916) journalist*
There may have been disillusionments in the lives of the medieval saints, but they would scarcely have been better pleased if they could have foreseen that their names would be associated nowadays chiefly with racehorses and cheaper claret.

Robert Sangster – *(b 1936) 5 times leading owner [1977–84]*
Horseflesh is an international commodity. It is an asset you can always shift: *1977*

Secretariat – *US Eclipse horse of the year [1972 & 1973]*
He looks as if he could jump over a barn:
          Richard Stone Reeves

Secretariat and Riva Ridge are the most famous pair of stablemates since Joseph and Mary:
          Dick Schaap – US sportswriter

Shergar – *Epsom Derby winner [1981]*
On the Derby win – I was a passenger on a very good horse. It was an easy ride:
          Walter Swinburn (1981)

Willie Shoemaker – *(b 1931) US jockey*
More horses are whipped out of the money than into it: *1978*

Slip Anchor – *Epsom Derby winner [1985]*
On the Derby win – It was a nice change for some of us to be identified with a horse that applies the Garbo principle at the right end of the field:
          Hugh McIlvanney – sportswriter (1985)

Christopher Smart – *(1722–71) poet*
Strong is the horse upon his steed;
Strong in pursuit the rapid glede,
Which makes at once his game: *1763*

Mark Twain – *(1835–1910) US writer*
It is a difference of opinion that makes horse races.

Horace Walpole – *(1717–97) Prime Minister*
The world should be postponed for a whore and a horse race.

Geoffrey Wheatcroft – *writer*
It has been said that racing is classless, only in the sense of bringing together the worst elements of every class: *1980*

Bill Williamson – *jockey*
If I was ice-cool, Bill Williamson was deep frozen: *Scobie Breasley – jockey*

Harry Wragg – *trainer*
All jockeys make mistakes, good jockeys make the fewest.

NATIONAL HUNT

The Aintree Grand National
It was a tremendous race, with four finishers out of 30 starters, so by the end there were far more BBC commentators than horses:
          Clive James – writer & humorist (1980)

Bell's Life
Why do the cavalry officers in England and France encourage steeple-chasing amongst their subordinates? Because it excites that courage, presence of mind, and skills in horsemanship without which their glorious achievements of Balaclava or Inkerman would never have been recorded.

Rintoul Booth – *writer*
A hunter needs to be tireless, tubeless, able to gallop on; but more important stop, and find out where are the best gaps, lanes, and pubs which open outside licensing hours: *1975*

When the hunting season comes to an end, usually in the month of March, there begins a round of Hunter Trials. To the uninitiated this might conjure up a courtroom scene: *1975*

Bob Champion – *jockey*
On recovering from cancer – As far as I'm
concerned there was no point in living if I
couldn't be a jockey: *1981*

Cottage Rake – *Cheltenham Gold Cup winner
[1948–50]*
Aubrey's up, the money's down,
The frightened bookies quake.
Come on, my lads, and give a cheer,
Begod, it's Cottage Rake: *Anon*
[*Aubrey was jockey Aubrey Brabazon*]

Dick Francis – *jockey & novelist*
A jump jockey has to throw his heart over the
fence – and then go over and catch it.

John Francome – *jockey*
Being a champion over the sticks isn't a patch
on the same thing on the Flat. It's a different
class, not even second class – more like working
class: *1977*

He was sometimes too outspoken for his own
good. His bluntness could make your eyes
water: *Monty Court (1985)*

David Gandolfo – *trainer*
David Gandolfo is racing's answer to
Shakespeare: *Barry Brogan – jockey*

Adam L. Gordon – *(1833–70) Australian poet*
Here's health to every sportsman, be he
stableman or lord,
If his heart be true, I care not what his pocket
may afford.

Clive James – *writer & humorist*
A loose horse is any horse sensible enough to
get rid of its rider at an early stage and carry on
unencumbered: *1980*

Lord William P. Lennox – *(1799–1881)
Army Officer*
Steeple-chasing is very popular in February,
but we own that it is with much regret that we
find this break-neck pursuit so much in the
ascendancy, for our ideas it cannot come under
the denomination of legitimate sport: *1871*

Gervaise Markham – *(1568–1637) writer*
Again, for infinite labour and long endurance,
which is to be desired in our hunting matches. I

have not seen any horse to compare with the
English. He is of tolerable shape, strong, valiant
and durable: *1607*

Dick Marsh – *official starter at Aintree*
If a man with short leathers is to get safely
round Liverpool, it will be because he is lucky
and flukes are on his side.

'Nimrod' [Charles Appleby] – *(1778–1843)
journalist*
The steeple-chase is the relic of ancient
foolhardiness and cruelty. It is ridden at the
evident hazard of the life of the rider, and
likewise that of the life and enjoyment of the
horse.

Hurdle races, although childish and silly
exhibitions, cannot perhaps come under the
denomination of cruel, but they serve to show
the cruelty of steeple races by the numerous
falls of the horses that contend them.

[Lord] John Oaksey – *TV commentator &
jockey*
In racing to insult a man's horse is worse than
insulting his wife.

There are, they say, fools, bloody fools, and
men who remount in a steeplechase.

George S. Patton Jr – *(1885-1945) US
military officer*
The element of personal risk is not a drawback,
but a decided advantage. No sport, save steeple-
chasing and football, is so good a school in this
respect.

Jenny Pitman – *trainer*
If you want to get rich, Flat racing is your
scene. But if you want to be happy,
steeplechasing is the thing.

If you want to understand the effect of weight
on a horse try running for a bus with nothing in
your hands. Then, try doing it again with your
hands full of shopping. Then, think about doing
that for four and a half miles: *1985*

Red Rum – *Grand National winner [1973, 1974
& 1977]*
The greatest thing on four hooves since
Pegasus: *Jean Rook – columnist*

Sir Walter Scott – *(1771–1832) Scottish novelist & poet*
Woe worth the chase, woe worth the day,
  That costs thy life, my gallant grey.

Sporting Life
In racing reports it is oftentimes said
That a jockey has cleverly won by a head.
But Yates has performed, when other arts fail,
  A more wonderful feat, for he won by a tail.
[*Yates fell off, grabbed the horse's tail, remounted and won the race at Croydon*]

The Times
The swindling, dangerous and absurd practice of steeple-chasing, things merely got up by publicans and horse-dealers to pillage the unwary and enrich themselves: *1838*

RACECOURSES

Ascot
It is scandalous that they allow horses in here!:
                          Anon actress

Ascot is so exclusive that it is the only racecourse in the world where the horses own the people: *Art Buchwald – US writer*

Jumping at Ascot is like Blackpool with the tide out: *John Hislop – sportswriter*

Apart from the still gloriously groomed Royal Drive down the course, Ascot in the last five years, had slumped from a 'My Fair Lady' spectacle into a vulgar and tatty farce:
                Jean Rook – columnist (1983)

Cheltenham
I find it fairly sickening to reflect that one has to be a rugby player of almost international standard to get to the bars:
              Jeffrey Barnard – writer (1979)

Cheltenham race-course is the beauty spot on the rugged face of world steeple-chasing:
          John Trickett – sportswriter (1989)

Epsom
Some people are born in circumstances which resemble being saddled in the enclosure at Epsom when the race is at Ripon:
                      Tom Crabtree

Epsom is the worst and most dangerous course we have: *London News (1864)*

The Downs are very famous for horse-matches as there is not a properer place in the world for this sport: *James Toland (1711)*

Huntingdon
Weighing room – dreadful. Changing room – cold and damp. Bad horses run there. Bad racing, and a bloody awful place to get to. Apart from that, there's nothing wrong with it:
              John Francome – jockey

Towcester
The only racecourse in the country with wooden seats on the toilet: *John Francome*

BETTING

Anon
A racehorse is an animal that can take several thousand people for a ride at the same time.

A very smart lady named Cookie
Said, 'I like to mix business with nookie.
  Before every race
I go home to my place
  And curl up with a very good bookie.'

Nobody has ever bet enough on the winning horse.

Proverbs
He that would have good luck in horses must kiss the parson's wife.

Richard Armour – *US writer*
They head the list,
Of bad to bet on;
But I insist,
They're worse to get on.

Jeffrey Barnard – *writer*
In most betting shops you will see three windows marked 'Bet Here', but only one window with the legend 'Pay Out'.

Hilaire Belloc – *(1870–1953) poet*
Lord Hippo suffered fearful loss,
  By putting money on a horse;
Which he believed, if it were pressed,
  Would run faster than the rest.

Richard Blackmore - *(1825-1900) novelist*
Betting is the manure to which the enormous
crop of horse-races and race-horse breeding in
this and other countries is to a large extent due:
The Jockey Club and its Founders (1891)

L. H. Curzon
It has to be said of the Sport of Kings that, so
long as it is surrounded by that army of
gamblers which now so fatly flourishes on all
our courses, it will continue to be what it has
long since become, a monstrous game of
speculation: *1892*

Duke of Devonshire
To pretend that the bookmakers are not vital to
racing is like pretending that the lions are not
in Trafalgar Square.

W. C. Fields - *US comedian*
Remember - Lady Godiva put all she had on a
horse.

Bernard Fergusson
  The lower classes are such fools
They waste their money on the pools.
I bet, of course, but that's misleading,
  One must encourage bloodstock breeding.

George Gissing - *(1857-1903) novelist & critic*
Everyone knows that horse racing is carried on
mainly for the delight and profit of fools,
ruffians and thieves: *1903*

George Herbert - *(1593-1633) poet*
Gamesters and racehorses never last long.

Elbert Hubbard - *(1856-1915) US humorist*
The only man who makes money following the
races is one who does it with a broom and a
shovel.

Franklin P. Jones - *US humorist*
Anybody who finds it easy to make money on
the horses is probably in the dog food business.

H. A. Jones & H. Herman - *US writers*
I backed the right horse, but the wrong horse
went and won.

Joe E. Lewis - *(b 1926) US comedian*
I met with an accident on the way to the track;
I arrived safely.

Edward V. Lucas - *(1868-1938) novelist &
poet*
In betting on races, there are two elements that
are never lacking - hope as hope, and an
incomplete recollection of the past: *1951*

Robert Lynd - *(1889-1949) Anglo-Irish essayist*
In choosing the winner of a horse race, a good
guess may beat all the skill and all the special
knowledge in the world.

Danny McGoorty - *(1901-70) US writer*
One of the worst things that can happen in life
is to win a bet on a horse at an early age.

Henry Morgan
A bookie is just a pickpocket who lets you use
your own hands.

Robert Morley - *(b 1908) actor & owner*
If in the paddock the owner is surrounded by a
herd of young children, don't back his horse.
But if the owner is accompanied by a beautiful
lady, plunge to the hilt.

Ogden Nash - *(1902-71) US poet & humorist*
The people who think they can wind up ahead
of the races are everybody who has ever won a
bet.

Dan Parker - *US sportswriter*
Millions of words are written annually,
purporting to tell how to beat the races,
whereas the best possible advice on the subject
is found in the three monosyllables 'Do not try'.

Lester Piggott - *jockey*
Punters are all stupid bastards, aren't they?

Frank Richardson
Any money I put on a horse is a sort of
insurance policy to prevent it winning.

Admiral Rous
Horse racing has always been, and always will
be, a gambling speculation.

William Shakespeare - *(1564-1616)
playwright*
I have heard of riding wagers, where horses
have been nimbler than sands: *Cymbeline*

Blackie Sherrod - *US writer*

If you bet on a horse, that's gambling. If you bet you can make three spades, that's entertainment. If you bet cotton will go up three points, that's business. See the difference?

S. Sidney
To pretend that modern race meetings are held for the purpose of improving the breed of horses is merely hypocrisy. They do indirectly improve the quality of horses, but races are held, in reality, to afford the world of betting men an opportunity of winning or losing millions: *1875*

John A. Spender - *(1862-1942) journalist*
Never back the horses you admire the most, for the horses you admire the most never win.

Sporting Review
No fair bet can be made on a steeple-chase

owing to the number of accidents which can take place.

William M. Thackeray - *(1811-63) novelist*
He attended to his game commonly, and didn't much meddle with the conversation except when it was about horses and betting:
Vanity Fair

Noel Whitcombe
I am not one of the people who believe that the main reason why a chap becomes a bookmaker is because he is too scared to steal and too heavy to become a jockey: *1969*

Lord Wyatt - *Chairman of the Tote*
Betting is the most moral thing you can do. It is an intellectual pursuit, as good as the Times crossword. For millions it is the only uninfluenced democratic decision they take:
1986

HUNTING

GENERAL

Anon
His hound is to the hunting gane,
His hawk to fetch the wild-fowl hame,
His lady's ta'en anither mate,
So we may take our dinner sweet.

Saying
Tally Ho!

Proverbs
Our ancestors grew not great by hawking and hunting.

He that will have Hare to breakfast must Hare overnight.

One does not catch rabbits with a dead ferret.

To run with the hare and hunt with the hounds.

All are not hunters that blow the horn.

If hawking and paramours, for one joy, a

hundred displeasures.

A southerly wind and a cloudy sky proclaim the hunting morning.

He who hunts two hares leaves one and loses one: *Chinese*

The hindmost dog may catch the hare.

The last dogge often times catcheth the hare, though the fleetest turne him.

Dogs that put up many hares, kill none.

The dog that hunts foulest, hits at most faults.

If three dogs chase a rabbit, they cannot kill it: *English*

The Koreans hunt the tiger during half of the year; while the tiger hunts the Koreans during the other half: *Chinese*

Thomas Adams - *(d 1620) poet & writer*
Hunting is one of the most sensual of pleasures

by which the powers of the body are strongly exerted, but those of the mind remain unemployed.

Joseph Addison – *(1672-1719) poet & critic*
Hunting is not a proper employment for a thinking man.

William Allingham – *(1828-1889) Irish poet*
    Up the airy mountain, down the rushy glen,
We daren't go a hunting, for fear of little men.

Aristotle – *(384-322 BC) Greek philosopher*
If some animals are good at hunting and others are suitable for hunting, then the Gods must clearly smile on hunting.

W. H. Auden – *(1907-1973) US poet*
Over the green pastures there, you shall go hunting the beautiful deer.

Happy the hare at morning, for she cannot read the Hunter's waking thoughts.

William Blake – *(1757-1827) poet*
    Each out-cry of the hunted hare,
A fibre from the brain does tear: *1801*

Wilfrid S. Blunt – *(1840-1922) poet & explorer*
I like hunting of the hare, better than that of the fox.

Assassins find accomplices. Man's merit Has found him three, the hawk, the hound, the ferret.

C. Nestelle Bovee – *(1829-1904) US writer & lawyer*
Hunting is a relic of the barbarous spirit that thirsted formerly for human blood, but is now intent with the blood of birds and animals.

Robert Burns – *(1759-96) Scottish poet*
My heart's in the Highlands, my heart is not here;
    My heart's in the Highlands a-chasing the deer;
Chasing the wild deer, and following the roe,
    My heart's in the Highlands wherever I go.

Lord Byron – *(1788-1824) poet*
Ah, nut-brown partridges! Ah, Brilliant

pheasants!
And, ah ye poachers! – 'Tis no sport for peasants.

William Cowper – *(1731-1800) poet*
Hunting, a detested sport, that owes its pleasure to another's pain.

Clarence Day Jr. – *(1874-1935) US writer*
Animals that want to live a life of their own, we call wild. If wild, then no matter how harmless, we treat them as outlaws, and those of us who are specially well brought up shoot them for fun.

Charles Dickens – *(1812-70) novelist*
There is a passion for hunting, something deeply implanted in the human breast:
                                        Oliver Twist

Michael Drayton – *(1563-1631) poet*
The greyhounds forth are brought, for coursing them in case,
    And choicely in the slips, one leading forth a brace.

John Dryden – *(1631-1700) poet & dramatist*
Better to hunt in fields, for health unbrought;
    Than fee the doctor for a nauseous draught.

Sam W. Foss – *(1858-1911) US editor & humorist*
The woods are made for the hunters of dreams,
The brooks for fishers of song;
To the hunters who hunt for the gunless game,
    The streams and woods belong.

Benjamin Franklin – *(1706-90) US statesman*
Don't think to hunt two hares with one dog.

James A. Froude – *(1818-1894) historian*
Wild animals never kill for sport. Man is the only one to whom the torture and death of his fellow creatures is amusing in itself.

Matthew Green – *(1696-1737) civil servant & poet*
    Hunting I reckon very good,
To brace the nerves and stir the blood.

Sir A. P. Herbert – *(1890-1971) MP & poet*
For when I'm not shootin' or ridin',
    I'm hunting' or fishin' or shootin'.

Well, a chap must do something I always tell
the chaps,
For if a chap doesn't a chap will collapse:
1930

Rowland Heylin - *(1562-1631) Sheriff of
London*
'Dry meal, it is!' said the country fellow, when
he lost the hare: *1659*

William Holden - *US actor*
If there is one word in the English language I
hate, it is 'game'. It seems to imply that other
creatures are about for our sport: *1972*

David Hume - *(1711-76) Scottish philosopher*
Everyone has observed how much more dogs
are animated when they hunt in a pack, than
when they pursue their game apart.

Even bear-baiting was esteemed heathenish and
unchristian; the sport of it, not the inhumanity,
gave offence.

Samuel Johnson - *(1709-84) lexicographer*
Hunting was the labour of the savages of North
America, but the amusement of the
'Gentlemen' of England.

It is very strange, and very melancholy, that the
paucity of human pleasures should persuade us
ever to call hunting one of them.

Rev Charles Kingsley - *(1819-75) novelist &
poet*
There's blood on the game you eat.

Joseph Wood Krutch - *(1893-1970) US critic
& teacher*
When a man wantonly destroys one of the
works of man, we call him a vandal. When he
wantonly destroys one of the works of God, we
call him a sportsman.

How anyone can profess to find animal life
interesting and yet take delight in reducing the
wonder of any animal to a bloody mass of fur or
feathers is beyond my comprehension: *1957*

Lao-Tzu - *(c 600 BC) Chinese philosopher*
Racing and hunting excite man's heart to
madness.

Stephen Leacock - *(1869-1944) Canadian
humorist & scientist*
A sportsman is a fellow who, every now and
then, simply has to go out and kill something.

Edward V. Lucas - *(1868-1938) novelist*
Nature never did a crueler thing than when she
gave rabbits white tails; it makes it possible to
shoot them long after it is too dark to see other
quarry: *1913*

Lord Thomas Macaulay - *(1800-59)
statesman & historian*
The Puritan hated bear-baiting, not because it
gave pain to the bear, but because it gave
pleasure to the spectators.

Ovid - *(43 BC-17 AD) Roman poet*
And even as when the greedy Gallic dog*
course the sillic hare,
Amidst the plain and a champion field without
all covert, bare.
[*A Gallic dog is an ancient name for a greyhound]

Pope Pius V - *[1566-72]*
Hunting is fit recreation for a Pope.

Plato - *(429-347 BC) Greek philosopher*
There can be no more important kind of
information than the exact knowledge of a
man's own country; and for this as well as for
more general reasons of pleasure and
advantage, hunting with hounds and other
kinds of sports should be pursued by the young.

William Shakespeare - *(1564-1616)
playwright*
Come shall we go and kill some venison?:
As You Like It

Huntsman, I charge thee tender well my
hounds: *The Taming of the Shrew*

Say thou wilt course, thy greyhounds are swift,
As breathed stags, ay, fleeter than the roe:
The Taming of the Shrew

We hunt not, we, with horse or hound
But hope to pluck a dainty doe to ground:
Titus Andronicus

Hunting he loved, but love he laughed to scorn:
Venus & Adonis

To-morrow he intends
To hunt the boar with certain of his friends:
Venus & Adonis

George Bernard Shaw - *(1856-1950) Irish dramatist & critic*
No sportsman wants to kill a fox or the pheasant as I want to kill him when I see him doing it.

Everyone can see that the people who hunt are the right people and the people who don't are the wrong ones.

Captain John Smith - *(1580-1631) explorer*
Will any go to catch a hare with a Taber and a Pipe?: 1624

William Somerville - *(1675-1742) poet & writer*
Each animal
By natural instinct taught, spares his own kind,
But man, the tyrant man, revels at large,
Free-booter unrestrained, destroys at will,
The whole creation, men and beasts his prey:
1742

Edward Stillingfleet - *(1635-99) Bishop of Worcester*
If hunting be a more genteel species of butchery, it is certainly a more cruel one.

Douglas Sutherland - *(b 1919) writer*
The gentleman must realise that once he is in the saddle he must be as rude as possible to anyone who crosses his path:
The English Gentleman (1978)

James Thomson - *(1700-48) Scottish poet*
Poor is the triumph o'er the timid hare: 1730

Thomas Tickell - *(1685-1740) poet*
How every nerve the greyhound's stretch displays
The hare, preventing in her airy maze.

Guillaume Twici - *poet*
And there ben other beasts, five of the chase;
The buck for the first, the second is the do;
The fox the third which hath ever hard grace;
The fourth the martyn, and the last the roe:
1340

Peter Wilson - *sportswriter for the Daily Mirror*
For, as long as one hears the anguished wailing of a hare as the blood gushes from its ears, and its eyes come out on stalks under the pressure of a hound's teeth, then our countryside can never be the green and pleasant place of our birthright.

I hate all blood pursuits involving animals whose panting death provides a thrill for the pursuers. But at least those who hunt the fox and the noble stag do put their own limbs at some risk. I loathe bull-fighting - but the great matador is not a coward. Hare-coursing puts no one, save the hare, at any worse risk than over-indulgence in eating and drinking can bring.

Xenophon - *(428-354 BC) Athenian writer*
The first pursuit that a young man just out of boyhood should take up is hunting, and afterwards, he should go on to other branches of education.

FOX HUNTING

Anon
Without foxes there would be no fox-hunting and without fox-hunting many would find it impossible to live through an English winter.

Proverbs
The tail does not often catch the fox.

The fox knows much, but more he that catcheth him.

He that will get the better of a fox must rise early: *French*

Peter Beckford - *(1740-1811) Master of Foxhounds*
Fox hunting is a kind of warfare, its uncertainties, its fatigues, its difficulties, and its dangers, rendering it interesting above all other diversions: 1899

William Cowper - *(1731-1800) poet*
Though the fox he follows may be tamed,
A mere fox-follower never is reclaimed.

***The Field* magazine**
If foxes could hear all sides of the debate on hunting, I think they would vote solidly for its

continuance.

John Gay - *(1685-1732) poet & playwright*
Soon as Aurora drives away the night
And edges eastern clouds with rosy light,
The healthy huntsman, with the cheerful horn,
Summons the dogs, and greets the dappled morn.

Konrad Lorenz - *(b 1903) Austrian behavioural physiologist*
The fox's hunting is quite as legitimate and a great deal more necessary to his existence than it is that of the game- keeper: *1952*

Captain J. Otho Paget - *(1860-1934) journalist*
A Master of Foxhounds to be perfect, must embody all the virtues of a saint with the commanding genius of a Kitchener, and the tact of a diplomat. *The Field magazine*

Plautus - *(254-184 BC) Roman comical playwright*
It is folly to take unwilling dogs out to hunt.

Hounds and the hunted have different smells.

Punch magazine
It ain't the 'unting, as 'urts 'un. It's the 'ammer, 'ammer, 'ammer along the 'ard, 'igh road: *1856*

Sir Walter Scott - *(1771-1832) Scottish novelist & poet*
Back limped, with slow and crippled pace,
The sulky leaders of the chase.

William Shakespeare - *(1546-1616) playwright*
We'll make you some sport with the fox ere we case him: *All's Well That Ends Well*

Rev Sydney Smith - *(1771-1845) Canon of St Paul's*
The fox, when caught, is worth nothing; he is followed for the pleasure of following.

William Somerville - *(1675-1746) poet & writer*
My hoarse sounding horn invites thee to the chase, the Sport of Kings.

Robert S. Surtees - *(1803-64) sportswriter & novelist*
It would be not a bit more absurd for a man to punish himself by keeping a yacht, who hates sailing and the sight of the sea, than it is for a man to keep a pack of fox-hounds, who has no ardent predilection for the chase.

The horse loves the hound, and I loves both.

Tell me a man's a fox hunter, and I loves him at once.

Jorrocks! Who is not afraid of the 'pace', so long as there is no leaping.

It ain't that I loves the fox less, but that I loves the hound more.

Sussex Express
Letters page - I am convinced that if a fox could vote, he would vote Tory.

John N. P. Watson - *biographer & writer*
Like the athlete's exacting career, that of the fox-hound is a short one: *1977*

Oscar Wilde - *(1854-1900) Irish dramatist & poet*
One knows so well the poplar idea of health. The English country gentleman galloping after the fox – the unspeakable in full pursuit of the uneatable: *A Woman of No Importance*

SHOOTING

Anon
A big game hunter is a man who can spot a leopard.

Proverbs
Short shooting loses the game.

Hilaire Belloc - *(1870-1953) poet*
I shoot the hippopotamus, with bullets made of platinum,
Because if I use leaden ones, his hide is sure to flatten 'em.

Jilly Cooper - *(b 1937) journalist*
If I were a grouse, I'd complain to the Brace Relations Board.

Walter Cronkite - *(b 1916) US TV presenter*
The perils of duck hunting are great, especially for the duck.

Ralph Waldo Emerson - *(1803–82) US philosopher & poet*
It is a proverb in England that it is safer to shoot a man than a hare.

Sir William S. Gilbert - *(1836–1911) humorist & lyricist*
Deer hunting would be fine sport, if only the deer had guns.

Philip Guedella - *(1889–1944) historian & biographer*
Biography, like big-game hunting, is one of the recognised forms of sport, and it is as unfair as only sport can be.

Heinrich Heine - *(1797–1856) German poet & satirist*
Love's torment made me seek the chase,
  Rifle in hand, I roam'd apace.

Ernest Hemingway - *(1898–1961) US novelist*
Shooting gives me a good feeling. It is faster than baseball and you are out on one strike.

Thomas Hood - *(1799–1845) poet*
  What he hit is history,
  What he missed is mystery.

John Marchington- *sportswriter*
Regard shooting as a means to an end and not an end in itself: *1981*

That men are clearly attracted by guns is beyond dispute; what is less clear is why: *1981*

Monty Python's Flying Circus - *BBC TV comedy show*
I always like the outdoor life, out there with the guns slaughtering a few of God's creatures, tramping about the moors blasting their heads off.

Lewis Mumford - *(b 1895) US philosopher & historian*
Hunting is an occupation in which the incidents are as much a part of the object as the final result; everything about it, from the kind of clothes worn to the manner of the weapon used, enhances, in some degree, the hunter's pleasure.

Alexander Pope - *(1688–1744) poet & satirist*
See from the brake the whirring pheasant springs
  And mounts exciting on triumphant wings.
  Short is his joy, he feels the fiery wound,
Flutters in blood, and panting beats the ground.

Punch magazine
You call pheasant shooting a sport, do you? Why? What is it? Up gets a guinea – off goes a penny-farthing – and, if you're lucky, down comes two-and-six! Bah!:   *1889*

George Bernard Shaw - *(1856–1950) Irish novelist & critic*
When a man wants to murder a tiger he calls it sport; when a tiger wants to murder him he calls it ferocity.

Sir Osbert Sitwell - *(1892–1969) poet & writer*
On Jesus Christ – He was never, well, what I call a sportsman. For forty days he went out into the desert and never shot anything.

Rev Sydney Smith - *(1771–1845) Canon of St Paul's*
The birds seem to consider the muzzle of my gun as their safest position.

Henry David Thoreau - *(1817–62) US poet*
A gun gives you the body, not the bird.

P. G. Wodehouse - *(1881–1975) writer & humorist*
The fascination of shooting as a sport depends almost wholly on whether you are at the right or wrong end of a gun.

ICE HOCKEY

Saying
Let's get the puck out of here.

Harold Ballard - *Toronto Maple Leafs*
On the Winter Olympics - If the Russkies win, they go home and find better conditions in their house, like two electric light bulbs instead of one. If the Americans win, it makes no difference at all for at a very minimum Hockey League wage you are making fifty grand before you even get started: *1980*

Jimmy Cannon - *(1910–73) sportswriter*
A puck is a hard rubber disk that hockey players strike when they can't hit one another.

Wayne Cashman - *Boston Bruins*
The key to a hockey match is the first punch. When you're left-handed and they're looking for the right, it helps a lot.

Don Cherry - *coach*
When I was a coach at Rochester they called me in and said, 'We are making a change in your department.' I was the only one in my department.

Rodney Dangerfield - *comedian*
I went to a fight the other night and an Ice Hockey game broke out: *1978*

Robert Fachet - *sportswriter*
Hockey is where a fan pays his money and almost a fifth of the time, sees nothing decided: *1978*

Wayne Gretzky - *(b 1961) Edmonton Oilers & Los Angeles Kings*
It's rough. It's physical. But if you think about it when you're playing, then you're in trouble.

Gordie Howe - *Detroit Red Wings*
I never broke my nose playing Ice Hockey, but eleven other guys did: *1981*

Colin M. Jarman - *(b 1958) British sportswriter*
Scars on ice: *1988*

Emory Jones - *General manager of St Louis Arena*
Hockey players are like mules. They have no fear of punishment and no hope of reward: *1963*

Stephen Leacock - *(1869–1944) humorist & scientist*
Hockey captures the essence of Canadian experience in the New World. In a land so inescapably and inhospitably cold, hockey is the chance of life, and an affirmation that despite the deathly chill of winter we are alive.

John Mariucci- *USA Olympic coach*
Every day you guys look worse and worse. And today you played like tomorrow: *1980*

Sammy Pollock - *Montreal Canadiens manager*
I would gnaw through a goalpost for Sammy Pollock: *John Ferguson*

Bill Torrey - *New York Islanders manager*
This team bends, but we don't break.

Ian Turnbull - *Toronto Maple Leafs*
Ice Hockey is a spontaneous game, but you have to be able to do things automatically.

MARTIAL ARTS

K. Higashi - *Japan*
American wrestlers are strong – much stronger than any of us pretend to be in muscular strength. After all, wrestling is wrestling.

However, against ju-jitsu, it is mere child's play.

Richard Hughes - *(1900–76) poet & writer*

Ju-jitsu (or Judo), being the art of using unbearable pain for the conquest of brute force, has an irresistible attraction for the young imagination, boys' almost as much as girls'.

Gerald Stanley Lee – *(1862-1944) US clergyman & critic*
Turning the other cheek is a kind of moral ju-jitsu: *Crowds*

J. P. McEvoy
The Japanese have a word for it. It's Judo – the art of conquering by yielding. The Western equivalent of Judo is, 'Yes, dear.'

Benjamin Raphael
Karate is like Christianity. Its history has been so riven by disputes between rival sects that some times the object of the devotion has been obscured.

MOTOR CAR

GENERAL

Fred Horsley – *writer*
In the motor world, as in the boxing ring, a sensational contender may look like a champion, with speed, power and style – everything except the winning punch. Around such a machine lays the aura of that intriguing world of 'if':   *The World's Fastest Cars*

GRAND PRIX

Chris Amon – *New Zealand*
There are people in this business who worry me.

Mario Andretti – *(b 1940) US world champion [1978]*
Racing gives you nothing but fun, anything else you have to take.

You can really talk to that car. She's handling like she's painted to the road.

Rene Arnoux – *France*
A real whacko from Grenoble, lacked the one essential quality of the modern racing driver – intelligence: *Keith Botsford – sportswriter*

At times he produces semi-precious drives – lots of glitter, but not much real worth:
Louis T. Stanley – sportswriter

Albert Ascari – *(1918-55) Italian world champion [1952-3]*
I don't want my children to become too fond of me. One of these days, I may not come back,

and they will suffer less if I keep them a bit at arm's length.
[He died in a crash at Monza, in 1955]

If men might be judged by their friends, Ascari could always be sure of a place among the greatest: *John Bentley – sportswriter*

Joe Bonnier – *President of FISA*
When a car starts sliding under you, it's a terrific sensation to feel that you are in control, until the moment you are not: *1970*

You're on the wrong road if you try to approach racing from the point of view of accidents, because accidents don't really mean anything: *1972*

Maxwell Boyd – *sportswriter*
Grand Prix motor racing is like Punch. It is never as good as it was: *1983*

Tony Brooks – *world championship runner-up [1959]*
We accepted that Grand Prix racing was a challenge. A good analogy is that of mountaineering; if you provide a safety net, no challenge remains.

Tony Brooks was the greatest 'unknown' racing driver there's ever been: *Stirling Moss*

Francois Cevert – *(d 1973) France*
As for the accidents and tragedy – the circus goes on. There is no room for tears: *1973*
[He was killed the following day – on the track]

Jim Clark - *(1936-68) world champion [1963 & 1965]*
On his death - As well as the grief, there was another dimension. If it could happen to Jim Clark, what chance did the rest of us have:
Chris Amon

E. Hunter Davies - *(b 1936) writer & broadcaster*
On the track, death is a subject the drivers put to the bottom of their consciousness. Off the track, they admit it exists, and take out huge insurance policies, then forget it.

Juan Fangio - *(b 1911) Argentine world champion [1951 & 1954-57]*
In my day it was 75 per cent car and mechanics, 25 per cent driver and luck. Today is is 95 per cent car. A driver can emerge in a good new car, become world champion and a year later disappear to the back of the queue. Driving skill hardly counts any more: *1983*

Enzo Ferrari - *(1898-1988) founder of Ferrari*
Anon executive - I wish the Pope would make you a Cardinal, Enzo.
Enzo Ferrari - Why a Cardinal?
Anon executive - Because then we'd only have to kiss your ring!

Richard Garrett - *sportswriter*
Grand Prix drivers, in contrast to the majority, seem to live rather ascetic lives - if not downright puritanical. Few of them smoke, they consume large quantities of soft drinks, but rarely touch alcohol, and mostly lead remarkably blameless married lives: *1970*

Barrie Gill - *writer and TV commentator*
Motor racing has had more than its share of legends, more than its fill of tragedy: *1972*

Mike Hawthorn - *(1929-59) world champion [1958]*
Motor racing is dangerous; but what is danger? It is dangerous to climb a mountain. It is dangerous to cross main roads. It is dangerous to explore a jungle. One cannot frame regulations to make everything safe: *1959*
[He died a few weeks later in a car crash]

Lord Hesketh - *Hesketh racing team owner*
Perilously fat, he waddled about like a giant

with the face of a child. He was fortunate to blend the brains of [Harvey] Postlethwaite with the skill of [James] Hunt, a formidable combination of talents that barely needed directions, just financial succour:
Louis T. Stanley - sportswriter

Graham Hill - *(1929-75) world champion [1962 & 1968]*
It is like balancing an egg on a spoon while shooting the rapids.

James Hunt - *(b 1947) world champion [1976]*
I don't get frightened when I am driving because if I am in a nasty situation I'm too busy sorting it out. It's cold calculation. If you're frightened you're not capable of looking after yourself. When I sit at home and think what can happen, then I'm scared.

James Hunt thinks he's king of the goddam world:
Mario Andretti

Jackie Ickx - *(b 1945) Belgian world championship runner-up [1969 & 1970]*
Ickx clicks, nicks Prix:
Newspaper headline after the Canadian Grand Prix (1969)

Alan Jones - *(b 1946) Australian world champion [1980]*
Racing is a form of commitment; once the flag drops, that's it. There's something important to me about having my back to the wall.

An average sort of man with the average man's lack of equipment for coping with sudden success. His track personality was very like the real one: *Louis T. Stanley - sportswriter*

Niki Lauda - *(b 1949) Austrian world champion [1977 & 1984]*
You appreciate that it is very easy to die and you have to arrange your life to cope with that reality.

People whose 'needs are satisfied by speed' are wankers, not racing drivers. Any joy is from fascination with perfection, not from a thrill of driving fast.

He is a single-minded chap. If he found you lying on the ground, he would sooner walk over you than round you: *James Hunt*

Stirling Moss – *(b 1929) world championship runner-up [1953-6]*
Motor racing to me is a sport, not a technical exercise.

The cars, I know, are incredibly sophisticated these days, but I don't believe the sport is.

It has taken thirty-three years and a bang on the head to get my values right.

It is necessary to relax your muscles when you can. Relaxing your brain is fatal.

I believe that if a man wanted to walk on water, and was prepared to give up everything in life, he could do it.

If Stirling Moss had put reason before passion, he would have been World Champion – he was more than deserving of it: *Enzo Ferrari*

Juan Fangio was the great man of racing; whilst Stirling Moss was the epitome of a racing driver: *Jackie Stewart*

Timeri Murari – *Indian novelist & journalist*
Drivers go to extremes to ignore the fact of death; it's taboo to them and something too dangerous to think about.

Nelson Piquet – *(b 1952) Brazilian world champion [1981, 1983 & 1987]*
Tell you the truth, I hate Monaco.

Alain Prost – *(b 1955) French world champion [1985, 1986 & 1989]*
I am indeed a believer, but at the start of a Grand Prix, with 156 litres of fuel behind me, I don't entirely rely on God. I rely on Prost to negotiate the first corner and the rest of it.

He looks more like a scrum-half than a Grand Prix driver: *Nigel Roebuck – sportswriter*

Keke Rosberg – *(b 1948) Finnish world champion [1982]*
After winning the World Drivers' title, it was like a balloon. You let the air out and all there is left is a pile of rubber. That's how I felt:
                                                    1984

He is as calculating as a slot-machine:
                        Louis T. Stanley – sportswriter

Jody Scheckter – *(b 1950) South African world champion [1979]*
It's all about going fast. You're very clever till you come off. Then you're stupid. 'What a Rock Ape,' people say. But if you go slow, they don't comment at all.

Ayrton Senna – *Brazilian world champion [1988]*
Ayrton has this problem – he thinks that he can't kill himself:
                Alain Prost – McLaren team-mate (1989)

Tom Sneva – *US Indianapolis 500 winner [1983]*
You just have to treat death like any other part of life: *1977*

Jackie Stewart – *(b 1939) world champion [1969, 1971 & 1973]*
To me, motor racing is a sport rather than a business. Some people say it should be banned because people get killed. OK, it's dangerous, but people who express these views are the most uninteresting people you'll ever meet. I do think that the Europeans have had this attitude that no one could really impregnate their superiority.

One of the weaknesses of racing drivers is that they are fickle, fickle in their own business.

An accident is when you lose control of the car.

Not too long ago, I lay awake in bed and counted all the people I've known who died racing, and after a while, maybe an hour, I counted fifty-seven: *1972*

To drive a racing car, you must be conservative. You cannot be a radical, someone who's given to spontaneity or enthusiasms.

A Formula One car is really an animal because it responds to different kinds of treatment. A highly bred racehorse, a thoroughbred in its sensitivity and nervousness.

There's enough Ferraris here to eat a plate of spaghetti.

Jackie Stewart is an enigma, a man who contributes perhaps more than any other to the cause of motor racing, yet is scorned by many of those who have most to gain from his efforts:
Bill Galvin - sportswriter (1972)

In spite of his phenomenal success, he never needed a bigger size in helmets:
Louis T. Stanley - sportswriter

Gilles Villeneuve - *Canadian world championship runner-up [1979]*
Gilles Villeneuve did everything in his life at 200 mph. Everything! Skiing, driving the speedboat, playing backgammon:
Patrick Tambay

Murray Walker - *TV commentator*
Anything happens in Grand Prix racing and it usually does.

The lead car is absolutely unique, except for the one behind it, which is identical.

Whatever is wrong with Arnoux's engine would be irremediable in the time it takes to do it.

Patrick Tambay's hopes, which were nil before, are absolutely zero now.

Do my eyes deceive me, or is Senna's Lotus sounding a bit rough?

John Watson - *world championship runner-up [1982]*
I want to be world champion, not for the things it would give me, but because I want the championship to satisfy something inside me. I'm like a hydrogen bomb waiting to explode. When it goes off, the fallout will be felt for miles. All I need to trigger it is success: *1980*

In motor racing the ever present danger is always there.

LAND-SPEED RECORD

Anon
A jet-propelled vehicle would not be a motor-car, it would be a sort of aeroplane dragging its wheels along the course.

Craig Breedlove - *US world record holder*

[1963-65]
The world landspeed record has meaning. It's an international thing. The rich Englishman used to hold all the records, but now I hold them. I'm patriotic. That's why I named my car 'The Spirit of America'.
[In 1965 'Spirit of America' set its last record - 600.6 mph]

Henry Ford - *(1863-1947) US industrialist*
On his new 'speed-machine' - Winning a race or making a record was then the best kind of advertising. So I fixed up the Arrow.
[In 1904 the 'Arrow' set a new record - 91.4 mph]

Gary Gabelich - *US world record holder [1970]*
On his record-breaking 'Blue Flame' - It is basically a long piece of pipe.
[In 1970 'Blue Flame' set a new record - 622.4 mph]

Hal Needham - *US owner of 'Budweiser Rocket'*
On his controversial record attempt - I sure hope people don't compare this to Evil Knievel trying to jump a dump-truck. This is a scientific and engineering achievement.
[In 1979 the 'Rocket' set an unratified record - 739.7 mph]

Tommy Wisdom
The World landspeed record requires the minimum of skill, and the maximum of courage.

OTHER

Autocar magazine
RAC Rally competitors should remember not to make a noise by rushing about unnecessarily on the lower gears and generally making a nuisance: *1931*

Lady Docker - *(b 1900)*
She was to post-war motoring as Salvador Dali was to between-war painting; she outraged and, at the same time, delighted:
Richard Garrett (1971)

John Gott - *writer*
When rally-driving was more a sport and less a win-at-all-costs business such things (necessary route deviations) used to be accepted as part of the game: *1959*

David J. Neuman – *writer*
When the first horseless carriage was timed for
acceleration, Drag Racing began: *1974*

MOTOR CYCLE

Alan Cathcart – *sportswriter*
Put the three words – Italy, motor-cycles and
racing – together and you automatically think
of a fourth – Monza.

Evil Knievel – *US 'explorer', stuntman &*
daredevil cyclist
I'm not a stuntman. I'm not a daredevil. I'm an
explorer.

Thomas McGuane – *(b 1939) US essayist*
A contending moto-crosser can expect to play
out sooner than a fighter or a football player.
There is no retirement plan.

Motocross is very properly considered a sport.

It requires strength, the balance of a slack-wire
walker, incredible co-ordination, and
endurance. The paunches and bubble-buts of
other motor sports are not seen here.

Martin Rogers – *sportswriter*
Unlike many other popular spectator sports,
speedway allows the emphasis upon
entertainment to equal that laid upon the final
result: *1978*

Barry Sheene – *world 500cc champion [1976 &*
1977]
On safety at the Nurburgring – You'd have to be
William Tell to hit a straw bale around here.

NETBALL

Malcolm Stanley – *Managing Director of Fads*
[DIY store]
Soccer is a sick sport, we would rather sponsor
netball: *1982*

ORIENTEERING

Anon
Cunning running.

The thought sport.

Orienteering is playing chess while jogging.

Martin Hyman – *Chairman, British*

orienteering squad
Many orienteers are joggers who are looking for
something more.

William Shakespeare – *(1564–1616)*
playwright
Run his compass: *Julius Caesar*

POLO

Anon
Horse Hockey.

A game played by Peers at the far end of the field.

Rintoul Booth – *writer*
Polo ponies are not really ponies at all and are not a breed but a type. Like Polo players they can be of any size and are frequently well-bred, though you would never guess from the shocking language they use: *1975*

Phyllis Critchley
  The game is won, they all retire,
For a long post-mortem in the bar.
  But do not pity Polo wives,
Because they really love their lives: *1954*

H. St C. S.
Chukka by chukka, the game is played,
So goal by goal, point by point is made.
  I hope I am never too old or staid,
    To play the game of Polo: *1922*

Juan Carlos Harriott – *Argentina*

Polo is a gentle game. There is risk and danger involved. We know that if each of us was not a gentleman out on the field, we would injure one another.

Polo is a game to be played with hot blood and a cool head.

Will H. Ogilvie
How the tingle of the strike,
Through arm and shoulder spins!
A hefty hit, a deadly line,
  A goal! The goal that wins.

Fame and the Anglo-Saxon pride,
In a goal to get,
  And a horse to ride.

Sylvester Stallone – *US actor*
Playing polo is like trying to play golf during an earthquake: *1990*

J. K. Stephen
  Let other people play at other things,
The King of Games is still the Game of Kings.

POOL

Minnesota Fats – *USA*
Dressing a pool player in a tuxedo is like putting whipped cream on a hot dog.

Meredith Willson – *US lyricist*
Pool – that game with fifteen numbered balls is the devil's tool: *The Music Man*

POWER BOAT

Simon Barnes – *sportswriter*
Power-boats are streamlined, advertisement-spattered, potential coffins: *1985*

Donald Campbell – *(1885–1949) world water speed record holder*
There is no hope of bailing out of a speedboat. You hit the water and become so much pulp.

RODEO

Gordon Hansen – *US writer*
The rodeo cowboy represents the last frontier
of the pure, unpampered athlete: *1970*

Bill Linderman – *(1922-61) US all-round
cowboy world champion [1950 & 1953]*
Rodeoing is about the only sport you can't fix.
You'd have to talk to the bulls and the horses,
and they wouldn't understand you: *1954*

William Shakespeare – *(1546-1616)
playwright*
Those that tame wild horses,
Pace 'em not in their hands to make 'em gentle,
But stop their mouths with stubborn bits and
spur them,
Till they obey the manage: *Henry VIII*

ROWING

GENERAL

Anon
It's not easy to teach a rowing man to think,
because if he could think he probably wouldn't
row.

Rowing isn't the most important thing in the
world. But, to do it well you have to perform an
act of faith and convince yourself that, from the
moment you step into the boat, nothing else
matters as much as moving it fast:
Harvard coach

Proverbs
Nodding the head does not row the boat: *Irish*

Robert Browning – *(1812-89) poet*
Not a jest, not a jorum; we bent to our yoke,
Neck by neck, swing by swing, never changing
our stroke.

Captain F. T. Desmond Coke – *(1879-1931)
author*
His blade struck the water a full second before
any other, until, as the boats began to near the
winning post his own was dipping in the water
twice as often as any other.
[*This is popularly misquoted as* – All rowed so fast
but none so fast as stroke]

Kenneth Grahame – *(1859-1932) novelist*
Believe me, my young friend, there is nothing –

absolutely nothing – half so much worth doing
as simply messing about in boats:
The Wind in the Willows (1908)

William Johnson Cory – *(1823-92) poet*
Jolly boating weather
  And a hay-harvest breeze,
Blade on the feather,
  Shade off the trees;
Swing, swing together,
With your bodies between your knees.
Swing, swing together,
With your bodies between your knees:
Eton Boating Song (1865)

Tom Egan – *University cox*
Our favourite science, rowing, ought to be the
first object of our love: *1852*

Ralph Waldo Emerson – *(1803-82) US
philosopher & writer*
No member of a crew is praised for the rugged
individuality of his rowing.

George Meredith – *(1828-1909) novelist, poet
& critic*
Quicker fell the blades as the grim Stroke
  stretches
  In his scant zephyr, calling on the crew,
Arms out, he lengthens. O bluish oar-blades!
O the stark aloofness of the star-skied blue!

'Ouida' [Marie Louise de la Ramee] –

(1838–1908) novelist
All rowed so fast, but none so fast as stroke:

Roy Plomley - *radio presenter*
Rowing shares with motor-racing the advantage of being practised while sitting down.

Alexander Pope - *(1688–1744) poet*
Spread the thin oar and catch the driving gale:
Essay on Man

Gordon Ross - *sportswriter*
Strokes, like Prime Ministers, and creators of works of art on political prisoners, are born only occasionally: *1954*

HENLEY REGATTA

Anon
But what has come out of the chatter,
Is that the Stewards aren't really old fools.
They've run the Regatta for ages,
And are always revising the rules: *1953*

Joseph Ashby-Sterry - *(1838–1917) writer*
I fly to the cheery Athena for shelter,
The pâté is perfect, the Giesler is dry
And think while I gaze undismayed at the pelter
That Henley's still joyous in dripping July:
c 1880

Mrs Ena Canvey
Henley Regatta without a fair is like a woman without hair.

John Cooper - *Hon Treasurer*
I cannot imagine how Henley Regatta costs such a large sum to run: *1920*

Frank Keating - *(b 1937) sportswriter*
Henley is full of haughty happiness, hats, haves and very few have-nots: *1983*

Nicholas Wapshott - *writer*
A full-scale British Day Out, a honeypot for the hoipolloi in leisure wear: *1983*

THE BOAT RACE

Anon
'Bottoms up!' is a toast not to be made to the crew of the Boat Race.

Sue Brown - *Oxford University cox*
The only occupant of the Oxford boat smaller than a house was the coxette . . . Weighing about as much as the stroke's left thigh:
Clive James - writer & humorist (1981)

Harry Carpenter - *BBC TV commentator*
Ah! Isn't that nice, the wife of the Cambridge President is kissing the cox of the Oxford crew:
1977

Miles Kington– *(b 1941) humorist*
The Boat Race would be much more attractive if the rules were changed to allow the boats to ram each other.

Terence 'Spike' Milligan - *(b 1918) comedian*
After having the race course outlined to him – Don't you think it's going to be rather wet for the horses?

Punch magazine
On the dead-heat - Oxford won, Cambridge too!:
1877

R. C. Robertson-Glasgow - *sportswriter*
There's nothing like the Boat Race. I have seen spectators at ball games try to light their hats and put a cigarette on their head. But, the Boat Race knocks them all. You seem to see half the world watching with their eyes, and you seem to feel the other half waiting with their souls.

Gordon Ross - *sportswriter*
What a blessing that men row; who ever heard of a University man playing billiards!: *1954*

Frederick Skey - *President of the Royal College of Surgeons*
The University Boat Race as at present established is a national folly: *1845*

John Snagge - *(b 1904) radio commentator*
I can't tell who's leading - it's either Oxford or Cambridge: *1949*

Anthony Trollope - *(1815–82) novelist*
Boat Race - it's dogged as does it. I ain't thinking about it.

RUGBY LEAGUE

Anon
To play Rugby league you need three things; a good pass, a good tackle, and a good excuse.

Brian Bevan - *Australia, Warrington & Blackpool [1945-64]*
As bald as a coot. No tooth in his head. A skeleton in braces.   *Arthur Clues - Leeds*

Brian Bevan could jink like a crazed pin-ball and hare like a barmy rabbit:
Frank Keating - sportswriter

Henry Cooper - *(b 1934) heavyweight boxer*
I've never seen a modern-day boxer, one who has boxed over the past ten years, who has a cauliflower ear even. And I've seen more punch-drunk Rugby League players than

fighters: *1972*

Alex Murphy - *Wigan & St Helens coach*
I wouldn't play the French at marbles, never mind Rugby League. All we will ever learn off them is how to fight and spit and bite each other.

Eddie Waring - *TV commentator*
Rugby League football is still not a national game and the only people who love it are Rugby League folk themselves: *1948*

Catchphrase - It's an oop-an-under.

Eddie Waring has done as much for our sport as Cyril Smith would do for hang-gliding:
Reg Bowden

RUGBY UNION

Anon
Rugby is a game played by men with odd-shaped balls.

New Zealand rugby is a colourful game - you get all black and blue.

Old rugby players never die - they simply have their balls taken away.

Mottoes
Rugby football is a game for gentlemen in all classes, but never for a bad sportsman in any class: *Barbarians RFC*
[*Attributed to Rev. W. J. Carey*]

Subdue and penetrate: *New Zealand All Blacks*

Sayings
A pastime for ruffians enjoyed by gentlemen:
Victorian

Fred Allen
Show me a team with high-scoring wings, and

I'll show you a team with good centres.

Rob Andrew - *England*
There is no such thing as 'a lack of confidence'. You either have it or you don't.

Bill Beaumont - *(b 1952) England*
Playing in the second row doesn't require a lot of intelligence really. You've got to be bloody crazy to play there for a start.

If I had been a winger, I might have been day-dreaming and thinking about how to keep my kit clean for next week.

The lads say my bum's equivalent to one 'Erica'!

He's John Wayne and Goliath, with blue eyes and curly hair like Samson: *Jean Rook - writer*

Upon seeing a topless Erica Roe - Bill, there's a guy just run on the park with your backside on his chest:
Steve Smith - England [v Australia] (1982)

He was like a St Bernard, a lovable, bulky, gentle old thing possessing great strength under the gracefully floppy exterior, someone who would always come to your rescue: *Clem Thomas*

Michael Benazet - *French sportswriter*
Forward play is like a funeral. You have to get in front, with the family; not behind with the friends.

George Best - *soccer player*
I went to a grammar school for a few months, but I didn't like it there, because they played rugby.

Max Boyce - *Welsh entertainer*
When it comes to the one great scorer,
 To mark against your name,
He'll not ask how you played the game,
But . . . whether you beat England.

Arthur Budd- *President of the RFU [1888-89]*
A player who could not take and give hacks was not considered worth his salt and to put one's head down in a scrummage was regarded as an act of high treason: *1878*

Peter Cranmer- *England*
It would be a very dull game without any individual brilliance, but it would cease to be a game if the whole team didn't benefit by it.

Danie Craven - *South Africa*
Danie Craven would himself axe the devil if he threatened rugby: *Donald Woods - writer*

Alfred E. Crawley - *(1869-1924) social anthropologist*
The tactical differences between association football and rugby with its varieties seems to be that in the former the ball is the missile, in the latter men are the missile: *1913*

Pierre Danos - *France*
Rugby players are either piano shifters or piano players. Fortunately, I'm one of those who can play a tune.

Gareth Davies - *Wales*
We've lost seven of our last eight matches. Only team that we have beaten was Western Samoa. Good job we didn't play the whole of Samoa: *1989*

Albert Ferrasse - *President of the French Rugby Federation*
Albert Ferrasse is a formidable man, the Harry Houdini of rugby union:
David Oxley - Chief Executive of the Rugby League

Charles B. Fry - *(1872-1956) England*
The game is so full of plot - interest and drama.

Clarrie Gibbons
A forward's usefulness to his side varies as to the square of his distance from the ball.

Sid Going - *New Zealand*
You don't beat Wales in Wales - you just happen to score more points than them.

Virginia Graham - *writer*
The women sit, getting colder and colder, on a seat getting harder and harder, watching oafs, getting muddier and muddier.

Ray Gravell - *Wales*
You've got to get your first tackle in early, even if it's late.

Banner at Cardiff Arms Park - Ray Gravell eats soft centres.

Michael Green - *writer*
A game played by fewer than fifteen a side, at least half of whom should be totally unfit:
Coarse Rugby

A. G. Hales - *(1870-1936) writer*
A Springbok back would work hands and arms like a deaf mute signalling for a fire escape:
1907

A bony shoulder would connect with his ribs, and he would be making more marks on Scottish soil than Robert Burns on Scottish history.

Anthea Hall
Choirs may look devout in action, but on tour they can behave like rugby clubs.

Rowe Harding - *Wales*
The rugby player during the course of a game is living life at its most intoxicating: *1929*

Like all fascinating things, however, rugby has

its dangers. To say that, 'Rugby is good for the health' is wrong; so many of the greatest exponents of rugby have fallen into an early grave: *1929*

Bob Hiller – *England*
He had the hair of a city slicker, and the hoofing toecap of a Tunisian mule:
Frank Keating – sportswriter

Phil Horrocks-Taylor – *England*
Every time I went to tackle him, Horrocks went one way, Taylor the other, and all I got was the bloody hyphen: *Nick England – Ireland*

'Dickie' Jeeps – *England & President of the RFU*
There is far too much talk of good ball and bad ball. In my opinion, good ball is when you have possession and bad ball is when the opposition have it.

Vivian Jenkins – *Welsh player & sportswriter*
The one-handed 'palmer' can always reach higher, they say. They may be right, but the result is that nearly every line-out is like a tropical island – all waving palms.

Barry John – *(b 1945) Wales*
Living in a 'goldfish bowl' is not living at all – adulation is alienating me from the human race.

I was able to stay in my natural environment and develop there as a respected member of the community. If I had been fifteen years old and pulled off the streets of Belfast onto the pitch at Old Trafford, I feel I'd have ended up as George Best has: *1972*

Chris Laidlaw – *New Zealand*
Rugby is a rolling barrel of history.

Rugby may have many problems, but the gravest is undoubtedly that of the persistence of summer.

Dennis LaLanne – *New Zealand*
Rugby is not like tea, which is good only in England, with English water and English milk. On the contrary, rugby would be better, frankly, if it were made in a Twickenham pot and warmed up in a Pyrenean cauldron: *1960*

Robert Lynd – *(1879-1949) Anglo-Irish essayist*
The only doubt in my mind was whether rugby isn't too dangerous a game – for the spectators.

Dr David MacSweeney – *Ireland*
It's the nearest you can get legally nowadays to coming home with flesh on your shoulders and blood on your hands.

Joe McPartlin – *Scotland & Oxford University*
On his successors in the Varsity back division – I've seen better centres in a box of Black Magic.

Colin Meads – *New Zealand*
I get very brassed off with All Blacks who say rugby has cost them a lot. Rugby has been the greatest thing that has ever happened to me.

John Morgan – *Wales*
An international at Twickenham is more than mere spectacle. It is the gathering of the clan.

Old Stager
To compare the rugby football of 1881 with the game as we know, would be about as absurd as instituting a comparison between the old Snider rifle of the period and the up-to-date magazine 'death-dealer': *1893*

O. L. Owen – *sportswriter*
The rugby game is full of possibilities and it is hard to pin-point the one absolute essential. But one thing at least is certain. No-one wants to see more than an occasional match lost and won by penalty points: *1954*

Maxwell Price
A touring team, especially an unbeaten one on a long tour, is the Aunt Sally of the rugby world in which it is travelling: *1961*

Wallace Reyburn – *New Zealand sportswriter*
There is, of course, something special about England as far as Rugby is concerned. After all, they invented it.

Andy Ripley – *England*
On selection for M. R. Steele-Bodger's XV – I had this strange phone call from this geezer, saying to report to Cambridge next Thursday to play for some departmental store side or something, name of Bodger and Steele, or something – should I go?

Rugby is picking the ball from the back of the scrum in 1974 and scoring a try against Wales at Twickenham and realising that, 'I sort of hit it and it was in the back of the net, Brian' is fairly appropriate.

Jean Pierre Rives – *France*
The whole point of rugby is that it is, first and foremost, a state of mind, a spirit.

J.W. Robinson
In my time I've had my knee put out, broken my collar-bone, had my nose smashed, a rib broken, lost a few teeth, and ricked my ankle, but as soon as I get a bit of bad luck I'm going to quit the game.

South Wales Reporter
To any sport, amusement or pastime, indoor or outdoor, bar rugby football, bad weather simply spells no gate and empty benches: *1893*

Elizabeth Taylor – *(b 1932) actress*

It seems a neat game, but do they really bite ears off?

Gwyn Thomas – *(1913–81) Welsh playwright*
I wanted a play that would paint the full face of sensuality, rebellion and revivalism. In South Wales, these three phenomena have played second fiddle to the Rugby Union, which is a distillation of all three: *1963*

Lord Wakefield – *England player & politician*
There is something in the spirit of rugger that is worth defining, difficult though it is to express.

Mike Williams – *coach*
All the problems of sevens arise from the basic fact of space.

Ray Williams – *Welsh coach*
If winning possession is to be regarded as the foundation stone of the game, then using it should be regarded as the super-structure.

SAILING

BOARD-SAILING

Major Hall – *US writer*
Board-sailing has the freedom of sailing, the speed and excitement of skiing and surfing, the beauty of gymnastics, the grace of figure skating, and the free-flight sensation of sky-diving and hang-gliding: *1985*

YACHTING

Proverbs
It is hard to sail over the ocean in an egg-shell.

David Blagden – *yachtsman & writer*
There is never a 'right' time to sail across the Atlantic alone. There is only 'now' or 'never':
      1973

Jilly Cooper – *(b 1937) writer*
I never liked sailing men. They yell blue murder at you all day, but then, when the boat is moored, the whisky comes out, 'Captain

Bligh' turns Casanova and is all ready to play 'deck coitus'.

John Fisher – *yachtsman & writer*
Sailing offers greater thrills than many sports, with less risk than most, for it provides a sensation of great speed without the necessity for travelling fast: *1953*

Michael Green – *writer*
A coarse sailor is one who in a crisis forgets nautical language and shouts, 'For God's sake turn left!':   *1962*

Coarse sailing is not mucking around in boats, but boating around in muck.

Edward Heath – *(b 1916) Prime Minister & yachtsman*
Ocean racing is like standing under a cold shower tearing up £5 notes.

Jack Knights – *yachtsman & writer*

Sailing is full of unstraightforward names for quite straightforward things: *1961*

'Ring' Lardner - *(1885-1933) US humorist*
Watching an America's Cup is like watching the grass grow.

D.A. Rayner - *yachtsman & writer*

The endless contest with the sea is the finer for being obscure; for being fought without the plaudits of spectators: *1961*

Hugh Whall - *US writer*
The things that drive a man to ocean sailing must be pretty much the same as those that drive him to drink: *1966*

SHOOTING

Proverbs
A good marksman may miss.

Shooting often hits the mark.

Never shoot, never hit.

He that's always shooting must sometimes hit.

It is not enough to aim, you must hit.

A. Bogardus

No shot is big enough to stop the target without hitting it.

Harry W. Johnson
Definition of Target Shooting skill -
Skill = Speed × Accuracy × Form × Adaptability.

Sir Philip Sidney - *(1554-1586) poet*
Who shoots at the mid-day sun, though he be sure he shall never hit the mark; yet, as sure as he is he shall shoot higher than who aims at a bush.

SKATING

FIGURE

Anon
The Rotterdam Dutchman, with fleet-cutting scates
To please the crowd shows his tricks and his feats;
Who, like a rope dancer (for his sharp steels),
His brains and activity lies in his heels:
c 1683

Notice at Eton School - No boy may go ice-skating on any water not passed by the headmaster.

Josh Billings [Henry Wheeler Shaw] - *(1818-85) US humorist*
The thinner the ice, the more anxious everybody is to see if it will bear.

Alan Coren - *(b 1938) editor & humorist*

Pairs skating relies for its effect upon manufacturing an illusion of romantic sexuality: *1989*

John Curry - *world & Olympic champion [1976]*
To Liberace - You've got so much ice on your hands, I could skate on them.

John Curry is appearing in the play, but he's not wearing his skates - he's got a completely different hat on his head this time: *Peter Levy*

Linda Fratianne - *US world champion [1979]*
Sometimes I get too 'thinky'. I don't skate as free as I can: *1978*

Heinrich Heine - *(1797-1856) German poet & satirist*
Skating is a chilly pleasure, and therefore, no sin.

Sonja Henie - *(1912-69) Norwegian Olympic champion [1928, 1932 & 1936]*
All my life I have wanted to skate and all my life I have skated.

Robert Lowell - *(b 1917) US poet*
Only Armageddon will suffice,
To turn the hero skating on thin ice.

Brian Orser - *Canadian world champion [1987]*
On taking the Olympic silver medal - Brian Orser was good, but not good enough to beat Boitano in Calgary. The hosts thought their Brian would be the winner, but Boitano skated figure eights, Orser skated only figure sevens:
Mike Downey (1984)

Samuel Pepys - *(1633-1703) diarist*
People sliding with their skates is a very pretty art.

Oleg & Lyudmila Protopopov - *Russian Olympic champions [1964 & 1968]*
Art cannot be measured by points. We skate from the heart. To us it is the spiritual beauty that exists between a man and a woman. That

is what we try to show: *Oleg*

The Protopopovs are a Russian couple whose name sounded like a moped misfiring:
Clive James - writer & humorist

SPEED

Ralph Waldo Emerson - *(1803-1882) US philosopher & poet*
In skating over thin ice, our safety is in our speed.

Eric Heiden - *(b 1958) US Olympic champion [1980]*
Five gold medals! What can you do with them? I'd rather have a warm-up suit, at least you could wear that.

Maybe if things had stayed the way they were, and I could still be obscure in an obscure sport, I might want to keep skating. I really liked it best when I was a nobody.

Eric Heiden is to ice what Mark Spitz was to chlorinated water: *New York Times (1980)*

SKIING

DOWNHILL

Anon
On modern apres-ski - People say it's piste-bashing by day and duvet-bashing all night:
New Society

Corey Ford
Skiing? Why break my leg at 40 degrees below zero when I can fall downstairs at home?

William H. Gass - *(b 1924) US philosopher & writer*
We always ski on the higher slopes when we can: *1971*

Marc Hodler - *President of the FIS*
Skiing has changed, the weather has not.

Bill Johnson - *US Olympic downhill champion*

[1984]
Before the Olympic downhill - It's a race for second place, I'm going to win: *1984*

Before the same race - Top three? I think I'll finish in the top one!: *1984*

Jean-Claude Killy - *(b 1943) French triple Olympic champion [1968]*
Skiing is a battle against yourself, always to the frontiers of the impossible. But most of all, it must give you pleasure. It is not an obligation: *1968*

Franz Klammer- *Austrian Olympic downhill champion [1976]*
I have never skied in Franz Klammer's shadow
– I was too good for that:
Peter Mueller - Switzerland

None of us should forget that Franz Klammer put ski-racing on the world television screen:
Ken Read – Canada

Champions are men who deliver on the day. Great champions are men who face crushing odds and still deliver on the day. And there are immortal champions. Such a champion is Franz Klammer: *Ian Wooldridge – sportswriter*

Klaus Leitner – *Austrian ski instructor*
You can play tennis anywhere in the world. You cannot ski anywhere.

John Lennon – *(1940–80) musician & songwriter*
After ten minutes on the St Moritz slopes – That's enough for today. Let's all go back to the restaurant.

Ernano Noggles – *ski trainer*
In skiing you win in the mind. You lose there too.

Steve Podborski – *Canadian joint World Cup champion [1982]*
Downhill skiing is the classic 'fight or fright' syndrome. The only thing I want to do when I am going fast is – to go faster.

You don't think. There is no thought process in skiing. You react like an animal.

Pope John Paul II – *(b 1920)*
It is unbecoming for a Cardinal to ski badly.

James Riddell
Good boots and average skis are better than average boots and good skis.

Maria Sterling – *US fashion writer*
On ski-wear – The idea is to look like a cross between subway graffiti and Papua New Guinea. The skier, even at a dead stop, will snap, sizzle and smoke: *1987*

G. Weltner
It would be a poor play indeed if it ever lost its most dramatic and spell-binding quality, the quality of danger – real, genuine, leg-breaking danger.

SPEED

Steve McKinney
It's a whole life trip, it beats the hell out of drugs.

Graham Wilkie – *world speed record holder [1987]*
Many thought us eccentrics, freaks, kamikaze people. Driving a London cab is more dangerous.

SKI JUMPING

Eddie 'The Eagle' Edwards – *British record holder & last in both Olympic ski-jumps [1988]*
His glasses are pink and white and as thick as the bottom of a Coca-Cola bottle and when he puts his goggles over them they mist up:
Chris Brasher (1988)

Eddie is the symbol of de Coubertin's ideal – a man whose only triumph is the struggle:
Chris Brasher

He has done for British winter sports what Screaming Lord Sutch has done for the British electoral system: *Colin M. Jarman (1988)*

You must not laugh at Eddie, he is good for our sport:
Matti Nykaenen – double Olympic gold medallist

'Eddie The Eagle' has shown the world that lack of ability need be no barrier to success on the slopes: *Barry Waters (1988)*

Mr Edwards' performance was the equivalent of a first ball duck in a Test match, two own goals in a Wembley Cup Final, or a first round of 168 in the Open Golf championships:
Ian Wooldridge – sportswriter

We have thousands of Eddie Edwards in

Norway, but we never let them jump:
Torbjorn Yggeseth (1988)

Shirley Sullivan - *US writer*
There are no natural jumpers, because what they do is unnatural.

SNOOKER

Steve Davis - *(b 1957) 6 times world champion [1981–89]*
Title of autobiography - Frame and Fortune.

Steve may be a man and a champion to millions, but at home he's still our boy and if he sits in my chair, I'll tell him and he gets out quickly: *Bill Davis - father (1981)*

Steve Davis is acknowledged by his peers to be the peerless master: *John McCririck - TV pundit*

You have as much class as my backside:
Cliff Thorburn - Canada (1981)

Terry Griffiths - *Welsh world champion [1979]*
Compared to the jobs I used to do, this is money for old rope.

Stephen Hendry - *Scottish world champion [1990]*
One of Stephen Hendry's greatest assets is his ability to score when he's playing well:
Ted Lowe - TV commentator

Alex 'Hurricane' Higgins - *Irish world champion [1972 & 1982]*
I was in tears when Ali lost. Apart from Lester Piggott and Georgie Best he was the only guy I ever really looked up to. People have criticised me in the past for behaving like the Ali of snooker. Well that's OK with me. Ali is in a class of his own. He is supreme, he is the greatest: *1981*

A lot of people are using two-piece cues nowadays. Alex Higgins hasn't got one, because they don't come with instructions:
Steve Davis - England

It is all very attractive, the talent, the tears, the tantrums, the highs and lows, and all that so-called human stuff, but underneath there is a selfishness and ruthlessness that makes me look

like a choir boy: *Steve Davis*

'Hurricane' Higgins did for snooker what Guy Fawkes did for fireworks:
Colin M. Jarman - sportswriter (1988)

Snooker's played on 'the green', and it pays to be bold,
Each click of the balls sounds like cricket.
The crowd rise as they did to the Bradman of old,
When Hurricane 'comes to the wicket':
John Jarvis

Alex Higgins has gone to Belfast to launch a ship, but he won't let go of the bottle:
Dennis Taylor - Ireland

Bernard Hollowood - *writer*
There's something wrong with a young chap who doesn't play games. Not even snooker:
Scowle in the Sixties

Clive James - *(b 1939) writer & humorist*
Whoever called snooker 'chess with balls' was rude, but right.

Ted Lowe - *TV commentator*
Cliff Thorburn has been unsettled by the erratic, but consistent potting of Perry Mans.

It's not easy to get a snooker when there's only one ball on the table.

John Pulman - *English world champion [1957–68]*
No one ever became so good at a ball game that they could play it like a machine.

Ray Reardon - *Welsh 6 times world champion [1970–78]*
If I had to make the choice between staying married and playing snooker, snooker would win.

Ray Reardon, one of the great Crucible champions, won it five times – when the championship was played away from the Crucible: *David Vine – TV presenter*

Dennis Taylor – *Irish world champion [1985]*
The deciding frame's always the toughest to win.

Jimmy 'The Whirlwind' White – *Masters champion [1984]*
Jimmy White has the nervous system of a fighter pilot on amphetamines:
Clive James – writer & humorist

A little pale in the face, but then his name is White: *Ted Lowe – TV commentator*

SQUASH

Jonah Barrington – *(b 1941) 6 times British Open champion [1967–73]*
Squash is boxing with rackets.

Before I arrived, no one trained specifically for squash; it was just a means of keeping fit for other sports such as rugby and football.

At the moment the gap between me and these other fellows is marginal. I want to make it a gulf as big as the Grand Canyon: *1967*

Fitness means you don't take risks to finish a rally quickly.

There is a fantastic and savage and unrivalled and unbelievable satisfaction the moment you know you have beaten your opponent. You look into his eyes and see the defeat, the degradation, the humiliation and there isn't anything in the world like it.

He has always been a fascinating evangelist for the game. He's the most important figure in the entire history of the game:
Rex Bellamy – sportswriter

Before Barrington,there were cobwebs on the courts of Pakistan. If you stopped somebody in the street and asked him what squash was, he would have said Robinsons make it and it comes in bottles. Jonah Barrington was the man who created the squash boom:
Dicky Rutnagur – sportswriter

Rex Bellamy – *sportswriter*
The essence of squash could, with care, be

written on the back of a postage stamp. But one can spend a lifetime failing to master it.

Sir Noel Coward – *(1899–1973) actor, composer & playwright*
Squash – that's not exercise, it's flagellation.

Gavin 'Peter' Hildick-Smith – *South African British amateur champion [1951]*
'Peter' was no stylist, but he was a strong, gritty player and had a knack of 'mishitting' winners. After he'd done it six or seven times you began to suspect it was no fluke:
Brian Phillips

John Hopkins – *sportswriter*
Squash is less frustrating than golf, less fickle than tennis. It is easier than badminton, cheaper than polo. It is better exercise than bowls, quicker than cricket, less boring than jogging, drier than swimming, safer than hang-gliding: *1980*

Geoff Hunt – *Australian World Open champion [1976–80]*
Australia is the only country where the game is opened up and available to the average person in the street.

Doug Ibbotson – *sportswriter*
A squash ball is no ordinary ball – ordinary balls bounce.

Hashim Khan – *Pakistani 7 times British Open champion [1950–7]*
In short time squash is best exercise. Fun game. Just follow the ball and forget everything: *1976*

My first impression of Hashim was of a short dumpy little man with a barrel chest. Inside that chest was a pump that cirulated blood with oxygen in it and continued to circulate blood long after his opponent had gone home:
Roy Wilson - British Amateur champion [1954 & 1956]

I'm sure that his plimsolls were three sizes too large. He started off and the shoes followed. Then the shoes stopped and Hashim went on – inside the shoes. There was a squeal of shoes on the floor, then a squeal of feet in the shoes:
Roy Wilson

Jahangir Khan - *Pakistani World Open champion [1981-85]*
Jahangir Khan seemed prodigal, unbeatable –

Hagler, Leonard and Curry rolled into one:
Frank Keating - sportswriter

This is a great sport. I have dedicated my life to it, squash and the Khan family are synonymous:
Nasrullah Khan - Pakistan

Almost without exception, squash players deep down are power crazy egomaniacs, with a profound inner need to dominate something. These are the people who, if they weren't executives or housewives or taxi-drivers, would probably be Public Executioners: *Barry Waters*

Mohamed Yasin - *Pakistan*
A springy little chap with bushy eyebrows and a solemn mien – a Victor Borge without the humour:
Rex Bellamy - sportswriter

SURFING

E. Burdick - *US writer*
The essence of surfing is the delicate balance between control and chaos, and it works on surfers like a drug.

R. Prytherch
Is it a sport, an art form, or a personal involvement between man and the elements? Perhaps it touches, even if it fails to combine, all three:
1972

SWIMMING

POOL

Anon
In swimming a person remembers that he is a child of nature.

It is said that swimming develops poise and grace, but have you seen how a duck walks?

Whoever said, 'Swimming is the best exercise for keeping the body slim and trim' had obviously never seen a whale.

Mother, may I go out to swim?
Yes, my darling daughter.
Hang your clothes on a hickory limb,
But don't go near the water!

A person drowns if he allows the water to win.

Woody Allen - *(b 1935) US comedian & actor*
I wanted to be an Olympic swimmer, but I had some problems with buoyancy.

Dr E. Baynard
Of exercises, swimming's best,
Strengthens the heart and the chest,
And all their fleshy parts confirms.
Extends and stretches legs and arms:
Health (1764)

John Betjeman - *(1906-1984) Poet Laureate*
When Captain Webb the Dawley man,
Captain Webb from Dawley,
Came swimming along the old canal
That carried the bricks to Lawley

We saw the ghost of Captain Webb,
   Webb in a water sheeting,
Come dripping along in bathing dress
To the Saturday evening meeting:
                              A Shropshire Lad

Matt Biondi – *US world & Olympic champion
[1986–8]*
It's the getting there that counts, not the cheese
at the end of the maze.

Lewis Carroll – *(1832–98) writer*
They told me you had been to her and
   mentioned me to him;
   She gave me a good character, but said I
   could not swim.

Cecil Colwin – *writer & coach*
The development of the crawl stroke is the
history of man's effort to swim better and
faster.

Samuel Croxall – *(1680–1752) Archdeacon of
Salisbury*
Never throw away your corks till time has
given you strength and experience enough to
swim without them.

Dawn Fraser – *Australian multi-Olympic
champion [1956–64]*
I have my fun and I think I'm a better swimmer
because of it.

Thomas Fuller – *(1654–1734) physician &
writer*
Good swimmers are oftenest drowned: *1732*

Shane Gould – *(b 1956) Australian double
Olympic champion [1972]*
All that glitters is not Gould:
                              T-shirt slogan (1972)
[Worn by US swimmers at the Munich Olympics]

Clive James – *(b 1939) writer, humorist &
broadcaster*
On the correctly formed pubescent girl, a
Speedo looked wonderful. When it was wet, it
was an incitement to riot.

Richard Jeffries – *(1848–87) novelist*
I swam and what is more delicious than
swimming? It is exercise and luxury at once.

Anne M. Lindbergh – *(b 1906) US poet &
essayist*
Swimming – exercise in its most condensed
form.

Anita Lonsborough – *Olympic breaststroke
champion [1960]*
It's obvious these Russian swimmers are
determined to do so well on American soil.

Anke Mohring – *East German world 10,000
metres record holder*
The secret of swimming? If I knew, I wouldn't
tell you.

N. W. Sarsfield
It is the swimmer not the water that moves.

William Shakespeare – *(1564–1616)
playwright*
If he fall in, good night, or sink or swim!:
                              Henry IV – Pt I

James Thomson – *(1700–48) poet*
This is the purest exercise of health; the kind
refresher of the summer heats.

Virgil – *(70–19 BC) Roman poet*
Odd figures were glimpsed in the waste of
waters.

David Wilkie – *Olympic 200m breaststroke
champion*
If David Wilkie goes on like this he'll be home
and dry: *Alan Weekes – TV commentator*

SYNCHRONIZED

David Hunn – *sportswriter*
A girl with a plastic smile and gelatined hair
will win the penultimate gold at these games. It
will be awarded for an outstanding performance
in holding your breath underwater and
waggling your legs in the air: *1984*

Colin M. Jarman – *(b 1958) sportswriter*
Synchronized swimming is to sport what
Formica is to the Antiques Roadshow: *1988*

Frank Keating – *(b 1937) sportswriter*
What on earth has this synchronised swimming
got to do with anything, let alone sport?

George Rackham - *(b 1914) writer & national technical officer, Swimming Teachers Association*
Synchronized swimming is a skilful art.

Demmie Stathoplos - *US sportswriter*
Synchronized swimmers may look cup-cakes, but they are tough cookies.

DIVING

C. J. Alderson
Springboard diving is a unique activity, a combination of aquatics and acrobatics: *1964*

Wally Orner
There is a world of difference between what the diver thinks he is doing and what he is doing.

TABLE TENNIS

Leslie Woollard
In no other sport is there so broad and universal an appeal which, in its higher phases, combines the psychology of bridge, the grace of eurythmics, the footwork of dancing, the lightning cut-and-thrust of fencing, the waywardness of golf, the ball cunning of billiards and the agility of athletics: *1952*

TENNIS

PLAYERS

Boris Becker - *(b 1967) West Germany*
Boris Becker's serve achieves upward thrust like a space shuttle: *Mark Cox (1989)*

Bjorn Borg - *(b 1956) Sweden*
Borg ran like a deer, leapt as if on springs, and served and smashed like a low-flying bomber:
Rex Bellamy - sportswriter

I'll chase that son of a bitch Borg to the ends of the earth. I'll be waiting for him. I'll dog him everywhere. Every time he looks around, he'll see my shadow: *Jimmy Connors - USA*

Bjorn Borg looks like a hunch-backed, jut-bottomed version of Lizabeth Scott, impersonating a bearded apache princess:
Clive James - writer & humorist

Like a Volvo, Bjorn Borg is rugged, has good after-sales service, and is very dull: *Clive James*

They should send Borg away to another planet. We play tennis. He plays something else:
Ilie Nastase - Rumania

Jean Borotra - *France*
The only possible regret I have is the feeling that I will die without having played enough tennis.

Louise Brough - *USA*
Louise Brough cannot serve at the moment, because she hasn't got any balls:
Rex Alston - commentator

Jimmy Connors - *(b 1952) USA*
After winning the US Open at Flushing Meadows -
The fans here are nuts, but so am I. They may not know a lot about whatever, but they enjoy guys who break their back and spill their guts and give everything that they have got. I've done that since I was 15 and they appreciate me: *1982*

New Yorkers love it when you spill your guts out there. Spill your guts at Wimbledon and they make you stop and clean it up.

When you're hot, anything can happen.

Connors likes the ball to come at him in a straight line, so that he can hit it back in another straight line. When it comes to him in a curve, he uses up half of his energy straightening it up again: *Clive James - writer*

Connors' seeding here at Wimbledon was affected by his wife having a baby. There was some doubt about his entry:
Peter West - commentator

Jimmy Connors is loud, aggressive and with the face and hairstyle of a medieval varlet, he personifies a generation which tips its hat to no man: *Ian Wooldridge - sportswriter*

Bradford Dillman - *US actor*
I prefer golf to tennis, all tennis courts look alike: *1980*

Francois Durr - *France*
I am glad I have not got a big serve - because I fear for the size of my shoulders: *1972*

Chris Evert - *(b 1954) USA*
You get labelled. People tell me every day how great I am, and they don't know me. I'm no angel. I'm a control freak - on and off the court.

Desire is the key. I don't feel it consistently, but when I have it I can't be beaten.

Chris Evert is the young lady who would rather be famous for being a girl than for being a tennis player: *Rex Bellamy - sportswriter (1972)*

If tailored is in, so is boring:
Mr Blackwell - US fashion critic (1977)
[*Miss Evert was on his list of worst-dressed women*]

Chrissie is the Sugar Plum fairy of the lot:
Ted Tinling - US fashion designer

Neale Fraser - *Australia*
If you put monkeys on to play they'd still pack Centre Court at Wimbledon.

Timothy Gallewey - *US player & writer*
I know intellectually that being good at tennis wasn't a valid test of manhood - or of anything of importance - but I was still tight before a match: *1975*

Althea Gibson - *(b 1927) USA*

I don't want to be put on a pedestal. . . . I've always wanted to have identity. I'm Althea Gibson - the tennis champion. I hope it makes me happy: *1958*

The Gullikson Twins [Tim & Tom] - *USA*
Both from Wisconsin:
Dan Maskell - TV commentator

Lew Hoad - *Australia*
Every year you say you'll never play Paris again. Your arm nearly falls off. The balls are heavy. They water the courts. You're always playing some guy you've never heard of and he keeps you out there for well over three and a half hours. But it's a great tournament.

Art Hoppe - *(b 1925) US writer*
The proper method of playing mixed doubles is to swipe the ball accidentally and straight at the woman opponent as hard and as accurately as possible. Male players must not only retain equanimity on their side of the net, but create dissension on the other.

Kathy Jordan - *USA*
Kathy Jordan has a frying pan grip:
Rex Bellamy - sportswriter

Kathy Jordan's racket arm bears not only a wristlet, but also an elbow bandage; which means that her arm looks like a lagged cold-water pipe: *Rex Bellamy*

Billie Jean King - *(b 1943) USA*
Ask Nureyev to stop dancing, ask Sinatra to stop singing, then you can ask me to stop playing: *1982*

The ultimate power trip for me, for any athlete, is to give those watching, to inspire, motivate, bring joy.

My ego operates this way - every time you tell me I can't do something, that ego tells me I not only can, but must.

Self-awareness is the most important thing towards being a champion.

I'm not sure if it's the environment in which you play or if it's innate, because I've always played better under pressure, even when I was

171

a youngster.

What saddens me about some young players is not merely that they lack devotion to the history of the game, but that they have little curiosity about anything around them.

If Colgate is just a kid's cavity fighter, how come Billie Jean won't brush with anything else?:
Advertising slogan

You'll be good, because you're ugly, Billie Jean:
Frank Brennan

Billie Jean has to work three times as hard as the rest of us to stay even. When I get out of bed stiff, the morning after a long, tough match, I can't imagine what it must be like for her:
Chris Evert

She was born to be an entertainer. She has to perform for a crowd, and she will as long as people clap. I'm afraid people like this sometimes equate adulation with love:
Larry King – husband

Billie Jean King has always been conscious of wind on the centre court:
Dan Maskell – commentator

We wouldn't be where we are without Billie Jean King:
Martina Navratilova

Madame Superstar is too susceptible to moods, too turbulent to ever be happy for very long. She self-destructs:
Ted Tinling – US fashion designer

Johann Kriek - *USA*
Kriek, receiving service, spun his racket as if using a manual food mixer:
Rex Bellamy – sportswriter

Rod Laver - *(b 1938) Australia*
An otherwise happily married couple may turn a mixed doubles game into a scene from *Who's afraid of Virginia Woolf.*

Ivan Lendl - *(b 1960) Czechoslovakia*
If I smile I have to think about smiling and that would break my concentration.

Lendl remains as calm as the proverbial

iceberg:
Dan Maskell – commentator

John Lloyd
Not since Betty Grable has so much been written about a pair of legs as John Lloyd's:
Taki (1978)

John McEnroe - *(b 1959) USA*
People pay to watch me and if they want to boo me, that's fine. I'd rather get some attention than no attention. If it's bad, that's life.

So many times the crowd never understand what I am trying to say and just never give me a chance. I have a perfect right to point out to an umpire politely he has made an error.

If I see something that's wrong I just have to say so. You could say I have a temper. I'm Irish you know.

People get very nervous when they officiate me. Anyone who doesn't think so is an absolute jerk. I'm partly to blame, but they're, like, jumping out of their pants half of the time.

I've probably played 10,000 games in my career and I've been annoyed by a call in about 9,999. There is probably one match when I wasn't angry. You're not talking to Bjorn Borg: *1989*

I wouldn't like to be an umpire for me, that's for sure.

Against Connors and Borg you feel like you're being hit with a sledgehammer. But this guy is a stiletto. He has great balance and he just slices people up. He's got a ton of shots. It's slice here, nick there, cut over there. Pretty soon you've got blood all over you, even though the wounds aren't deep. Soon after that you've bled to death:
Arthur Ashe – USA

The game is so simple for him, he just gets mad when anything goes wrong:
Mary Carillo – former mixed doubles partner

I'm telling you, this guy can't pick his nose without people booing him:
Peter Fleming – former men's doubles partner

McEnroe serves around the corner of an imaginary building and his wind-up must perforce be extra careful. He has a sniper's caution: *Clive James – writer*

Hair like badly-turned broccoli: *Clive James*

Bob McPhee
Behind every tennis player there is another tennis player.

Dan Maskell – *TV commentator*
On a doubles partnership – The British boys are adopting the attacking position – Cox up.

Kerry Melville – *Australia*
Kerry Melville hits the line so often, that we sometimes suspect she has an inbuilt reluctance to assault anything green:
Rex Bellamy – sportswriter

Fred Mulhauser – *US coach*
Every tennis doctor at some time or another will be called upon to treat a case of virulent foot-faulting: *1980*

Ilie Nastase – *Rumania*
Tennis is a very dangerous life. To spend nine years with a person and to have a child; to lose them because of a game, is a big, big price to pay.

Tennis is the strangest game ever. It is all in your head. Little things can bother you, destroy your game. So think what a big thing can do.

How wonderful it is to look over after smashing the ball he cannot see, and watch how he cannot move, and see him split in half: *1972*

After complaints about his abusive language – You don't go to an X-rated movie if you don't want to watch it: *1981*

When Ilie Nastase plays John McEnroe, it's the only time the crowd call for silence:
Jerry Girard (1979)

When he demanded to be addressed as 'Mr' – Look, Nastase, we used to have a famous cricket match in this country called *Gentlemen versus Players*. The Gentlemen were put down on the scorecard as 'Mister' because they were gentlemen. By no stretch of the imagination can anybody call you a gentleman:
Trader Horn – Wimbledon umpire

Nastase is a Hamlet who wants to play a clown. He is no good at it: *Clive James (1975)*

Nastase rarely grins and bears it. More commonly he grins, groans, shrugs, slumps, spins around, shakes his head, puffs out his cheeks, rolls on the ground and bears it. Even more common, he does all that and doesn't bear it: *Clive James*

The problem with Ilie Nastase is that you never know what he's thinking. He's like Muhammad Ali. You just never know what he's up to and it psyches you out: *Bob Kreiss*

Sometimes something happens. He goes mad, I guess. I think there are times when he does not know what he is doing, when he does not know where he is: *Dominique Nastase – wife*

Never has sport produced such an enigmatic man. For while nature endowed him with the golden gift of instinctive athleticism, she left him a little short in stability:
Laurie Pignon – sportswriter

There are some wonderfully strange people in sport. But, in trying to find comparisons with Nastase, I can only come up with three I know of – Ali, Bobby Fischer and, to a lesser extent, Lee Trevino: *George Plimpton – US writer*

You cannot change Nastase, and if you did, he would not be Nastase:
Ion Tiriac – former Davis Cup partner

Martina Navratilova – *(b 1956) USA*
I'm not involved in tennis, I am committed. Do you know the difference between involvement and commitment? Think of ham and eggs. The chicken is involved, the pig is committed!

Chris Evert and I are more like fine wine. We get better with age. The older we get, the more you appreciate us. So, I think we'll stick around for another decade: *1988*

Navratilova charges the net like a ship under full sail, with a following wind:
Rex Bellamy – sportswriter

Martina's smashes and volleys are the kind that punctuate a rally with a full stop rather than a comma: *Rex Bellamy*

When Martina is tense it helps her to relax:
Dan Maskell – commentator

People sitting behind Martina Navratilova on the roller have the best view of her receiving service: *Max Robertson – commentator*

The only way to beat Martina now is to run over her foot in the car park:
Pam Shriver – doubles partner

Todd Nelson – *USA*
Todd Nelson is coffee coloured – medium roast – and has such well developed muscles, that one wonders how his skin takes the strain:
Rex Bellamy – sportswriter

Yannick Noah – *(b 1960) France*
Having the No. 1 hung on me doesn't interest me at all; you end up thinking you're God. That's dangerous.

Noah always beats Curren, he has a sort of Houdini against him:
David Lloyd – player and commentator

Charlie Pasarell – *USA*
Charlie Pasarell moves so slowly between points, that at times he seems to be flirting with reverse gear: *Rex Bellamy – sportswriter*

Raffaella Reggi – *Italy*
When Raffaella Reggi goes out of a tournament, it is as if someone switched out the Christmas lights: *Rex Bellamy – sportswriter*

Eugene Scott – *USA*
Instead of being used to commence a rally, the serve is now being used to abort a rally. It is an instrument of destruction in its own right.

Speed in tennis is a strange mixture of intuition, guesswork, footwork and hair-trigger reflexes. Many of the players famed for quickness on court would finish dead last in a field of schoolgirls in a race over any distance more than ten yards.

Betty Stove – *Holland*
Miss Stove seems to have gone off the boil:
Peter West – commentator

Roscoe Tanner – *USA*
Roscoe Tanner is the kind of man who keeps ringing the bell on fairground strength machines: *Rex Bellamy – sportswriter*

Bill Tilden – *(1893–1953) USA*
The primary objective of match tennis is to break up the other man's game.

The player owes the gallery as much as an actor owes the audience.

Anticipation at the net is just a woman's fancy word for guessing right.

Amateur is a term used to indicate an inferior performer – but this is not true in the world of tennis.

Bill Tilden's silhouette as he prepares to serve suggests an Egyptian pyramid King about to administer punishment: *Anon*

He is more of an artist than nine-tenths of the artists I know. It is the beauty of the game that Tilden loves; it is the chase always, rather than the quarry: *Franklin P. Adams*

To opponents it was a contest; with Tilden it was an expression of his own tremendous and overwhelming ego, coupled with feminine vanity: *Paul Gallico – US writer*

When he came into the room it was like a bolt of electricity hit the place. The atmosphere became charged, and there was almost a sensation of lightness when he left. You felt completely dominated and breathed a sigh of relief for not having ventured an opinion of any sort: *George Lott – USA*

Teddy Tinling – *US fashion designer*
Teddy Tinling added glamour and class to the game. He thought of tennis as show-biz and that we were all actresses: *Chris Evert*

Mats Wilander – *Sweden*
During the French Open – Wilander reminded the strong-armed German that playing shots is not the same as playing tennis. Becker played draughts, while Wilander played chess:
Rex Bellamy – sportswriter

Guillermo Vilas - *Argentina*
For Nastase, tennis was all game, all play. For
Vilas, it is all work: *Ion Tiriac - manager*

Vilas strong? I play ice hockey, I think I am
strong. If we arm wrestle, this guy snap my arm
off quick. Laver strong? This guy snap Laver in
two pieces: *Ion Tiriac*

Helen Wills-Moody - *USA*
If you see a tennis player who looks as if he is
working very hard, then that means he isn't
very good.

LITERARY

Anon
When as the hand at Tennis plays,
    And men to gaming fall;
Love is the court, Hope is the house,
And Favour serves the ball: *1782*

Franklin P. Adams - *(1881-1960) US editor
& humorist*
Of tennis I played one or two sets
On a court at Richmond, Massachusetts.

J. M. Barrie - *(1860-1937) Scottish novelist &
dramatist*
What a polite game tennis is. The chief word in
it seems to be 'sorry' and admiration of each
other's play crosses the net as frequently as the
ball.

John Betjeman - *(1906-84) Poet Laureate*
Pam, you great big mountainous sports girl.
Whizzing them over the net, full the strength of
five: *Pot Pourri*

What strenuous singles we played after tea
    We in the tournament - you against me!
Love-thirty, love-forty, oh! weakness of joy,
    The speed of a swallow, the grace of a boy.
    The warm-handled racket is back in its press,
But my shell-shocked victor, she loves me no
    less: *A Subaltern's Love Song*

Robert Frost - *(1875-1963) US poet*
Writing free verse is like playing tennis with the
net down.

Virginia Graham - *writer*
Good shot, bad luck and hell are the five basic
words to be used in tennis.

James Hogg - *(1770-1839) Scottish poet*
A vain, idle and sinful game at which there was
much of the language of the accursed going on.

William Shakespeare - *(1564-1616)
playwright*
There falling out at tennis: *Hamlet*

When we have match'd our rackets to these
    balls,
    We will, in France, by God's grace play a set:
        Henry V

Molly Tyson - *US writer*
In a sport where 'love' means nothing, it's not
surprising that etiquette means everything:
        1978

John Webster - *(1580-1625) dramatist*
We are merely the stars' tennis balls, struck and
bandied, which way may please them: *1623*

VOLLEYBALL

Gail Parent - *(b 1941) US writer & scenarist*
Volleyball is a Jewish sport. It's fun, and
nobody can get hurt: *Sheila Levine is Dead and
Living in New York (1972)*

WEIGHT-LIFTING

Anon
Dumb-bells will get colour in a girl's face, and colour in a girl's face will get dumb-bells.

Paul Anderson – *US multi-world record holder*
For me this man has always been not only the personification of strength, but that of inspired strength, of lofty human qualities:
Yuriy Vlasov – Russian Olympic champion

Tommy Kono – *US world & Olympic champion [1952–59]*
When Tommy Kono looks at me from the wings, he works on me like a python on a rabbit: *Anon*

Al Murray – *weight trainer*
The one sport which will lay the foundation of success in all others – the one alone which can ensure pre-eminence in all others.

WRESTLING

ANCIENT

Anon
The other wrestlers are stylists, I win by my strength, as is only right and fitting for a Spartan.

Saying
A wrestler who dies in the contest earns entry to heaven just as surely as the soldier who falls in battle: *Turkish*

Ovid – *(43 BC–17 AD) Roman poet*
The fresh wrestler on the yellow sand is stronger than the one whose arms are worn out by a long wait.

MODERN

Anon
If someone died in the ring, they'd still claim it was faked.

Badminton Library
A Lancashire wrestling match is an ugly sight; the fierce animal passions of the men which mark the struggles of maddened bulls, the savage yelling of their partisans, and finally the clog business which settles all disputes and knotty problems, are simply appalling.

**George 'The Russian Lion'
Hackenschmidt** – *Greco-Roman wrestler*
Professional wrestling is just rehearsed acrobatics. It's not the sort of thing you would let your children go to see.

Luke Neely – *writer*
Professional wrestling's most mysterious hold is on its audience: *Saturday Evening Post (1953)*

William Shakespeare– *(1564–1616) playwright*
Like an Olympian wrestling: *Troilus & Cressida*

Joseph Strutt – *(1749–1802) writer & engraver*
To give a Cornish Hug is a proverbial pleasure: *1801*

'Gorgeous' George Wagner – *(1915–63) USA*
Catchphrase – I am the greatest!

I saw 15,000 people coming to see this man get beat. His talking did it. This is a g-o-o-o-o-o-o-d idea!: *Cassius Clay (1961)*
[*Clay used the 'Greatest' catchphrase to good effect*]

Andy Warhol – *(1927–88) US artist & film-maker*
On the WWF Wrestlemania – It's excitement, it's show business, it's chic.

ADVICE

Anon
If you wish to be a good sport, you must let people teach you a lot of things that you already know.

ATHLETICS

Sam Mussabini - *coach*
Only think of two things - the gun and the tape. When you hear the one, just run like hell until you break the other.

Emil Zatopek - *(b 1922) Czechoslovakian long distance runner*
You can't climb up to the second floor without a ladder. When you set your aim too high and don't fulfil it, then your enthusiasm turns to bitterness. Try for a goal that's reasonable, and then gradually raise it. That's the only way to get to the top.

BASEBALL

Tommy LaSorda - *LA Dodgers manager*
Always give an autograph when somebody asks you. You never can tell. In baseball, anything can happen.

Leroy 'Satchel' Paige - *(1906-82) St Louis Browns pitcher*
Six Rules for a Happy Life -
1. Avoid fried meats which angry up the blood.
2. If your stomach disputes you, lie down and pacify it with cool thoughts.
3. Keep the juices flowing by jangling around gently as you move.
4. Go very light on vices such as carrying on in society. The social ramble ain't restful.
5. Avoid running at all times.
6. Don't look back. Something may be gaining on you.
[*Paige used to hand out an autograph card with these six rules printed on the reverse*]

BOXING

Fritzie Zivic - *US welterweight*
Always work the ref's blind side.

CARDS

Nelson Algren - *(1909-81) US novelist*
Never play cards with a man called 'Doc'!

CLIMBING

Edward Whymper - *(1840-1911) alpinist*
Do nothing in haste, look well to each step, and from the beginning think what may be the end:
1871

CRICKET

W. G. Grace - *(1848-1915) Gloucestershire*
When you win the toss - bat.
If you are in doubt, think about it - then bat.
If you have very big doubts, consult a colleague - then bat.

Prince Ranjitsinhji - *(1872-1933) Sussex*
Find out where the ball is, get there; hit it.

EQUESTRIANISM

Xenophon - *(428-354 BC) Athenian soldier*
The Golden Rule in dealing with a horse is never to approach him angrily.

FOOTBALL

Brian Clough - *(1935) Nottingham Forest manager*
Say nowt, win it, then - talk your head off.

GOLF

Henry Cotton
I would not advise any pro to marry until after the age of thirty. Marriage demands a division of interests and golf, particularly tournament golf, demands every minute of a man's time.

Walter Hagen - *(1892-1969) USA*
You're only here for a short visit, so don't hurry, don't worry, and be sure to stop and smell the flowers along the way.

Ken Keniston - *US rower*
So much for a beautiful swing in golf if the ball ends up in the rough. It doesn't matter how you do it, as long as you do it better than your opponent: *1854*

Jack Nicklaus - *(b 1940) USA*
Tee the ball high. Because years of experience have shown me that air offers less resistance to dirt: *1977*

Edward Ray
On how to hit a golf ball further - Hit it a ruddy sight harder.

Lee Trevino - *(b 1939) USA*
On personal safety in a lightning storm - Hold up a one-iron and walk. Even God can't hit a one-iron.
[*Trevino had been struck by lighting in 1976*]

GYMNASTICS

Dale Flanasas - *US coach*
Reach out towards a goal. When you reach it, set another.

HORSE RACING

Lester Piggott - *(b 1935) jockey*
Never catch a loose horse. You could end up holding the fucking thing all day.

MOTOR RACING

Bill Vukovich - *USA*
After winning the Indianapolis 500 for the second successive year - There's no secret. You just press the accelerator to the floor and steer left: *1954*

[*He was killed in the following year's race, while leading*]

SHOOTING

Dead Shot magazine
In shooting with a young sportsman or a stranger, always allow him to precede you in getting over the fences; it may be that you save your life, or a limb, by the precaution: *1861*

SKIING

Rosie Mittermaier - *West Germany*
The main thing to remember is not to take sport too seriously. I have learned that because I have been beaten too often: *1976*

TENNIS

Hugo L. Black - *(1886-1971) US politician*
When I was forty my doctor advised me that a man in his forties shouldn't play tennis. I heeded his advice carefully and could hardly wait until I reached fifty to start again.

Billie Jean King - *(b 1943) USA*
Be Bold. If you're going to make an error, make a doozy, and don't be afraid to hit the ball.

If you're up against a girl with big boobs, bring her to the net and make her hit backhand volleys.

Rod Laver - *(b 1938) Australia*
Don't compose eulogies to yourself when you get ahead. Concentrate on staying there.

When you've got your man down, rub him out.

AGE

Anon
We do not stop playing because we are old; we grow old because we stop playing.

Proverb
Age is jocund; it makes sport for death.

Benjamin Franklin - *(1706-90) US statesman & philosopher*
Keep flax from fire, and youth from gaming.

Cornelia Otis Skinner - *(1901-79) US actress & humorist*
There are compensations for growing older.

One is the realisation that to be sporting isn't at all necessary. It is a great relief to reach this stage of wisdom.

Robert Walpole – *(1676–1745) Prime Minister*
My chief regret for the advance of life is that the infirmities of age compel me to renounce the enjoyment of field sports.

ANGLING

Izaak Walton – *(1593–1683) writer*
It is an act worthy the knowledge and patience of any old man: *The Compleat Angler*

ATHLETICS

Zola Budd – *South African/British middle distance runner*
Zola Budd looks like a twelve year old, runs like a twenty-five year old, and is only seventeen: *Ingrid Kristiansen – Norway*

Sir James Cantlie – *(1851–1926) physician*
Running races shuld be absolutely forbidden to men over 27 years of age. Between 30 and 40 a man may indulge in running at a moderate pace for exercise, but not in races. Men over 60 years of age should never run at all for anything, not even to catch a train: *Physical Efficiency (1906)*

Mary Decker – *(b 1958) US middle distance runner*
By the time I was sixteen I was a has-been.

Miruts Yifter – *Ethiopian long distance runner*
I no count the years. Men may steal my chickens, men may steal my sheep. But no man can steal my age.

BASEBALL

Joe Garagiola – *(b 1926) Pittsburgh Pirates & TV commentator*
Being traded is like celebrating your hundredth birthday. It might not be the happiest occasion in your life, but consider the alternatives.

'Casey' Stengell – *(1891–1975) New York Yankees & Mets manager*
On being sacked by the Yankees, for being too old –
I'll never make the mistake of being seventy again.

Charles de Gaulle is older than me, and he's running a country.

Most people my age are dead at the present time, and you can look it up!

Old-timers, weekends, and airplane landings are alike. If you can walk away from them, they're successful.

There comes a time in every man's life, and I've had plenty of them.

BOWLS

Derek Bell – *national coach*
Children who don't like contact sports find themselves more at home in the quieter, concentrated atmosphere of a Bowling green:
1985

David Bryant – *world Lawn Bowls champion*
Bowls is a young man's game which old men can play.
[*Age was of no concern to Bryant as he won the world title in 1980, fourteen years after his previous championship victory*]

Humphrey J. Dingley – *author*
So many young men are bowlers now that the appellation 'old man's game' does not hold good: *1893*

BOXING

Wilfrid Diamond – *US writer*
Age is a mighty important subject for a boxing champion, because it is the one opponent he can't lick.

CARDS

Alexander Pope – *(1688–1744) poet & satirist*
See how the world its veterans rewards!
A youth of frolics, an old age of cards.

GOLF

Andra Kirkaldy
Golf is not an old man's game. It is also an old woman's game. We can almost play golf as long as we can see and walk.

HORSE RACING

Dick Beddoes - *Canadian sportswriter*
Horses and jockeys mature earlier than people
– which is why horses are admitted to race
tracks at the age of two, and jockeys before they
are old enough to shave.

SQUASH

Heather McKay - *(b 1941) Australia*
Part of the problem with sport today is that the
parents want their kids to be what they weren't,
and are trying to live through them.

TENNIS

Tracy Austin - *USA*
When I was ten, all I ever dreamed of was
playing at Wimbledon, with the greats, and
having my ears pierced.

Ilie Nastase - *Rumania*
Everyone keeps telling me I'm 31, and now I
start to worry about my strokes. Now I'm
thinking, two or three times, before I hit each
shot. Before I just used to play and everything
came naturally.

ANTI-SPORT

John Betjeman - *(1906–84) Poet Laureate*
The greatest dread of all, the dread of games.

Jean-Marie Brohm - *French gym coach*
Sport is an armoured apparatus for coercion, an
instrument of bourgeois hegemony in a
Gramscian sense, dominated by a phallocratic
and fascitoid idea of virility. It is mechanisation
of the body conceived as a robot, ruled by the
principle of productivity: *1975*

Roger Caillois - *writer*
Organised sport is an occasion of pure waste –
waste of time, energy, ingenuity, skill, and often
money: *Men Play Games*

Dr H. Campbell - *physiologist*
Sports and games are entirely non-creative; no
game yet played had any lasting effect on
human well-being.

Galen - *(c 200) Greek philosopher*
Athletes live a life quite contrary to the
precepts of hygiene, and I regard their mode of
living as a regime far more favourable to illness
than to health.

While athletes are exercising their profession,
their body remains in a dangerous condition,
but, when they give up their profession, they
fall into a condition more parlous still; as a fact,
some die shortly afterwards; others live for
some little time but do not arrive at old age.

Aldous Huxley - *(1894–1963) US novelist &*
satirist
Like every other instrument man has invented,
sport can be used for good and evil purposes.
Used badly, it can encourage personal vanity
and group vanity, greedy desire for victory and
even hatred for rivals, an intolerant *esprit de
corps* and contempt for people who are beyond
an arbitrary selected pale.

Robert Lynd - *(1879–1949) Anglo-Irish essayist*
It may be that all games are silly. But then, so
are humans.

Games are the last recourse of those who do
not know how to be idle.

Henry L. Mencken - *(1880–1956) US editor*
I hate all sports as rabidly as a person who likes
sports hates common sense.

George Nathan - *(1882–1958) US editor &*
critic
Athletic sports, save in the case of young boys,
are designed for idiots: *1931*

Jeremy Taylor - *(1613–67) chaplain to*
Charles I
He that spends his time in sports is like him
whose garment is all made of fringes, and his
meat nothing but sauces; they are healthless,
chargeable and useless.

Peter Wilson – *sportswriter*
We do not want youngsters modelling themselves, in all sports, on stars who do not so much flout as utterly ignore the conventions of civilized society.

William B. Yeats – *(1865-1939) Irish poet*
I was useless at games, I cannot remember tha I ever kicked a goal or made a run.

AMERICAN FOOTBALL

Andrew White – *(1832-1918) President of Cornell University*
On refusing Cornell leave to play a game in Michigan – I will not permit 30 men to travel 400 miles to agitate a bag of wind.

BOXING

Howard Cosell – *(b 1920) US TV commentator*
Professional boxing is no longer worthy of civilised society. It's run by self-serving crooks, who are called promoters. Professional boxing is utterly immoral. It's not capable of reformation. I now favour the abolition of professional boxing. You'll never clean it up. Mud can never be clean: *1982*

CRICKET

Sir Alec Douglas Home – *(b 1903) Prime Minister*
Oh God, if there be cricket in heaven, let there also be rain.

George Orwell – *(1903-50) novelist & critic*
Cricket is not a twentieth century game and nearly all modern-minded people dislike it:
1944

William Temple – *(1881-1944) Archbishop of Canterbury*
Personally, I look upon cricket as organised loafing.

Oscar Wilde – *(1854-1900) Irish dramatist & humorist*
I do not play cricket, because it requires me to assume such indecent positions.

FOOTBALL

George Orwell – *(1903-50) novelist & critic*
I loathed the game, and since I could see no pleasure or usefulness in it, it was very difficult for me to show courage at it. Football, it seemed to me, is not really played for the pleasure of kicking a ball about, but is a species of fighting. The lovers of football are large, boisterous, nobby boys who are good at knocking down and trampling on slightly smaller boys.

GOLF

Sir Max Beerbohm – *(1872-1956) caricaturist*
On subscribing a shilling to W. G. Grace's testimonial – It's not in support of cricket, but as an earnest protest against golf.

Michael Parkinson – *(b 1935) TV presenter & writer*
I'd rather watch a cabbage grow, than a man worrying his guts over a two-foot putt.
[*He is a former president of the anti-golf league*]

HORSE RACING

Anthony Trollope – *(1815-82) novelist*
Horse-racing I hate.

COACHING

Anon
There is no bad coaching – only bad coaches.

Alexander Gomelsky – *Russian coach*
It is a good axiom that good players without a good coach made a mediocre team.

Joe Lapchick – *US coach*
The players make the coach. The coach who thinks his coaching ability is more than his talent is an idiot.

ATHLETICS

Bud Baldaro - *coach*
If you coach well, you should make yourself redundant.

Marti Liquori - *US long distance runner*
Much of running is mental, and the guru coaches probably have been successful more because they knew how to harness a runner's heart and mind, than because of any mysterious secret training formula: *1980*

Franz Stampfl - *coach*
The coach's job is twenty per cent technical and training, and eighty per cent inspirational. He may know all there is to know about tactics, technique and training, but if he cannot win the confidence and comradeship of his pupils he will never be a good coach: *1955*

Stuart Storey - *coach*
Stuart Storey has been a mother and a father to me. He's more than a coach. I learnt from him, from his experiences just as most kids learn from their folks: *Geoff Capes - shot-putter*

BASKETBALL

Ken Loeffler - *coach*
There are only two kinds of coach – those who have been fired and those who will be fired.

CRICKET

Rachael Heyhoe-Flint - *(b 1939) England ladies captain*
Professional coaching is a man trying to get you to keep your legs together when other men have spent a lifetime trying to get them wide apart.

A. E. Knight - *(1872–1946) Leicestershire & writer*
Coaching which is good simply sharpens up a player, as wide travel and experience will.

FOOTBALL

Danny Blanchflower - *(b 1926) Spurs*
If you are playing a match for an hour and a half on Saturday, you shouldn't spend two hours a day training. You don't want to leave all your vitality on the training track: *1960*

Ron Greenwood - *West Ham & England manager*
Ron Greenwood is such a great coach that he could make a field of cows do something other than chew grass: *Anon West Ham player*

Gordon Jago - *Millwall & Tampa Bay Rowdies manager*
Coaching is to inform, educate and encourage: *1974*

GYMNASTICS

Nik Stuart - *national coach*
The coach will find that one of his more important roles is to dispel the fear in his pupil.

ICE HOCKEY

Don Cherry - *coach*
The hungry coach is the best coach

RUGBY UNION

Fran Cotton - *England*
I'm a great believer in coaching. But I believe in players even more. Look back at all the great coaches and you'll find they had some pretty useful players to work with: *1989*

Mike Williams - *coach*
Every game has problems. Understanding them and planning ways to overcome them is at the very centre of coaching: *1975*

SQUASH

Jonah Barrington - *(b 1941)*
The coaching manual is sterile, because so many sports need improvisation.

SWIMMING

Harry Gallagher - *coach*
To coach is to create and a thing of which to be proud.

VOLLEYBALL

Peter Wardale - *coach*
No player likes to think of himself as a puppet with the coach in the background manipulating the strings: *1964*

COLEMEN

DAVID COLEMAN – BBC TV COMMENTATOR

And with an alphabetical irony Nigeria follows New Zealand.

Some names to look forward to – perhaps in the future.

He's 31 this year; last year he was 30.

The late start is due to the time.

The pace of this match is really accelerating, by which I mean it is getting faster all the time.

One of the great unknown champions, because very little is known about him.

His brother failed, so let's see if he can succeed and maintain the family tradition.

You've got to hand it to Gonzalez, once he saw it was possible, he saw his chance and made it possible.

The big guns haven't pulled all the stops out.

There'll only be one winner now, in every sense of the word.

For those of you watching who haven't TV sets, live commentary is on Radio Two.

This man could be a dark horse.

He just can't believe what's not happening to him.

ATHLETICS

During the Moscow Olympics – Lasse Viren, the champion, came in fifth and ran a champion's race: *1980*

And this line up for the final of the women's 400 metres hurdles includes three Russians, two East Germans, a Pole, a Swede and a Frenchman.

It's a battle with himself and with the ticking finger of the clock.

Alan Pascoe could have won the gold, but he simply ran out of time.

There's going to be a real ding-dong when the bell goes.

This could be a repeat of what will happen at the European Games, next week.

Charlie Spedding believes in an even pace and hopes to run the second part of the race faster than the first.

Panetta was the silver medallist in the European championships, when he led all the way.

She's not Ben Johnson, but then who is?

The reason she's so fast over the hurdles is because she's so fast between them.

This race is all about racing.

The news from the javelin is that it was won by the winning throw that we saw earlier.

It doesn't mean anything, but what it does mean is that Abde Bile is very relaxed.

David Bedford is the athlete of all-time in the 1970s.

Her time was 4 minutes 13 seconds, which she's capable of.

They come through absolutely together, with Allan Wells in first place.

There is Brendan Foster, by himself, with twenty thousand people.

He is even smaller in real life than he is on the

track.

He won the bronze medal in the 1976 Olympics, so he is used to being out in front.

Lillian Board's great strength is her great strength.

Bradford, who had gone up from 200 metres to 400, found it hard going and for the last 100 metres was always going backwards.

Coe has made absolutely no move at all down the back straight.

FOOTBALL

Manchester United are buzzing around the goalmouth like a lot of red blue-bottles.

Nottingham Forest are having a bad run, they've lost six matches now without winning.

Both of the Villa scorers – Withe and Mortimer – were born in Liverpool, as was the Villa manager – Ron Saunders – who was born in Birkenhead.

Kevin Reeves, who's just turned 22, proving that an ill wind blows nobody any good.

The ball has broken 50–50 for Keegan.

Don't tell those coming in the final result of that fantastic match, but let's just have another look at Italy's winning goal.

RUGBY UNION

Dusty Hare kicked 19 of the 17 points.

Anything that matters so much to David Coleman, you realise, doesn't matter so much at all: *Clive James – writer*

JERRY COLEMAN – BASEBALL ANNOUNCER & MANAGER – SAN DIEGO PADRES

Hi folks! I'm Gerry Gross.
[*Gerry Gross is another San Diego radio announcer!*]

Young Frank Pastore may have just pitched the biggest victory of 1979, maybe the biggest victory of the year.

We're all sad to see Glen Beckert leave. Before he goes, though, I hope he stops by so we can kiss him good-bye. He's that kind of guy.

He slides into second with a stand-up double.

We've got an absolutely perfect day here at Desert Sun Stadium, and we're told it's going to be even more perfect tomorrow.

With one out in the first, Dave Roberts looks a lot better than the last time he pitched against the Padres.

Houston has its largest crowd of the night here this evening.

There's someone warming up in the bull-pen, but he's obscured by his number.

Rich Folkers is throwing up in the bull-pen.

There's a fly ball to deep centre field. Winfield is going back, back. . . . He hits his head against the wall. It's rolling back toward second base.

From the way Denny's shaking his head, he's either got an injured shoulder or a gnat in his eye.

The way he's swinging the bat, he won't get a hit until the 20th century.

That's Hendricks' 19th home run, one more and he hits double figures.

At the end of six innings play, it's Montreal 5, the Expos 3.

Hector Torrez, how can you communicate with Enzo Hernandez when he speaks Spanish and you speak Mexican?

On being appointed the Padres manager – I think Ray Kroc [owner] told 'em to give the job to Gary Coleman [child actor] and they misunderstood him: *1980*
[*He lasted one season and returned to announcing*]

DRINK, DRUGS, FOOD & TOBACCO

DRINK

AMERICAN FOOTBALL

Harry Carson - *New York Giants*
While training in Fresno, California - Fresno? I
thought that was a diet soft drink!

ANGLING

Jimmy Cannon - *(1910-73) US sportswriter*
Ernest Hemingway was a sportswriter - he was
the only guy who could make fishing seem
interesting to me. Fishing, with me, has always
been an excuse to drink in the daytime: *1973*

ATHLETICS

Alf Shrubb - *long distance runner*
Never touch spirits of any kind. They are the
worst thing an athlete can go in for: *1910*

BASEBALL

'Dizzy' Dean - *(1911-74) St Louis Cardinals*
Sure I eat what I advertise. Sure I eat Wheaties
for breakfast. A good bowl of Wheaties with
bourbon can't be beat.

'Casey' Stengel - *(1891-1975) New York
Yankees & Mets manager*
They say some of my stars drink whiskey, but I
have found out that the ones who drink milk-
shakes don't win many ball games.

We are in such a slump that even the ones that
are drinkin', aren't hittin'.

My guys only had four beers after the game,
but each beer came in a pail.

Hack Wilson - *Chicago Cubs*
I never played drunk; hungover, but never
drunk.

Wilson was a highball hitter on the field and off
of it: *Warren Brown*

BOWLS

Anon
Life isn't all beer and skittles; some of us
haven't touched a skittle in years.

Thomas Hughes - *(1822-96) jurist*
Life isn't all beer and skittles; but beer and
skittles, or something better of the same sort,
must form part of every Englishman's
education.

BOXING

Johnny Cooke - *welterweight*
You can get two guys from the boozer who can
fight. But boxing - well that's a bit different:
1968

CRICKET

Geoff Boycott - *(b 1940) Yorkshire*
I don't think I should be judged on how good a
talker I am, or how many pints of beer I drink.

Rachael Heyhoe-Flint - *(b 1939) England
ladies captain*
On crowd trouble in the West Indies - If the crowd
throw bottles at us, we'll hurl 'em straight back
- unless they are full of course: *1970*

'Quid' (Robert A. Fitzgerald) - *writer*
A cricket umpire should be above all suspicion
of bias, and free from all odours of the tavern:
Jerks in from Square Leg (1866)

Sir Charles Percy Snow - *(1905-80) novelist
& scientist*
Drinking the best tea in the world in an empty
cricket ground - that, I think, is the final
pleasure left to man: *1932*

DARTS

Alun Evans - *Wales*
I need six or seven pints and a half dozen trips
to the gents before I'm ready to play.

Bobby George - *England*
I learnt to play darts before I learnt to drink.
For some players, darts and booze are linked.
It's psychological.

Leighton Rees - *Wales*
I had a bash at positive thinking, yoga,
transcendental meditation, even hypnotism.
They only screwed me up, so now I'm back to
my normal routine – a couple of lagers.

FOOTBALL

Anon
I used to play football for Scotland until I
discovered Smirnoff: *Graffiti*

George Best - *(b 1946) Manchester United*
On his drink problem – I might go to Alcoholics
Anonymous, but I think it'd be difficult for me
to be anonymous: *1980*

As recently as the late Seventies, to woo our top
players home, the authorities introduced all-day
drinking in Scottish pubs; a valiant effort that
succeeded only in enticing George Best to Hibs:
Only an Excuse – BBC Radio Scotland
comedy show (1986)

Jimmy Greaves - *(b 1940) Spurs*
While with Spurs I drank heavily to help
relieve the pressure of big-time football. My
career covered an era when the game suddenly
went sick and defeat became a dirty word. We
used to get really stoked up for the games, with
our adrenalin pumping so high that a lot of us
needed an after-match drink to bring us back to
earth: *This One's On Me (1979)*

Wallace Mercer
In Scotland, football hooliganism has been met
by banning alcohol from grounds, but in
England this solution has been
circumnavigated.

Charlie Nicholas - *(b 1961) Arsenal*
If I go into a bar and have a lager shandy, word

gets back that I'm knocking back bottles of
champagne. By the time it gets back to the
papers or my manager at Arsenal, it's me lying
in the gutter: *1984*

Graeme Souness - *(b 1953) Glasgow Rangers*
They serve a drink in Glasgow called the
Souness – one half and you're off:
Tommy Docherty

GOLF

Patty Berg - *USA*
If I were a man I wouldn't have half a dozen
Tom Collinses before going out to play golf,
then let profanity substitute for proficiency on
the golf course: *1945*

Dean Martin - *(b 1917) US actor*
If you drink, don't drive. Don't even putt.

ROWING

Frank Keating - *(b 1937) sportswriter*
If the Government banned alcohol, then the
Henley Regatta would fold up its tents
overnight: *1989*

G. Morrison - *President of the Oxford University*
boat crew
Large wine glasses and such things will lose
you a race sooner than anything else: *1865*

RUGBY

Tom David - *Wales & Cardiff City*
The main difference between League and
Union is that now I get my hangovers on
Monday instead of Sunday.

J. Dickinson - *behavioural analyst*
The pub is as much a part of rugby as the
playing field: *1976*

Doug Ibbotson - *sportswriter*
The Holy Writ of Gloucester Rugby Club
demands: first, that the forwards shall win the
ball, second that the forwards shall keep the
ball, and third, the backs shall buy the beer.

SHOOTING

***Dead Shot* magazine**

Any person who has been drinking freely
should not touch a gun until sober: *1861*

The young sportsman must always shun spirits,
the old one sometimes requires a stimulus of
the kind to help him over the hedges and to lift
his legs out of the heavy soil: *1861*

SNOOKER

Bill Werbeniuk - *Canada*
I need six pints to get to the table, even for a
practice.

Snooker is my livelihood and I like a pint, so it
is a way of combining business with pleasure:

DRUGS

Chris Brasher - *(b 1928) sportswriter*
Death is the final penalty, but the life of a
sportsman on drugs is a perpetual living
penalty because he is offending against himself:
1978

Russell Fleming
It should be noted that the drug problem will
not leave sports of its own accord: *1981*

Colin Moynihan - *(b 1955) Minister for Sport*
A universal fight must be waged now against
drugs in sport, if we are to avoid a 21st century
of chemical freaks instead of athletes: *1988*

Jack Scott
Drug abuse is only one of the many symptoms
that show that something is terribly wrong with
the role sport is playing in society today: *1970*

AMERICAN FOOTBALL

Joe Namath - *(b 1943) New York Jets*
On being asked if he preferred grass or Astro-turf - I
don't know, I've never smoked Astro-turf!

ATHLETICS

Geoff Capes- *shot-putter*
There is no point in the British athlete
competing against a Communist bloc athlete in
the field events. He will be beaten by steroids:
1978

Robert G. Finberg - *US runner*
Running gives the mind a boost worth all the
tranquillisers in the world.

Charley Francis - *Canadian track coach*
I can tell you that Ben Johnson is very much
against drugs. He has never taken them and he
never will: *1987*

Howard Payne - *hammer thrower*
There are two alternatives to anabolic steroids
– don't take them and be second class, or give
up athletics: *1974*

CRICKET

Robin Williams - *US comedian*
Cricket is baseball on valium.

GOLF

Isao Aoki- *Japan*
The PGA tour has a simple test to see if a
player is on drugs – if Isao Aoki speaks and the
player understands him, the player is on
something: *Bob Hope*

Deane Beman - *US PGA tour commissioner*
The chances of the PGA tour developing a drug
problem are about the same as Gary Player and
Tom Watson sharing a cabin on the 'Love
Boat': *1974*

Bob Hope - *(b 1903) US comedian*
Drugs are very much a part of professional
sports today, but when you think about it, golf
is the only sport where the players aren't
penalized for being on grass.

Tony Jacklin - *Open Champion*
The great intellectual fact about golf is that it is
a cold-blooded activity, in which your mind is
completely bereft of the drugs and stimulants
which nature provides in other sporting
competitive activities: *1974*

HORSE RACING

Bruce Hobbs - *trainer*
If I had my way, I'd throw all the hypodermic
needles into the Atlantic.

FOOD

Proverbs
Good sport that fills the belly.

No sport, no pie.

Nick Seitz – *US writer*
The breakfast of champions is not cereal, it's the opposition.

ATHLETICS

Herb Elliott – *(b 1938) Australian middle distance runner*
If Americans want to run they will have to deny themselves other things the body wants – like chocolates.

Wilma Rudolph – *(b 1940) US sprinter*
I had to be fast, otherwise there was nothing left to eat on the dinner table.
[*She was the 20th of 22 children*]

S.H. & W.R. Short – *US nutritional scientists*
There is no area of nutrition where faddism, misconception and ignorance are more obvious than in athletics: 1983

BASEBALL

'Yogi' Berra – *(b 1925) New York Yankees player & manager*
On a packed New York restaurant – No wonder nobody comes here to eat – it's too crowded.

After ordering a pizza, he was asked if he wanted it cut into 4 or 8 pieces – Better make it four, I don't think I can eat eight.

Jimmy Cannon – *(1910–73) sportswriter*
Baseball players who are first into the dining room are usually last in the statistics.

Oscar Homolka – *actor*
Baseball may be America's national pastime, but dieting is a close second.

Tug McGraw – *Philadelphia Phillies*
If the Food and Administration ever walked into the Phillies' club-house, they'd close down baseball.

'Babe' Ruth – *(1895–1948) Orioles & Yankees*
Asparagus makes my urine smell.

BOXING

Muhammad Ali – *(b 1942) US heavyweight*
We'd be better off if we obeyed God's command
And ate vegetables and grain and fruit of the land.
You may think fresh pork is a very rare treat
But our bodies are made of what we eat.
And the food that the hog has eaten,
Which is the filth of the land,
Goes into our body second-hand.

Denis Andries – *light-heavyweight*
I don't feel I've tasted success yet. I'm hungry for it, and I'll eat anywhere in the world.
[*He got his fill – winning the world title in 1986 & 1988*]

John Conteh – *light-heavyweight*
After winning his world title – No more chip butties!: 1974

Archie Moore – *(b 1913) US light-heavyweight*
Eat spaghetti – look what it done for Rocky Marciano. It made him tough enough to take any kind of punch and gave him the strength of a mule.

CRICKET

Geoff Boycott – *(b 1940) Yorkshire*
Boycott, somewhat a creature of habit, likes exactly the sort of food he himself prefers:
Don Mosey – writer & commentator

Ray East – *(b 1947) Essex*
We used to eat so many salads, there was a danger of contracting myxomatosis: 1983

Sunil Gavaskar – *(b 1949) India*
Everywhere I go in the world, my host offers me only curry.

Ian Gould – *(b 1957) Sussex*
My main problem is that through being rather short, I only have to look at a pint or a pork pie to put weight on.

Rachael Heyhoe-Flint – *(b 1939) England*

ladies captain
On seeing a pack of pastry with directions 'Makes a
pie for four people, or twelve little tarts' – I hadn't
realised that it would be such an opportunity to
invite the current England women's cricket
team.

Derek Randall – *(b 1951) Nottinghamshire*
Tasting caviar on tour in India – The
champagne's all right, but the blackcurrant jam
tastes of fish: *1976*

FOOTBALL

Anon
At the 1986 World Cup opening ceremony –
Queremos frijoles no goles [We want beans not
goals]: *Mexican protesters*

John Barnes – *Liverpool*
After Everton fans greeted him with bananas –
Some fruit and vegetable dealers did very well:
1987

Luther Blissett – *(b 1958) Watford & AC
Milan*
On life in Italy – My only problem seems to be
with Italian breakfasts. No matter how much
money you've got, you can't get any Rice
Krispies: *1983*

GOLF

Ray C. Hutchinson – *(b 1907) novelist*
A man must be fed to play golf. It is ill going
golfing on an empty interior.

Sam Snead – *(b 1912) USA*
If people gripped a knife and fork like they do a
golf club, they'd starve to deth.

Lee Trevino – *(b 1939) USA*
When I first hit the Pro tour my caddie
suggested I might use a 'Sand-wedge'. I replied,
'Sure, get me a ham-on-rye!'

HORSE RACING

Lester Piggott – *(b 1935) jockey*
The most famous recipe in racing is the one for
Lester Piggott's breakfast – a cough and a copy
of The Sporting Life:
Simon Barnes – sportswriter

ROWING

Rudie Lehmann – *poet*
Thinner and thinner grows each tiny coxswain,
Fed upon husks, but ever complaining,
He fades and fades, and thus fulfils his training:
1900

TOBACCO

BASEBALL

Napoleon Lajoie – *Cleveland Indians manager*
'Nap' was a rough customer. If he didn't like an
umpire's call, he'd give him a faceful of tobacco
juice: *Roger Angell – sportswriter*

BOXING

Primo Carnera – *Italian heavyweight*
On a fictional character – In physique, he was
not unlike what Primo Carnera would have
been if Carnera had not stunted his growth by
smoking cigarettes as a child: *P. G. Wodehouse*

CRICKET

W. G. Grace – *(1848-1915) Gloucestershire*
You can get rid of drink, but you can never get
rid of smoke.

Colin M. Jarman – *(b 1958) sportswriter*
If Benson and Hedges sponsored the England v
Australia Test match series, would the
Government put a health warning on the
'Ashes'?: *1988*

DARTS

Olly Croft – *President of the British Darts
Organisation*
If they ban smoking, it won't be long before
some nut wants to ban drinking with darts:
1979

MOTOR RACING

Peter Cooper – *RAC Motor Sports Association
Chief Executive*
I don't believe anybody will start smoking
simply because a tobacco manufacturer has
sponsored a race or rally.

SNOOKER

Steve Davis – *England*
On winning the 1981 Embassy World

Championships – I'd like to thank Embassy but unfortunately I don't smoke: *1981*

EXERCISE

FOR

ANCIENT

Cicero – *(106–43 BC) Roman orator & statesman*
Whatever is over-wearied by the day's exercise is, as it were, new born by the night's rest and quiet.

The body when over-laboured becomes heavy and jaded; but it is exercise alone that supports the spirits, and keeps the mind in vigour.

Exercise and temperance can preserve something of our early strength even in old age.

Cleobulus – *(c 600 BC) Greek sage*
Keep the body in health by exercise.

Confucius – *(551–497 BC) Chinese philosopher*
He that in his studies wholly applies himself to labour and exercise, and neglects meditation, loses his time; and he that only applies himself to meditation, and neglects labour and exercise, only wanders and loses himself.

Demophilus – *(c 100) Latin playwright & philosopher*
In exercise study to avoid fatigue.

Diogenes – *(400–325 BC) Greek philosopher*
By consistent exercise one develops freedom of movement – for virtuous deeds.

Epictetus – *(55–135) Stoic philosopher*
Every faculty is conserved and increased by its appropriate exercise.

Hippocrates – *(460–377 BC) Greek physician*
Fat people who want to reduce should take their exercise on an empty stomach and sit down to their food out of breath. Thin people

who want to get fat should do exactly the opposite and never exercise on an empty stomach.

Sport is a preserver of health.

Juvenal – *(60–140) Roman satirist*
Our prayers should be for –
A sound mind in a sound body. [Mens sana in corpore sano]

Plato – *(429–347 BC) Greek philosopher*
As for the man who laughs at naked women exercising their bodies from the best of motives, in his laughter he is plucking 'a fruit of unripe wisdom'.

Lack of activity destroys the good condition of every human being, while movement and methodical physical exercise save it and preserve it.

We should not exercise the body without the joint assistance of the mind; nor exercise the mind without the joint assistance of the body.

Pythagoras – *(584–504 BC) Greek mathematician*
Let exercise alternate with rest.

Socrates – *(469–399 BC) Greek teacher*
Moderate exercise is indispensable; exercise till the mind feels delight in reposing from the fatigue.

Xenophon – *(428–354 BC) Athenian soldier*
He who has a weak constitution becomes stronger by manual exercise than a robust man without it.

MODERN

Anon

There are many troubles which you cannot cure by the Bible and the hymnbook, but which you can cure by a good perspiration and a breath of fresh air.

It is exercise alone that supports the spirits and keeps the mind in vigour.

Physical activity is the cure for most modern ailments.

To live a life, free from gout, pain, and phthisic,
    Athletic employment is found the best physic;
The nerves are by exercise hardened and strengthened,
    And vigour attends it by which life is lengthened.

Those who do not find time for exercise will have to find time for illness.

A man too busy to take care of his health is like a mechanic too busy to look after his tools.

Francis Bacon - *(1561-1626) philosopher & statesman*
Men ought to beware that they use not exercise and spare diet both; but if much exercise, a plentiful diet; if sparing diet, little exercise.

Ambrose Bierce - *(1842-1914) US journalist & poet*
A pastime is a gentle exercise for intellectual debility: 1906

Josh Billings [Henry Wheeler Shaw] - *(1818-1885) US humorist*
Health is like munny, we never hav a true idea ov its value until we lose it.

Hugh Blair - *(1718-1800) Scottish clergyman*
Exercise is the chief source of improvement in all our faculties.

Andrew Boorde - *(1490-1549) Carthusian Monk*
Before you go to your reflection, moderately exercise your body with some labour, or playing tennis, or casting a bowl, to open the pores and to augment natural health.

Erma Brombeck - *(b 1927) US writer &*

humorist
The only reason I would take up jogging is so that I could hear heavy breathing again.

Alistair Cooke - *(b 1908) US journalist & broadcaster*
For all forms of exercise theoretically designed for recreation and relaxation, none can be so unerringly guaranteed to produce nervous exhaustion and despair leading to several mental illnesses and in some cases petulance.

Thomas Kirk Cureton Jr. - *US professor of physical fitness*
Over the years, I have come to look upon physical fitness as the trunk of a tree that supports the many branches of life; intellectual life, spiritual life, occupation, love and social activities: 1965

Norman Douglas - *(1868-1952) novelist & travel writer*
There is beauty in fitness which no art can enhance.

John Dryden - *(1631-1700) poet*
    The wise the cure, on exercise depend;
God never made his work, for man to mend.

Daniel Ellis - *(1775-49) philosopher*
Immoderate labours weaken the body; but a temperate kind of exercise conserveth the same in health.

Dr S. Fitch
Exercise should be taken at the same hour every day.

Samantha Fox - *'Page Three' model & pop singer*
I've got ten pairs of training shoes. One for every day of the week.

Mark Hopkins - *(1802-87) US professor of philosophy*
If a man would strengthen his intellectual faculties, he must exercise them.

Samuel Johnson - *(1709-84) lexicographer*
I take the true definition of exercise to be labour without weariness.

Exercise is labour used only when it produces

pleasure.

Thomas à Kempis - *(1380-1471) German monk*
Bodily exercises are to be done discreetly; not to be taken evenly and alike by all men: *1426*

Norman Mailer - *(b 1923) US novelist*
Any workout which does not involve a certain minimum of danger or responsibility does not improve the body - it just wears it out.

J. W. Mailler
The benefits of exercise, to those whose occupations does not lead them to make any physical exertion, cannot be too highly estimated.

Mao Tse-Tung - *(1893-1976) Chinese political leader*
In general, any form of exercise, if pursued continuously, will help to train us in perseverance.

Jean Baptiste Massillon - *(1663-1742) French Bishop of Clermont*
Health and good humour are to the human body like sunshine to vegetation.

Arthur Newton - *long distance runner*
Training is, in some ways at any rate, just cleaning the channels through which energy flows: *1947*

Natural exercise is physical as well as mental development and makes the whole machine more capable. When your physique is about near perfect as nature can make it, all your abilities become greatly enhanced; you can work better, think more clearly and play more actively and intensely than before: *1949*

Lloyd Percival
The physically fit can enjoy their vices.

Jim Peters - *marathon runner*
Train little, train hard, train often: *1955*

Thomas de Quincey - *(1785-1859) essayist & critic*
There is a necessity for a regulating discipline of exercise that, whilst evoking the human energies, will not suffer them to be wasted.

Dr Benjamin Rush - *(1745-1813) US physician & statesman*
Moderate exercise and toil, so far from prejudicing, strengthens the body and consolidates it.

William Shakespeare - *(1564-1616) playwright*
The rich advantage of good exercise: *King John*

So long as nature will bear up this exercise, so long I daily vow to use it: *A Winter's Tale*

Dr George Sheehan - *US cardiologist*
Health is something a runner goes through on his way to fitness. A way station he hardly notices in his pursuit of the twenty or thirty per cent of his capacity that lies untouched: *1975*

Sir Philip Sidney - *(1554-1586) poet & scholar*
You will never live to my age without you keep yourself in breath with exercise.

Mrs Lydia Sigourney - *(1791-1865) US author*
Vigorous exercise will often fortify a feeble constitution.

Rev Robert South - *(1634-1716) chaplain to Charles II*
God made no faculty, but he also provided it with a proper object upon which it might exercise itself.

Sir Richard Steele - *(1672-1729) Irish founder of Tatler*
Reading is to the mind what exercise is to the body.

James Thomson - *(1700-1748) poet*
Health is the vital principal of bliss and exercise of health.

AGAINST

Neil Armstrong - *(b 1930) US astronaut*
I believe every human has a finite number of heart-beats. I don't intend to waste any of mine running around doing exercises.

The Bible
Bodily exercise profiteth little: *Timothy 4:8*

Phyllis Diller – *(b 1917) US comedienne*
Health is what my friends are always drinking
to before they fall down.

Henry Ford – *(1863–1947) US industrialist*
Exercise is bunk. If you are healthy, you don't
need it; if you are ill, you shouldn't take it.

Robert M. Hutchins – *(1899–1977) US
educator*
Whenever I feel like exercise, I lie down until
the feeling passes.

Ring Lardner – *(1885–1933) US humorist*
The only exercise I get is when I take the studs
out of one shirt and put them in another.

G. Legwold – *US fitness writer*
The loudest part of the fitness boom is over:
1985

Mickey Lolich – *overweight US baseball player*
The only thing running and exercise can do for
you is make you healthy.

Henry L. Mencken – *(1880–1956) US
journalist & critic*
The popular belief in athletics is grounded
upon the theory that violent exercise makes for
bodily health and that bodily health is
necessary for mental vigour. Both halves of this
theory are highly dubious. Athletes, as a class,
are not above the normal in health, but below
it: *1951*

Dolly Parton – *(b 1946) US singer*
I bought all those Jane Fonda videos. I love to
sit and eat cookies and watch 'em.

Sean Penn – *US actor*
I prefer the bar to the gym any day. I like to
drink and I like to brawl.

Joan Rivers – *(b 1933) US comedienne*
I'm Jewish. I don't work out. If God had
wanted us to bend over he'd put diamonds on
the floor.

Francois, duc de La Rochfoucauld –
(1613–80) French writer
What a troublesome affliction to have to
preserve one's health by too strict a regime.

George Santayana – *(1863–1952) US
philosopher & poet*
The need for exercise is a modern superstition,
invented by people who ate too much and had
nothing to think about. Athletics don't make
anybody either long-lived or useful.

Red Skelton – *(b 1913) US actor*
Exercise? I get it on the golf course. When I see
my friends collapse, I run for the paramedics.

Simeon Strunsky – *(1879–1948) US editor*
The beneficial effects of the regular quarter of
an hour's exercise before breakfast is more than
offset by the mental wear and tear in getting
out of bed fifteen minutes earlier than one
otherwise would: *The Patient Observer*

Alec Yuill Thornton – *US writer*
I consider exercise vulgar. It makes people
smell.

Mark Twain – *(1835–1910) US humorist &
writer*
I have never taken any exercise, except for
sleeping and resting, and I never intend to take
any. Exercise is loathsome.

Bill Vaughan – *US writer*
As a nation we are dedicated to keeping
physically fit – and parking as close to the
stadium as possible.

JOGGING

Anon
Jog and die healthier: *Graffiti*

Dr Meyer Friedman
Jogging is a form of exercise in which man
transforms himself into a machine.

Abe Lemmons – *US college basketball coach*
I don't jog. If I die I want to be sick.

Robert Morley – *(b 1908) actor & writer*
Yes, I go to the funerals of friends who have
been doing this jogging thing!

Ogden Nash – *(1902–71) US poet*
At another year, I would not boggle,
  Except that when I jog, I joggle.

Kenneth Robinson – *writer*
Show me a man who jogs every morning and
I'll show you a breaking marriage.

Harcourt Roy – *writer & sports administrator*
Jogging is as natural as breathing:
The Anytime Exercise (1978)

Mike Royko – *US sportswriter*
It's unnatural for people to run around city
streets unless they are thieves or victims. It
makes people nervous to see someone running.
I know that when I see someone running on my
street, my instincts tell me to let the dog out
after him.

Charles M. Schulz – *(b 1922) US cartoonist*
Jogging is very beneficial. It's good for your legs
and your feet. It's also very good for the
ground. It makes it feel needed.

Laurence Sterne – *(1713–68) vicar & novelist*
As we jog on, either laugh with me, or at me, in
short do anything – only keep your temper.

Joseph Strutt – *(1749–1802) author*
There is no kind of exercise that has more
uniformly met the approbation of authors in
general than running: *1830*

Lee Trevino – *(b 1939) US golfer*
My doctor told me my jogging could add years
to my life. I told him 'Yeah, since I began, I
already feel ten years older!'

Victoria Wood – *comedienne*
Jogging is for people who aren't intelligent
enough to watch Breakfast TV: *1989*

WALKING

Anon
Walking may be good exercise, but did you ever
see a postman as well built as a truck driver?

Proverbs
After dinner rest a while,
 After supper walk a mile: *Arabian*

Fred Allen – *(1894–1956) US comedian*
I like long walks, especially when they are taken
by people who annoy me!

Evan Esar – *(b 1899) US writer*
Walking isn't a lost art; one must, by some
means, get to the garage.

Eric Leyland – *(b 1911) writer*
Like all sports, and walking is a sport if tackled
the right way rhythm is the first key: *1960*

You can't hit a cricket ball properly without
rhythm, you can't play tennis or golf or ride a
horse without it. Neither can you walk
properly: *1960*

Alfred L. Rowse – *(b 1903) historian*
Walking is a favourite sport of the good and the
wise.

Oscar Wilde – *(1854–1900) Irish dramatist &
humorist*
The only possible form of exercise is to talk, not
walk.

FAIR PLAY & RULES

Anon
 Every dog shall have his day,
But let both sides have what's fair play.

Proverbs
Fair play's a jewel.

If you must play, decide upon three things at
the start; the rules of the game, the stakes and
the quitting time: *Chinese*

Friendship first, competition second: *Chinese*

The Duke of Beaufort
One point I find lacking in sport today is
gentlemen vs. players. It is not easy to find a

team of gentlemen: *1978*

Thomas Chatterton – *(1752-1770) poet*
The man that has no friend at court,
Must make the laws confine his sport,
But he that has, by dint of flaws,
May make his sport confine the laws.

Sir Winston Churchill – *(1874-1965) Prime Minister*
In sport, in courage, and in the sight of Heaven,
all men meet on equal terms.

Sam Dish – *US lawyer*
When you play a game you have to play by the
rules. Otherwise there can be no game: *1973*

Paul Gardner – *US sportswriter*
A sport is, at base, nothing but a set of rules
and if they are too flagrantly flouted the sport
that is built on them collapses: *1974*

Sir Michael Havers – *(b 1923) Attorney General & life peer*
Anyone who engages in competitive sport
accepts that there must be rules and referees
and umpires to enforce them. If the rule book is
torn up or vicious fouls go unpunished then the
sporting element is destroyed and the fun for
both the player and the spectator is lost: *1978*

Capt. W. E. Johns – *(1893-1968) novelist*
I teach sportsmanship according to the British
Idea. I teach that decent behaviour wins in the
end as a natural order of things.

Herman L. Masin – *US sportswriter*
Justice does not always triumph in sports.
Sometimes it is lucky to gain even a tie. And
sometimes it can go down like the *Titanic*: *1983*

Don Murray – *US sportswriter*
People understand contests. You take a bunch
of kids throwing rocks at random and people
look askance, but if you go and hold a rock-
throwing contest – people understand.

Grantland Rice – *(1880-1954) US sportswriter*
For when the great scorer comes to write
  against your name,
He marks: Not that you won or lost, but how
  you played the game.
[*Possibly the most quoted reference to sport*]

K. Rysdorp
Sportsmanship is the union of I and you into
we.

N. Terekhov – *Russian coach*
Sport is a school of honest competition.

AERIAL SPORT

Chris Brasher – *(b 1928) sportswriter*
Aero-modelling is a recreation, but put some
rules on it and it becomes a sport: *1982*

AMERICAN FOOTBALL

Tommy Bell – *attorney & NFL referee*
During the week I practised law. On Sunday I
was the law.

Pat Culpepper – *University of Texas*
Sportsmanship is hard to define, especially in
football, which starts with premeditated
mayhem: *1983*

Glenn Dobbs – *Tulsa coach*
If you spend a lot of time on sportsmanship,
you're going to spend a lot of time losing.

ATHLETICS

Steve Ovett – *(b 1955) middle distance runner*
Gamesmanship, if it's in the mind, is beautiful
in the sense that you can use your mind and
body in conjunction. You're using them in the
same way as you can imagine chess – your body
is the piece and your mind is the player.

BASEBALL

Heywood Broun – *(1888-1939) humorist*
The tradition of baseball always has been
agreeably free of chivalry. The rule is 'Do
anything you can get away with.'

Leo Durocher – *(b 1906) Brooklyn Dodgers manager*
Show me a good sportsman and I'll show you a
player I'm looking to trade: *1950*

'How you play the game' is only for college
boys. When you're playing for money, winning
is the only thing that counts.

Win any way you can, as long as you can get away with it.

What are we out at the park for? I'd trip my mother. I'll help her, brush her off, tell her I'm sorry. But mother don't make it to third.

Charles W. Eliot - *(1834-1926) President of Harvard*
I understand that a curve ball is thrown with a deliberate attempt to deceive. Surely that is not an ability we should want to foster at Harvard.

Bob Federic - *umpire*
When I blow one, I never admit it. I sure don't tell the team involved, although they know it and I know it. But then, as officials, we're supposed to be perfect. So I guess I never made a mistake.

Bill Veeck - *(1914-86) St Louis Browns owner*
I try not to break the rules, merely to test their elasticity.

Lee Walls - *coach*
Players like rules. If they didn't have any rules, they wouldn't have anything to break.

BASKETBALL

Tom Canterbury - *player*
The trouble with referees is that they just don't care which side wins.

Manny Goldstein - *University of New Mexico recruiter*
I thought I was an honest guy, and just doing what everyone else was doing - bending the rules.

BOXING

Sir John Douglas - *(1844-1900) 8th Marquis of Queensberry*
Queensberry Rules K.O.: *Graffiti*

As for myself I regarded every part of my anatomy above the waist as a weapon. It may not have been what the Marquis of Queensberry intended when he wrote up the rules all those years ago, but the Marquis didn't have to do the fighting, did he?: *John Conteh*

The trouble was that in prohibiting such tactics as kicking, gouging, butting and biting, the revised code was taking a great deal of the harmless fun and good sportsmanship out of a recreation whose followers included a great many for whom the vicarious joys of kicking, gouging, butting and biting were, in the manly fulfilment they afforded, second only to the act of witnessing the ritual dismemberment of a fox: *Benny Green*
[*Although the Marquis was the patron of the 'rules', they were written by a member of the Amateur Athletic Union - John Graham Chambers*]

CRICKET

Anon
Cricket has added a new conception of fairness and chivalry to the common stock of our national ideas, since everyone English knows at once what is meant by such statements as 'this is cricket' and 'that is not cricket':
Harrow schoolmaster

Fred Trueman - *(b 1931) Yorkshire*
Use every weapon within the rules, and stretch the rules to breaking point, say I.

If you are summoned to court in England, you are told why your presence is required. You know the crime for which you stand accused. This is something you never get from the MCC.

FOOTBALL

Anon
To regulate the game, to earn expenses and a guinea fee!
Yes! There is great attraction in the name of Referee: *1893*

Danny Blanchflower - *(b 1926) Spurs*
The off-side law seems to me to be like the bunker shot in golf; it causes an interesting and infuriating hazard in the course of play, and creates healthy argument about the game.

Joseph Blatter - *secretary-general of FIFA*
One of the secrets of football is the simplicity of its laws: *1987*

Corinthian Casuals F. C.
Amateurism and good sportsmanship . . . for
this club one is valueless without the other and,
if either is surrendered, even in the present
difficult world, in the cause of success, the time
has surely been reached for the club's life to be
brought to a close. Euthanasia must come
before corruption: *1983*

Charles B. Fry - *(1872-1956) sportsman*
In football, it is widely acknowledged that if
both sides agree to cheat, cheating is fair: *1911*

Alan Hardaker - *Football League Secretary*
Referees should arrive by the back door and
leave by the back door.

Graham Taylor - *Watford manager*
After losing 7-3 to Nottingham Forest - There's no
rule to say a game can't finish 9-9:   *1982*

J. C. Thring
Rules of Football: No. 3 - Kicks must be aimed
only at the ball: *The Simplest Game (1862)*

GOLF

Walter Travis - *USA*
To brag little; to show well,
To improve gently given luck.
To pay, to own up
And to shut up if beaten –
These are the virtues of the sporting man.

HUNTING

H. Langford Brown
The definition of 'Sport' is the taking of a wild

animal in such a way that the said animal has a
fair chance of escape: *1926*

RUGBY LEAGUE

Keith Macklin - *TV commentator*
Lighthouse keepers have lonely jobs – so do
referees.

RUGBY UNION

Derek Robinson - *sportswriter*
The advantage law is the best law in rugby,
because it lets you ignore all the others for the
good of the game: *1969*

The laws of the game are written down for all
to see. There may be a lot of secrets about how
to win, but there is no secret about how to play:
                                             1969

One of the biggest differences between rugby
and soccer is the assumption that in rugby the
players will do their best to play to the laws;
while in soccer the players follow the laws until
it is to their advantage to break them: *1971*

Admiral Sir Percy Royds - *(1874-1955)*
Laws may come and laws may go, but the game
goes on for ever:
          History of The Laws of Rugby Football (1949)

SQUASH

Jack Barnaby
Playing a cheater is the real test of
sportsmanship: *1979*

FAMOUS LAST WORDS

ATHLETICS

Harry Andrews - *coach*
The man who has made the mile record is
W. G. George. His time was 4 minutes 12.75
seconds and the probability is that this record
will never be broken: *1903*
Walter George's 'unbeatable' time, set in 1886, has

*been reduced by almost half a minute. In fact, the
current women's world record is only slightly above
George's mark!*

David Bedford - *long distance runner*
The difference between me and other athletes
who go to the Olympics is that I go to win and
they go to compete: *1972*
He came sixth in the 10,000 metres

197

Daily Mail
Zola Budd will become a great British athlete, her heart lies here: *1984*
In 1988 she revoked her citizenship and returned to South Africa

Marti Vaiinio - *Finnish long distance runner*
There are no short-cuts to the top: *1972*
Ten years later, he was disqualified from second place in the 10,000 metres at the European championships for drug abuse

BOXING

Nat Fleischer - *US boxing editor*
The judge and the referee must be guided by what they see, and not by what others would have them see: *1962*
Three years after this statement, Fleischer intervened in the Ali v Liston re-match in 1965. After Ali had floored Liston, referee Jersey Joe Walcott lost the count and allowed Liston to rise after more than ten seconds. Fleischer, from his ringside seat, shouted – Joe! The fight is over! – On this unofficial instruction, Walcott stopped the fight and Ali retained his title

Tom O'Rourke
Before the world heavyweight title fight between Jess Willard [champion] and Jack Dempsey –
Dempsey fighting Willard is like a bull trying to butt a locomotive off the track: *1919*
Dempsey took the title

After the fight Arthur 'Bugs' Baer gave his opinion –
Jess Willard had about as much chance in this fight as a dish-faced chimpanzee in a beauty contest!

CRICKET

Ian Botham - *(b 1955) England captain*
Before a Test match v West Indies – There's no way at all we should lose. If we do, then a few heads will roll. You could bat for ten days on this pitch and not get a result: *1981*
England lost by an innings

Greg Chappell - *(b 1948) Australia*
Australia has been accused of using a lot of gamesmanship and I'm sure, at times, we've been guilty of utilising it to try to gain an advantage, but I don't think we've got

anywhere near what we've been accused of doing, and I don't feel that I've been responsible for much of it.
Despite his high self-esteem, Chappell went on to perpetrate one of the least sporting efforts in cricket history, when he asked his brother Trevor to bowl the last ball of a limited over game against New Zealand, who needed a six to win, underarm along the ground

Tony Greig - *(b 1946) England captain*
If the West Indies are on top, they're magnificent. If they are down, they grovel. I intend to make them grovel: *1976*
West Indies won the series 3-0

Keith Miller - *(b 1919) Australia*
Jeff Thomson looks like a flash in the pan: *1974*
Thomson took 200 Test wickets between 1972-85

Sir Malcolm Sargent - *concert conductor*
While in Australia, on a concert tour, he was asked if he would like to see Clem Hill – Love to. How high is it?
Clem Hill was an opening batsman for Australia and a classical music lover

FOOTBALL

Brian Clough - *(b 1935) Nottingham Forest manager*
I have decided to quit as a full-time manager four years from now. That statement is not meant to shock people, to stir them up or to frighten them. It is a fact: *1978*
He is still managing more than a decade later

Martin Edwards - *Manchester United chairman*
The chairman should never say, 'If we don't win the League, the manager's out.' You have to judge things like that at the end of the season: *1986*
He sacked Ron Atkinson two months into the following season

Terry McDermott - *Liverpool*
Arsenal? Spurs? No chance! The best two clubs in London are still Stringfellow's and the Hippodrome: *1988*
Arsenal beat Liverpool, in the final game of the 88/89 season, to clinch the League Championship

Malcolm Macdonald - *(b 1950) Huddersfield*

Town manager
On a promising start against Manchester City –
I think I'll have a cigar – if we keep this up
we'll get double figures: *1987*
Huddersfield lost 10–1

Margaret Thatcher – *(b 1925) Prime Minister*
On being asked to name the best player in the FA
Cup final – I thought the No. 10, Whymark,
played exceptionally well: *1978*
Although he was named in the programme Trevor
Whymark did not play

Tommy Woodruffe – *BBC radio commentator*
On the very poor showing in the 1938 FA Cup
Final – If there's a goal now, I'll eat my hat!
There was and he did

GOLF

Horatio Hutchinson – *Amateur champion*
Constitutionally and physically women are
unfitted for golf. The first women's
championship will be the last. They are bound
to fall out and quarrel on the slightest, or no,
provocation: *1893*
The ladies PGA now runs a multi-million dollar
tour

HORSE RACING

Charles Benson – *racing tipster*
Form guide to the Grand National – Foinavon has
no chance. Not the boldest of jumpers, he can
be safely ignored, even in a race noted for
shocks: *1967*
Foinavon won at 100–1

SKATING

Carlo Fasbi – *coach*
Robin Cousins is a great skater, but he's
chicken. I don't think he'll win the Olympics
because of it: *1980*
Cousins won the individual gold medal

SWIMMING

Mayor of Dover
After Matthew Webb's first Channel crossing –
I make so bold to say that I don't believe that in
the future history of the world any such feat
will be performed by anybody else: *1875*
Over 2000 people have now swum the channel

TENNIS

Anne Jones – *commentator*
Billie Jean King left Wimbledon yesterday for
the last time: *1973*
Billie Jean not only returned but won the singles
title in 1975 and doubles in 1979

Bobby Riggs – *USA*
On the Battle of the Sexes challenge v Billie Jean
King – She's a great player, for a gal. But no
woman can beat a male player who knows what
he's doing. I'll put Billie Jean and all the other
Women's Libbers back where they belong – in
the kitchen and the bedroom: *1973*
Billie Jean beat him in straight sets

[*Riggs later said –* There is no doubt that Billie
Jean's victory was a big one for the women's
movement and for all women. One guy said to
me, after the match, 'That set my marriage
back ten years – and I've only been married
two'.]

GENERAL

ANCIENT [B.C.]

Aristotle – *(384–322 BC) Greek philosopher*
The athlete's habit of body neither produces a
good condition for the general purposes of civic
life, nor does it encourage ordinary health and
the procreation of children.

The Bible
The race is not to the swift:
                              Ecclesiastes 9:11

Write the vision, and make it plain upon tables,
that he may run that readeth it:
                          Book of Habakkuk 2:2

Bion - *(c 280 BC) Greek poet*
Though boys throw stones at frogs in sport, the frogs do not die in sport, but in earnest.

Horace - *(65-8 BC) Roman poet & satirist*
Sport begets tumultuous strife and wrath, and wrath begets fierce quarrels.

After serious matters, let us indulge in a season of sport.

The happy state of getting the victor's palm without the dust of racing.

The man who knows nothing of games keeps away from the weapons of the campus, and being ignorant of ball play, the discus or the hoop, he remains quiet, for fear that spectators may justifiably roar with laughter at his efforts.

Thus, to turn serious matters to sport.

The shame is not having sported, but in not having broken off the sport.

If Roman pursuits wear you out because you are used to playing the Greek, try the quick ball play, which its excitement makes you forget your exhaustion.

Philomatius - *Greek sportsman*
For it is impossible for a player to join in a team game and retire at his pleasure.

Plato - *(427-348 BC) Greek philosopher*
The mere athlete becomes too much of a savage.

Plautus - *(254-184 BC) Roman comic playwright*
The Gods play games with men as balls.

He will never be dull to strangers who joins in sport with his own family.

Lao Tzu - *(c 500 BC) Chinese religious teacher*
The best charioteers do not rush ahead, the best fighters do not make displays of wrath:
Tao Te Ching

ANCIENT [A.D.]

Anon - *(c 1700)*

A hound and hawk no longer shall be tokens of disaffection,
A cockfight shall cease,
To be a breach of the peace,
And a horse-race an insurrection.

Artemidorus - *(c 200) Greek soothsayer*
Ball players play in rivalry, and whenever they receive the ball they hit it back again.

Cardinal Damiani - *(1007-72) Bishop of Ostia*
I restrain my pen, for I blush with shame to add the more disgraceful frivolities, to wit –
hunting, hawking, and especially the madness of dice and chess: *1061*

Juvenal - *(60-140) Roman satirist*
Two things only the people anxiously desire; bread and the circus games.

He wears his athletic trophies on his oil-smeared neck.

Nicharchus - *(c 100) Greek satirist & epigrammist*
Charmos, a long distance runner, finished seventh in a field of six! A friend ran alongside him shouting, 'Keep going Charmos!', and although fully dressed, beat him. And if he had had five friends he would have finished twelfth.

Phoedrus - *(c 100) Roman fabulist*
After a season of sport the mind is prepared to resume its studies with increased vigour.

Quintilian - *(35-100) Spanish/Roman orator*
The teacher of rhetoric will make the same distinction between his pupils as an athletics coach, who will make a runner of one pupil, a boxer or wrestler of another, or an expert at one of the other events of the Sacred Games of a third.

St Jerome - *(342-420) 'Father of the Western Church'*
Athletes as a rule are stronger than their backers; yet the weaker presses the stronger to part forth all his efforts.

No athlete gains his crown without sweat.

LITERARY PROSE

Anon
Sport is an aspect of psychology and psychology is an aspect of sport.

Dwell not too long upon sports; for as they refresh a man that is weary, so they weary a man that is refreshed.

Proverbs
In sports and journeys, men are known.

Sport is the sweetest when there are no spectators.

The best of the sport is to do the deed and say nothing.

Mischief the better for sport.

If the ball doesn't stick to the wall, it will at least leave a mark.

He who cannot make sport, should mar none:
Scottish

Jane Austen – *(1775-1817) novelist*
For what do we live, but to make sport for our neighbours, and laugh at them in our turn?:
Pride and Prejudice

Anna L. Barbauld – *(1743-1825) poet & essayist*
Finding out riddles is the same kind of exercise to the mind which running and leaping and wrestling and sport are to the body.

Maurice Baring – *(1874-1945) journalist*
There is a vast difference between games and play. Play is played for fun, but games are deadly serious and you do not play them to enjoy yourself:
1922

Dr Arnold R. Beisser
The reluctance to penetrate into comprehending the meaning of sports is understandable. We prefer not to know too much about what we treasure:
Madness in Sport (1967)

Lord Birkenhead – *(1872-1930) Attorney-General*

Were cricket and football abolished, it would bring upon the masses nothing but misery, depression, sloth, indiscipline and disorder:
1911

C. Nestelle Bovee – *(1829-1904) US writer & lawyer*
The pleasure of playing games comes from the small vanity of beating our opponents.

Mary Breese
Life without sport is not life.

Heywood Broun – *(1888-1939) US humorist & writer*
Sports do not build character. They reveal it.

Edmund Burke – *(1729-97) statesman & author*
Gaming is a principle inherent in human beings:
1780

Sir Richard Burton – *(1821-90) explorer*
And who, 'mid e'en the Fools, but feels that half the joy is in the race.

Sports and gaming, whether pursued from a desire of gain or love of pleasure are as ruinous to the temper and disposition of the party addicted to them, as they are to his fame and fortune.

Robert Burton – *(1577-1640) vicar & scholar*
Let the world have their May games, wakes, and whatever sports and recreations please them, provided they be followed with discretion.

Lewis Carroll – *(1832-98) US writer*
Now, here, you see, it takes all the running you can do, to keep in the same place:
Through The Looking Glass

If you want to get somewhere else, you must run at least twice as fast as that:
Through The Looking Glass

Agnes De Mille – *(b 1909) US choreographer*
Sports require skill, co-ordination and strength, but they are not dancing nor the stuff of dancing. Even when pleasing to watch, their real meaning lies in the practical results; the food caught, the game won, the record set: *1963*

John Dryden - *(1631-1700) poet & dramatist*
Science distinguishes a man of honour from one of those athletic brutes whom undeservedly we call heroes.

Finley Peter Dunne - *(1867-1936) US humorist*
'Slug-yer-spouse' is an international sport that has niver become popular on our side iv the wather. An American lady is not th' person that anny man but a trained athlete wud care to raise his hand again', save by way iv smoothin' her hair: 1906

Ralph Waldo Emerson - *(1803-82) US writer & philosopher*
Sport is the bloom and glow of perfect health.

Richard Espy - *writer*
Sport symbolizes the international environment and is also a pragmatic tool of the environment: 1979

Benjamin Franklin - *(1706-90) US statesman & philosopher*
Games lubricate the body and mind.

Paul Fussell - *(b 1924) US humorist*
The balls used in top class games are generally smaller than those used in others.

Stephen Gosson - *(1554-1624) ecclesiastic & writer*
Our wrestling at armies is turned to wallowing in ladies' laps, our courage to cowardice, our running to ryot, our bowes to bowls and our darts to dishes: 1579

Baltasaar Gracian - *(1601-58) Spanish writer & Jesuit priest*
In any game where the players are equally matched it is a great advantage to have the first move.

Henry Graves - *(1871-1951) US professor*
There are few words in the English language which have such a multiplicity of divergent meaning as the word 'sport'.

Robert Graves - *(1895-1985) poet*
In love as in sport, the amateur status must be strictly maintained.

William A. Harper
Whether he is hurling a javelin, soaring off a ski-jump, performing a double back flip off a diving board, or screaming towards earth in a free fall sky dive, man is alone. He is beyond the world of public determinations; of official identities; of functions; of self-deceptions and of everydayness. And in the solitary state of oneness, man can meet himself.

H. A. Harris - *sportswriter*
Most games have their origin in the spare-time activities of a leisured class: 1975

William Hazlitt - *(1778-1830) essayist & critic*
I have a much greater ambition to be the best racket player than the best prose writer.

It may be said that there are things of more importance than striking a ball against a wall – there are things indeed which make more noise and do as little good, such as making war and peace, making speeches and answering them, making verses and blotting them, making money and throwing it away.

George Herbert - *(1593-1633) poet*
It is a poor sport that is not worth a candle.

Oliver Wendell Holmes - *(1809-94) US jurist*
Man is a sporting as well as a praying animal.

Edgar W. Howe - *(1853-1937) US editor*
Some men are so mean that when they attend a ball game, they want to see the home team beaten.

William Inge - *(1860-1954) Dean of St Pauls*
Gaming is a disease of barbarians superficially civilized.

Games are the best safety-valve for the spirit of mere pugnacity.

Karl Jaspers - *(1883-1969) German philosopher*
Sport is not only play and the making of records; it is likewise a soaring and a refreshment.

Lori Johnson
I haven't hit a square ball all afternoon.

Samuel Johnson - *(1709-84) lexicographer*
Who can run the race with death?

James Jones - *(1921-72) US writer*
I think people invent and play games in order to kid themselves at least for a time, into thinking that life is a game; in order to forget that at the end of life there is nothing but a big blank wall.

Rudyard Kipling - *(1865-1936) novelist & poet*
For the race is run one and one, and never by two and two.

Charles Lamb - *(1775-1834) essayist*
Man is a gaming animal. He must always be trying to get the better in something or other.

I play over again for love, as the gamesters phrase it, games for which I once paid so dear.

L. L. Levinson - *US lexicographer*
Spring is the season of balls – golf, tennis, base and moth.

Eric Linklater - *(b 1899) Scottish novelist*
He prepared the lady to cricket – though he was an accomplished bat, fielded boldly at cover-point, and she found him more comforting than cards, though she played very good bridge indeed.

Sir Richard Livingstone - *(1880-1960) scholar*
Onlookers have a clearer view of the game than the players.

Robert Lynd - *(1879-1949) Anglo-Irish essayist*
It is in games that many men discover their paradise.

Almost any game with any ball is a good game.

Olaus Magnus - *(1490-1558) Swedish historian & cleric*
Sports are a most excellent device with which to test a man's character.

Rene Maheu - *United Nations Director General*

Sport is an order of chivalry, a code of ethics and aesthetics, recruiting its members from all classes and all peoples. Sport is a truce.

James A. Manson - *(1851-1921) poet*
Every sport on which the curse of gambling and the blight of excessive drinking have fallen is doomed sooner or later: *1912*

John May - *(1890-1959)*
A game, to be an all-round, good game, should have three main qualities. It should provide healthy recreation; should reward skill sufficiently to encourage serious effort, and have enough luck in it to give even the poorest competitor some sort of a chance: *1947*

Henry L. Mencken - *(1880-1956) US editor*
It's impossible to imagine Goethe or Beethoven being good at billiards or golf.

Edward Meyerstein - *(1889-1952) writer*
It seems to me that the real attractions of varsity life are reserved for the sportsman and the loafer: *1908*

Alice Meynell - *(1847-1922) essayist & poet*
With the first dream that comes with the first sleep, I run, I run.

Martin Opitz - *(1597-1639) German poet & critic*
What is sport to a cat is death to the mouse.

George Orwell - *(1903-50) novelist & critic*
Sport is an unfailing cause of ill-will: *1945*

John Pearson
The word 'sport' has been so widely used that any exact meaning which the term may have had has been eroded: *1982*

Vasili D. Philarete - *(1782-1867) Russian author*
Sports are necessary to divert the mind as well as the body.

Pope Pius XII - *(1876-1958)*
Sport, rightly conceived, is an occupation carried out by the whole man: *1945*

K. Privalor
The ball is neutral.

John Ray - *(1627-1705) naturalist*
Give o'er when the play's gude.

He'll play a small game rather than stand out.

Louis A. Reid - *(b 1895) writer*
Sometimes there is an element of art in sport
and scope for the artist in the sportsman,
though it is a limited one.

David Riesman - *(b 1909) US social scientist*
Play can easily vanish when people have to
strain for competence.

Robson
We may take example by three sorts of men
which hazard themselves in danger, and often
perish. The best swimmers are drowned. The
best climbers do fall. The best fencers are
wounded: *1585*

Mary P. Roby
History and art have recorded sports in words
and beauty; science and philosophy are tugged-
at by its means and meanings; but the soul of
sports remains uncaptured.

Abraham S. Rosenbach - *(1876-1952) US
bibliophile*
After love, book-collecting is the most
exhilarating sport of all:
A Book Hunter's Holiday (1936)

Royal Commission on public schools
The cricket and football fields are not merely
places of exercise and amusement; they help to
form some of the most valuable social qualities
and manly virtues: *1864*

Dr Benjamin Rush - *(1745-1813) US
physician*
Sports are often resorted to, with good effect, to
relieve anguish of the mind.

Antoine de Saint-Exupery - *(1900-44)
French novelist*
Games always cover something deep and
intense, else there would be no excitement in
them, no pleasure, no power to stir us.

Friedrich von Schiller - *(1759-1805)
German dramatist & poet*
The last perfection of our faculties is that their

activity, without ceasing to be sure and earnest,
become sport.

Man only plays when in the full meaning of the
word he is a man, and he is only completely a
man when he plays.

William Shakespeare - *(1564-1616)
playwright*
If thou dost play him at any game,
Thou art sure to lose; and, of that natural luck
He beats thee 'gainst the odds:
Antony & Cleopatra

To sports, to wilderness and much company:
Julius Caesar

Now bid me run, and I will strive with things
impossible: *Julius Caesar*

Faith, I ran when I saw others run:
Henry IV - Part I

If all the year were playing holidays, to sport
would be as tedious as work: *Henry IV*

Nay, if you get it you shall get it with running:
King Lear

Why dost thou run so many miles about?:
King Richard III

Playing patient sports in unrestrained gyves:
A Lover's Complaint

There's no such sport as sport by sport o'er
thrown: *Love's Labours Lost*

That sport best pleases that doth least know
how: *Love's Labours Lost*

Let me for ever be your table-sport:
Merry Wives of Windsor

Thou thinkst I am in sport:
Much Ado About Nothing

George Bernard Shaw - *(1856-1950) Irish
dramatist*
Games are for people who can neither read nor
think.

Percy B. Shelley - *(1792-1822) poet*

There is no sport in hate, when all the rage is on one side: *1821*

Howard Slusher - *(b 1937) US writer & attorney*
The understanding of being is clarified by sport: *1967*

Stow's Survey of London
The lower classes divert themselves at football, wrestling, cudgels, ninepins, shovel-board, cricket, stowball, ringing of bells, quoits, pitching the bar, bull and bear baitings, throwing at cocks and lying in ale-houses: *1700*

Robert S. Surtees - *(1803-64) sportswriter & novelist*
No man is fit to be called a sportsman what doesn't kick his wife out of bed on an average once in three weeks.

Sir Henry Taylor - *(1800-86) poet*
There's no game so desperate that the wisest of the wise will not take freely up for the love of power, or love of fame, or merely love of play.

Alfred Lord Tennyson - *(1809-92) Poet Laureate*
Sport went hand in hand with science.

James Thomson - *(1834-88) poet*
Give a man a horse he can ride,
Give a man a boat he can sail:
Sunday up the River

Thorstein Veblen - *(1857-1929) US sociologist & philosopher*
The addiction to sports, therefore, in a peculiar degree marks an arrested development of man's moral nature: *1899*

LITERARY RHYME

Lord Byron - *(1788-1824) poet*
He learned the arts of riding, fencing, gunnery,
And how to scale a fortress - or a nunnery.

Humphrey J. Dingley - *lawn bowler & writer*
All the village train from labour free,
Led up their sports beneath the spreading tree:
1893

Thomas D'Urfey - *(1653-1723) dramatist & song writer*
Her was the prettiest fellow.
At foot-ball or at cricket,
At hunting chase,
Or nimble race,
Cots-plus how her cou'd prick it: *1719*

Edward Fitzgerald - *(1809-83) translator*
The Ball no question makes of Ayes and Noes,
But Here or There as strikes the Player goes,
And He that toss'd it down into the Field;
He knows about it all - He knows - He knows!: *The Rubayait of Omar Khayyam*

Oliver Goldsmith - *(1730-74) poet & playwright*
The pictures placed for ornament and use.
The twelve good rules, the Royal game of Goose: *1770*

By sports like these are all their cares beguil'd
The sports of children satisfy the child.

Adam L. Gordon - *(1833-70) Australian poet*
No game was ever worth a rap
For a rational man to play,
Into which no accident, no mishap,
Could possibly find its way.

George Herbert - *(1593-1633) poet*
Play not for gain but sport, who plays for more,
Than he can lose for pleasure, stakes his heart -
Perhaps his wife too, and who she hath bore.

Thomas Hood - *(1799-1845) poet & humorist*
Dice will run the contrary way,
As well is known to all who play,
And cards will conspire as in treason;
And what with keeping a hunting box,
Following fox - friends in flocks,
Eurgundies, hocks - From London Docks,
Stultz's frocks - Manton and Nocks,
Barrels and locks - Shooting blue rocks,
Trainers and Jocks - Busking and socks,
Pugilistical knocks - And fighting cocks,
If he found himself short in funds and stocks,
These rhymes will furnish the reason
Miss Kilmansegg

Soame Jenyns - *(1704-87) MP & writer*
Here you'll be ever sure to meet,

A hearty welcome, through no treat;
A house, where quiet guards the door,
  No rural wits smoke, drink or roar,
Choice books, safe horses, wholesome liquor.
Billiards, backgammon and the vicar: *1735*

Charles Kingsley - *(1819-75) poet &*
clergyman
  When all the world is old, lad
And all the trees are brown,
And all the sport is stale, lad,
And all the wheels run down: *1863*

Rudyard Kipling - *(1865-1936) novelist &*
poet
  Then ye contented souls,
With flannelled fools at the wickets or
The Muddied oafs at the goals: *The Islanders*

In all of our distress,
And in our triumph too,
The game is more than the player,
And the ship is more than the crew.

John Milton - *(1608-74) poet*
  Sport that wrinkled Care derides
And laughter holding both his sides: *L'Allegro*

Sir Walter Scott - *(1771-1832) dramatist &*
poet
  His limbs were cast in manly mould,
For hardy sports or contests bold.

William Shakespeare - *(1546-1616)*
playwright
A summer's day will seen an hour but short
Being wasted in such time-beguiling sport:
                      Venus & Adonis

Edmund Spenser - *(1552-1599) poet*
  In wrestling nimble, and in running swift;
In shooting steady, and in swimming strong;
Well made to strike, to leap, to throw, to lift,
And all sports that shepherds are among.

How Mutability in them doth play
Her cruel sports, to many men's decay: *1596*

MODERN

George Allan - *sportswriter*
In cricket it separated Bradman and Sobers
from the rest; Pele had it in football, Borg had

it in tennis, Ali had it in boxing, Barry John
had it in rugby. Those who try to pin down
everything in life like so many butterflies to a
board would call it genius. I prefer it nameless:
                                    1983

Simon Barnes - *sportswriter for The Times*
Sportsmen are always trying to make
comebacks; it is part of the rhythm of every
sporting year. Perhaps they cannot stand the
drabness of living in the shadow of their own
youth. Always they believe it is possible to find
within themselves one more last hurrah.

Danny Blanchflower - *footballer*
Sport is a wonderfully democratic thing, one of
the few honourable battle-fields left. It is a
conflict between good and bad, winning and
losing, praise and criticism. Its true values
should be treasured aand protected: *1968*

Chef de Partie - *Monaco Casino*
At play, anything may happen.

Olga Connolly [Fikotova] - *(b 1932) Czech/*
US Olympic discus champion [1956]
Humans have been equipped with a wondrous
range of creative movement. Motion is a basic
element of life, and sports are the milieu
wherein a human being can express her
physical genius.

Dan Devine - *American football coach at Notre*
Dame
A team is a team is a team. Shakespeare said
that many times.

Carlton Fisk - *baseball player*
If the human body recognized agony and
frustration, people would never run marathons,
have babies or play baseball.

Jim Fixx - *US runner & writer*
Because sport offers no hiding places, it teaches
honesty and authenticity.

Lucinda Green - *(b 1953) three-day eventer*
Sport is a university of life.

David Hemery - *hurdler*
Sport is one very good avenue for self-
expression, self-awareness and personal growth.

Colin M. Jarman - *(b 1958) sportswriter*
Sport is an activity where feats are measured in
inches and first place won by seconds: *1988*

A. E. Knight - *(1872-1946) Leicestershire
cricketer & writer*
All sport, if it is to be a delight, giving as it may
be, must embody an element of creative art, of
generation, not of technical skill alone: *1906*

John Lardner - *US sportswriter*
The roller derby is a sport. Defenestration is
also a sport for those who like it.

Bill 'The Spaceman' Lee - *baseball pitcher*
When cerebral processes enter into sports, you
start screwing up. It's like the Constitution,
which says separate church and state. You have
to have a separate mind and body.

Michael Novak - *(b 1933) US critic, writer &
philosopher*
To diagnose sport as the source of machismo is
like diagnosing love as the source of selfishness:
1976

Angela Patmore - *sportswriter*
Sport is not like a novel or a play, with the
ending already decided. It is alive and dynamic.

Anything can happen.

Ron Pickering - *TV commentator*
Sport was born of man's highest ideals and has
been around for 33 centuries, which is longer
than any religion, culture or subculture; it must
be defended and harnessed for its values.

Michael Roberts - *US writer*
The Athletic aesthetic is a tricky thing: *1977*

J. Russell - *yachtsman*
The highest reward of all sports, even
competitive ones, is the conscious savouring of
perfect performance: *1977*

Lee Trevino - *(b 1939) US golfer*
When you play a sport, you have two things in
mind. One is to get into the Hall of Fame and
the other is to go to heaven when you die.

Gene Upshaw - *(b 1945) American footballer*
If you didn't have humour you couldn't have
sport.

Maurice Yaffe - *sports psychologist*
The sports arena is a wonderful laboratory for
observation.

MEDIA

Anon
Sport is anything they can make competitive or
entertaining enough to be good television.

Sports writing is easy. You sit in front of a
typewriter until little drops of blood run down
your forehead.

George Allan - *sportswriter*
You can recognize minority sports by the
bland, uncritical way they're reported: *1985*

John Bromley - *TV sports producer*
At its best, sport is living drama: *1982*

Jimmy Cannon- *(1910-73) US sportswriter*
We work in the toy department.

A sportswriter is entombed in a prolonged
boyhood.

Sportswriting only survives because of the guys
who don't cheer.

A rabid sports fan is one that boos a TV set.

Howard Cosell - *(b 1920) US TV commentator*
Unquestionably, TV is saving sports, although I
am not sure if sports is worth saving.

Bernard Darwin - *sportswriter*
Sports writing is a job into which men drift,
since no properly constituted parent would
agree to his son starting his career in that way.
Having tried something else which bores them

they take to this thing which is lightly esteemed by the outside world but which satisfies in them some possibly childish but certainly romantic feeling.

Writing about sport is worth nothing without gusto.

Peter Dobereiner - *(b 1925) sportswriter*
Bernard Darwin and Neville Cardus took the shine off the ball in the battle against penny-a-line journalese and then Henry Longhurst came along to win the match: *1978*

Robert Lipsyte - *US writer*
Well-meaning people often ask sportswriters, even middle-aged sportswriters, what they are going to do when they grow up.

Desmond Lynam - *(b 1942) TV sports presenter*
There's a simple recipe about this sports business. If you're a sporting star, you're a sporting star. If you don't quite make it, you become a coach. If you can't coach, you become a journalist. If you can't spell, you introduce Grandstand on a Saturday afternoon.

Desmond Lynam is so laid back he's almost horizontal - which is exactly how his legions of fantasising housewifey fans imagine him to be:
Frank Keating

Rene Maheu - *United Nations Director General*
Not in literature or in music must we seek the image of sport, but in the press, in photography and television.

Derek Malcolm - *(b 1932) critic*
The capacity of sporting journalists to wax lyrical in face of the exceptional is only matched by the speed with which they run out of adjectives in doing so.

Steve Miller- *US sportswriter*
Television turns uniform numbers into personalities: *1984*

Jim Murray - *US sportswriter*
Sportswriting has never been a matter of schools. When a guy is wonderful you can say he is wonderful. When he isn't, just say that he stinks.

Judge Earl Warren - *(1891-1974) Governor of California*
The sports page records people's accomplishments; the front page has nothing but man's failures.

AMERICAN FOOTBALL

Bob Costas - *TV commentator*
Don't fix your sets. I've been waiting for this all day. Mosi Tatupu runs into the arms of Manu Tuiasosopo: *1980*

Bill Curry - *Colts & TV sports announcer*
Sports announcers are as colourless as a glass of gin. Most of them are like a bunch of barbers cutting each other's hair.They emulate each other and fawn over each other on the air. The same dull, successful ones show up everywhere. The broken-down old ball-players are the worst, but almost all are equally appalling.

Art Modell - *Cleveland Browns owner*
The days of quantum leaps in TV revenue may have ended not only for professional football, but for all sports. Even if the party isn't over, the champagne has ceased to flow.

Bo Schembechler - *University of Michigan coach*
I don't have anything against media people. I just don't want my daughters going to school with them.

Pat Summerall - *TV commentator*
On his vocal delivery - If ever I got cancer, I would want Pat Summerall to be the one to tell me: *Beano Cook - TV commentator*

Norm Van Brocklin - *coach & quarterback*
After having surgery - It was a brain transplant. I got a sportswriter's brain, so I could be sure I had one that hadn't been used: *1980*

ATHLETICS

Russell Davies - *writer*
Plainly no way has yet been found to stop long-jump commentaries sounding like naughty stories after lights-out in the dorm - 'Ooooh! It's enormous. It was so long!'

Steve Ovett - *(b 1955) middle distance runner*
I hate this attitude the media have that just because someone is good at sport means that their opinion on any topic is of fantastic importance.

That 'Superstars' programme – talented sportsmen being asked to jump through hoops when somebody blows a whistle. I think that cheapens sport. People say it makes sportsmen look human. I think it makes them look foolish.

BASEBALL

Joe DiMaggio - *(b 1914) New York Yankees*
I remember a reporter asking for a quote, and I didn't know what a quote was. I thought it was some kind of drink.

'Ring' Lardner - *(1885-1933) humorist*
Nothing is more depressing than an old baseball writer.

Jim Murray - *sportswriter*
By and large baseball writers and baseball managers get along like man and wife. They respect each other, but not much.

William 'Bucky' Walters - *(b 1909) Boston Red Sox & Cincinnati Reds*
If baseball was half as complicated as some of these writers make out it is, a lot of us boys from the farm would never have been able to make a living at it.

BOXING

Tyrell Biggs - *US heavyweight*
On his drug habit – How did I get hooked? Well, it's something like a journalist having a drink after work: *1988*

Joe Bugner- *heavyweight*
On British jounalists – They ring me up from London, smooth-talk you for half an hour, hang up and then slag you off as if you were some mad rapist.

The Press are gin-swilling, beer-swilling slobs.

'Tex' Cobb - *US heavyweight*
Sportswriters are probably the only individuals in our universe who actually have less

constructive jobs than I do. I don't do nothing but hit people. And they don't do nothing but talk about what I do.

Eugene Corri - *US referee*
Sport is one of the great factors in the lives of tens of thousands of Britishers, and yet there are supercilious gentlemen who speak and write of sport as though it were just the merest side issue: *1915*

Barney Eastwood - *Irish promoter & manager*
I'm convinced that, in the long term, live TV is very harmful to boxing. It has already half-killed the game in America.

B. J. Evans - *journalist*
I do not consider any writer on boxing fully equipped for his job unless he can advise a trainer on how to prepare his man for the championship:
How to Become a Sporting Journalist

George Foreman - *US heavyweight*
The Press has been real nice to me. There is no George Foreman without the Press. People can knock you sports guys all they want, but I'm a creation of you. When you get tired of me, there's no more George Foreman in anybody's mind.

Frank Keating - *(b 1937) sportswriter*
My method of covering boxing is simple – pare down the prelims to the simple basic of Goodie versus Baddie. The British boy is always the Goodie.

Norman Mailer - *(b 1923) US novelist*
The popular assumption that professional boxers do not have brains comes from sportswriters, but then sportswriters' brains are themselves damaged by the obligation to be clever every day. And the quantities of booze necessary to lubricate such racing of the mental gears ends up giving sportswriters the equivalent of a good many punches to the head.

Sylvester Mittee - *welterweight*
There's a myth that fighters are monosyllabic buffoons. And that myth is perpetuated when fighters are thrown in front of a microphone and they freeze.

CLIMBING

Claire Engel – *writer*
Every sport, including mountaineering, gets the literature and the adepts it deserves: *1971*

CRICKET

John Arlott – *(b 1914) writer & commentator*
I talk about what I see. A lot of commentators tend to talk about what they are thinking than what they are watching.

Ted Dexter – *(b 1935) Sussex*
Journalism and batting are not so different – a few good strokes are often better remembered than all the padding in between: *1974*

Ted Dexter is to journalism what Danny La Rue is to Rugby League: *Michael Parkinson*

Brian Glanville – *(b 1931) sportswriter*
Much that passes for literature in the lauded realm of cricket now often seems whimsical or over-written.

Sir A.P. Herbert – *(b 1890) poet & humorist*
And when you rub the ball on rump or belly,
  Remember what it looks like on the telly.

E. W. Swanton – *(b 1907) Middlesex &*
sportswriter
One could make a good case for the proposition that more has been written about Dr W. G. Grace than any sporting figure in history.

Fred Trueman – *(b 1931) Yorkshire*
At a dinner engagement – I'm here to propose a toast to sportswriters and it's up to you if you stand up.

DOGS

Ralph Ryan – *US greyhound owner & trainer*
On the special 'hares' he uses in training – I use sportswriters and when we get a broken-down dog, we give him a typewriter.

FOOTBALL

Malcolm Allison – *manager*
A lot of people in football don't have much time for the press; they say they're amateurs. But I say to those people, 'Noah was an amateur, but the Titanic was built by professionals!':   *1980*

Sir Dennis Follows – *Minister for Sport*
With the dominance of TV, the influence of sponsors, the interference of manufacturers, public-relations officers and entrepreneurs, I see no future for sport at top level. It is not too alarming a glimpse into the future to see professional football playing to empty stadia for the benefit of TV and the football pools: *1983*

Emmanuel Gambardella – *sportswriter*
After Sweden had beaten Cuba 8-0 – Up to five goals is journalism; after that it becomes statistics: *1938*

Cesar Menotti – *manager of Argentina*
On the local sporting press – Not only do they know nothing about football, but if you were to shut them up in a room by themselves, they couldn't even write a letter to mother: *1982*

Jack Taylor – *referee*
It was when old ladies who had been coming into my shop for years started talking about sweepers and creating space that I really understood the influence of TV: *1974*

GOLF

David Brenner – *US comedian*
I don't like to watch golf on TV because I can't stand people who whisper: *1977*

Peter Dobereiner – *(b 1925) sportswriter*
When TV first focused a cyclopean eye on American professional sport, the golf match-play form of the game was turned to stone.

HORSE RACING

Dick Francis – *(b 1920) jockey & novelist*
I approach Chapter One each year with a deeper foreboding than I ever felt facing Becher's.

Lord Wigg – *Chairman of the Jockey Club*
Instead of a month's jail someone should be sentenced to read the *Sporting Life* on non-racing days: *1959*

SAILING

Herman L. Masin - *US sportswriter*
The coverage of the America's Cup is
unbelievable. Never have the media done so
much for so few: *1980*

SNOOKER

Geoffrey Nicholson - *sportswriter*
If snooker hadn't existed, TV would surely have
had to invent it.

TENNIS

John Barrett - *BBC TV commentator*
We don't always get from slow-motion the pace
at which they play.

MONEY

Jim Benagh - *US sportswriter*
Getting an athlete to sign a contract can be a
very expensive venture. But getting him to sign
anything else - a photograph, a baseball, a
personal letter or just a scrap of paper - can be
like getting him to write you a check: *1980*

Lord Chesterfield [Philip Stanhope] -
(1694-1773) statesman & wit
A man may play, with decency; but if he games,
he is disgraced.

Irvin S. Cobb - *(1876-1944) US humorist*
As I understand it, sport is hard work for which
you do not get paid.

E.N. Gardiner - *sportswriter*
When money enters into sport, corruption is
sure to follow: *1930*

Paul Gardner - *US sportswriter*
When you talk about the link between
television and sport, you start thinking in terms
of millions of dollars, because that is what the
link is all about. Millions of dollars: *1974*

Johan Huizinga - *(1877-1945) Dutch historian*
Now with the increasing systemisation and
regimentation of sport, something of the pure
play quality is inevitably lost. The spirit of the
professional is no longer the true play spirit, it
is lacking in spontaneity and carelessness. This
affects the amateur too.

Vivian Jenkins - *Welsh rugby player &
sportswriter*
The only real amateur is one who pays his own
expenses.

Jack Kelly Jr. - *US Olympic committee member*
The difference between an amateur and a
professional athlete is the latter is paid by
cheque: *1983*

Life magazine
The commercial standard, which governs the
great world of business and most of the
practical concerns of life, keeps elbowing its
way into college sports, and trying to drive the
gentleman's standard out: *1907*

Gary Pomerantz - *US sportswriter*
Money has done more than make the sports
world go round, it has made it spin off its axis.

AMERICAN FOOTBALL

James Lawton - *British sportswriter*
American Football is about many things. Most
of all, it is about money.

Carl Lewis - *(b 1961) Olympic sprinter & long-
jumper*
On his refusal to join the Dallas Cowboys - He

couldn't afford to take the pay-cut:

Joe Douglas – agent (1982)

Norm Van Brocklin - *LA Rams quarterback*
There's no tougher way to make easy money
than to play pro football.

ATHLETICS

Geoff Capes - *shot-putter*
Amateurism in athletics is dead. It has been a
ghost of its original self for years: *1981*

Linford Christie - *sprinter*
They are prepared to pay Ben [Johnson] and
Carl [Lewis] ridiculous sums, but promoters
want me to come on Oxfam: *1988*

Sebastian Coe - *middle distance runner*
Sport has to remain sport, a concept rooted on
the track and not in the balance sheet.

E. N. Gardiner - *sportswriter*
The Nemesis of excess in athletics is
professionalism, which is the death of all true
sport: *1930*

Venissa Head - *discus thrower*
On the lack of discus events for women – I keep
hearing athletes screaming for more money, but
I would scream just to compete.

Ben Jipcho - *Kenyan middle distance runner*
Running for money doesn't make you run fast.
It makes you run first: *1975*

Carl Lewis - *(b 1961) US sprinter & long
jumper*
It's unbelievable how amateurs are looked
down on for accepting money. Stevie Wonder
signs a $40 million recording contract and the
world rejoices; I make a token of that and they
say 'You dog!'

Frank Horwill - *coach*
The athletes are caught between the devil and
the deep blue sea, and usually the agent wins
because the athlete doesn't want to upset him.

Jackie Mekler - *South African long distance
runner*
Professionalism is being paid to rest.

Bob Tisdall - *Irish hurdler*
As soon as money comes into sport, the fun
goes out and the greedier you are, the less you
enjoy it.

Emil Zatopek - *(b 1922) Czech long distance
runner*
An athlete cannot run with money in his
pockets. He must run with hope in his heart
and dreams in his head.

BASEBALL

Anon
The hot dog is king. For every one dollar we get
paid in admission, our total cost of operating
the club is $1.06. If we didn't have extra income
from concessions, we'd have to lock our gates.

Chicago Cubs official

Dizzy Dean - *(1911-74) St Louis Cardinals*
I throw a ball around and get paid for it. Others
do it by throwing the bull.

Samuel Goldwyn - *(1882-1974) movie
producer*
The third baseman gets that? I wouldn't even
pay the first baseman that!

'Lefty' Gomez - *New York Yankees*
*On being asked to take a pay-cut from $20,000 to
$7,500* – Tell you what, you keep the salary and
pay me the cut.

Ray Kroc - *(1902-84) owner of the San Diego
Padres & McDonald's food chain*
I can make more money out of one hamburger
stand than I can out of baseball.

Walter 'Rabbit' Maranville - *Boston Red
Sox & sportswriter*
Nobody gets a kick out of baseball anymore,
because big salaries and the pension fund have
made it more serious business than running a
bank.

Harold Parrott - *sportswriter*
Baseball owners are little boys with big wallets.

'Babe' Ruth - *(1895-1948) Orioles & Yankees*
A man who knows he's making money for other
people ought to get some of the profit he brings
in. Don't make any difference if it's baseball or

a bank or a vaudeville show. It's business.
There ain't no sentiment to it. Forget that stuff.

John B. Sheridan
Money chasing is the great American game.
Professional baseball is based on money
chasing: 1922

Paul Waner – *(b 1903) Pittsburgh Pirates*
They say money talks, but the only thing it ever
says to me is good-bye.

BASKETBALL

Bob 'Mr Basketball' Cousy – *(b 1928)*
Boston Celtics
Viewers attach financial rewards as an
incentive, but in reality, you never think of it
once the whistle blows.

BOXING

Muhammad Ali – *(b 1942) US heavyweight*
I'll do anything for publicity. I'll bring a pretty
girl to the gym every day, if it is going to get me
another $50,000 in eating money.

Dave Anderson – *US sportswriter*
The fast money attracts the boxers and the
schemers. But the boxers bleed, the schemers
smirk. The boxers depart, the schemers survive.
It has always been that way in boxing, and it
always will be: 1977

'Tex' Cobb – *US heavyweight*
I'm a whore who sells his blood instead of his
ass. I never made much money being good
looking, but there's always somebody who'll
pay me to take a punch.

John Conteh – *light-heavyweight*
For someone who was obsessed with making
millions of pounds, I never was much good at
counting the pennies.

I looked upon all the boxing purely as a
business. As a means to an end. Getting the
money.

Jack Dempsey – *(1895-1983) US heavyweight*
When you're fighting, you're fighting for one
thing – money.

Dempsey hit me hardest, 'cos Dempsey hit me
two hundred eleven thousand dollars' worth,
while Louis only hit me thirty-six thousand
dollars' worth:
Jack Sharkey – US heavyweight

Wilfrid Diamond – *US writer*
On the Tunney/Dempsey fight – Two million
dollars gate at one fight! That's some cabbage
in any man's language: 1926

Virgil Hill – *US light-heavyweight*
Boxing is a sport for the man with no money. It
is an opportunity for a man who is from the
street and has had to scuffle to make it.

Larry Holmes – *(b 1949) US heavyweight*
I came from a dirt farm. Now I'm filthy rich.

Frank Keating – *(b 1937) sportswriter*
Sport is business and business is business. It's
nothing really new – Kid Cain would not have
put his title on the line against Boy Abel if the
money hadn't been right.

Sugar Ray Leonard – *(b 1956) US multi-
weight*
I know it would be easy to carry on fighting and
pick up another 12 or 15 million dollars. But, I
will never be able to spend the money I've got
already for as long as I live, so cash doesn't
exactly inspire me.

Joe Louis – *(1914-81) US heavyweight*
I don't like money, actually, but it quiets my
nerves.

Gary Mason – *heavyweight*
We have different aims in boxing. Frank Bruno
wants to be world champion and I just want the
money.

Mike Tyson – *US heavyweight*
I ride around in a luxury car, but I didn't pay
for it. The money that I made, I bled for it, and
I don't part with it easy.

CRICKET

Charles Booth – *writer*
Cricketers, especially first class men, may be
ranked among the lowest paid of all
professional men. In power of drawing a crowd,

a well known eleven probably equals any music hall combination, and yet, their remuneration will be at best but one quarter of that given to artistes: *1903*

Pat Gibson – *writer*
Cricket must be the only business where you can make more money in one day than you can in three: *1975*

Thomas Kenneally – *(1879-1954) Australian politician*
Despite the big money, cricket in Australia has become merely a game. And when that happens, we're in trouble.

Barry Richards – *(b 1945) South Africa*
When I'm too old to earn a living playing cricket, how much will a bank manager give me for my Springbok cap? What kind of reaction will I get when I push my pads over the counter and say 'What are these cheques worth?'

E. W. Swanton – *(b 1907) Middlesex & sportswriter*
If, as has been said, Mailey bowled like a millionaire and Grimmett like a miser, Rhodes was the hard-headed financier, ready to buy his wickets, but never at an extravagant price.

Fred Trueman – *(1931) Yorkshire*
I've been very lucky, Freddie Trueman has made a lot of money out of cricket, but for every player like me, there's a hundred who struggle on a shoe-string.

CROQUET

Richard Rodgers
The game is passionate enough without money.

FOOTBALL

Danny Blanchflower – *(b 1926) Spurs*
I personally don't hold with those players who say they'd play for England for nothing. So would I in one way. I'd play for Ireland for nothing, if they let everybody in for nothing. If they're collecting a £50,000 gate, playing for hope and glory has nothing to do with the facts: *1960*

Tommy Docherty – *(b 1928) much travelled*

manager
On getting the sack from Preston North End – They offered me a handshake of £10,000 to settle amicably. I told them they would have to be a lot more amicable than that: *1981*

Anton Johnson – *Rotherham United Chairman*
I've heard claims that I'm supposed to be using Mafia money. Some football clubs are in such a mess right now, you could buy them out of Brownie funds: *1983*

Tommy Trinder – *Fulham Chairman*
On breaking the minimum wage – Johnny Haynes is a top entertainer and will be paid as one from now on. I will give him £100 a week to play for Fulham: *1961*

GOLF

Sayings
Drive for show, putt for dough.

Frank Beard – *USA*
Golf is a business with me. It's like going to the office from nine to five. It's my livelihood. When I'm at my office – on the course – I like to apply myself to my work. When I fail to do this, I think I'm cheating myself out of money.

Walter Hagen – *(1892-1969) USA*
I never wanted to be a millionaire, I just wanted to live like one.

All the professional golfers who have a chance to go after the big money today, should say a silent thanks to Walter Hagen each time they stretch a cheque between their fingers:
Gene Sarazen

Gene Sarazen – *(b 1902) USA*
Money, after all, is incidental. That goes. You use it up. You lose it on the Stock Market or other investments, but the titles are yours, you keep them for life.

Lee Trevino – *(b 1939) USA*
I plan to win so much this year, my caddie's gonna finish in the top 20 money-winners.

I'm making money, so when I retire I hope I'll be set up. If not, I'll go back to picking up golf balls somewhere.

GYMNASTICS

Mike Jacky - *Director of the USGF*
We have one rule to follow – everything we do has a price tag and we have to carefully evaluate this.

MOTOR RACING

Colin Chapman - *(1928–82) Lotus team manager*
Money is how we keep the score in motor racing nowadays: *1974*

Charles Jarrott
The curse of commercialism is the ruin of sport and the degeneracy of motor racing as a sport is

due to the financial issues now involved: *1905*

RUGBY UNION

Bill Beaumont - *(b 1952) England*
Money would probably have made me a dirtier player.

TENNIS

Gordon Forbes - *sportswriter*
Tennis has changed – come into money and absolutely gone public. It's the day of the superstar, the supercoach, the how-to books, the tennis universities and the tracksuits with the stripes down the sides.

NATIONAL

COUNTRY OF ORIGIN UNLESS OTHERWISE STATED

GLOBAL

E. M. Forster - *(1879–1970) British novelist*
It is international sport that helps kick the world downhill. Started by foolish athletes, who thought it would promote understanding, it is supported today by the desire for political prestige and by the interests involved in gate monies. It is completely harmful: *1957*

Frederick W. Hackwood - *British sportswriter*
The sports of the people afford an index to the character of the nation: *1907*

Peter C. McIntosh - *US sociologist*
The desire for international competition is not confined to the richer and more highly developed countries but is shared by those countries which might be thought to be preoccupied with the basic needs for survival:
1963

E. W. Swanton - *(b 1907) British sportswriter*
Of all the talking points which make international sport fascinating, selecting a team to represent the country surely takes pride of place.

AFRICA

G. Fenwick - *British writer*
The attitude to physical activity is still very different in rural Africa – it would be worthwhile running miles to find your cows, but not for a silver cup.

Marina Sulzberger - *(1920–76)*
Where but in Kenya can a man whose grandfather was a cannibal watch a really good game of polo?

AUSTRALIA

John A. Daley
Australia's National Sport – Winning!

K. Dunstan
Sport is the ultimate Australian super-religion; the one thing every Australian believes in passionately.

Jack Fingleton - *cricketer*
Australians will not tolerate class distinctions in sport: *1946*

Thomas Kenneally - *(1879–1954) politician*

215

In the manner in which soccer is the great way up for the children from the economic sumps of Brazil, so cricket was the great way out of Australian cultural ignominy. No Australian had written *Paradise Lost*, but Bradman had made a hundred before lunch at Lord's.

We may be a small race, but there's divinity in our cricket.

Michael McKernan – *sports historian & writer*
Australians are a race of 'sports'.

John Snow – *(b 1941) English cricketer*
Melbournians are like piranha fish when it comes to sport. They will devour anything that will satisfy their appetite for competition.

BRAZIL

Jornal Da Tarde – *national newspaper*
Our football is like our inflation – 100%.

CANADA

George Chuvalo – *heavyweight boxer*
I'm the best heavyweight fighter in Canada and I'll still be the best when I'm dead seven years:
1979

CHINA

Bobby Charlton – *(b 1937) English football player*
China will certainly have a soccer team in the not-too-distant future. They're working on a squad of 100 million kids: 1988

EASTERN BLOC

Jean Marie Brohm – *French gym coach*
East Germany cultivates a sporting conception of the state, and a state conception of sport:
1978

'Buster' Mottram – *British tennis player*
I've played behind the Iron Curtain, and those squalid East European countries are disastrous. I hate it there. I mean, it's a luxury if you can eat eggs for breakfast.

EIRE

Mike England – *(b 1941) Welsh soccer manager*
If you have a fortnight's holiday in Dublin you qualify for an Eire cap: 1986

Noel Henderson – *rugby player*
The state of British sport is mostly serious, but never hopeless. The state of Irish sport is usually hopeless, but never serious.

FRANCE

Jean Fayard – *(b 1902) novelist*
If the French were to play cricket they would all want to be "batsman' - the cynosure of all eyes – at the same time, just as nearly all of them want to be Prime Minister.

Chris Laidlaw – *New Zealand rugby player*
Rugby has always captured the imagination of the French, just as the French have always captured the imagination in their rugby.

Ron Pickering – *British TV commentator*
The French are not normally a Nordic skiing nation.

GREAT BRITAIN

Sir Herbert Beerbohm – *(1872–1956) caricaturist*
The national sport of England is obstacle-racing. People fill their rooms with useless and cumbersome furniture, and spend the rest of their lives trying to dodge it.

Brian Dobbs – *sportswriter*
A Welsh defeat at soccer or a Scottish defeat at rugby can be treated by the local population with relative shoulder-shrugging indifference, but for the Welsh to lose at Rugby or the Scots to lose at soccer is akin to a national disaster:
1973

Andre Drucker – *(b 1909) author*
Foreigners suspect that cricket is some form of English lunacy. They will never understand there is a method in this English madness. It is what keeps them sane.

Ralph Waldo Emerson – *(1803–82) US novelist & philosopher*

The English are the most voracious people of prey that ever existed. Every season turns out the aristocracy into the country to shoot and fish.

Ronald Firbank – *(1886–1926) novelist*
It is said that to behold the Englishman at his best one should watch him play tip-and-run.

Frederick W. Hackwood – *sportswriter*
To an Englishman sport is as the salt of life – particularly the field sports of country life:
1907

Margaret Halsey – *(b 1910) US writer*
Listening to Britons dining out is like watching people play first-class tennis with imaginary balls.

Lord Mancroft – *(1872–1942)*
Cricket is a game which the British, not being a spiritual people, had to invent in order to have some concept of eternity.

George Mikes – *(1912–87) Hungarian-born author*
Many continentals think that life is a game. The English think cricket is just a game:
How To Be An Alien

George Orwell – *(1903–50) novelist*
The English themselves are not outstandingly good at all games but they enjoy playing them, and, to an extent that strikes foreigners as foolish, they enjoy reading about them and betting on them.

Ron Pickering – *TV commentator*
We nurture our losers better than any other country.

David Sutherland – *athletics coach*
It seems as a nation we are too keen to laud the athletes of other nations to the detriment of our own.

GREECE

Anon
Baseball was a favourite game among the Greeks – back then they had something called a 'Homer'.

INDIA

Aslam Sher Khan
Sport in India is a gravy train that catapults you to popularity.

Eric Silver – *British writer*
Indians are perhaps the only people who still place the austere skills of billiards above the gaudy promiscuity of snooker:
1985

ITALY

Bunny Sterling – *British middleweight boxer*
Any British boxer fighting in Italy has to knock his opponent out to be even worth a draw.

Jackie Stewart – *(b 1939) British racing driver*
Italians are distinguished by their disrespect for speed limits and preference for flair over civil obedience:
1983

NEW ZEALAND

Frank Keating – *(b 1937) British sportswriter*
In quaint, friendly New Zealand – where church is low, tea is high and brows are middling – rugby football is the enduring passion:
1983

Dennis LaLanne – *rugby union player*
I believe that pelote, bowls, politics, love, religion, urban housing, the atomic bomb, the war in Algeria and potato chips do not fill the thoughts of people in France as much as rugby stirs the souls of New Zealanders:
1961

PAKISTAN

Ian Botham – *(b 1955) English cricketer*
Pakistan is the sort of place every man should send his mother-in-law to, for a month, all expenses paid:
1984

RUSSIA

Anon
You must give the Russians credit, they haven't claimed yet that they invented baseball.

Henry W. Morton – *(b 1929) British writer*
Sport is used by the Party as a lever of social control, offering the Soviet regime a wonderful

opportunity to exploit genuine enthusiasm and at the same time channel leisure-time activity toward party-inspired goals: *1963*

Galina Shavrova - *athlete*
In our country men and women are treated equal in sport. We need to be strong to build the Mother country: *1975*

SPAIN

Richard Ford - *(1796-1858) British travel writer*
Bull-baiting in any shape is irresistible to the Spaniard: *Handbook For Travellers In Spain*

USA

Anon
We have to have impact, and action, and instant reward, and punishment. Soccer is too subtle for most Americans.

Francis Allen - *University of Nebraska gym coach*
In the USA, unlike China and Russia, you cannot tell an athlete he has to go to the gym.

Jacques Barzun - *(b 1902) Provost of Columbia University*
Whoever wants to know the heart and mind of America had better learn baseball.

Dr Arnold R. Beisser
Whether we view sports as a reflection of the mores of American life or as the promoter of these mores, it is a sobering analysis to consider that they may represent the end result of American pragmatism: *1977*

The concepts and language of sports are so familiar and pervasive that they are used as metaphors to clarify other aspects of American life: *1977*

Sir Maurice Bowra - *(1898-1971) British scholar & historian*
With one or two exceptions, colleges expect their players of games to be reasonably literate.

E. H. Cady - *sportswriter*
Though nobody in the modern world holds a monopoly on sports frenzy, the Big Game

happens only in America: *1978*

Jimmy Cannon - *(1910-73) sportswriter*
Philadelphia is an old wino sleeping it off in the doorway littered with busted dreams. Its teams are doomed to lose and its fans are cruel and crabbed.

Angelo Dundee - *boxing trainer & manager*
Philadelphia is not a town, it's a jungle. They don't have gyms there; they have zoos. They don't have sparring sessions; they have wars.

Paul Fussell - *(b 1924) humorist*
On the US and USSR - The two societies are becoming identical in terms of athleticism, the idea of finding national identity in athletic victory. The Soviets happen to be good at chess and weight-lifting and we're good at football, but it's the same kind of stupid, mind-blowing imbecility on both sides which is projected as national policy. Two great big, muscle-bound giants with little pea brains on top.

James Lawton - *British sportswriter*
The football coach has become much more than another functionary of sport. He is expected to embody the very deepest Americans' perceptions of themselves. He is expected to be authoritative, tough but fair, philosophical but imbued with a hunger for action. Ideally, he is a soldier-priest: *1984*

General Douglas MacArthur - *(1880-1964) military leader*
If I were to indicate today that element of American life which is most characteristic of our nationality, my finger would unerringly point to our athletic escutcheon.

Henry L. Mencken - *(1880-1956) journalist & critic*
The United States, to my eye, is incomparably the greatest show on earth. We have clowns among us who are as far above the clowns of any great state as Jack Dempsey is above the paralytic - and not a few dozen or score of them, but whole droves and herds.

Martina Navratilova - *(b 1956) tennis player*
On her Czech roots - I'm an American. You can't go on where we were born. If you do that John McEnroe would be a German.

[*McEnroe was born in Wiesbaden, West Germany*]

Frederic L. Paxson - *(1877-1948) historian*
Spectator sports found lodgement in American society earlier than did those in which participation is the price of enjoyment.

Judson P. Philips
It is a curious fact that you can give an American man some kind of ball and he will be thoroughly content.

Will Rogers - *(1879-1935) humorist*
America became a great nation under baseball. And began to decline the moment it took up a lot of poor substitutes.

Albert G. Spalding - *(1850-1915) baseball manufacturer*
Two hours is as long as an American will wait for the close of a baseball game - or anything for that matter: *1950*

John Steinbeck - *(1902-68) novelist*
All Americans believe that they are born fishermen. For a man to admit a distaste for fishing would be like denouncing mother-love or hating moonlight: *1954*

Edward Walsh - *writer*
Americans are experts at winning, but still amateurs at losing: *1977*

OLYMPICS

THE ANCIENT GAMES

William T. Brande - *(1788-1866) writer*
The games of the Ancient Greeks were, in their original institutions, religious solemnities.

Epictetus - *(55-135) Greek philosopher*
There are enough irksome and troublesome things in life; aren't things just as bad at the Olympics festival?

Lucian - *(120-200) Greek satirist*
If the Olympic Games were being held now, you would be able to see for yourself why we attach such great importance to athletics. No one can describe in mere words the pleasure derived from them and which you yourself would enjoy if you were seated among the spectators, feasting your eyes on the prowess and stamina of the athletes, the beauty and power of their bodies, their incredible dexterity and skill, their incredible strength, their courage, ambition, endurance and tenacity. You would never stop applauding them.

Michel de Montaigne - *(1533-1592) French moralist*
Pythagoras used to say that life resembles the Olympic Games; a few men strain their muscles to carry off a prize, others bring

trinkets to sell to the crowd for a profit and some there are who seek no further advantage than to look at the show and see how and why everything is done. They are the spectators of other men's lives in order better to judge and manage their own.

Pausanias - *(c 200) Greek travel writer*
It is the custom for athletes, their fathers and their brothers, as well as their trainers, to swear an oath upon slices of boar's flesh that in nothing will they sin against the Olympic Games.

On the road to Olympia, there is a precipitous mountain with lofty cliffs; the mountain is called Typaeum. It is a law of Elis that any woman who is discovered at the Olympic Games will be pitched from this mountain.

Philostratus - *(170-245) Greek philosopher*
If you have worked hard enough to render yourself worthy of going to Olympia, if you have not been idle or ill-disciplined, then go with confidence; but those who have not trained in this fashion, go where they will.

Pindar - *(518-438 BC) Greek poet*
The sun warms more than any lesser star, and no festival outshines Olympia.

Whoever wins your shining prize, Olympia, wears glory always.

Truly Zeus is god of Olympia; the hero Hercules began these Games spending gold he'd seized in war.

William Shakespeare *(1564–1616)*
playwright
And if we thrive, promise them such rewards
As victors wear at the Olympian Games:
Henry VI

THE MODERN GAMES

Olympic Motto
Citius, Altius, Fortius [Swifter, Higher, Stronger]:
[Taken from the coping stone over the doorway of a French lycee run by a friend of Baron de Coubertin]

Olympic Oath
Sport to me is nothing more than a recreation without material gain of any kind, direct or indirect.

The important thing in the Olympic Games is not winning, but taking part, for the essential thing in life is not so much conquering, as fighting well: *Bishop of Pennsylvania (1908)*

Per-Olaf Astrand – *Swedish athletic researcher*
To be an Olympic champion, I am convinced you must choose your parents carefully.

Tyrell Biggs – *US boxer*
This is the college of boxing. The kind of degree you get depends on how far you go. If you win the Olympics, you get a doctorate:
1984
[Biggs earned his doctorate by becoming the super-heavyweight champion in 1984]

Chris Brasher – *athlete*
There is something in the Olympics, indefinable, springing from the soul, that must be preserved: *1968*

Jean-Marie Brohm – *French gym coach*
The primary aim of the organisers of sports or Olympic competitions is not sport for its own sake but sport for capitalist profit; or rather, their aim is capitalist profit through sport: *1978*

Avery Brundage – *(1887–1975) US President of the IOC*
The Olympic Games are contests between individuals not between nations: *1956*

The biggest problem today is that the Olympic Games have become so important that political people want to take control of them. Our only salvation is to keep free from politics: *1964*

The Olympic Movement is a twentieth-century religion. Where there is no injustice of caste, of race, of family, of wealth: *1972*

Dr H. Campbell
The Olympics create no enduring benefit for the world, they simply represent a gigantic organised playground.

John Carlos – *US 200 metres silver medallist*
Why do you have to wear the uniform of your country?
Why do they play the National Anthem?
Why do we have to beat the Russians?
Why do the East Germans have to beat the West Germans?
Why can't everyone wear the same colours, but wear numbers to tell them apart?
What happened to the Olympic ideal of man against man?: *1968*

Philippe Chartier – *President of the International Tennis Federation*
Some Olympic officials insist that the Olympics should be reserved for amateurs. This is like a very bad joke.

Baron de Coubertin [Pierre de Fredi] – *(1863–1937) founder of the modern Olympics*
If young men are active and in good health, incited by the instinct of emulation, they will desire to contend, in the name of their country, against men of other lands.

Personally, convinced as I am that amateurism is one of the first conditions of the progress and prosperity of sport, I have never ceased to work for it.

Richard Espy – *writer*
The modern Olympic Games symbolise the struggle between man's ideals and the reality within which he must live: *1979*

Nationalism was never a stranger to the Olympics: *1979*

Sq Ldr Mike Freeman - *British Olympic bobsleigh team*
We may not be the greatest nation at winning Winter Olympics, but at least we can carry our bloody flag properly: *1972*

Murray Halberg - *New Zealand*
After winning the 5,000 metres - I had always imagined an Olympic champion was something more than a mere mortal, in fact a God. Now I know he was just a human being: *1960*

Norman Harris - *writer*
Murphy's Law and Parkinson's Law have both contributed to an Olympics Law which says that the bigger a thing becomes, the more problems it attracts and the sooner it hastens its own demise: *1984*

Adolf Hitler - *(1889-1945) German dictator*
Sporting and chivalrous competition awakens the best human qualities. It does not sever, but on the contrary, unites the opponents in mutual understanding and reciprocal respect. It also helps to strengthen the bonds of peace between nations. May the Olympic Flame therefore never be extinguished: *1936*

The Americans ought to be ashamed of themselves for letting their medals be won by Negroes. I myself would never even shake hands with one of them: *1936*

I didn't come to Berlin to shake hands anyway:
Jesse Owens (1936)
[*Owens was not in fact the original US black athlete snubbed by Hitler. It was high-jump gold medallist Cornelius Johnson*]

Frank Keating - *(b 1937) sportswriter*
California shared the Olympics with the athletes of the world, I suppose, but first and foremost it shared them with ABC TV: *1984*

Jim Plunkett - *American football player*
After running one kilometre with the Olympic flame relay - That's probably the farthest I'll run this year without being hit: *1984*

Wilma Rudolph - *(b 1940) US 100 and 200 metres champion [1960]*
They talk about an 'open' Olympics. No amount of money could pay me for the thrill I got.

Peter Wilson - *sportswriter*
The Games need to take the Pill before the sporting explosion gets entirely out of hand:
1968

PLAYERS

Andrew Bailey - *sportswriter*
Sport is a lifelong ticket to a private theatre in which the player can act out as many roles as he likes: *1982*

J. J. Bentley - *Football League & Football Association official*
It is all very well to say that a man should play for the pure love of the game. Perhaps he ought, but to the working man it is impossible.

Herman L. Masin - *US sportswriter*
Pressure does crazy things to athletes. Some love it, thrive on it. Others choke on it. Most learn to live with it. A few go nuts!: *1980*

Peter Richmond - *US sportswriter*
Being a role model is as integral a part of the athlete's world as artificial turf: *1984*

Henry Roxburgh
Sport is one area where no participant is worried about another's race, religion or wealth, and where the only concern is, 'Have you come to play?'

Howard Slusher - *(b 1937) US writer & attorney*
Athletes hang loose, but tough. They relax and let sport turn them on:
Man, sport & existence (1967)

AMERICAN FOOTBALL

Hank Stram – *coach*
A football player has always been referred to as a football player. He's not. He's a man who happens to play football.

ATHLETICS

Howard Payne – *hammer thrower*
The engineer of a racing car would despair at the unpredictable response of a human racing model.

BASEBALL

Enos Cabell – *(b 1949) Baltimore Orioles & Houston Astros*
I don't want to be a star. Stars get blamed too much.

Harry Edwards – *Sociology professor at the University of California, Berkeley*
From little-league sports up through the professional ranks, the athlete's role is fixated in institutionalised adolescence: *1973*

Peter Gent – *American footballer & writer*
Baseball players are the weirdest of all. I think it's all that organ music.

Dave Kingman – *New York Mets*
Athletes are pieces of meat. No matter who you are, the second your ability to produce is not up to what they expect it to be, you're disposable.

Joe Morgan – *Cincinnati Reds*
I have never seen a great player who wasn't cocky and a little arrogant.

Branch Rickey – *(1881–1965) Brooklyn Dodgers manager*
Only in baseball can a team player be a pure individual first and a team player second, within the rules and spirit of the game.

CRICKET

Peter Pollock – *(b 1941) South Africa*
You have not lived in the world of competitive sport until you have fought a battle that is not against an opponent, but against yourself.

E. W. Swanton – *(b 1907) Middlesex & writer*
The truest of all axioms about cricket is that the game is as good as those who play it.

FOOTBALL

Brian Clough – *(b 1935) Nottingham Forest manager*
It doesn't matter if the players like you or dislike you. It's when they respect you that they play for you.

Show me a talented player who is thick and I'll show you a player who has problems.

Bobby Ferguson – *West Ham United manager*
Players win games and players lose games – it's all about players really.

GOLF

Billy Casper – *USA*
Athletes have a great influence on every phase of man's life. And that is why an athlete must conduct himself in an exemplary way, always.

GYMNASTICS

Klaus Huhn – *East German sports administrator*
We get the right people into the right sports.

Nik Stuart – *national coach*
The real champion does not compete with the others for high status but with himself to achieve that goal.

ICE HOCKEY

Gordie Howe – *Red Wings*
American professional athletes are bi-lingual; they speak English and profanity: *1975*

RUGBY UNION

Lord Wakefield – *player & politician*
On the rugby field, though you are chasing a piece of leather, the game is basically about people.

TENNIS

Jimmy Connors – *(b 1952) USA*
The public will never fully understand about

sports celebrities. They see them only when
they are competing and therefore under stress.

John McEnroe - *(b 1959) USA*
Being a celebrity is like being raped, and there's
absolutely nothing a player can do about it.

WEIGHT-LIFTING

Yuriy Vlasov - *Russian world champion
[1959-63]*
An athlete's sporting career is determined by
the length of time he can go on striving for
better results: *1976*

POLITICS

John Arlott - *(b 1914) writer & commentator*
Politics governs everything we do - the games
we play, the way we play them, who we play:
                                                   1980

Avery Brundage - *(1887-1975) US President
of the IOC*
In an imperfect world, if participation in sports
is to be stopped every time the politicians
violate the laws of humanity, there will never
be any international contests. Is it not better to
try to expand the sportsmanship of the athletic
field into other areas: *1956*

Winston Churchill - *(1874-1965) Prime
Minister*
In my experience officers with high athletic
qualifications are not usually successful in the
higher ranks: *1941*

Benjamin Disraeli - *(1804-81) Prime
Minister*
England is unrivalled for two things - sport and
politics.

Geof Gleeson - *writer*
Sport is a part of society, therefore politics
must be a part of sport.

Dr Piet Koornhof - *South African Minister of
Sport*
Sport has three main aspects - physical well-
being, entertaining and social interchange. It is
a God-given thing which should be used to the
good of mankind: *1974*

Peter C. McIntosh - *US sociologist*
The desire to win is sometimes so strong that
sport cannot contain it; when this natural
desire is reinforced with political pressures it is

small wonder that on occasions the structure of
sporting events bursts asunder: *1963*

Alex Natan
It is significant that throughout the world, the
only people who deny the political nature of
competitive sport are those whose livelihood
depends on such lies, who are more interested
in holding their positions in international sports
organisations: *Sport & Society (1958)*

Alan Paton - *(1903-88) South African writer &
political leader*
To my mind, sportsmanship and the colour bar
are incompatible. Sport is supposed to teach us
to admire the prowess of others, not to want to
restrict it: *1959*

Pravda - *Russian newspaper*
An important factor in our foreign policy is the
international relations of our sportsmen. A
successful trip by the sportsmen of the USSR
or of the people's democratic countries is an
excellent vehicle of propaganda in capitalist
countries: *1958*

Sir Osbert Sitwell - *(1892-1969) poet &
writer*
Everywhere in England and America statesmen
were already preparing their triumphs of 1914
and '39, by spending long days on the golf
course and long nights at the bridge table.

Pierre Trudeau - *(b 1919) Canadian Prime
Minister*
Canada is a country whose main exports are ice
hockey players and cold fronts. Our two main
imports are baseball players and acid rain.

AMERICAN FOOTBALL

Eugene McCarthy - *(b 1916) US Senator*
Being in politics is like being a football coach;
you have to be smart enough to understand the
game, and dumb enough to think it's important.

BOARD GAMES

Tony de Angeli - *political commentator*
Butter is just the pawn in the political game of
draughts.

Thomas Carlyle - *(1795-1881) Scottish
historian*
Councillors of state sit plotting and playing
their high chess-game where the pawns are
men.

Arthur H. Dean- *(1898-1987) US diplomat*
A Soviet diplomat, like a skilled chess-player,
does not expect his opposite number to give up
something for nothing, not even a pawn.

Harry Golombek - *World War II code-breaker
& world chess arbiter*
Breaking codes is a bit like playing blindfold
chess with a hidden adversary.

John Perkins - *political commentator*
Sir Peter Parker [Chairman of British Rail]
played the final card in what's been a tricky
game of chess.

BOXING

Idi Amin - *(b 1925) Ugandan President &
heavyweight champion*
Politics is like boxing - you try to knock out
your opponents.

'Tex' Cobb - *US heavyweight*
The people in boxing are as honest and
trustworthy as individuals in politics.

Gerrie Coetzee - *South African heavyweight*
I can't change the apartheid laws back home.
All I can do is call a spade a spade.

I don't pay no attention to this racial talk. I see
no colour except the red of the gloves and the
red of the blood. It is not black or white that
matters, but whether you throw a left or a

right: *1987*
I'm not fighting in South Africa. I wouldn't do
that. But fighting Coetzee, who is against
apartheid, is my way forward to the title.
Supposing I did pull out - I'd soon be forgotten
by all those anti-apartheid people. And
supposing, because I pulled out, I went broke. I
can imagine what their response would be if I
asked them to pay my electricity bill:
Frank Bruno

John Conteh - *light-heavyweight*
No amount of money in the world could have
persuaded me to condone a political system like
apartheid. Anyway, my dear old dad would
never have let me go to a rough place like that.

Eder Jofre - *Brazilian world boxing champion &
city councillor*
Boxing has an advantage over politics. In the
ring you know exactly what your opponent's
intentions are.

BOWLS

R. G. Briscow - *MP*
If only Hitler and Mussolini could have a good
game of bowls once a week at Geneva, I feel
that Europe would not be as troubled as it is.

CARDS & DICE

William E. Gladstone - *(1809-98) Prime
Minister*
I do not object to Gladstone's always having
the Ace of Trumps up his sleeve, only to his
pretence that God had put it there:
Henry Labouchere

CRICKET

Bill Alley - *(b 1919) Australian player &
umpire*
If you made Ian Botham Prime Minister
tomorrow, he'd pick this country up in ten
minutes: *1980*

John Arlott - *(b 1914) writer & commentator*
Say that cricket has nothing to do with politics
and you say that cricket has nothing to do with
life.

Clement Attlee - *(1883-1967) Prime Minister*
Clement Attlee brings to the fierce struggle of
politics the tepid enthusiasm of a lazy summer
afternoon at a cricket match:
Aneurin Bevan MP

Geoff Boycott - *(b 1940) Yorkshire*
Most cricket critics, who have more power than
any other writers in sport, would see Chairman
Mao as British Prime Minister before they
would give Boycott the vote as England's
captain. *Ian Wooldridge - sportswriter*

Canberra Times
If a computation were to be made, it is probable
that as many cheers have been evoked
spontaneously for Bradman, as were organised
or demanded by Hitler.

Dr Richard Downey - *(1881-1953) Bishop of
Liverpool*
If Stalin had learned to play cricket, the world
might now be a better place: *1948*

David Graveney - *(b 1953) Gloucestershire*
Cricket shouldn't be used as a political football:
1986

Barry Richards - *(b 1945) South Africa*
When I first picked up a cricket bat as a child,
politics and sport were simply two subjects at
opposite ends of a newspaper.

Jam Sahib [Prince Ranjitsinhji] - *(1872-
1933) Sussex*
How often have I wished that all the political
leaders in all the countries of the Empire were
cricketers! For if they had undergone the
training and the discipline of the great game, I
am sure they would find it easier than they
appear to do at present to think first and last of
the team: *1930*

Lord Wyatt
No country which has cricket as one of its
national games has yet gone Communist: *1979*

EQUESTRIAN

Peter Robeson - *show jumper*
On the Olympics - It's a complete farce. The
way politicians keep running what is basically
the greatest sporting concept in the world: *1976*

I've been riding in major competitions for many
years and I reckon we've played a greater role
in international understanding than ten
thousand politicians: *1976*

FOOTBALL

Brian Clough - *(b 1935) Nottingham Forest
manager*
There are more hooligans in the House of
Commons than at a football match: *1980*

Tommy Docherty - *(b 1928) much travelled
manager*
There's a hell of a lot of politics in football. I
don't think Henry Kissinger would have lasted
48 hours at Old Trafford: *1982*

Frank Keating - *(b 1937) sportswriter*
Sport, let's be honest, doesn't really matter.
Over the years we have had General Elections
won or lost by the Poor Laws, the Corn Laws,
never the Denis Laws.

Pele - *(b 1940) Brazil*
Football's appeal and magnitude is such that it
ignores race, religion and politics. Soccer has
one real goal and that is to create friendship.

Harold Wilson - *(b 1916) Prime Minister*
Have you ever noticed how we only win the
World Cup under a Labour government?: *1971*

I know more about football than politics: *1974*

GOLF

Alec Bedser - *(b 1918) cricketer & selector*
On the Commonwealth anti-apartheid agreement -
Gleneagles? What's a golf course got to do with
it?

George Bernard Shaw - *(1856-1950) Irish
dramatist*
The Englishman is at his best on the links, and
at his worse in the cabinet.

GYMNASTICS

Norbert Rogalski - *East German director of the
Leipzig college of physical culture*

Proceeding from Marxism, the only method to develop the whole human being is to unite teaching, polytechnic training and gymnastics.

HORSE RACING

Henry Candy - *trainer*
I never like getting involved with racing politics. I leave other people to talk about that sort of thing and take the dogs for a walk.

Eddie Harty - *Irish trainer*
Racing is like politics - it's full of good rogues:
1972

HUNTING

Sir Fred Burrows - *(1887-1973) Governor of Bengal*
On his retirement - Unlike my predecessors, I have devoted more of my time to shunting and hooting, than to hunting and shooting.
[*He had previously been the President of the National Union of Railwaymen*]

RUGBY UNION

Albert Ferrasse - *President of the French Rugby Federation*
I prefer the low blows of rugby to the low blows of politics.

SAILING

Edward Heath - *(b 1916) Prime Minister & yachtsman*
I have no interest in sailing round the world. Not that there is any lack of requests for me to do so:
1977

UNITED STATES OF AMERICA

Anon
We have a crisis of leadership in this country. Where are all the Washingtons, the Jeffersons, and the Jacksons? I'll tell you where they are – they are playing professional basketball and football.

Muhammad Ali - *(b 1942) heavyweight boxer*
After his third visit to the White House - If there is a black man to be President, they might just run me. I'm getting used to this place!:
1980

Aaron B. Champion - *President of Cincinnati Reds baseball team*
I would rather be President of the Cincinnati baseball club than President of the United States:
1869

Thomas Hicks - *athlete*
After winning the Olympic marathon - I would rather have won this race than be President of the United States:
1904

Hubert H. Humphrey - *(1911-78) Vice-President*
On the baseball Leagues - I take a national view of the American League and an American view of the National League:
1967

I don't like that Hubert H. Humphrey Metrodome [*in Minnesota*]. It's a shame a great guy like Humphrey had to be named after it:
Billy Martin - baseball manager (1985)

John Schulian - *sportswriter*
To watch athletes is to know who, and what, they are; it is to know them better than anyone we will ever elect President.

Adlai Stevenson - *(1900-65) Ambassador to the United Nations*
Golf is a fine release from the tensions of Office, but we are a little tired of holding the bag.

Gore Vidal - *(b 1925) novelist*
These Presidential ninnies should stick to throwing out baseballs and leaving the important matters to serious people.

PRESIDENTS

Dwight D. Eisenhower - *(1890-1969)*
An atheist is a guy who watches a Notre Dame–SMU football game and doesn't care who wins.

Golf has long symbolised the Eisenhower years – played by soft, boring men with ample waistlines who went around rich men's country club courses in the company of wealthy businessmen and were tended by white-haired dutiful negroes:
David Halberstam

As an intellectual, Eisenhower bestowed upon

the games of golf and bridge the enthusiasm
and perseverance that he withheld from books
and ideas: *Emmett John Hughes*

Gerald Ford - *(b 1913)*
Whenever I can, I always watch the Detroit
Tigers on the radio.

I've had a lifelong ambition to be a professional
baseball player, but nobody would sign me.

Outside of a national character and an educated
society, there are few things more important to
a country's growth and well-being than
competitive athletics: *1974*

Before becoming President - I had offers from the
Lions and Packers, who were pretty hard up for
linemen in those days. If I had gone into
professional football the name Jerry Ford might
have been a household word today: *1974*

I would like to deny all allegations by Bob
Hope that during my last game of golf, I hit an
eagle, a birdie, an elk and a moose.

It's not hard to find Jerry Ford on a golf course,
you just follow the wounded:
Bob Hope - comedian

Jerry Ford has made golf a contact sport:
Bob Hope

Jerry Ford - the most dangerous driver since
Ben Hur: *Bob Hope*

There are 42 golf courses in the Palm Springs
area and nobody knows which one Ford is
playing until after he tees off: *Bob Hope*

There's nothing wrong with Gerald Ford,
except he played football too long without his
helmet on: *Lyndon B. Johnson*

James A. Garfield - *(1831-81)*
On being told that Garfield had been shot - Yeah!
What League was he in?:
Pete Browning - baseball player

Warren G. Harding - *(1865-1923)*
I never saw a baseball game without taking
sides and never want to see one. There is the
soul of the game.

Herbert Hoover - *(1874-1964)*
Sportsmanship, next to the Church, is the
greatest teacher of morals.

There are only two occasions when Americans
respect privacy, especially Presidents. These
are prayer and fishing. So that some have taken
to fishing: *1944*

All men are equal before a fish: *1951*

Thomas Jefferson - *(1743-1826)*
Games played with the ball, and others of that
nature, are too violent for the body, and stamp
no character on the mind.

Lyndon B. Johnson - *(1908-73)*
One lesson you'd better learn if you want to be
in politics is that you never go out on a golf
course and beat the President.

You'd better be careful any time you play golf
with President Johnson - he always brings his
own birdies: *Hubert H. Humphrey*

On a visit to the struggling New York Mets - He
wanted to see poverty, so he came to see my
team: *'Casey' Stengel - manager*

John F. Kennedy - *(1917-63)*
Politics is an astonishing profession. It has
enabled me to go from being an obscure
member of the junior varsity at Harvard to
being an honorary member of the Football Hall
of Fame.

We are inclined that if we watch a football
game or baseball game, we have taken part in
it: *1961*

We are under-exercised as a nation. We look
instead of play. We ride instead of walk. Our
existence deprives us of the minimum of
physical activity essential for healthy living:
1961

There is nothing more unfortunate than to have
soft, chubby, fat-looking children, who go to
watch their school play basketball every
Saturday and regard that as their week's
exercise: *1962*

Physical fitness is not only one of the most

227

important keys to a healthy body, it is the basis for dynamic and creative intellectual activity.

Abraham Lincoln - *(1809-65)*
Lincoln went down in history as 'Honest Abe', but he never was a jockey. If he had been a jockey, he might have gone down as just 'Abe':
Will Rogers - humorist

Ronald Reagan- *(b 1911)*
When Governor of California - We're looking forward to a great season at the University of California - if we can find a way to put cleats on their sandals.

Ronald Reagan has held the two most demeaning jobs in the country - President of the United States and radio broadcaster for the Chicago Cubs:
George Will

Franklin D. Roosevelt - *(1882-1945)*
I played for Washington five different times. That beat Franklin Delano Roosevelt's record. He was only elected four times:
Bobo Newsome - baseball player

Theodore Roosevelt - *(1858-1919)*
Brutality and foul play should receive the same summary punishment given to a man who cheats at cards:
1905

I do not, in the least, object to a sport because it is rough:
1907

Both in ring-style and image, Ray Mancini [US boxer] is Teddy Roosevelt charging up San Juan Hill:
Mort Sharnik - TV presenter

William H. Taft - *(1857-1930)*
On an anonymous baseball player - He ran the bases as if he was hauling William H. Taft in a rickshaw:
Heywood Broun - humorist

Taft was a bad President, but a good sport:
Felix Frankfurter - jurist

Harry S. Truman - *(1884-1972)*
It's a lot tougher to be a football coach than a President. You've got four years as a President, and they guard you. A coach doesn't have anyone to protect him when things are going wrong:
1958

ROYALTY

Ben Jonson - *(1573-1637) dramatist & poet*
They say Princes learn no art truly, but the art of horsemanship. The reason is the brave beast is no flatterer. He will throw a Prince as soon as his groom.

Philip Massinger - *(1583-1640) dramatist*
Hawking is a Pretty pastime - 'tis Royal sport.

Blaise Pascal - *(1623-66) French philosopher & mathematician*
The master is sincerely concerned, then hunting is agreed, nay, a Royal pleasure; his beaters are not of that opinion.

Samuel Pepys - *(1633-1703) diarist*
To the Tennis Court, and there saw the King play at tennis and others; but to see how the King's play was extolled, without any cause at all, was a loathsome sight:
4 Jan 1664

George Taylor
I set not by the King's crown and, if I had it here, I would play football with it:
1535

George M. Trevelyan - *(1876-1962) historian*
Without aristocratic patronage, sporting events would have lost their zest and picturesqueness, and would have degenerated into orgies of brutality and fraud, for the lower type of sporting men who surrounded the ring, included too many like Thurtell, the murderer:
1929

ROYAL PERSONS

Princess Anne - *(b 1950)*
Golf seems to me an arduous way to go for a walk. I'd prefer to take the dogs out.

I didn't like netball. I used to get wolf-whistles

because of my short skirts.

When I appear in public, people expect me to neigh, grind my teeth, paw the ground and swish my tail – none of which is easy: *1977*

When I'm approaching a water jump, with dozens of photographers waiting for me to fall in, and hundreds of spectators wondering what's going to happen next, the horse is just about the only one who doesn't know I am a Royal!

I'd have been quite happy, if I'd been given the chance, to have had a shot at playing Polo.

If only those in authority realised what it means to a sportsman to train for four years and then be told that they cannot go, they wouldn't be so fast to make decisions that can totally destroy someone's hopes. There is nothing like the Olympics.

Generally, what dictates whether you are going for one sport or another is its availability to you personally; whether you live next door to a football stadium or running track, or whatever, may well influence the way you approach your own sport. I grew up with ponies: *1984*

'Identifying' an anonymous mud-splattered jockey [Princess Anne] on TV's 'A Question of Sport' – It's John Reid: *Emlyn Hughes*

Queen Anne – *(1665–1714)*
Cricket is not illegal, for it is a manly game: *1710*

King Canute – *(994–1035)*
I will that every man be entitled to his hunting in wood and in field of his possession, and let everyone forego my hunting.

Prince Charles – *(b 1948)*
We British must ski on: *1979*

I have a feeling that most of us nowadays have become rather blasé about conquering Everest: *1977*

Princess Diana – *(b 1961)*
On his team's promotion prospects – We're like Lady Di. She's not Queen yet. She's not even

married. But like us, she's nicely placed:
Jimmy Sirrell – manager of Notts County FC (1981)

King Edward II – *(1284–1327)*
Footballe, wherein nothing but beastlie furie and extreme violence; wherefore it is to be put in perpetual silence: *1314*

For as much as there is great noise in the city caused by hustling over large balls, from which many evils might arise; which God forbid: *1314*

King Edward IV – *(1442–83)*
All fair terms of hunting cometh of the seeking and hunting of the hare.

When men seek in cover for a fox and the hounds happen to find him, then the hunter rejoicest for the exploit of the hounds, and also because it is vermin they run to.

King Edward VII – *(1841–1910)*
Goodwood – A garden party with racing tacked on.

King Edward VIII – *(1894–1972)*
The word 'England' suggests many different ideas to different kinds of Englishmen; the greater part of our juvenile population, for instance, think of it simply as that portion of the globe which, from time to time, produces eleven good cricketers to play Test matches (and sometimes win them) against Australia or South Africa: *1923*

If you can't ride, I'm afraid people will call you a duffer: *King George V*

On a Royal hunting trip – The Prince is going to shoot wild animals as fast as they come out of their cages: *Will Rogers – US humorist*

Queen Elizabeth I – *(1533–1603)*
No foteball player be used or suffered within the City of London and the liberties thereof upon pain of imprisonment: *1572*

Queen Elizabeth II – *(b 1926)*
If it were not for my Archbishop of Canterbury, I should be off in my plane to Longchamp every Sunday.

After Sir Stanley Rous had asked if she had thought anyone had played well in a disappointing FA Cup Final - Yes, the band!

Queen in brawl at Palace:

The Guardian (1970)

[*The headline referred to a Crystal Palace football player - Gerry Queen*]

There is so much class in our boardroom that some of my directors call the Queen 'Mate'!:
Lawrie McMenemy - manager of Southampton FC

King Farouk of Egypt - *(1920-65)*
There will soon be only five Kings left - the Kings of England, Diamonds, Hearts, Spades and Clubs: *1951*

King Frederick II [The Great] of Prussia - *(1712-86)*
A man who can in cold blood hunt and torture a poor innocent animal, cannot feel much compassion for the distresses of his own species.

King George II - *(1683-1760)*
No English coachman could drive, nor English jockey ride, nor were any English horses fit to be ridden or driven.

King George V - *(1865-1936)*
Golf always makes me so damned angry.

On his death -
Spirits of well-shot woodcock, partridge, snipe
Flutter and bear him up to the Norfolk sky:
John Betjeman

King Henry VIII - *(1491-1547)*
No man in the dominions drew the English bow more vigorously than Henry himself; no man shot further with a more unerring aim:
Paulus Jovius

Queen Isabella I of Spain - *(1451-1504)*
As for Bullfighting. After I had consented to them, I had the fullest determination never to attend them again in my life nor be where they were held: *1493*

King James I - *(1566-1625)*
I debarre all rough and violent exercises, as the foot-ball, meeter for mameing than making able

users thereof: *1603*

As for Chesse, I think it over fond, because it is over wise and philosophicke a folly.

Princess Margaret - *(b 1930)*
Liverpool manager Bill Shankly's story of the 1966 FA Cup Final
HRH - But Mr Labone, where is Everton?
Brian Labone - In Liverpool, Ma'am.
HRH - Of course, we had your first team here last year.
[*Liverpool had won the Cup in 1965*]

Princess Nukuda of Japan *(fl. 665-669)*
The moon is up, the tide is high;
Away, let us row out speedily.

Queen Elizabeth, the Queen Mother - *(b 1900)*
On horse racing - It's one of the real sports that's left to us; a bit of danger and a bit of excitement, and the horses, which are the best thing in the world.

Prince Philip - *(b 1921)*
There is a widely and quite erroneously held belief that cricket is just another game.

Cricket without *Wisden* is almost as unthinkable as batting without pads.

It seems to be a characteristic of the British to take a perfectly ordinary, even juvenile amusement and convert it into a highly organised, competitive sport or recreation: *1976*

The association between man and horse must go back thousands of years, but it is somewhat ironic that so many of the horse sports only really began to flourish long after the horse had lost its practical utility.

A horse which stops dead before a jump and thus propels its rider into a graceful arc provides a splendid excuse for general merriment. It has happened to me: *1984*

I am convinced that the greatest contribution Britain has made to the national life of Uruguay was to teach the people football.

Philip II King of Macedon - *(382-336 BC)*

Philip of Macedon reckoned a horse race won at Olympus among his three fearful felicities:
Sir Philip Sidney – poet (1580)

Prince Rainier III of Monaco – *(b 1923)*
I didn't like cricket. It was the fielding I

couldn't get used to.
[*He was forced to play at Stowe School, England*]

William IV – *(1765-1837)*
I consider horse racing to be a national sport – the manly and noble sport of a free people.

SEX

Bumper stickers
American Footballers do it with larger helmets:
Colin M. Jarman – sportswriter

Archers do it with a bull: *CMJ*

Chess players do it very slowly – one move at a time – and finish by mating: *CMJ*

Climbers do it halfway up a mountain: *CMJ*

Darts players do it from 8 feet away: *CMJ*

Divers do it deeper than anyone else. *CMJ*

Fencers always do it with protection: *CMJ*

Gliders can keep it up all day.

Goalkeepers never do it near the other half: *CMJ*

Hang-gliders do it on their own.

Jockeys do it on horseback: *CMJ*

Polo players do it in public – without scaring the horses: *CMJ*

Shot putters do it on one leg.

Show jumpers do it against a clock: *CMJ*

Skiers do it on the piste.

Snooker players do it bending over a table.

Snooker players sometimes do it with a long rest: *CMJ*

Squash players do it against the wall.

Swimmers do it with the breaststroke.

Some swimmers do it at great lengths: *CMJ*

Synchronised swimmers do it with a smile on their face: *CMJ*

Tennis players start with love.

Ten-pin bowlers do it with something to spare: *CMJ*

Water-skiers do it in rubber suits.

Weight-lifters sometimes do it with a jerk: *CMJ*

Windsurfers do it standing up.

Cary Grant – *(1904-86) US actor*
I never jog. Love is still a better and more pleasurable sport.

Piet Hein – *Danish philosopher*
The human spirit sublimates the impulses it thwarts;
A healthy sex life it mitigates, the lust for other sports: *1966*

Lord Stonham
During a fairly active life, including 25 years playing team games, I have never encountered a homosexual: *1965*

AMERICAN FOOTBALL

Paul Hornung – *(b 1935) Green Bay Packers*
I think that I would still rather score a touchdown on a particular day than make love to the prettiest girl in the United States.

Joe Namath – *(b 1943) New York Jets*

On one area of 'Broadway' Joe's legend – In another century someone with his chronic droop-eyed leer would have been pegged the village idiot. I remember when a quarterback's most famous appendage was his arm!:

Mike Royko – sportswriter

ANGLING

Clark Gable – *(1901-60) US actor*
If I'd jumped on half the dames I'm supposed to have jumped on, I'd never have had the time to go fishing.

ATHLETICS

Noel Carroll – *Irish double Olympian*
Runners may make the best lovers but sometimes lousy spouses: *1981*

BASEBALL

Reggie Jackson – *(b 1946) Yankees & Athletics*
I love competition. It motivates me, stimulates me, excites me. It is almost sexual. I just love to hit that baseball in a big game.

'Casey' Stengel – *(1891-1975) Yankees & Mets manager*
Being with a woman all night never hurt no professional baseball player. It's the staying up all night looking for one that does him in.

BOXING

Muhammad Ali – *(b 1942) US heavyweight*
When asked about sex before a fight –
Only the nose knows,
Where the nose goes,
When the door close.

I'd like to borrow his body for just 48 hours. There are three guys I'd like to beat up and four women I'd like to make love to:

Jim Murray – US sportswriter (1964)

He is a pelvic missionary. He's laid more ugly women than you'd ever believe. Ali wants to be liked. He has a great capacity to give and receive, and it carries over into exchanging bodies. He thinks the woman will remember it all her life: *Dr Ferdie Pacheco*

John Conteh – *light-heavyweight*
Contrary to the old wives' tales that bloody-minded trainers put around, a little love-in before the main event can do you more good than a rub-down with the *Sporting Life.*

Angelo Dundee – *US trainer & manager*
Without sex a fighter gets mean, angry, anxious to fight. Keep a fighter away from women, keep him in camp pounding bags, punching fighters day in, day out, and when he gets in the ring he's ready to take it all out on his opponent.

Sonny Liston – *(1932-71) US heavyweight*
On his other sporting activities – I enjoy broad-jumping!

CRICKET

Linda Lovelace – *US porn movie star*
Cricket is like sex films – they relieve frustration and tension: *1974*

Harold Pinter – *playwright*
I tend to believe that cricket is the greatest thing that God ever created on Earth . . . certainly greater than sex although sex isn't too bad either. But everyone knows which comes first when it's a question of cricket or sex: *1980*

Jeff Thomson – *(b 1950) Australia*
I don't try to be Joe Blow, the super-stud – it just happens: *1981*

DARTS

Eric Bristow – *world champion*
I'm young and healthy and free and you'd be amazed at the number of dishy birds at big darts events these days.

FOOTBALL

Peter Ackroyd – *(b 1949) writer & critic*
Like sex, the movements in football are limited and predictable: *1982*

Malcolm Allison – *manager*
John Bond has blackened my name with his insinuations about the private lives of football managers. Both my wives are upset.

Nicola Berti – *Inter Milan & Italy*

To score in front of 70,000 fans at San Siro is like finding a place in a woman's heart – No! It's better: *1988*

George Best – *(b 1946) Manchester United*
Once I started playing football I realized I was in the perfect position for pulling birds. I had the limelight, the publicity, the money. Where could I go wrong?

If you want the secret of my success with women, then don't smoke, don't take drugs and don't be too particular.

Once you get the taste of George Best you never want to taste anything else: *Angie Best*

Stan Bowles – *(b 1948) Queens Park Rangers*
If I had the choice of a night with Raquel Welch or going to a betting shop, I'd choose the betting shop.

Ken Brown – *Norwich manager*
With our luck one of our players must be bonking a witch!: *1987*

Maurice Johnston – *(b 1963) Celtic & Rangers*
If Rod Stewart can't pull the best-looking girls in the world, what chance do the rest of us have?: *1988*

Charlie Nicholas – *(b 1961) Arsenal & Scotland*
I don't have a drink problem, though if it helps to not touch a drop I'll try. But if sex ruined your game, all the married players would be out of a job: *1984*

We talked about football, but really all he wanted to talk about was sex . . . I hear he's not been scoring many goals recently and that's why he left Arsenal, but all I can tell you is he certainly scored a hat-trick with me that night: *Therese Bazar – pop singer (1988)*

Ferenc Puskas – *Hungary*
After scoring against Yugoslavia in the Olympic final – I got so many kisses after this goal, that they would have sufficed a modest woman for a lifetime: *1952*

Bill Shankly – *Liverpool manager*
Of course a player can have sexual intercourse

before a match and play a blinder. But if he did it for six months, he'd be a decrepit old man. It takes the strength from the body: *1971*

Graeme Souness – *(b 1953) Rangers manager*
To suggest a player shouldn't have sex the night before a match is the height of silliness. I've had enjoyable nights and mornings before a game and it never affected me. But before a match I won't put a lot of energy into it: *1985*

Peter Storey – *(b 1945) Arsenal*
The orgies, the birds and the fabulous money – football is just a distraction: *1980*

Douglas Sutherland – *(b 1919) writer*
Association football is no longer considered a gentleman's game. The practice of footballers kissing each other after a goal is scored has lowered the tone. Kissing in public, even between consenting gentlemen, is not considered the done thing:
The English Gentleman (1978)

GOLF

Anon
Golf is the most fun you can have without taking your clothes off.

Seve Ballesteros – *(b 1957) Spain*
On why he didn't have a steady girlfriend – That would be too much like playing on the same golf course all the time!

Arthur Daley – *(1904–74) sportswriter*
Golf is like a love affair; if you don't take it seriously, it's no fun; if you do take it seriously, it breaks your heart.

HORSE RACING

Anon
It's hell dancing with jockeys. It's 'Ouch! Don't put your hand there' and 'Mind my bad shoulder' all the time – and it's the same in bed, I may say.

John Francome – *National Hunt jockey*
Most jockeys I know would have sex on the morning of the Grand National, if they could.

Jenny Pitman – *National Hunt trainer*

No sex before a race? That's a load of old cobblers. No one who knows jockeys could imagine them saying, 'Not tonight, darling, I am riding in the National tomorrow.'

HUNTING

Robert Mead
A lover is like a hunter; if the game be got with too much ease, he cares not for it.

MOTOR RACING

Hunter Davies - *writer*
Racing drivers are not sex maniacs. In fact, they are less interested in sex than any other group of sportsmen.

Emerson Fittipaldi - *(b 1946) Brazil*
Part of my skill is treating the car like a woman. To get the best performance, you coax her, cajole her, persuade her, seduce her. Instead of caressing the flesh of a woman, I am caressing the controls.

Nigel Mansell
After his first Grand Prix victory - Your first win is like making love; you enjoy it so much the first time that you want to do it again and again: 1985

Stirling Moss - *(b 1929)*
There are two things no man will admit he can't do well - drive and make love.

Louis T. Stanley - *sportswriter*
When Tommy Docherty was manager of Rotherham he banned his players from having sex before a big match. It is just as well he never managed a motor-racing team: 1985

Jackie Stewart - *(b 1939)*
Making love before a race has the same effect upon my metabolism as food upon hunger. It leaves me contented. It takes off the anticipatory, even slightly nervous edge I need to perform well in a racing car: 1972

Cornering is like bringing a woman to climax.

SNOOKER

Fred Allen - *(1894-1956) US humorist*

On sex in the movies - The British Board of Censors will not pass any seduction scene unless the seducer has one foot on the floor. Apparently sex in England is something like snooker.

Steve Davis - *(b 1957) England*
I think it's a great idea to talk during sex, as long as it's about snooker: 1988

Alex Higgins - *Northern Ireland*
I know I've got a reputation like George Best. I've found that it helps being world champion, especially at snooker. I always tell them I'm a great potter. They know what I mean.

TENNIS

Billie Jean King - *(b 1943) USA*
If I had been caught making love to a male movie star at high noon in Times Square, it wouldn't even have made the six o'clock news. But Billie Jean and a woman. . . .

Ilie Nastase - *Rumania*
You know what they say about sex being bad for your game. Well, I can tell you it's rubbish. Sex before tennis brings me luck.

SKATING

Gamaliel Bradford - *(1863-1932) US biographer*
Skating I never really cared much for, except as it gave an excellent opportunity for making love to girls: 1916

Alan Coren - *(b 1938) humorist*
Pairs skating is doing it in public without scaring the horses: 1989

SKIING

Hans Jorg-Badrutt
Apres-ski is now all up in the rooms.

WRESTLING

Brian Maxime
A lot of wrestlers think they're God's gift to women. I'm different. I know I am!

VICTORY & DEFEAT

DEFEAT

Rob Coombes
Many a match is lost by want of training: *1852*

John Donne – *(1571–1631) poet*
If I lose at play, I blaspheme; if my fellow loses, he blasphemes. So, God is always the loser:
1623

Thomas Fuller – *(1654–1734) physician*
It signifies nothing to play well and lose: *1732*

Charles E. Hughes – *(1862–1948) Governor of New York*
Why they call a fellow that keeps losing all the time a 'Good Sport' gets me.

Stanley Keeley – *US academic*
Last guys don't finish nice.

AMERICAN FOOTBALL

Duffy Daugherty – *Michigan State University coach*
My only feeling about superstition is that it's unlucky to be behind at the end of the game.

Joe Kapp – *Minnesota Vikings*
Do you know what happens after you lose a Super Bowl? The world ends. It just stops:
1970

Curtis McClinton – *Kansas City Chiefs*
On losing Super Bowl I – I felt like one of the losers at Pompeii. It was like being on a death bed. Everything you've accomplished up to that point didn't mean a thing.

Sam Rutigliano – *Cleveland Browns coach*
On losing too many close ones – It's like having heart attacks. You can survive them, but there's always scar tissue: *1978*

Murray Warmath – *coach*
If lessons are learned in defeat, our team is really getting a great education: *1958*

Bud Wilkinson – *coach*
The man who tried his best and failed is superior to the man who never tried: *1954*

ATHLETICS

Yevgeny Arzhanov – *Russian Olympic 800 metres silver medallist [1972]*
After losing the gold medal to Dave Wottle [USA] by 0.03 seconds – It is very disappointing to lose in the very last stride by the length of your nose: *1972*

Dr Arnold R. Beisser
The history of sports is filled with reports of bad-luck athletes who always faltered on the threshold of victory: *1967*

Stuart Storey – *coach*
Geoff Capes [shot-putter] finally mellowed into a nice guy. Sometimes I wish he hadn't. Nice guys begin to accept defeat.

BASEBALL

Ken Brett – *Chicago White Sox*
Things were so bad in Chicago last summer, that by the fifth inning the White Sox were selling hot dogs to go: *1977*

Leo Durocher – *(b 1906) Dodgers manager*
There's Mellot. Take a good look at him. A nicer sort of guy never put shoes on. Fine fellow, but he didn't come here to win; that's the answer. Nice guys finish last: *1952*

Show me a good loser and I'll show you an idiot: *1950*

Billy Martin – *New York Yankees manager*
There's no excuse for happy losers.

'Casey' Stengel – *(1891–1975) manager of the New York Yankees & Mets*
You gotta lose 'em some time. When you do, lose 'em right.

BASKETBALL

Bill Musselman - *NBA coach*
Defeat is worse than death, because you have to
live with defeat: *1972*

BOWLS

Mavis Steele - *EWBA champion*
It doesn't do anyone any harm in sport to have
a damn good hiding. It proves you're not as
good as you thought you were.

BOXING

Joe Louis - *(1914-81) US heavyweight*
Every man's got to figure to get beat some time.

FOOTBALL

John Lyall - *West Ham manager*
In terms of the Richter scale, this defeat was a
force 8 gale.

Bob Paisley - *(b 1919) Liverpool manager*
Yes, we've had bad times at Anfield; one year
we came second.

HORSE RACING

Tony Murray - *Flat racing jockey*
If you lose a horse-race, it's a matter of passing
the buck; the owner blames the trainer, the
trainer blames the jockey, and the jockey
blames the poor old horse.

SNOOKER

Ray Reardon - *Wales*
I cannot remember anyone ever asking 'Who
came second?' Can you?

SQUASH

Jonah Barrington - *(b 1941) British Open
champion*
When I lose, it's like a knife wound in the
stomach.

VICTORY

Proverbs
In all games it is good to leave as the winner.

He plays best that wins.

You can't win them all.

Slow but sure wins the race.

Francis Bacon - *(1561-1626) philosopher &
statesman*
A cripple in the right way may beat a racer in
the wrong one. Nay, the fleeter and better racer
is, who once missed his way, the farther he
leaveth it behind.

Ed Barner - *US golf manager*
In entertainment, talent has very little bearing
on success; whereas in sport, regardless of how
you look or talk, if you can do it, you can be
Number One.

R. K. Elliott
The goddess of sport is not Beauty but Victory,
a jealous goddess who demands an absolute
homage.

Charles B. Fry - *(1872-1956) sportsman*
A man can do no better than beat the best
around in his time.

Thomas Fuller - *(1654-1734) physician*
It is a silly game where nobody wins.

The race is got by running.

George Herbert - *(1593-1633) poet*
At the game's end we shall see who gains.

Hugh E. Keough
The race is not always to the swift, but that is
where to look.

Vernon Law
If you don't play to win, why keep score?

Desmond Lynam - *TV sports presenter*
That performance would have won him the
Olympic gold medal in the championship four
years ago, which he won anyway.

Tony Mason - *social history lecturer*
Losing has often been likened to death but it is
only a small death and it is one of sport's
enduring attractions that there is almost always
a second chance: *Sport in Britain (1988)*

R. C. Robertson-Glasgow – *sportswriter*
Success at games demands a total freedom from
care: *1952*

Gordon Ross – *sportswriter*
To win is to have done enough; it is better still
to have beaten a good 'un: *1954*

Philip Roth – *(b 1933) US novelist*
The sooner we get rid of losing, the happier
everyone will be:
                  The Great American Novel (1986)

Alec Waugh – *(1898-1981) writer*
Success lay in a blind pursuit at the shrine of
the God of athleticism.

AMERICAN FOOTBALL

Bud Grant – *Pittsburgh Steelers coach*
We don't win with mirrors or gimmicks. There
are no short cuts. You win with hard work and
good players.

Vince Lombardi – *(1913-70) Green Bay
Packers coach*
Winning isn't everything, but making the effort
is.
[*Attributed as* – Winning isn't everything, it's the
only thing. *See Bill Veeck* – BASEBALL]

Everyone has a will to win, but very few have a
will to prepare to win.

Winning is life and death, my life and your
death.

Al McGuire – *coach*
Winning is over-emphasized. The only time it
is really important is in war and surgery.

Joe Namath – *(b 1943) New York Jets*
When you win, nothing hurts.

O. A. 'Bum' Phillips – *Houston Oilers coach*
Wins are like women, some of them are prettier
than others, but they're still the best things I
can think of.

Buddy Ryan – *Philadelphia Eagles coach*
Some games you win 52-50. Some games 7-6.
The main thing is to win them: *1989*

ATHLETICS

Mary Decker – *(b 1958) US middle-distance
runner*
The more I win, the more I want to win.

Juma Ikangaa – *Tanzanian marathon runner*
Until you've come to the finish line, you can't
say you've won: *1989*

Carl Lewis – *(b 1961) US sprinter & long
jumper*
Winning is not the aim, only a part of the
whole. You have talent, you work within that
talent and that's it. We're not out here to win,
we're out here to do our best and winning is
part of it.

Marti Liquori – *US long-distance runner*
If you want to be a champion, you will have to
win every race in your mind one hundred times
before you win it in real life, that last time:
                                                              1981

Tom McNab – *coach*
If we define a winner as someone who tries
their hardest to do their best, then we can have
a lot more winners.

Steve Ovett – *(b 1955) middle-distance runner*
I used to think winning was everything. Being
injured has made me appreciate the other side
of the coin.

Gordon Pirie – *middle-distance runner*
My aim has been to win, first against myself,
and my reluctant body, and secondly against
the best athletes, not by stop-watch timing but
in races: *1961*

Rick Wohlhutter – *US middle-distance runner*
I'm willing to accept any kind of pain to win a
race.

BASEBALL

Anon
In baseball the best team always wins because
the other side got all the breaks.

Johnny Pesky – *Boston Red Sox manager*
When you win you eat better, sleep better and
your beer tastes better. And your wife looks like

Gina Lollobrigida: *1963*

Phil Rizutto – *(b 1918) Yankees announcer*
After announcing the death of Pope Paul VI – Well, that kind of puts the damper on even a Yankee win!

Bill Veeck – *(1914–86) Browns owner*
I do not think that winning is the most important thing. I think it is the only thing.
[*Attributed to Vince Lombardi as* – Winning isn't everything, it is the only thing]

BASKETBALL

Bill Bradley – *(b 1943) New York Knicks*
Becoming Number One is easier than remaining Number One.

Gail Goodrich
The tempo, the essential beat of the game, ultimately will be controlled by one team – the winning one.

BOARD GAMES

Savelly Tarkatower – *(1887–1956) Russian Grandmaster*
Moral victories don't count.

Victory goes to the player who makes the next-to-last mistake.

CANOEING

Tamas Wichmann – *Hungarian world champion*
Sporting dignity and victory are concepts that rank on the same level: *1980*

CYCLING

Steele Bishop – *(b 1953) Australian world cycling champion*
If you can't win fairly, you don't deserve to win: *1983*

FOOTBALL

Steve Archibald – *(b 1956) Scotland*
Team spirit is an illusion you only glimpse when you win: *1988*

David Pleat – *Spurs manager*
Winning isn't the end of the world.

Bobby Robson – *(b 1933) England manager*
Football is a game called 'win'. If a man misses a six-yarder, the manager takes the can back. If he scores, the player gets the glory.

Jimmy Sirrel – *Notts County manager*
The best team always wins. The rest is only gossip: *1985*

Howard Wilkinson – *(b 1943) Sheffield Wednesday & Leeds United manager*
I'm a firm believer that if you score one goal, the other team have to score two to win.

GOLF

Arnold Palmer – *(b 1929) USA*
Winning isn't everything, but wanting to is.

Paul Runyan – *USA*
A champion is as good as he has to be.

HORSE RACING

Lester Piggott – *(b 1935) Flat racing jockey*
Everyone keeps asking me 'Are you going to win?' How on earth do you know if you're going to win or not?

At least sixty per cent of horses don't really want to do their best. Winning doesn't mean all that much to them.

Charlie Smirke – *Flat racing jockey*
The test of a good jockey isn't the races that he should win; it's the ones he wins that he shouldn't win.

MOTOR RACING

Alan Jones – *(b 1946) Australia*
The really good drivers win races in the slowest times, not the quickest.

SAILING

Rodney Pattisson – *yachtsman*
Winning is easy. It's far harder, once you've won, to be honourable.
[*The Hon. Rodney Patisson won the Olympic*

Flying Dutchman class in 1968 & 1972]

J. Russell – *yachtsman*
The triumph of being first past the finishing post is transient, the faultlessly timed and co-ordinated output of the last ounce of energy into the sport that took you there is imperishable: *1977*

SQUASH

Dick Hawkey – *player & writer*
The whole aim of any sport is to prove that on a particular day you can beat someone else at that sport: *1976*

SWIMMING

Duncan Goodhew – *(b 1957)*
To me, competing to win is the ultimate self-interest.

Mark Spitz – *(b 1950) USA*
For me winning a gold medal was as important as winning a million dollars, because the medal was all I had to aim for.

TENNIS

Althea Gibson – *(b 1927) USA*
In sports, you simply aren't considered a real champion until you have defended your title successfully. Winning it once can be a fluke; winning it twice proves you are the best.

Bob Lutz – *USA*
When you're a point or two away from winning, it's very difficult to convince yourself that it's just another point. How do you get yourself to believe what is, isn't?

VICTORY & DEFEAT

Anon
The difference between winners and losers is that winners tell the jokes and the losers talk about the run of the ball.

Proverbs
Win some, lose some.

Lord Byron – *(1788-1824) poet*
In play there are two pleasures for your choosing;
The one is in the winning and the other the losing.

Dave Cowans – *US coach*
I don't look for excuses when we lose, and I don't buy excuses when we win.

George Crabbe – *(1754-1832) poet*
The game is never lost till won.

Charles H. Goren – *(b 1901) US columnist*
Men like to win, but women hate to lose. The difference can be summed up in one word – bridgemanship: *1961*

Heath
Some play for gain, to pass time others play
For nothing; both play the fool I say,
Nor time, nor coin, I'll lose, or idly spend,
Who gets by play, proves loser in the end.

C.M. Jones – *journalist*
Success is important but defeats are valuable: *1972*

George S. Kaufman – *(1889-1961) US humorist & playwright*
I'd rather be a poor winner than any kind of loser.

Bud Werner
There are only two places in a race – first and last.

AMERICAN FOOTBALL

Len Dawson – *Kansas City Chiefs*
I had a taste of winning and losing Super Bowls, and believe me, winning was better.

Eddie Erdelatz – *Naval Academy coach*
After a game against West Point finished 7-7 – A tie game is like kissing your sister.

Vince Lombardi – *(1913-70) Green Bay Packers coach*
The pressures of losing are awful. It kills you eventually. But the pressure of winning is even worse, infinitely worse, because it keeps on torturing you and torturing you.

Duane Thomas – *Dallas Cowboys*

After losing the Super Bowl – There is something noble in defeat. You cannot find victory unless you first understand defeat: *1971*

Johnny Unitas – *(b 1933) Baltimore Colts*
You're a hero when you win and a bum when you lose. That's the game. They pay their money and they can boo if they feel like it.

BASEBALL

Bill James – *statistician*
It's better to be involved with a loser. A winning team doesn't need you as much.

John McGraw – *New York Giants manager*
Be in a hurry to win. Don't be in a hurry to lose.

Pete Rose – *(b 1941) Cincinnati Reds & Philadelphia Phillies*
Somebody's gotta win and somebody's gotta lose – and I believe in letting the other guy lose.

'Casey' Stengel – *(1881-1975) New York Yankees & Mets manager*
Without losers, where would the winners be?

Most ball games are lost, not won.

George Weiss – *Yankees executive*
There is no such thing as second place. Either you're first or you're nothing.

BOXING

Floyd Patterson – *(b 1935) US heavyweight*
It's easy to do anything in victory. It's in defeat that a man reveals himself.

Peter Wilson – *sportswriter*
Boxing can be a cruel business and I know no contrast so savage as that between the winner's and the loser's dressing room: *1982*

CRICKET

Ted Dexter – *(b 1935) Sussex*
If you're going to lose, you might as well lose good and proper, and try and sneak a win.

W. G. Grace – *(1848-1915) Gloucestershire*
Looking at Mr Grace's playing, I am never able to tell whether that gentleman was playing a winning or a losing game: *Lord Charles Russell*

Rachael Heyhoe-Flint – *(b 1939) England ladies captain*
It is most pleasing when you win, but rather noticeable when you lose!

Meatloaf – *US rock musician*
I want to play cricket, it doesn't seem to matter whether you win or lose: *1984*

FOOTBALL

Ian Greaves – *Huddersfield Town manager*
If you're winning you get a snowball of the right attitudes. The average player becomes a good player, and the good player becomes excellent. When you fail, it's the same principle in reverse. The good player becomes average and the average player becomes a very, very poor player.

Tony Waddington – *Stoke City manager*
We are living in a society which increasingly demands success and no longer has time for the good loser: *1973*

GOLF

Jack Nicklaus – *(b 1940) USA*
While some championships are won, most of them are lost. What I've really done is failed a little less than other people who have had the chance to win.

Tom Weiskopf – *USA*
I am absolutely delighted to have come second. Who cares about winning when you can be second? I love being runner-up: *1978*

HORSE RACING

Terry Biddlecombe – *National Hunt jockey*
Jockeys are only there to win on the ones that aren't meant to win.

RUGBY UNION

Lord Wakefield – *player & politician*
If defeat comes our way, it is a lesson rather than a loss; while if we win, we are satisfied that our best should have proved good enough.

SNOOKER

Terry Griffiths - *Wales*
I have always said that the difference between winning and losing is nothing at all.

TENNIS

Bjorn Borg - *(b 1956) Sweden*
If you're afraid of losing, then you daren't win.

Jimmy Connors - *(b 1952) USA*
I hate to lose more than I like to win. I hate to see the happiness on their faces when they beat me: *1977*

Bill Tilden - *(1893-1953)*
Never change a winning game: always change a losing one.

VIOLENCE

Don Atyeo - *writer & editor*
Sport legitimises violence . . . the mugger in the parking lot is a villain; the mugger on the playing field a hero.

George Chapman - *(1559-1634)*
Without danger the game grows cold.

E. Dunning
Many aspects of sport are aggressive, but it is a socially accepted form of expression - civilised violence.

Paul Fussell - *(b 1924) US humorist*
The more violent the body contact of the sports you watch, the lower the class.

David Rhys Jones - *TV commentator & writer*
Gentle games like snooker, bowls and croquet have hidden qualities. Seemingly sedate, even solemnent, a match can suddenly ignite. Aggressive tactics can destroy a carefully built-up advantage and initiative can pendulum at a stroke: *1986*

William Shakespeare - *(1564-1616)*
playwright
As flies to wanton boys are we to the Gods,
They kill us for their sport: *King Lear*

AMERICAN FOOTBALL

Michael Oriard - *writer*

It is not just violence we like in football. It's that meeting of violence and artistry, the tension between the two, that so appeals. It's that instant when ball, receiver, and defender converge, when artistry is threatened by violence and the outcome is in doubt, that epitomizes the game's attraction.

Dr Thomas Tutko & Dr Umberto Tosi -
sports psychologists
Football people may tell you about the skills and the beauty of the game, and we know they exist, but don't lets kid ourselves; most people go to a football game for the violence.

Bob Ward - *Dallas Cowboys strength coach*
Pro football is the most violent of all games. In no other sport is bodily contact so pronounced, explosive power of such repeated use and total body power of such importance.

George Will - *writer*
American Football is like committee meetings; called huddles, separated by outbursts of violence.

BOARD GAMES

Reuben Fine - *(b 1914) US Grandmaster*
Chess is a contest between two men which lends itself particularly to the conflicts surrounding aggression: *1967*

BOXING

Denzil Batchelor – *sportswriter*
The boxer, if he would be champion, must strive to destroy his opponent – not, of course to kill him (for that would be a waste of energy), but to wipe him out of the world for ten seconds: *1954*

Ernst Jokl – *US professor of physical education at Kentucky University*
Boxing is not a sport, it is a criminal activity:
                                    1970

R. A. McCormick
Professional boxing is the only sport whose primary objective toward victory is to batter and damage an opponent into helplessness and the incapacity to continue.

Sugar Ray Robinson – *(1920–89) US middleweight*
I ain't never liked violence.

Lord [Thomas J.] Taylor of Gryfe – *(b 1912)*
Boxing is glamorised violence: *1981*

CRICKET

Dennis Lillee – *(b 1949) Australia*
I don't want to do the batsman permanent injury, just to cause him concern – to hurt him a bit.

Jeff Thomson – *(b 1950) Australia*
I enjoy hitting a batsman more than getting him out. It doesn't worry me in the least to see a batsman hurt, rolling around screaming and blood on the pitch.

FOOTBALL

Jack Charlton – *(b 1935) Leeds United*
I have a little black book with two players in it, and if I get a chance to do them I will. I will make them suffer before I pack this game in. If I can kick them four yards over the touch-line, I will: *1970*

Jack Dunnett – *(b 1922) President of the Football League*
I don't watch TV myself. But my family do and they tell me the most popular programmes are the ones which are full of violence. On that basis football ought to do rather well: *1985*

Charles B. Fry – *(1872–1956) sportsman*
It is a standing insult to sportsmen to have to play under a rule which assumes that players intend to trip, hack and push their opponents, and to behave like cads of the most unscrupulous kidney. The lines marking a penalty area are a disgrace to the playing fields of a public school: *1907*

Norman Hunter – *(b 1943) Leeds United*
Norman Hunter bites yer leg!:   *Banner*

Norman Hunter does not tackle opponents so much as break them down for resale as scrap:
                                    Julie Welch

Phillip Stubbes – *(1543–91) puritan*
Football causeth fighting, brawling, contention, quarrel-picking, murder, homicide, and a great effusion of blood, as daily experiences teaches:
                                    1583

Concerning football playing, I protest unto you it may be rather called a friendly kind of fighting than recreation.

RUGBY LEAGUE

John Raper
Rugby League is violent for most of the time and, I'd say, a lot harder than professional boxing.

RUGBY UNION

Albert Ferrasse – *President of the French RFU*
Rugby must not become a game to which you bring your knife and revolver: *1978*

Wilfrid Wooller – *sportswriter*
Man is a fighting animal and rugby is a civilised (almost always, anyway) blood sport.

WAR

Anon
If you want to interest a Frenchman in sport, you tell him it's a war; if you want to interest the British in a war, you tell them it's a game.

Proverbs
War is the sport of Kings.

Denis W. Brogan – *(1900–74) political scientist*
For Americans war is almost all of the time a nuisance and military skill is a luxury like mahjong. But when the issue is brought home to them, war becomes as important, for the necessary period, as business or sport. And it is hard to decide which is likely to be more ominous for the Axis – an American decision that this is sport, or that it is business.

Henry L. Mencken – *(1880–1956) US editor*
War is the only sport that is genuinely amusing. And it is the only sport that has any intelligible use.

Drew Middleton – *US writer*
Those who know little about either like to see parallels between war and sports: *1977*

Stan Obodiac – *Canadian writer*
I shudder to think what would have happened to the Canadian World War II effort if we had depended on track and swimming participants, instead of mannish [ice] hockey players.

George Orwell – *(1903–1950) novelist & critic*
Serious sport has nothing to do with fair play. It is bound up with hatred, jealousy, boastfulness, disregard of all rules and sadistic pleasure in witnessing violence. In other words, it is war minus the shooting: *1950*

Dr George Sheehan – *US cardiologist*
People outside of sport may only see the game, just as those outside of war only see the horror. Yet, in that horror a man may be better than he will ever be the rest of his life. And in that game a man may find what life is really about:
1978

Duke of Wellington – *(1769–1852) military leader*
The Battle of Waterloo was won on the playing fields of Eton.   *Attrib.*

AMERICAN FOOTBALL

House of Representatives Committee on Armed Services
Pearl Harbour, and the subsequent lessons we learned, day by day, until September 1945, should have taught all military men that our military forces are one team – in the game to win regardless of who carries the ball. This is no time for 'fancy dans' who won't hit the line with all they have on every play, unless they can call the signals. Each player on this team – whether he shines in the spotlight of the backfield or eats dirt on the line – must be an All-American: *1949*

Terry Bradshaw – *Pittsburgh Steelers*
If America got into another war, I'd send San Diego out to run the offense. Air power, bombs, those big 'tanks' on the line – who'd stop them?

Boomer Esiason – *Cincinnati Bengals quarterback*
I'm like General Patton – I never retreat, I just keep going forward: *1988*

Frank Gifford – *(b 1930) New York Giants & TV commentator*
Pro football is like nuclear warfare; there are no winners, only survivors.

Forrest McDonald – *historian at the University of Alabama*
The Southerners are naturally violent, and football is the idealized ritual substitute for actual warfare. If you happen to be 10 years old, or 30, when war breaks out, instead of being lucky enough to be 20, the Southerner will feel deprived of his manhood. Football can fill that void.

Darrell Royal – *college coach*
A head coach is guided by this main objective –

you want them to play every Saturday as if they were planting the flag on Iwo Jima.

BASEBALL

Ty Cobb - *(1886-1961) Detroit Tigers*
I have observed that baseball is not unlike war, and when you come right down to it, we batters are the heavy artillery.

This great athlete seems to have understood early in his professional career that in the competition of baseball, just as in war, defensive strategy never produced ultimate victory and, as a consequence, he maintained an offensive posture to the end of his baseball days: *General Douglas MacArthur*

BOARD GAMES

Bobby Fischer - *(b 1943) USA*
Chess is like war. The object is to crush the other man's mind. I like to see them squirm.

BOWLS

Dr John W. Fisher - *player & writer*
Such records as are available establish bowls as the grandparent of all English sports, with the solitary exception of Archery. Bowls, however, is purely and solely a game, it makes no claim to being also a technique or training for combat: *1956*

BOXING

Muhammad Ali - *(b 1942) US heavyweight*
On refusing to be drafted to fight in the Vietnam War - I don't have no personal quarrel with them Vietcongs. The Vietcongs don't call me nigger: *1967*

War on nations change maps. War on poverty maps change.

Marvelous Marvin Hagler - *(b 1954) US middleweight*
When a man goes into the ring, he's going to war. It takes a man to go 15 rounds.

Saoul Mamby - *US light-welterweight*
I was in 'Nam for one year, six days and four hours. Did I see combat? Enough - and boxing

is easier.

Mike Tyson - *US heavyweight*
After knocking out Trevor Berbick - Hydrogen bombs! I threw hydrogen bombs out there! Every punch with murderous intent: *1986*

CARDS

Charles Lamb - *(1775-1834) essayist*
Cards are war in disguise of sport.

CRICKET

Brian Close - *(b 1931) Yorkshire*
If we had shown that kind of attitude and guts during the war that our cricketers have in the West Indies, Hitler would have walked over us: *1986*

Ray East - *(b 1947) Essex*
There should have been a last line of defence during the war. It would have been made up entirely of the more officious breed of cricket stewards. If Hitler had tried to invade these shores he would have been met by a short, stout man in a white coat who would have said, 'I don't care who you are, you're not coming in here unless you're a Member!' *1983*

Ian Peebles - *(1908-80) Middlesex & writer*
Field-Marshal Rommel would have made a great cricket captain if his birthplace had been slightly different.

Glenn Turner - *(b 1947) New Zealand*
When you come back from touring Australia, you almost feel like you've been to Vietnam.

Sir Pelham Warner- *(1873-1963) Middlesex*
A cricket match may be likened to a battle, for there are, as in battle, only three possible results - victory, defeat, or an indecisive encounter.

Duke of Wellington - *(1769-1852)*
My successes in the Army are owing in a great measure to the manly sports of Great Britain, and one sport above all - cricket.

FOOTBALL

Bryon Butler - *commentator & writer*

If Chamberlain had sent a couple of battalions of goal-keepers across the Channel in the autumn of 1939, the Second World War would not have lasted a fortnight: *1979*

Alfred E. Crawley – *(1869–1924) social anthropologist*
Football, in all of its varieties, is pre-eminently a game of military tactics: *1913*

John Gay – *(1685–1732) poet & playwright*
Oft' my course I bend, when lo! From far,
I spy the furies of the foot-ball war: *1716*

Socrates – *Brazil*
Football became popular because it was considered an art, but now too many pitches are becoming battlefields: *1981*

GOLF

Seve Ballesteros – *(b 1957) Spain*
Playing on the American PGA tour is like being in the Army.

HUNTING

Donald C. Peattie – *(1898–1964) botanist & writer*
We shoot geese and duck because they are so gamey, such good sports. As in war, it is the brave that die first: *1937*

Francis Quarles – *(1592–1644) poet*
The chase is a fair resemblance of a hopeful war, proposing to the pursuer a flying enemy.

Sir Walter Scott – *(1771–1832) writer & poet*
The chase I follow far,
'Tis miming of noble war.

Robert S. Surtees – *(1803–64) writer & poet*
Hunting is all that's worth living for – all time is lost wot is not spent in hunting – it is like the air we breathe – if we have it not we die – it's the 'Sport of Kings', the image of war, without its guilt, and only five and twenty per cent of its danger.

RUGBY LEAGUE

Anon
Rugby League is war without frills.

RUGBY UNION

John Hopkins – *sportswriter*
A major rugby tour by the British Isles to New Zealand is a cross between a medieval crusade and a prep school outing.

WOMEN

Saying
Horses sweat, men perspire, women glow.

Badminton magazine
Let young girls ride, skate, dance and play lawn tennis and other games in moderation, but let them leave field sports and rough outdoor pastimes to those for whom they are naturally intended – men: *1900*

Bailey's magazine
There are still among us a good sprinkling of true women, who have not bowed the knee to the mannish ways and nobly set the fashion of ladylike behaviour in sport: *1905*

Mary Boutilier & Lucinde SanGiovanni –
US writers
Mere participation in sport can cast a woman's sexual preference into question, just as participation in ballet can for men:
The Sporting Woman (1982)

Susan Brownmiller – *(b 1935) US feminist leader*
There are important lessons to be learned from sports competition, among them that winning is the result of hard, sustained, serious training, cool, clever strategy that includes the use of tricks and bluffs, and a positive mind-set that puts all reflex systems on go. This knowledge, and the chance to put it into practice, is precisely what women have been conditioned to abjure.

Kathryn Clarenbach - *(b 1925) US educator & feminist leader*
Girls are the spectators and cheerleaders. Perfect preparation for the adult role of women – to stand attractively on the sidelines of history and cheer the men who make decisions.

Doris Corbett - *US sports sociologist*
Black women face all the discrimination that all women face plus there is the additional burden of racism. This is especially true in sports.

Baron de Coubertin - *(1863–1937) French founder of the modern Olympics*
Women have but one task, that of crowning the winner with garlands: *1902*

Bill Gilbert & Nancy Williamson - *US writers*
Sports may be good for people, but they are considered a lot gooder for male people, than for female people: *1973*

Dr Elizabeth Harris
If being independent and having a good self-image with high self-esteem is masculine, then exercise does masculinize women: *1982*

Hollander v Connecticut inter-scholastic athletic conference - *US court case*
Athletic competition builds character in our boys. We do not need that kind of character in our girls – the women of tomorrow: *1971*

Shirbey Johnson - *(b 1941) US athletics director*
Women are carrying a new attitude. They've cast aside the old stereotypes. They don't believe you have to be ugly or have big muscles to play sports.

Kathryn Lance - *US runner & writer*
Women know they're too sedentary but no one tells them to go out and learn a sport, the way men are supposed to do. Women are told to get their exercise by bending over daintily while they're doing the housework. If you're a woman, people are always giving you silly exercises to do at home or at the office or on the way to the market. This is the result of cultural bias.

Robert Lypsyte - *US writer*

Sport was the first great separator of the sexes: *1982*

Harold Macmillan - *(b 1894) Prime Minister*
In my day one could go into sports without first having to go into a long test to discover whether you are man or woman. Those were the times when games were games and sport was sport: *1979*

Ann Moore - *show-jumper*
Girls who ride horses don't necessarily have big behinds: *1974*

Bruce Ogilvie - *US psychologist*
Women have no lack of natural ability; they are merely subject to cultural prejudices. Cultural pressures are created by what people think a woman should be.

Carole Oglesby - *US professor of sports psychology, Temple University*
Sport for women has been more myth than a reality, because the Western world has both accepted and rejected women in sport.

William Shakespeare - *(1564–1616) playwright*
It is the first that ever I heard breaking of ribs was sport for ladies: *As You Like It*

Christine L. Wells - *US physiologist*
The female of our species has been hindered by the propagation of myths regarding her abilities to withstand stress, to perform heavy work, to run, jump, or just plain play:
Women, Sport & Performance (1986)

AMERICAN FOOTBALL

Jeanne Moreau - *(b 1929) French actress*
Women will not be talking about football unless one of them is in love with a football player, and then suddenly you discover that they know everything that is to be known about it: *1976*

ATHLETICS

Anon
Watching the Russian female shot-putters, is like watching an eighteen stone ballet dancer.

The only time our girls looked good in Munich

was in the discotheque, between 9 and 11 every night: *US Olympic coach (1972)*

Shirley de la Hunty (neé Strickland) – *(b 1925) Australian hurdler*
Two things I felt I had to prove as a young woman in the post-war period. One was that I was feminine and an athlete, and the other that I was intelligent and an athlete.
[*She proved herself as an athlete, winning the Olympic 80 metres hurdles gold medal in 1952 and 1956*]

Nine Kuscsik – *US marathon runner*
Women need a firm bra, not one of the flimsy all-elastic ones. That's especially true if you have large breasts. Otherwise they'll bounce and you'll always be waiting for them to come down before you take your next step.

Andy Norman – *promoter*
The sports correspondents are jealous. It's not so bad if a talented male athlete makes more money than they do. But they can't stand it if it's a woman.

Bruce Ogilvie – *US psychologist*
The woman who wants to turn to athletics must make a leap – a psychological leap. She has to have the courage to redefine herself as a human being.

Eddy Ottoz – *Italian hurdler*
Italian men and Russian women don't shave before a race.

Dr Christine Pickard
Women athletes, except for very rare cases, are real women: *1972*

John T. Powell – *US coach*
Frequently track and field events are relegated to the realm of sweat and muscles, unsuitable for the 'gentler sex'. There is nothing wrong with sweat, and a strong woman whose figure stands up for itself is much to be admired: *1963*

Scientific American
Girls can run as well as boys, and while they cannot go as fast, they can run much more gracefully: *1883*

BOARD GAMES

Ruth Haring
I would prefer to become a good chess player, not a good woman chess player.

BOWLS

Frank Soars – *Australian player & writer*
Women have bumps in the wrong places for the ideal delivery: *1970*

BOXING

Muhammad Ali – *(b 1942) US heavyweight*
My toughest fight was with my first wife, and she won every round.

Henry L. Mencken – *(1880–1956) US editor*
When women kiss, it always reminds me of prize-fighters shaking hands.

CRICKET

Anon
Ladies playing cricket? Absurd. Just like a man trying to knit.

Sir Neville Cardus – *(1889–1975) writer*
If the best spin bowler in the country were a woman, what would be done about the dressing room at Lord's?

Nat Gubbins – *poet*
 The game of cricket is no joke
 To us who neither drink or smoke
 Games are won and runs are made
 By girls who stick to lemonade: *1951*

Rachael Heyhoe-Flint – *(b 1939) England ladies captain*
Remember, women were the first to bowl over-arm: *1975*

We have nothing against man cricketers. Some of them are quite nice people, even though they don't win as often as we do: *1975*

How to get 2,000 women's cricket clubs together with 20,000 men's clubs – All we need is an extra lavatory and a broom cupboard.

Denis Norden – *(b 1922) humorist*

It's a funny kind of month, October. For the really keen cricket fan it's when you realise that your wife left you in May.

Fred Trueman - *(b 1931) Yorkshire*
You should treat women the same way as any good Yorkshire batsman used to treat a cricket ball. Don't stroke 'em, don't tickle 'em, just give 'em a ruddy good belt.

FOOTBALL

Ron Atkinson - *manager*
Women should be in the kitchen, the discotheque and the boutique, but not in football: *1989*

Sarah Bernhardt - *(1844-1923) French actress*
On seeing a game of football in Manchester -
J'adore ce cricket; c'est tellement Anglais [I do love cricket. It is so English]:   *c 1905*

HORSE RACING

Richard Baerlein - *sportswriter*
Racehorses, like women, are entirely unpredictable.

Dick Francis - *(b 1920) jockey & novelist*
I am firmly against women riding in National Hunt races. I would deny them the equal right to cripple their limbs or disfigure their faces. Jump racing is as physically wrong for girls as boxing: *1972*

Jeff King - *jockey*
Women riding at Aintree don't worry me. There will be just as many amateurs going round who will be just as much a pain in the neck.

Elaine Mellor - *jockey*
I may sound tough, but I say to women riders who complain, 'If you don't like the heat, get out of the kitchen!':   *1980*

Roger Mortimer - *sportswriter*
I see no particular objection to giving women a chance to ride in races now and again . . . such races should be on the Flat and be placed last on the card so that those racegoers not

interested can return home for tea and 'Magic Roundabout'.

HUNTING

Robert S. Surtees - *(1803-64) sportswriter & poet*
Women never look so well as when one comes in wet and dirty from hunting.

Evelyn Waugh - *(1903-66) novelist*
I have often observed in women a tendency to regard all athletics as inferior forms of fox-hunting.

SWIMMING

Dawn Fraser - *Australia*
I hated the easy assumption that girls had to be slower than boys.
[Her winning time in the 1964 Olympic 100 metres freestyle was half a second slower than Johnny Weissmuller when he won the men's gold in 1924]

Jack Queen - *British women's coach*
Britain's swim girls are just not tough enough. At the World Championships, they were no more than a glee club for the men: *1975*

TENNIS

Martina Navratilova *(b 1956) USA*
I'm the only woman who doesn't have a sweat problem: *1982*

Suzanne Lenglen - *(1879-1938) France*
All women tennis players should go on their knees in thankfulness to Suzanne Lenglen for delivering them from the tyranny of corsets:
Elizabeth 'Bunny' Ryan

Bobby Riggs - *USA*
Since women don't play tennis as well as men do, they don't deserve to be paid as much as men.

Eugene Scott - *USA*
Women tennis players can't stand the pressure of playing against men. Girls are brought up from the time they are six to read books, eat candy, and go to dancing class. They can't compete against men, can't stand the strain.

INDEX

INDIVIDUALS QUOTED OR MENTIONED IN QUOTATION

———————————— A ————————————

B

C

─────────────────────────── **D** ───────────────────────────

E

F

G

H

I

J

L

M

INDEX

—————————————————— **N** ——————————————————

INDEX

P

INDEX

—————————————————— T ——————————————————

GENERAL REFERENCE